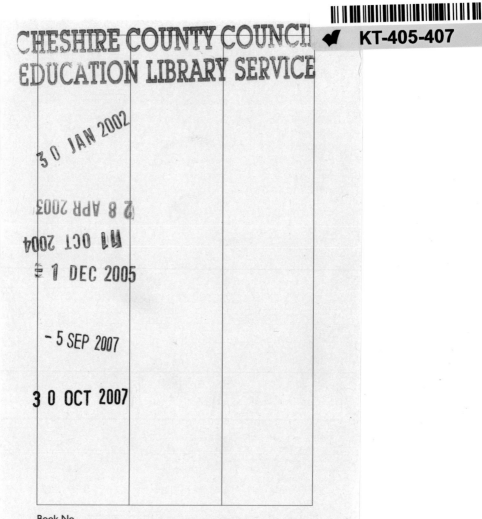

BUILDING A NEW MILLENNIUM

BAUEN IM NEUEN JAHRTAUSEND
CONSTRUIRE UN NOUVEAU MILLÉNAIRE

PHILIP JODIDIO

TASCHEN

KÖLN LONDON MADRID NEW YORK PARIS TOKYO

PREFACE / VORWORT / PRÉFACE

BUILDING A NEW MILLENNIUM

BAUEN IM NEUEN JAHRTAUSEND
CONSTRUIRE UN NOUVEAU MILLÉNAIRE

THE RULES HAVE CHANGED. AT THE DAWN OF THE 21ST CENTURY THERE IS A NEW WAY TO SEE ARCHITECTURE. NATIONAL BORDERS AND LOCAL STYLES STILL EXIST, BUT THERE IS AN EMERGING AWARENESS THAT TRANSCENDS CATEGORIES ESTABLISHED WHEN THE WORLD DIDN'T MOVE SO FAST. COMPUTERS AND THE RISE OF THE INTERNET HAVE SOMETHING TO DO WITH THIS AWARENESS, BUT SO DOES A PUBLICATION LIKE THIS ONE THAT IS DISTRIBUTED IN 80 COUNTRIES. THE KEY IS THE FLOW OF INFORMATION, NO MATTER WHAT FORM IT TAKES. SOME CALL IT **GLOBALIZATION**, AND FEAR THAT NEW, UNKNOWN

COMPETITORS WILL TAKE THEIR PLACE. OTHERS VIEW THE FLOW OF INFORMATION AS AN UNPRECEDENTED ENRICHMENT. THOSE WHO REJECT THE NEW CLAIM THAT STANDARDIZATION WILL ROB LOCAL CULTURES OF THEIR SPECIFICITY – **THOSE WHO GREET THE PRESENT AND FUTURE WITH AN OPEN MIND – UNDERSTAND THAT THIS REVOLUTION IS NOT ABOUT STANDARDIZATION BUT ABOUT DIVERSITY.** IT WAS THE INDUSTRIAL REVOLUTION THAT GAVE BIRTH TO THE MODEL T, AVAILABLE, AS HENRY FORD SAID, "IN ANY COLOR AS LONG AS IT'S BLACK." THIS REVOLUTION IS ABOUT FREELY AVAILABLE INFORMATION.

ANY ATTEMPT TO GATHER TOGETHER THE MOST SIGNIFICANT BUILDINGS CREATED IN THE WORLD IN THE PAST FEW YEARS IS DESTINED TO BE SUBJECTIVE. THE AUTHOR'S JUDGMENT INTERVENES, BUT SO DO MORE MUNDANE QUESTIONS LIKE THE AVAILABILITY OF PHOTOGRAPHS AND THE ARCHITECTS' WILLINGNESS TO COOPERATE. **BUILDINGS PUBLIC AND PRIVATE, LARGE AND SMALL, ARE PUBLISHED HERE IN THE SPIRIT OF THE DIVERSITY THAT IS THE KEY TO THE NEW CENTURY.** THEY RANGE FROM JAPAN TO PORTUGAL, FROM MOOBALL, NEW SOUTH WALES, TO SOCORRO, NEW MEXICO. ALTHOUGH THERE ARE SOME

EXCEPTIONS, **THIS BOOK IS INTENDED AS AN OVERVIEW OF WORK COMPLETED IN THE FINAL YEARS OF THE 1990S.** SOME ARE SLIGHTLY EARLIER, OTHERS ARE UNDER CONSTRUCTION, BUT TAKEN COLLECTIVELY THEY SHOULD PRO-VIDE SOME INSIGHT INTO THE VERY DIFFERENT WAYS IN WHICH ARCHITECTS ARE APPROACHING WHAT MUST BE RECOGNIZED AS A TIME OF **UNPRECEDENTED FREEDOM.**

THERE IS NO DOMINANT STYLE TODAY. RANGING FROM THE RIGOROUS MINIMALISM OF SWISS ARCHITECTS LIKE HERZOG & DE MEURON TO THE PRICKLY ECOLOGICAL DESIGNS OF THOMAS SPIEGELHALTER, THE FORMS OF TODAY'S ARCHITECTURE ARE ALMOST AS VARIED AS ITS PRACTITIONERS. WHILE **COMPUTER-AIDED DESIGN** MAKES IT INCREASINGLY EASY TO CREATE UNIQUE BUILDINGS, INTELLECTUAL FREEDOM HAS ALSO EXPANDED. WHEREAS THE FOUNDERS OF **MODERNISM** SOUGHT TO REJECT THE PAST, TODAY'S YOUNG ARCHITECTS DO NOT HESITATE TO ENRICH THEIR DESIGNS BY CALLING ON

THEIR KNOWLEDGE OF **HISTORY**, BE IT RECENT OR MORE DISTANT. THE **MINIMALISM** THAT SEEMS QUITE PRESENT IN SWITZERLAND OR JAPAN IS INFORMED BY KNOWLEDGE NOT ONLY OF THE ROOTS OF MODERNITY, BUT ALSO OF THE ART OF THE 20TH CENTURY. MATERIALS TOO HAVE TAKEN ON FLEXIBILITY UNHEARD OF JUST A FEW YEARS AGO. THE SCULPTED TITANIUM PANELS OF FRANK O. GEHRY'S GUGGENHEIM MUSEUM BILBAO ARE A TESTIMONY TO THE ARTISTIC AND TECHNICAL FREEDOM OF **CONTEMPORARY ARCHITECTURE AT THE DAWN OF A NEW CENTURY.**

BUILDING A NEW MILLENNIUM

Die Regeln haben sich geändert. An der Schwelle zum 21. Jahrhundert gilt eine neue Art der Architekturbetrachtung. Landesgrenzen und regionale Stile existieren zwar noch, aber zugleich gibt es ein zunehmendes Bewußtsein für die Überschreitung jener etablierten Kategorien, die aus einer Zeit stammen, als die Welt sich noch nicht so schnell veränderte. Computer und Internet haben mit diesem Bewußtsein zu tun, aber auch eine Publikation wie diese, die in 80 Ländern vertrieben wird. Der Schlüssel ist hier wie dort der Informationsfluß, gleich welche Form er annimmt. Einige nennen es Globalisierung und befürchten, daß neue, unbekannte Konkurrenten ihren Platz einnehmen werden. Andere wiederum betrachten den Informationsfluß als außerordentliche Bereicherung. Die Gegner des Neuen behaupten, die Standardisierung beraube regionale Kulturen ihrer Eigenständigkeit. Wer jedoch der Gegenwart und Zukunft aufgeschlossen begegnet, begreift, daß es bei dieser Revolution nicht um Standardisierung geht, sondern um Vielfalt. Es war die industrielle Revolution, die Henry Fords T-Modell ermöglichte – ein Modell, das, wie er sagte, »in jeder beliebigen Farbe, vorausgesetzt, es ist schwarz«, geliefert werden könne. Bei der gegenwärtigen Revolution geht es um die Bereitstellung und die freie Verfügbarkeit von Informationen.

Jeder Versuch einer Zusammenstellung der bedeutendsten Bauten, die in den letzten Jahren auf der Welt gebaut wurden, ist zwangsläufig subjektiv. Das Urteil des Autors tritt hinzu, aber ebensolchen Einfluß haben prosaischere Gründe, wie die Möglichkeit zur Nutzung von Fotografien und die Bereitschaft der Architekten zur Kooperation. In diesem Band sind öffentliche und private, kleine und große Gebäude im Geist jener Vielfalt vereint, die das Kennzeichen des neuen Jahrhunderts sein wird. Sie reichen von Japan bis Portugal, von Mooball in Neusüdwales, Australien, bis Socorro in New Mexico. Das Buch ist – von wenigen Ausnahmen abgesehen – als Übersicht über Bauten am Ende der 90er Jahre angelegt. Einige Projekte sind etwas älter, andere noch im Bau, aber insgesamt vermitteln sie einen Einblick in die sehr unterschiedlichen Weisen, wie Architekten sich einer Zeit annähern, die offenbar noch nie dagewesene Freiheiten bietet.

Heute gibt es keinen vorherrschenden Stil. Vom strengen Minimalismus der Architekten Herzog & de Meuron bis zu den spröden ökologischen Entwürfen von Thomas Spiegelhalter sind die Formen der gegenwärtigen Architektur beinahe so unterschiedlich wie ihre Urheber. Indem es durch computergestütztes Design (CAD) immer leichter wird, einmalige Gebäude zu entwerfen, hat auch die intellektuelle Freiheit zugenommen. Während die Begründer der modernen Architektur die Vergangenheit ablehnten, zögern junge Architekten heute nicht, ihre Entwürfe durch Rückgriffe auf die jüngere oder ältere Geschichte anzureichern. Der in der Schweiz und in Japan offenbar vorherrschende Minimalismus beruht nicht nur auf dem Verständnis der Ursprünge der Moderne, sondern auch der Kunst des 20. Jahrhunderts. Auch haben die Materialien eine bis vor wenigen Jahren unvorstellbare Flexibilität gewonnen. Die geformten Titanplatten von Frank O. Gehrys Guggenheim Museum Bilbao zeugen von der künstlerischen und technischen Freiheit zeitgenössischer Architektur im Aufbruch in ein neues Jahrhundert.

Les règles ont changé. À l'aube du XXIe siècle, l'architecture se regarde de façon différente. Si les frontières nationales et les styles locaux perdurent encore, on constate l'émergence d'une conscience qui transcende les catégories datant de l'époque où la terre ne tournait pas aussi vite. Les ordinateurs et la montée en puissance d'internet ne sont pas sans rapport avec cette nouvelle attitude, ce qui est d'ailleurs aussi le cas d'un ouvrage comme celui-ci, diffusé dans 80 pays. La clé de ce phénomène se trouve dans le flux d'information, quelle que soit sa forme. Certains l'appellent mondialisation et craignent que des concurrents nouveaux et inconnus ne viennent prendre leur place. D'autres y voient un enrichissement sans précédent, et rejettent cette peur qui veut que la standardisation dépouille à terme les cultures locales de leur spécificité. Ils saluent le présent et le futur dans un esprit ouvert, et comprennent que cette révolution n'a pas pour objet la standardisation, mais au contraire la diversité. C'est la révolution industrielle qui a donné naissance au Modèle T, disponible comme le disait Henry Ford «dans n'importe quelle couleur, pourvu que ce soit noir». La révolution actuelle est celle de la libre disponibilité de l'information.

Toute tentative pour réunir en un seul volume les réalisations architecturales les plus significatives de ces dernières années dans le monde ne peut qu'être subjective. Le jugement de l'auteur intervient, mais aussi des questions plus triviales comme la disponibilité des photographies ou le souhait de coopération de l'architecte. Les constructions publiques et privées, grandes et petites, publiées dans ces pages le sont dans l'esprit de cette diversité qui est la clé du siècle nouveau. Elles ont été sélectionnées du Japon au Portugal, de Mooball en Nouvelle-Galles du Sud, à Socorro, Nouveau-Mexique. À quelques exceptions près, ce livre se veut un survol de réalisations achevées à la fin de la dernière décennie du XXe siècle. Si certaines sont légèrement plus anciennes, d'autres encore en construction, elles fournissent collectivement une certaine vision de la multiplicité des approches pratiquées par les architectes, ce qui doit être reconnu comme une période de liberté sans précédent.

Aujourd'hui, il n'existe pas de style dominant. Du minimalisme rigoureux d'architectes suisses comme Herzog & de Meuron aux projets écologiques hérissés de Thomas Spiegelhalter, les formes de l'architecture contemporaine sont presque aussi variées que le nombre de ses pratiquants. Si la conception assistée par ordinateur facilite de plus en plus la création de bâtiments d'exception, la liberté créative s'est tout autant développée. Alors que les fondateurs du modernisme rejetaient le passé, les jeunes architectes actuels n'hésitent pas à enrichir leurs projets de rappels de l'histoire, qu'elle soit récente ou plus distante. Le minimalisme qui semble assez présent en Suisse ou au Japon se nourrit de la connaissance non seulement des racines de la modernité, mais aussi de l'art du XXe siècle. Le choix des matériaux a lui aussi conquis une souplesse encore inconnue il y a quelques années. Les panneaux sculpturaux en titane du musée Guggenheim Bilbao de Frank O. Gehry témoignent de la liberté artistique et technique de l'architecture contemporaine à l'aube d'un siècle nouveau.

PLACES TO LIVE

LEBENS-RÄUME
DES LIEUX OÙ VIVRE

No matter how much architecture evolves, its primary function is to provide shelter. "As long as there is a man who needs a house, architecture will still exist," says the Swiss-Italian architect Mario Botta. Botta has a marked preference for thick walls and clearly defined boundaries. Others are not of like mind. One of the most radical interpretations of the contemporary house is that of the Japanese architect Shigeru Ban. His "Wall-less House" (Karuizawa, Japan, 1997, see P 086.087) comes as close as any piece of architecture to doing away with the very boundaries that seem so essential to Mario Botta. Built on a steeply sloped, wooded site, the house consists of a 60 m² slab that is embedded into the hillside, curving up at the rear to support the light steel roof. This design permitted the architect to create an open living surface with just three 55 mm thick columns. Sliding panels can of course provide a degree of privacy, just as glass panels can give shelter from the elements, but Shigeru Ban here approaches a limit that others like Ludwig Mies van der Rohe or Philip Johnson flirted with, but without quite daring to go so far. This is an example of the newfound freedom of contemporary architects to deal with some of the preoccupations of Modernism

Wie weit sich die Architektur auch entwickelt haben mag – ihre primäre Aufgabe ist es immer noch, Schutz zu gewähren. »Solange es einen Menschen gibt, der ein Haus braucht, wird es auch Architektur geben«, sagt Mario Botta, der Architekt aus der italienischen Schweiz. Er hat eine ausgeprägte Vorliebe für dicke Mauern und deutliche Begrenzungen. Andere teilen diese Auffassung nicht. Eine der radikalsten Interpretationen des zeitgenössischen Wohnhauses stammt von dem japanischen Architekten Shigeru Ban. Sein »Haus ohne Wände« (Karuizawa, Japan, 1997, siehe P 086.087) ist das extreme Beispiel einer Architektur ohne jene Begrenzungen, die einem Mario Botta so wichtig erscheinen. Das auf einem steil abfallenden, bewaldeten Grundstück erbaute Wohnhaus besteht aus einer 60 m² großen Platte, die in den Hang eingebettet und an der Rückseite aufwärts gebogen ist, um das leichte Stahldach zu tragen. Dieser Entwurf ermöglichte dem Architekten die Anlage einer offenen Wohnfläche mit nur drei 55 mm starken Stützen. Zwar sorgen verschiebbare Platten für ein gewisses Maß an Privatsphäre, ebenso wie Glaswände Schutz vor den Elementen bieten, aber Shigeru Ban geht hier bis an eine Grenze, mit der andere – etwa Ludwig Mies

Quelle que soit l'évolution de l'architecture, sa fonction primaire reste d'offrir un abri. «Aussi longtemps que vivra un homme qui aura besoin d'une maison, l'architecture existera», affirme l'architecte suisse Mario Botta. Il manifeste une préférence marquée pour des murs épais et des limites clairement définies. D'autres diffèrent de cette position. L'une des interprétations les plus radicales de la maison contemporaine est celle de l'architecte japonais Shigeru Ban. Sa «Maison sans murs» (Karuizawa, Japon, 1997, voir P 086.087) est sans doute la création architecturale la plus éloignée de cette affirmation des limites jugée si essentielle par Mario Botta. Construite sur un site boisé escarpé, sa maison consiste en une dalle de 60 m² encastrée dans le flanc d'une colline, et recourbée à l'arrière pour soutenir un léger toit en acier. Ce concept permet à l'architecte de créer un espace de vie dégagé à peine rythmé par trois colonnes de 55 mm d'épaisseur. Des panneaux coulissants apportent un peu plus d'intimité lorsqu'on le souhaite, et des panneaux de verre protègent des éléments naturels. Shigeru Ban se rapproche ici d'une limite avec laquelle d'autres, comme Ludwig Mies van der Rohe ou Philip Johnson avaient flirté sans oser aller si

in their own way. For some decades after the height of Modernism "icons" like the Farnsworth House by Mies were considered so perfect that few talented architects dared to try to take up where such a master left off. That is no longer the case.

Ben van Berkel's Möbius House ('t Gooi, Netherlands, 1993-97, see P 094-099) is an example of a different kind of freedom. Here the goal was not to delve into historic Modernism, but to create a new model whose point of origin was the Möbius strip – a rectangular strip with a half-twist and ends connected to form a continuous-sided, single-edged loop, invented by the German mathematician August Ferdinand Möbius (1790-1868). The computer-aided design tools used by Ben van Berkel are naturally well adapted to working with such a mathematical model, but the architect has also provided a logical reason for doing so. Thus this striking house moves from day to night areas in a seamless sequence. Forms overlap and intertwine; interior blends with exterior, just as day turns to night. Ben van Berkel shows that the computer is coming of age not only as a design tool but also as a giver of form, and this is an important dimension in the new freedom of architecture.

van der Rohe oder Philip Johnson – höchstens liebäugelten, ohne ihr jedoch zu nahe zu kommen. Dies ist eines der Beispiele für die neu gewonnene Freiheit zeitgenössischer Architekten, sich auf je eigene Weise mit der Moderne auseinanderzusetzen. Jahrzehntelang wurden die Glanzlichter unter den modernen »Ikonen«, wie das Haus Farnsworth von Mies, als so perfekt angesehen, daß nur wenige begabte Architekten sich zutrauten, dort anzusetzen, wo einer der früheren Meister aufgehört hatte. Das ist nicht mehr der Fall.

Ben van Berkels Möbius-Haus ('t Gooi, Niederlande, 1993-97, siehe P 094-099) ist ein Beispiel für eine andere Art von Freiheit. Hier bestand das Ziel nicht im Ausloten der historischen Moderne, sondern im Entwerfen eines neuen Modells, das seinen Ursprung im Möbiusschen Band hat – einem von dem deutschen Mathematiker August Ferdinand Möbius (1790-1868) entwickelten, verschlungenen und gedrehten Band, bei dem man jeden Punkt seiner Oberfläche ohne Überschreiten des Rands erreichen kann. Die computergestützten Planungswerkzeuge, die van Berkel nutzt, sind von ihrer Anlage her natürlich gut geeignet, mit einem solchen mathematischen Modell zu arbeiten; der Architekt hat jedoch

loin. C'est un exemple de la liberté retrouvée des architectes contemporains qui n'hésitent pas à affronter certaines des préoccupations du modernisme à leur manière propre. Durant quelques décennies après l'apogée du modernisme, des «icônes» comme la Farnsworth House de Mies étaient considérées si parfaites que peu d'architectes de talent avaient osé en relever le défi après la disparition du maître. Ce n'est plus le cas aujourd'hui.

La maison Möbius de Ben van Berkel ('t Gooi, Pays-Bas, 1993-97, voir P 094-099), est un exemple d'une forme différente de liberté. Ici, le but n'était pas de remonter jusqu'au modernisme historique, mais de créer un nouveau modèle dont le point de départ serait l'anneau de Möbius – un ruban qui se retourne pour former une bande continue – imaginé par le mathématicien allemand August Ferdinand Möbius (1790-1868). Les outils de conception assistée par ordinateur utilisés par van Berkel sont naturellement adaptés au travail sur un tel modèle mathématique, mais l'architecte fournit également une raison logique à son choix: cette étonnante maison évolue de zone de jour en zone nocturne en une séquence sans rupture. Les formes se superposent et se chevauchent, l'intérieur se marie avec

PLACES TO LIVE

Two houses in Australia are evidence that architecture can retain a powerful local element without resorting to folklore in any sense. The Steel House (Mooball, New South Wales, 1996-97, see P 182-185) by the architects Grose Bradley is set to the south of Brisbane along the eastern coast of Australia. This design seeks to respect its natural environment while stating clearly that it stands apart. Horizontal and open like the Australian landscape itself, the Steel House is related to various forms of temporary architecture. Calling on an industrial vocabulary and creating a house specifically for this spectacular setting, James Grose affirms the vitality of Australian architecture in terms not unlike those set out by Glenn Murcutt, who is 18 years his senior. Murcutt's Private Residence (Mount Wilson, New South Wales, 1989-94, see P 360-363) is an exercise in austerity. Consisting of a house and an atelier connected by an elevated wooden walkway and a basin, the residence is made of aluminum, painted steel, glass, and polished concrete for the floors. Also very horizontal in its design, the plan takes into account an existing rocky outcrop. The problem posed to Steven Ehrlich in designing his House Extension (Santa Monica, California,

auch eine logische Begründung für ihren Einsatz geliefert. Dieses Haus bewegt sich demgemäß fließend von einem Tag- in einen Nachtbereich. Die Formen überschneiden sich und greifen ineinander, das Innere geht in das Äußere über. Ben van Berkel zeigt, daß der Computer nicht nur als Planungswerkzeug, sondern auch zur Formgestaltung eingesetzt werden kann. Das ist ein neue Dimension innerhalb der architektonischen Freiheit.

Zwei Wohnhäuser in Australien beweisen, daß Architektur sich mit einer kraftvollen lokalen Sprache behaupten kann, ohne in irgendeiner Weise folkloristisch zu sein. Das Steel House (Mooball, Neusüdwales, 1996-97, siehe P 182-185) der Architekten Grose Bradley liegt südlich von Brisbane an der Ostküste Australiens. James Grose, der verantwortliche Architekt, versuchte, die natürliche Umgebung zu respektieren: Horizontal und offen wie die australische Landschaft, hat das Steel House gewisse Elemente provisorischer Architektur. Indem James Grose ein industrielles Vokabular anwendet und ein speziell für diese spektakuläre Lage geeignetes Haus entwirft, bestätigt er die Vitalität der australischen Architektur in Ausdrucksformen, die der 18 Jahre ältere Glenn Murcutt geprägt hat.

l'extérieur comme le jour change imperceptiblement en nuit. Ben van Berkel montre que l'ordinateur accède à la maturité, non seulement comme outil de dessin, mais aussi comme générateur de formes, qui enrichit ainsi d'une importante dimension la nouvelle liberté architecturale.

Deux maisons construites en Australie prouvent que l'architecture peut conserver un puissant élément d'inspiration locale sans relever en aucune façon du folklore. La Steel House (Mooball, Nouvelle-Galles du Sud, 1996-97, voir P 182-185), des architectes Grose Bradley se trouve au sud de Brisbane sur la côte orientale de l'Australie. Ce projet cherche à respecter son environnement naturel tout en affirmant clairement son autonomie. Aussi horizontale et ouverte que le paysage qui l'entoure, la Steel House rappelle diverses formes d'architecture temporaire. Faisant appel à un vocabulaire industriel tout en créant une maison spécifiquement conçue pour ce site spectaculaire, James Grose affirme la vitalité de l'architecture australienne dans des termes qui ne sont pas très différents de ceux de Glenn Murcutt, de 18 ans son aîné. Sa résidence privée (Mount Wilson, Nouvelle-Galles du Sud, 1989-94, voir P 360-363) est un exercice de style

1996-98, see P 154-157) was not so much one of drawing on the experience of Modernism, as fitting in with a masterpiece in the shape of Richard Neutra's 1938 Lewin House. Although some critics faulted him for his attitude, Ehrlich determined that he need not attempt to imitate the Austrian master. "I'd like to think the pavilion, with the new materials and the evaporating glass walls, takes Neutra's ideas a step further," says Ehrlich. "It's much more minimal than he was ever able to achieve in those days." The new confidence shown by Shigeru Ban's "Wall-less House" also can be seen in Steven Ehrlich's respectful effort to go even further along a path first walked by Richard Neutra.

The Portuguese architect Álvaro Siza is well known for his personal brand of modern architecture, perhaps inspired by masters like Alvar Aalto, but always unexpected and innovative in its sculptural freedom. His Vieira de Castro House (Famalicão, Portugal, 1984-98, see P 454-457) is no exception. A long time in the making simply because Siza gave priority to public projects, the Vieira de Castro House is set on a hilltop against a rocky outcrop. Much as he did in early projects

Murcutts Einfamilienhaus (Mount Wilson, Neusüdwales, 1989-94, siehe P 360-363) ist eine Übung in Nüchternheit. Das Anwesen, das sich aus einem Wohnhaus und einem Atelier mit hölzernem Verbindungsgang sowie einem Wasserbecken zusammensetzt, besteht aus Aluminium, gestrichenem Stahl und Böden aus geschliffenem Beton. Der Grundriß des betont horizontal angelegten Gebäudes trägt einer vorhandenen Felsformation Rechnung.

Das Problem, das sich Steven Ehrlich bei der Erweiterung eines Wohnhauses (Santa Monica, Kalifornien, 1996-98, siehe P 154-157) stellte, war weniger das eines Rückgriffs auf die Moderne. Vielmehr ging es hier um die Anpassung an ein Meisterstück: Richard Neutras Haus Lewin von 1938. Obgleich einige Kritiker Ehrlich getadelt haben, erklärt er selbst hierzu, daß er nicht versuchen müsse, den österreichischen Meister zu imitieren: »Ich möchte meinen, daß der Pavillon mit den neuen Materialien und den sich verflüchtigenden Glaswänden Neutras Ideen einen Schritt weiterführt. Der Pavillon ist viel minimalistischer, als Neutra es zur damaligen Zeit erreichen konnte.« Das neue Selbstvertrauen, das Shigeru Bans »Haus ohne Wände« zeigt, drückt sich auch in Steven Ehr-

sur le thème de l'austérité. Constituée d'une maison et d'un atelier réunis par une allée de planches surélevée et d'un bassin, l'ensemble est construit en aluminium, en acier peint, en verre, et en béton poli pour les sols. Également très horizontal, le plan prend en compte un enrochement existant.

Le problème posé à l'architecte Steven Ehrlich par la conception de l'extension d'une villa à Santa Monica (Californie, 1996-98, voir P 154-157) ne consistait pas tant à s'appuyer sur l'expérience du modernisme, qu'à s'y intégrer puisqu'il devait opérer sur un chef-d'œuvre de cette époque, en l'espèce la Lewin House de Richard Neutra (1938). Bien que quelques critiques lui aient reproché son attitude, Ehrlich était déterminé à ne pas tenter d'imiter le maître autrichien. «J'aime penser que le pavillon, ses matériaux nouveaux et ses murs en verre qui s'évaporent font franchir aux idées de Neutra une étape supplémentaire», déclare-t-il. «Il est beaucoup plus minimaliste que ce qu'il pouvait imaginer atteindre à cette époque.» La nouvelle confiance affichée par la «Maison sans murs» de Shigeru Ban se retrouve dans l'effort respectueux de Steven Ehrlich d'aller plus loin encore sur un chemin ouvert à l'origine par Neutra.

PLACES TO LIVE

like his Boa Nova Tea House and Restaurant (Leça da Palmeira, Portugal, 1958-63), or the Swimming Pool he designed just up the coast along the Avenida Marginal (Leça da Palmeira, 1961-66), Siza uses these rocks in forming a narrow passageway toward the entrance. Within and without, this house shows just how orthodox Modernism can be enlivened by an architect who is not preoccupied with grids and alignments. This is a kind of sensual Modernism that is by no means dated. It is a measure of today's freedom that Siza's Vieira de Castro House is in many ways no less contemporary than a residence that might be considered its diametrical opposite, Thomas Spiegelhalter's Experimental Housing (Freiburg, Germany, 1996-97, see P 468-471). Spiegelhalter is a representative of a growing trend in contemporary architecture toward ecologically sensitive design. Passive solar energy, efficient insulation and thermal storage are used to reduce energy consumption, while the curving roof on the south-facing side of this structure houses photovoltaic panels and protects it from the sun. The aesthetics of such a building are in good part determined by its energy consciousness, a goal encouraged in this instance by local

lichs Bemühen aus, den von Richard Neutra vorgezeichneten Weg einen Schritt weiterzugehen. Der portugiesische Architekt Álvaro Siza ist für seine individuell geprägte moderne Architektur bekannt, die möglicherweise von Meistern wie Alvar Aalto inspiriert wurde, sich aber stets überraschend und innovativ in ihrer plastischen Freiheit äußert. Sizas Haus Vieira de Castro (Famalicão, Portugal, 1984-98, siehe P 454-457) bildet hier keine Ausnahme. Dieses Haus – das nur deshalb eine so lange Entstehungszeit hatte, weil Siza öffentlichen Bauvorhaben den Vorrang einräumte – ist auf einen Hügel gegen einen auskragenden Felsen gesetzt. Siza nutzt diese Felsen, um einen schmalen Durchgang zum Eingang zu gestalten, ähnlich wie bei früheren Projekten: dem Teehaus und Restaurant Boa Nova (Leça da Palmeira, Portugal, 1958-63) und dem Schwimmbad über dem Meer an der Avenida Marginal (Leça da Palmeira, 1961-66). Von innen und außen zeigt dieses Haus, wie ein Architekt, der sich nicht durch Raster und Fluchtlinien einschränken läßt, die orthodoxe Moderne beleben kann. Hier handelt es sich um eine mit den Sinnen erfahrbare Moderne, die keineswegs überholt ist.

L'architecte portugais Álvaro Siza est bien connu pour son approche personnelle du modernisme – peut-être inspirée de maîtres comme Alvar Aalto – toujours inattendue et novatrice dans sa liberté formelle. Sa Maison Vieira de Castro (Famalicão, Portugal, 1984-98, voir P 454-457) n'y fait pas exception. Longtemps en chantier, tout simplement parce que Siza donnait la priorité à des projets publics plus importants, cette résidence se situe au sommet d'une colline contre un enrochement. Un peu comme il le fit pour des projets antérieurs comme son Salon de thé – restaurant Boa Nova (Leça da Palmeira, Portugal, 1958-63) ou la piscine qu'il a dessinée en bordure de plage le long de l'Avenida Marginal (Leça da Palmeira, 1961-66), il utilise ces rochers pour délimiter un étroit passage vers l'entrée. À l'intérieur comme à l'extérieur, cette maison montre à quel point le modernisme non orthodoxe peut être revivifié par un architecte qui ne se préoccupe pas outre mesure de trames ou d'alignements. Cette forme sensuelle de modernisme n'est en aucun cas datée. Que la maison Vieira de Castro ne soit à de nombreux égards pas moins contemporaine qu'une résidence qui peut être jugée diamétralement

authorities. With the spread of public awareness of the importance of respecting the environment, it is entirely possible that ecologically driven designs will be judged aesthetically pleasing in the future. Thomas Spiegelhalter's prickly buildings may then be seen as the precursors of a new generation in architecture.

Es ist ein Gradmesser der heute möglichen Freiheit, daß Sizas Haus Vieira de Castro in vieler Hinsicht weniger zeitgemäß ist als Thomas Spiegelhalters Experimentalwohnungen (Freiburg, 1996-97, siehe P 468-471), die ein diametral entgegengesetztes Konzept vertreten. Spiegelhalter ist Repräsentant eines Trends zur ökologisch orientierten Architektur. Passive Solarenergie, effiziente Isolierung und Wärmespeicherung werden verwendet, um den Energieverbrauch zu reduzieren, während das gekrümmte Dach auf der Südseite Photovoltaiktafeln enthält und Sonnenschutz bietet. Die Ästhetik eines solchen Wohnhauses wird zu einem großen Teil von seinem Energiespareffekt bestimmt; hier wurde dieses Ziel von den örtlichen Behörden gefördert. Angesichts des wachsenden Umweltbewußtseins ist es durchaus möglich, daß Energiesparhäuser in Zukunft als ästhetisch ansprechend empfunden werden. Spiegelhalters spröde Bauten können als Vorläufer einer neuen Architekturgeneration betrachtet werden.

opposée donne une idée de la liberté actuelle, en l'occurrence le Logement expérimental de Thomas Spiegelhalter (Freiburg, Allemagne, 1996-97, voir P 468-471). Spiegelhalter illustre une tendance grandissante de l'architecture contemporaine vers une sensibilité écologique. L'énergie solaire passive, l'isolation thermique efficace et l'emmagasinement de la chaleur servent à réduire la consommation d'énergie, tandis que le toit incurvé qui surplombe la façade sud est équipé de panneaux photovoltaïques et protège du soleil. L'esthétique de ce type de construction est pour une bonne part déterminée par cette préoccupation énergétique, objectif encouragé en l'occurrence par les autorités locales. Au fur et à mesure que se répand la conscience de l'importance du respect de l'environnement, il est tout à fait possible que des projets de nature écologiques soient jugés esthétiquement de plus en plus acceptables. Les bâtiments hérissés de Thomas Spiegelhalter annoncent peut être une nouvelle génération architecturale.

PLACES TO GATHER

VERSAMMLUNGS-RÄUME
DES LIEUX POUR SE RASSEMBLER

Second only to architecture's role as a provider of shelter and residence is its ability to bring people together. Theaters, cinemas or convention centers have not yet replaced museums as the ultimate symbols of civic pride, but the glut of museum construction in the 1980s certainly has led many municipalities to ponder the virtues of buildings that do not require collections to function. One of the most spectacular movie theaters to be built in recent years was designed by the group Coop Himmelb(l)au in Dresden, Germany (UFA Cinema Center, 1996-98, see P 144-151). While its fractured, "Deconstructivist" forms may recall aesthetic choices more than a decade old, this 2,400 seat facility certainly has created a surprise in the Stalinist architectural environment of Dresden. According to the principal Wolf Prix, the building is "designed like a video-clip, and seeks to do away with centralized perspective." Whatever one thinks of its aesthetics the UFA Cinema shows again that architects are free both technically and morally to create astonishing new forms more akin to sculpture than so many symmetrical buildings of the past. Of course the degree of surprise that a work of contemporary architecture can create depends in good

Nach ihrer primären Aufgabe, Schutz und Wohnraum zu bieten, kommt Architektur die Rolle zu, Menschen zusammenzuführen. Noch haben Theater, Kinos oder Kongreßzentren die Museen als höchste Symbole des Bürgerstolzes nicht ersetzt, doch hat das Übermaß an Museumsbauten in den 80er Jahren sicher viele Kommunalverwaltungen veranlaßt, über die Vorzüge von Gebäuden nachzudenken, die keiner Sammlung bedürfen, um ihre Funktion zu erfüllen. Eines der spektakulärsten Multiplex-Kinos der letzten Jahre stammt von der Gruppe Coop Himmelb(l)au (UFA-Palast, Dresden, 1996-98, siehe P 144-151). Obgleich seine gebrochenen, dekonstruktivistischen Formen eher ästhetische Vorstellungen aufgreifen, die bereits über ein Jahrzehnt zurückliegen, hat diese Anlage mit ihren 2 400 Plätzen sicherlich für Überraschung in Dresden gesorgt, dessen Bebauung noch weitgehend vom Monumentalstil der ehemaligen DDR geprägt ist. Laut Wolf Prix von Coop Himmelb(l)au wurde das Gebäude »unter Verzicht auf Zentralperspektive geplant«. Wie immer man die Gestaltung des UFA-Palastes beurteilt, er ist wiederum ein Beweis dafür, daß Architekten sowohl über die technische als auch die moralische Freiheit verfügen, erstaunliche

Juste après la fonction première de l'architecture – fournir un abri et un lieu de vie – vient sa capacité à réunir les hommes. Théâtres, cinémas ou centres de congrès n'ont pas encore remplacé les musées dans la symbolique urbaine, mais la masse de ceux édifiés depuis les années 80 a certainement conduit de nombreuses municipalités à réévaluer les vertus de bâtiments qui, eux, n'ont pas besoin de collections pour fonctionner. L'un des cinémas les plus spectaculaires récemment construits est l'œuvre du groupe Coop Himmelb(l)au à Dresde, Allemagne (UFA Cinema Center, 1996-98, voir P 144-151). Si ses formes «constructivistes» fracturées peuvent rappeler des choix esthétiques datant de plus de dix ans, ce complexe cinématographique de 2 400 places, a certainement créé la surprise dans l'environnement architectural stalinien de la ville. Selon l'associé principal de Coop Himmelb(l)au, Wolf Prix, le bâtiment est «conçu comme un vidéo-clip et cherche à se libérer de la perspective par rapport à un axe central». Quoi que l'on pense de cette esthétique, le cinéma UFA prouve une fois encore que les architectes sont libres, aussi bien techniquement que moralement, de créer des formes nouvelles étonnantes plus pro-

part on its environment. Despite an attachment to tradition in many areas, the Japanese are surprisingly open to new forms in architecture. Arata Isozaki, one of the great masters of today's architecture, has had both the inventiveness and the durability to substantially mark building design in his country. His most recent structures, including the Shizuoka Convention and Arts Center "Granship" (Japan, 1993-98, see P 252-257), are evidence of a new, unexpected direction in his work. This very large (60,630 m²) facility has a hall capable of seating up to 5,000 persons. Its spectacular curved shape is visible from the main Shinkansen "Bullet train" lines going from Tokyo to Osaka. At one time rather "Post-Modern" in his style, Isozaki has moved on to the kind of "mega-structure" that the Japanese have long been fond of. Seen from some angles, the Shizuoka "Granship" recalls a samurai helmet, a device that others in Japan such as Fumihiko Maki have also called on. But this reference, even in an oblique form, together with the massive roof/walls present both in Shizuoka and in his Nara Convention Center, show that Isozaki is fully able to carry forward the synthesis between tradition and modernity that has made contemporary Japanese

neue Formen zu entwerfen, die – eher als so viele symmetrische Bauten der Vergangenheit – an eine Skulptur erinnern.
Natürlich hängt der Grad der Überraschung, den ein Werk der Gegenwartsarchitektur auslösen kann, in erheblichem Maß von seiner Umgebung ab. Trotz ihrer in vielen Bereichen spürbaren Traditionsgebundenheit sind die Japaner erstaunlich offen für neue Formen in der Architektur. Arata Isozaki, einer der großen Meister der Gegenwartsarchitektur, hat durch seine Phantasie und Durchsetzungskraft die Architektur in seinem Lande entscheidend mitgeprägt. Seine neuesten Bauten, etwa das Kongreß- und Kunstzentrum »Granship« (Japan, 1993-98, siehe P 252-257), sind Anzeichen einer neuen und unerwarteten Tendenz in seinem Werk. Die sehr große Anlage (60 630 m²) umfaßt eine Halle mit bis zu 5 000 Sitzplätzen. Ihre spektakuläre Silhouette ist vom Hochgeschwindigkeitszug Shinkansen zu sehen, der Tokio und Osaka miteinander verbindet. Von einer eher »postmodernen« Ära seines Stils ist Isozaki jetzt zu einer Art »Megastruktur« übergegangen, wie sie in Japan schon immer beliebt war. Von verschiedenen Seiten betrachtet, erinnert das »Granship« in Shizuoka an einem Samurai-Helm –

ches de la sculpture que d'innombrables œuvres du passé qui faisaient appel à la symétrie.
L'intensité de surprise que provoque éventuellement une œuvre architecturale contemporaine dépend pour une bonne part de son environnement. Malgré leur attachement à la tradition dans de nombreux domaines, les Japonais se révèlent étonnament ouverts aux formes architecturales nouvelles. Arata Isozaki, l'un des grands maîtres de l'architecture contemporaine, a fait preuve d'une telle inventivité pendant de si longues années, qu'il a substantiellement marqué l'art de construire de son pays. Ses plus récentes réalisations, dont le Centre d'arts et de congrès de Shizuoka «Granship» (Japon, 1993-98, voir P 252-257), témoignent de la direction nouvelle et inattendue prise par son œuvre. Ce très vaste édifice (60 630 m²) possède une salle de 5 000 places assises. Sa forme incurvée spectaculaire est visible du train à grande vitesse, le Shinkansen, qui relie Tokyo à Osaka. Lors de sa période assez postmoderne, Isozaki s'était rapproché de ces mégastructures dont les Japonais se sont longtemps montrés si friands. Sous certains angles, le «Granship» rappelle un heaume de samouraï, parti esthétique auquel certains autres architectes japo-

PLACES TO GATHER

architecture so fruitful in recent years. Again, these are new, thoroughly modern forms that do have relationships to the local past: to the great wooden temple roofs of ancient Japan, for example. Isozaki knows as well as anyone what is happening elsewhere in architecture, yet his work is far from showing signs of weakening its links to Japanese culture.

Slightly older than Isozaki, Fumihiko Maki has also created an innovative body of work blending modern and traditional influences. One of his latest works, the Kaze-no-Oka Crematorium (Nakatsu, Oita, Japan, 1995-97, see P 330-335), brings his capacity in this respect to new heights. Despite its surprising shapes, more akin to Minimalist sculpture than to the generally ornate Japanese funeral homes, this complex derives from the traditional approach to the cremation of the dead. It also uses landscaping to highlight the close bond that the Japanese feel with nature, despite its relative absence in the crowded urban centers. A large, angled Corten steel wall shields the area where relatives wait for the process to be completed. It is interesting to note that just as the sculptor Richard Serra has tended in his use of massive Corten sheets to a more and

ein Sinnbild, auf das bereits andere japanische Architekten wie Fumihiko Maki angespielt haben. Aber dieser Bezug, der sogar in seiner versteckten Form mit dem massiven Dach und den Wänden sowohl in Shizuoka wie im Kongreßzentrum von Nara erkennbar ist, zeigt, daß Isozaki in der Lage ist, jene Synthese aus Tradition und Moderne weiterzuentwickeln, die so viele japanische Bauten der vergangenen Jahre auszeichnet. Und wieder sind es neue, durch und durch moderne Formen, die einen Bezug zur regionalen Überlieferung herstellen – etwa zu den großen hölzernen Tempeldächern des alten Japan. Isozaki weiß so gut wie andere auch, was anderswo in der Architektur geschieht, und doch zeigt sein Werk keinerlei Anzeichen einer Abschwächung seiner Bindungen an die japanische Kultur. Der etwas ältere Fumihiko Maki hat ebenfalls eine Anzahl innovativer Werke geschaffen, in denen sich moderne und traditionelle Einflüsse vermischen. In einem seiner jüngsten Bauwerke, dem Krematorium Kaze-no-Oka (Nakatsu, Oita, Japan, 1995-97, siehe P 330-335), erreichen Makis Fähigkeiten in dieser Richtung einen neuen Höhepunkt. Der Gebäudekomplex leitet sich trotz seiner innovativen Formensprache von der traditionellen Art der Einäscherung

nais, tel Fumihiko Maki, ont déjà fait appel. Mais cette référence, même sous une forme détournée, ainsi que les murs et toits massifs que l'on trouve à la fois à Shizuoka et dans le Centre de congrès de Nara, montrent qu'Isozaki est pleinement en mesure de faire progresser la synthèse entre tradition et modernité qui a tellement enrichi l'architecture japonaise au cours de ces dernières années. Là encore, il s'agit de formes vraiment modernes qui entretiennent un dialogue avec le passé national, les grands toits de bois des anciens temples japonais par exemple. Isozaki sait aussi bien que quiconque ce qui se passe dans le monde de l'architecture, mais les liens entre son travail et la culture japonaise n'en sont pas affaiblis pour autant. Légèrement plus âgé qu'Isozaki, Fumihiko Maki a également créé un corpus qui associe des influences modernes et traditionnelles. A cet égard, l'une de ses œuvres les plus récentes, le crématorium Kaze-no-Oka (Nakatsu, Oita, Japon, 1995-97, voir P 330-335), porte ce talent à de nouveaux sommets. En dépit de ses formes surprenantes, plus proches de la sculpture minimaliste que des temples funéraires japonais généralement très ornés, ce complexe se réfère à l'approche traditionnelle de la crémation.

more architectural type of expression, Maki here takes a step in the reverse direction – from architecture toward sculpture.

The younger generation in Japan has naturally been more experimental and in tune with the greater possibilities of contemporary design and construction technology. One of the more inventive architects of his generation, Makoto Sei Watanabe (born in 1952) goes so far as to create very complete designs that have little or no chance of being built. This is the case with his National Diet Building (1996, see P 508.509), planned for the New Capital of Japan. Taking the idea of "transparency" in politics beyond its logical conclusion, he suggests that a new building for the Diet be literally transparent, with walls, ceilings and floors made of glass. Going even further, Watanabe suggests that the "exterior of the building is made of elastic covering, and minute actuators densely arranged on its inside maintain and adjust the form of the building. Consisting of small linked cells, the covering resembles the skin of a living organism. Photosynthesizing organs and chromatophores are built into the cells, and the cells are activated by sunlight ..." Mixing ecology, politics and technology, Watanabe reminds one that archi-

Verstorbener ab – er ähnelt eher einer minimalistischen Skulptur als den im allgemeinen reich verzierten japanischen Leichenhallen. Das Krematorium bezieht die Landschaft ein und betont so die Naturverbundenheit der Japaner, auch wenn die Natur in den überbevölkerten städtischen Zentren kaum präsent ist. Eine große, schräge Wand aus Corten-Stahl schirmt den Bereich ab, in dem die Angehörigen auf das Ende der Einäscherung warten. Während ein Bildhauer wie Richard Serra sich durch seine Verwendung massiver Platten aus Corten-Stahl immer stärker der architektonischen Ausdrucksform nähert, geht Maki hier interessanterweise einen Schritt in die umgekehrte Richtung: von der Architektur zur Skulptur.

Die jüngere japanische Architektengeneration arbeitet stärker experimentell und mehr mit den vielfältigen Möglichkeiten der modernen Planungs- und Bautechnologie. Einer der phantasievollsten Architekten seiner Generation, Makoto Sei Watanabe (geboren 1952), geht so weit, quasi baureife Entwürfe zu erarbeiten, die nur eine geringe oder gar keine Chance haben, realisiert zu werden. Dies ist etwa der Fall bei seinem National Diet Building (Parlamentsgebäude, 1996, siehe P 508.509) für

L'architecte se sert également de la mise en forme du paysage pour mettre en valeur le lien que les Japonais entretiennent avec la nature, malgré sa relative absence dans les centres urbains surpeuplés. Un grand mur en acier Corten protège la zone dans laquelle les parents attendent que le processus de crémation soit achevé. Il est intéressant de noter que tandis que le sculpteur Richard Serra tend à partir d'épaisses feuilles d'acier Corten vers un type d'expression de plus en plus architectural, Maki emprunte ici le chemin inverse, de l'architecture vers la sculpture.

Au Japon, une génération d'architectes plus jeune se trouve naturellement davantage tentée par l'expérimentation et les possibilités plus larges ouvertes par le design contemporain et les technologies de la construction. L'un des architectes les plus inventifs de sa génération, Makoto Sei Watanabe (né en 1952), va jusqu'à créer des projets complets qui ont peu ou pas de chance d'être jamais réalisés. C'est le cas de sa proposition d'immeuble pour la diète japonaise (1996, voir P 508.509), conçu par la nouvelle capitale. Poussant l'idée de «transparence» en politique au-delà de sa conclusion logique, il suggère qu'un nouveau bâtiment parlementaire

PLACES TO GATHER

tecture can also be a vehicle for thought and debate. Again, since the origins of Modernism in the pre-war Bauhaus, politics has often been dissociated from architecture. The goal of "improving" anyone, let alone corrupt politicians, through design would have seemed far removed from any possible architectural debate just a few years ago. The rise of green architecture in Europe does show that a quasi-political stance is admissible in the current climate of freedom and freely available information. Three recently built European places of gathering show something of the variety of styles and types of expression that are considered not only as acceptable but even as being in the spirit of the times. Mario Botta's Church of Saint John the Baptist (Mogno, Ticino, Switzerland, 1986/92-98, see P 110-113) is far off the beaten path, some 40 km up a winding mountain road from Locarno. Built on the site of a 17th-century church that was swept away by an avalanche in 1986, Botta's church is unusual in its form – oval in plan with a circular skylight set at an angle. As specialist of visual perception Rudolf Arnheim has written, "in designing a new church, Mario Botta avoided the paralyzing effects of the closed symbols of traditional

die in Planung befindliche neue Hauptstadt Japans. Indem Watanabe den Gedanken der »Transparenz« von der Politik auf die Architektur überträgt, schlägt er vor, das neue Unterhaus im wörtlichen Sinne durchsichtig zu gestalten: mit Wänden, Decken und Böden aus Glas. Er geht sogar noch weiter und erklärt, daß »das Äußere des Gebäudes aus einer elastischen Abdeckung besteht und an der Innenseite in geringen Abständen angebrachte winzige Spannvorrichtungen oder Auslöser den Bau in Form halten und regulieren. Die aus kleinen, miteinander verbundenen Zellen bestehende Hülle ähnelt der Haut eines lebenden Organismus. ›Organe‹, die Photosynthese vollziehen, und Farbstoffträger sind in die Zellen eingebaut, die bei Sonnenlicht aktiviert werden ...« Indem Watanabe Ökologie, Politik und Technologie miteinander verbindet, erinnert er daran, daß Architektur Ideen vermitteln und Diskussionen anstoßen kann. Auch hier gilt: Seit den Ursprüngen der modernen Architektur im Weimarer Bauhaus hat sich die Politik häufig von der Architektur distanziert. Das Ziel, Menschen durch Gestaltung zu »bessern« – korrupte Politiker nicht ausgenommen – scheint über jede mögliche Architekturdiskussion der letzten Jahre weit hinauszuge-

devrait être littéralement transparent, avec des murs, des sols et des plafonds en verre. Allant plus loin encore, il suggère que «l'extérieur du bâtiment soit réalisé dans un matériau élastique, ce qui permettrait à des activateurs instantanés disposés en réseau serré de maintenir et de réguler la forme du bâtiment. Composée de petites cellules reliées entre elles, cette couverture fait penser à la peau d'un organisme vivant. Des systèmes de photosynthèse et des chromatophores sont intégrés à ces cellules, activées par la lumière du jour ...» Associant écologie, politique et technologie, Watanabe nous rappelle que l'architecture peut aussi être un véhicule de réflexion et de débat. Depuis les origines du modernisme dans le cadre du Bauhaus d'avant-guerre, la politique a souvent été dissociée de l'architecture. L'objectif «d'amélioration» par le design, pour ne pas parler de la corruption de la classe politique, aurait semblé bien étranger à tout débat sur l'architecture il y a quelques années seulement. La montée en puissance de l'architecture écologique en Europe montre qu'une posture quasi politique est admise dans le climat actuel de liberté et de libre accès à l'information. Trois lieux de rassemblement récemment construits en Europe témoignent de la variété de styles et de

church architecture. His church is modern in style, shockingly different, but in no way struggling for sensational novelty. On the contrary, it aspires to meet the demands of a temple of worship by deriving them simply and directly from expressive traits of basic geometrical shapes." With its thick walls, clad in alternating bands of local gray granite and white marble, this church brings to mind the Romanesque architecture that Botta is avowedly fond of. Here is a work that proceeds from the geometric vocabulary of Modernism and yet somehow calls on the roots of European architecture. This is more than a question of cladding; it is one of form, function and concept. One of the newly discovered freedoms of contemporary architecture is that of looking to the past while still retaining the triumphs of modernity.

More resolute in its embrace of the new, Jean Nouvel's Lucerne Culture and Congress Center (Switzerland, 1992-99, see P 384-393) was partially opened in 1998. Set on the banks of the Vierwaldstätter See, the lake of Lucerne, it is also next to the railway station, whose facade and entrance were redesigned by Santiago Calatrava. A major distinguishing feature is the extremely thin roof,

hen. Die Konjunktur ökologischer Architektur in Europa zeigt, daß eine quasi-politische Haltung durchaus zulässig ist.

Drei jüngst in Europa fertiggestellte Versammlungsorte geben Einblick in die Vielfalt der Stile und Ausdrucksformen. Mario Bottas Kirche Johannes der Täufer (Mogno, Tessin, Schweiz, 1986/92-98, siehe P 110-113) ist etwa 40 km von Locarno entfernt. Sie ist nur über einen gewundenen Bergpfad zu erreichen. Bottas Bau wurde anstelle einer 1986 von einer Lawine zerstörten Kirche aus dem 17. Jahrhundert errichtet. Er hat die ungewöhnliche Form eines abgeschrägten Zylinders. Der Wahrnehmungstheoretiker Rudolf Arnheim schrieb darüber: »Bei der Planung der neuen Kirche hat Mario Botta die lähmende Wirkung der geschlossenen Symbolik traditioneller Kirchenarchitektur vermieden. Seine Kirche ist modern im Stil, schockierend anders, aber in keiner Weise auf sensationelle Neuartigkeit bedacht. Sie sucht im Gegenteil den Erfordernissen eines Andachtsraums zu entsprechen, indem sie diese schlicht und direkt aus den expressiven Eigenschaften geometrischer Grundformen ableitet.« Diese Kirche erinnert mit ihren dicken, abwechselnd aus grauem Granit und weißem Marmor

types d'expression qui sont considérés non seulement comme acceptables mais même comme relevant de l'esprit de l'époque. L'église Saint-Jean-Baptiste de Mario Botta (Mogno, Tessin, Suisse, 1986/92-98, voir P 110-113) loin des circuits touristiques, se trouve à quelque quarante kilomètres de Locarno et est accessible par une petite route sinueuse de montagne. Construit sur le site d'une église du XVIIe siècle balayée par une avalanche en 1986, le sanctuaire de Botta présente un plan ovale et un grand toit-verrière circulaire incliné de formes inhabituelles. Comme le grand théoricien de la perception visuelle Rudolf Arnheim l'a remarqué: «En dessinant cette nouvelle église, Mario Botta a évité les effets paralysants des symboles clos de l'architecture traditionnelle religieuse. Son église est de style moderne, différente au point de choquer, mais ne s'efforce en aucun cas de tendre vers le sensationnalisme. Au contraire, elle aspire à répondre aux exigences d'un temple de prière simplement et directement, à partir de l'expressivité des formes géométriques de base.» Avec ses murs épais, plaqués de bandeaux alternés de granite gris local et de marbre blanc, cette église rappelle l'architecture romane dont Botta est un admirateur avoué. C'est là une œuvre qui part du

which not only defines its profile, but also articulates the space of the square near the entrance. Like many new cultural facilities this is a multipurpose complex that will eventually have space for congress activities and art exhibitions as well as a concert hall. A wealth of materials ranging from aluminum to wood greet visitors in a surprisingly harmonious and innovative composition.

By way of comparison, Álvaro Siza's Portuguese Pavilion, Expo '98 (Lisbon, Portugal, 1996-98, see P 458-465) is rather less baroque in its use of materials. The defining feature of this building, intended as the central pavilion of the 1998 Lisbon Expo, is the unusual curved concrete "veil" that is suspended at either end of an outdoor square from steel cables. Siza denies any relationship between this form and the sails that might be expected in the context of the theme of exploration chosen for Expo '98. Be that as it may, in this, as in many of his other structures, Álvaro Siza shows that architecture derived from Modernism is still capable of generating an incredible variety of new forms.

gemauerten Wänden an die von Botta erklärtermaßen bewunderte romanische Architektur. Das Bauwerk greift auf das geometrische Vokabular der Moderne zurück und bezieht sich doch auf die Ursprünge der europäischen Architektur. Hier geht es um mehr als um die Frage der Fassadengestaltung: es ist eine Frage der Form, der Funktion und der Konzeption. Zu den neuentdeckten Freiheiten der Gegenwartsarchitektur gehört der Blick auf die Vergangenheit, ohne die Errungenschaften der klassischen Moderne aus dem Blick zu verlieren. Entschiedener in der Hinwendung zum Neuen ist Jean Nouvels Luzerner Kultur- und Kongreßzentrum (Schweiz, 1992-99, siehe P 384-393). Das Kongreßzentrum wurde 1998 bereits teilweise eröffnet. Es liegt am Ufer des Vierwaldstätter Sees neben dem Bahnhof, dessen Fassade und Eingang von Santiago Calatrava umgestaltet wurden. Ein hervorstechendes Merkmal des neuen Gebäudes ist das extrem dünne Dach, das nicht nur die Silhouette prägt, sondern auch den Platz vor dem Eingang bestimmt. Wie viele neue Kultureinrichtungen ist auch diese Anlage ein Mehrzweckkomplex, der Raum für Kongresse, Ausstellungen und Konzertveranstaltungen bietet. Eine Vielfalt unterschied-

vocabulaire géométrique du modernisme et prend cependant appui d'une certaine façon sur les racines de l'architecture européenne. Plus qu'une question de revêtement, il s'agit ici d'une réflexion sur la forme, la fonction et le concept. L'une des nouvelles libertés de l'architecture contemporaine est de savoir regarder vers le passé, tout en assimilant les victoires de la modernité.

Plus affirmé dans sa nouveauté, le centre culturel et de congrès de Lucerne de Jean Nouvel (Suisse, 1992-99, voir P 384-393) a été partiellement ouvert en 1998. Il est situé au bord du lac des Quatre Cantons, non loin de la gare centrale dont la façade et l'entrée ont été remodelées par Santiago Calatrava. Une de ses caractéristiques originales majeures est un toit extrêmement fin qui définit non seulement son profil, mais détermine et articule également l'espace de la place sur laquelle il donne. Comme de nombreux équipements culturels récents, il s'agit d'un complexe multifonctions qui abritera aussi bien des activités de congrès que des expositions artistiques et une salle de concert. Une multitude de matériaux, de l'aluminium au bois, accueillent le visiteur dans une composition étonnamment harmonieuse et novatrice.

licher Materialien von Aluminium bis Holz zeigt sich in einer erstaunlich harmonischen und innovativen Komposition.

Im Vergleich dazu ist Álvaro Sizas Portugiesischer Pavillon für die Expo '98 (Lissabon, Portugal, 1996-98, siehe P 458-465) weniger üppig im Materialgebrauch. Kennzeichnend für Sizas Bau, der der zentrale Pavillon der Expo war, ist das ungewöhnliche Beton-»Segel«, das zu beiden Seiten an Stahlseilen aufgehängt ist. Siza selbst leugnet allerdings jeglichen Bezug seiner Formen zu Segeln, der doch im Kontext des für die Expo '98 gewählten Themas »Entdeckungen« nahegelegen hätte. Wie auch immer, Siza zeigt in diesem wie auch in vielen anderen Bauwerken, daß eine von der Moderne inspirierte Architektur immer noch in der Lage ist, eine unglaubliche Vielfalt neuer Formen hervorzubringen.

Par comparaison, le Pavillon portugais d'Álvaro Siza pour Expo '98 (Lisbonne, Portugal, 1996-98, voir P 458-465) est nettement moins baroque dans son choix de matériaux. La forte identité de ce bâtiment-phare de l'Exposition universelle de Lisbonne de 1998, tient à l'étonnant voile de béton suspendu à ses deux extrémités par des câbles en acier recouvrant une place. Siza réfute toute relation entre cette forme et les voiles de bateau que l'on aurait pu attendre dans le contexte du thème de l'exploration retenu pour Expo '98. Ceci dit, comme dans beaucoup de ses autres réalisations, l'architecte démontre que l'architecture inspirée du modernisme est encore capable de générer une incroyable variété de formes.

PLACES FOR MOVEMENT

BEWEGUNGS-RÄUME
DES LIEUX DE MOUVEMENT

Railway stations were to the late 19th century what some airports were in the post-World War II period – symbols of progress, and rapid movement. The decline of rail travel brought about by the rise of the airplane also made the grandiose stations of another era seem inappropriate. An example of this attitude can be seen in New York, where Pennsylvania Station (1902-11), McKim, Mead & White's masterpiece, with its cathedral-like arcade and Main Waiting Room modeled after the Baths of Caracalla, was demolished in October 1963. It was replaced by an undistinguished concourse located beneath Madison Square Garden. Today, it is hoped that Penn Station will rise again in the walls of the former General Post Office, a scheme that highlights the new importance being given to railway stations worldwide. London's Waterloo International Terminal by Nicholas Grimshaw (1990-93), Madrid's Atocha Station by Rafael Moneo (1986-92), the Lille-Europe station in Lille (Jean-Marie Duthilleul, 1990-94), or Santa Justa in Seville (Antonio Cruz and Antonio Ortiz, 1988-92) confirm the European trend toward more spectacular stations, reminiscent of their 19th-century ancestors. So too air travel, once marked by such spectacular

Bahnhöfe hatten für das 19. Jahrhundert die gleiche Bedeutung wie Flughäfen in der Zeit nach dem Zweiten Weltkrieg – sie waren Symbole des Fortschritts und der schnellen Fortbewegung. Der mit dem Vordringen des Luftverkehrs einhergehende Rückgang der Bahnreisen ließ auch die grandiosen Bahnhöfe einer vergangenen Ära überholt erscheinen. Ein Beispiel für diese Entwicklung ist die New Yorker Pennsylvania Station (1902-11). Das Meisterwerk von McKim, Mead & White wurde im Oktober 1963 abgerissen. Als Ersatz entstand eine nichtssagende Bahnhofshalle unter dem Madison Square Garden. Heute besteht die Hoffnung, die Pennsylvania Station in den Mauern des früheren Hauptpostamts zu rekonstruieren – ein Plan, der dem weltweit wiedererwachten Interesse an Bahnhöfen Rechnung trägt. Der Londoner Waterloo International Terminal von Nicholas Grimshaw (1990-93), der Bahnhof Atocha in Madrid von Rafael Moneo (1986-92), der Europa-Bahnhof im französischen Lille (Jean-Marie Duthilleul, 1990-94) oder Santa Justa in Sevilla (Antonio Cruz und Antonio Ortiz, 1988-92) bezeugen den europäischen Trend zu spektakulären Bahnhöfen, die an ihre Vorgänger aus dem 19. Jahrhundert erinnern. Auch das Erleb-

Symboles de progrès et de déplacements rapides, les gares de chemin de fer ont été pour la fin du XIXe siècle ce que certains aéroports furent pour la période d'après-guerre. La croissance des transports aériens s'est accompagnée du déclin du voyage en train et a rendu un peu obsolètes les gares grandioses d'une autre époque. Exemple de ce phénomène, New York n'hésita pas en 1963 à démolir Pennsylvania Station (1902-11), chef-d'œuvre de McKim, Mead & White, aux voûtes et arcades de cathédrales et au grand hall d'attente inspiré des bains de Caracalla. Aujourd'hui, on espère que Penn Station renaîtra dans les murs de l'ancien General Post Office, projet qui éclaire l'importance nouvelle donnée aujourd'hui aux gares dans le monde entier. Le terminal international de Waterloo à Londres de Nicholas Grimshaw (1990-93), la gare d'Atocha à Madrid, de Rafael Moneo (1986-92), la gare Lille-Europe à Lille (Jean-Marie Duthilleul, 1990-94) ou la gare de Santa Justa à Séville (Antonio Cruz et Antonio Ortiz, 1988-92) confirment la tendance européenne en faveur de gares plus spectaculaires, qui rappellent leurs ancêtres du XIXe siècle. Il en est de même pour les aérogares, jadis marquées par des édifices aussi brillants que le terminal TWA

buildings as Eero Saarinen's 1961 TWA Terminal at Kennedy (then Idlewild) Airport, fell victim to the increasingly banal experience of flight.

Both railway travel and air travel have seen recent projects completed that are destined to give them back some of their glamour and excitement. The Japanese have long been convinced of the virtues of high-speed rail travel, with the Shinkansen system linking cities along the country's east coast. The JR Kyoto Railway Station by Hiroshi Hara (1991-97, see P 192-197) affirms the importance of the railway station in the life of the modern city. With at least 20 restaurants, a hotel, and a shopping center integrated into its admittedly considerable volume (470 m long and 59.5 m high, for a total floor area of 235,257 m²), the JR Kyoto Railway Station hints at the reality of the theories of Hara, who has written about future cities made of interconnected skyscrapers. Here, a central atrium that is neither fully exterior nor interior rises up in banks providing gathering space, areas for concerts, or places to simply enjoy the view. This area has become one of the favorite meeting spots of Kyoto residents, showing that a railway station need not be confined to the role of getting people in and out

nis einer Flugreise, einst begleitet von so markanten Bauwerken wie Eero Saarinens TWA-Terminal von 1961 auf dem Kennedy (bis 1963 Idlewild) Airport, wird heute immer alltäglicher.

Sowohl für den Bahn- als auch für den Flugverkehr sind neue Projekte ausgeführt worden, die diesen Formen des Reisens wieder etwas von ihrem Glanz und ihrer Faszination zurückgeben. Der Bahnhof der Japan Railway in Kioto von Hiroshi Hara (1991-97, siehe P 192-197) zeugt von der Bedeutung des Bahnhofs im Leben einer modernen Stadt. Mit ihren mindestens 20 Restaurants, einem Hotel und einem Einkaufszentrum, die in das beträchtliche Volumen (470 m Länge, 59,5 m Höhe und eine Gesamtfläche von 235 257 m²) integriert sind, spricht die Japan Railway Station von Kioto für die Theorien Haras, der über zukünftige Städte aus miteinander verbundenen Wolkenkratzern geschrieben hat. Hier erhebt sich in Abstufungen ein zentraler Atriumhof, der weder ein Außen- noch ein Innenraum ist. Die verschiedenen Ebene bieten Versammlungs- und Konzerträume oder einfach nur einen großartigen Blick über die Stadt. Dieser Bereich hat sich zu einem beliebten Treffpunkt der Kiotoer Bevölkerung entwickelt, und er beweist, daß die Aufgabe eines

d'Eero Saarinen en 1961 à Kennedy Airport (alors Idlewild), et victimes de la banalisation grandissante du voyage en avion.

Ces deux grands modes de transport que sont le train et l'avion ont récemment vu l'achèvement de projets destinés à leur faire renouer avec leur séduction et leur sens du spectaculaire antérieurs. Les Japonais sont depuis longtemps convaincus des vertus du train à grande vitesse, et le Shinkansen relie plusieurs villes notamment le long de la côte est de l'île principale. La gare JR de Kyoto, par Hiroshi Hara (1991-97, voir P 192-197), affirme l'importance de la gare dans la vie de la cité moderne. Comptant au moins 20 restaurants, un hôtel et un centre commercial intégrés dans son volume considérable (470 m de long, 59,5 m de haut, pour une surface au sol totale de 235 257 m²), cette gare matérialise les théories de Hara, qui a proposé des cités futures composées de gratte-ciel interconnectés. Ici, un atrium central qui n'est ni vraiment intérieur ni vraiment extérieur s'élève en gradins et offre des espaces de rassemblement, pour des concerts ou simplement des endroits d'où profiter de la vue. Cette gare est devenue l'un des lieux de rencontre favoris des habitants de Kyoto, ce qui montre

PLACES FOR MOVEMENT

of trains. In Japan, where many major stations are located underground, this is no small achievement. In Europe, Santiago Calatrava's Oriente Station (Lisbon, Portugal, 1993-98, see P 126-131) is as much a gateway to a new area of the city as it is a railway station. Situated at one of the main entrances to the Expo '98 fairgrounds, not far from the banks of the Tagus River, the Oriente Station includes a bus terminal, subway station and parking facilities. Since it is open on both ends at ground level, with the railway lines running above on an elevated mound, the Oriente Station is a point of passage for almost anyone entering or leaving the area now intended as a development zone for the city. This is about architecture and urban renewal on a large scale. No fewer than 200,000 persons a day pass through Oriente Station. Its light, airy presence speaks of a bright future in which contemporary architecture will have played a central role. As ambitious as the Oriente Station may seem in the context of an old European city like Lisbon, its scale fades in comparison to that of Lord Norman Foster's new Hong Kong International Airport, (China, 1995-98, see P 166-169). At nearly 520,000 m², the terminal building of Hong Kong

Bahnhofs nicht darauf beschränkt sein muß, Zugreisende ein- und aussteigen zu lassen. In Japan, wo viele große Bahnhöfe unterirdisch angelegt sind, ist dies keine geringe Leistung.
In Europa hat sich Santiago Calatravas Oriente Station (Lissabon, 1993-98, siehe P 126-131) sowohl als Tor zu einem neuen Stadtgebiet wie auch als Bahnhof bewährt. Zu dem Bauwerk, das an einem der Haupteingänge zum Gelände der Expo '98 nahe dem Tejo-Ufer liegt, gehören ein Busbahnhof, eine U-Bahn-Station und Parkplätze. Der Bahnhof ist auf Erdgeschoßniveau an beiden Seiten offen; die Züge werden über einen darüber gelegenen Damm geführt. Damit wird er zum Durchgangsbereich für jeden, der den neuen, nun zum Vorort Lissabons erklärten Stadtteil betritt oder verläßt. Hier handelt es sich um Architektur und Stadterneuerung in großem Maßstab. Mindestens 200 000 Personen passieren den Bahnhof täglich. Sein filigranes Erscheinungsbild verheißt eine glänzende Zukunft, in der die Architektur eine zentrale Rolle spielen wird. So ehrgeizig ein Projekt wie die Oriente Station in einer alten europäischen Stadt wie Lissabon auch erscheint, sein Maßstab verblaßt im Vergleich zu Lord Norman Fosters neuem Internationalen Flug-

bien qu'une gare n'est pas nécessairement confinée au rôle de plate-forme ferroviaire. Au Japon, où de nombreuses grandes gares sont souterraines, c'est une entreprise qui ne manque pas d'audace.
En Europe, la gare d'Oriente par Santiago Calatrava (Lisbonne, Portugal, 1993-98, voir P 126-131) fait autant office de porte d'accès à une nouvelle partie de la ville que de gare de chemin de fer. Située à l'une des entrées principales de l'Expo '98, non loin du Tage, elle comprend un terminal de bus, une station de métro et des parkings. Comme elle s'ouvre à ses deux extrémités au niveau du sol, et que ses voies sont surélevées, elle est le point de passage presque obligé pour quiconque entre ou sort de cette zone en plein développement. Elle concerne donc à la fois l'architecture et la rénovation. Pas moins de 200 000 personnes la traversent quotidiennement. Sa présence légère et aérienne parle d'un futur souriant dans lequel l'architecture contemporaine devrait jouer un rôle central.
Aussi ambitieuse que soit la gare de l'Oriente dans le contexte d'une vieille cité européenne comme Lisbonne, son échelle pâlit en comparaison de celle du nouvel aéroport international de Hongkong de Norman Foster (Chine, 1995-98, voir P 166-169).

International Airport has been called "the largest enclosed public space ever made." The structure, which is 1.27 km long, is designed to handle 35 million passengers a year. Before its opening, Lord Norman Foster made much of the remarkable transition plans from aging Kai Tak Airport in downtown Hong Kong to this new facility built essentially on reclaimed land. It was all to happen smoothly in a single night. The transition was of course not as smooth as planned, but the airport remains as a symbol of the economic power of Hong Kong, now in its first years of Chinese administration. Foster's architecture is about spaces that people are comfortable in, but it is in many ways an ode to technology – the very technology that permitted the construction of such a massive airport almost on time and on budget. Contemporary architecture is also about unprecedented access to construction materials and technology that were unavailable just a few years ago.

hafen in Hongkong (China, 1995-98, siehe P 166-169). Der fast 520 000 m² große Terminal ist als »größter je umbauter öffentlicher Raum« bezeichnet worden. In dem 1,27 km langen Gebäude sollen zunächst 35 Millionen Passagiere pro Jahr abgefertigt werden. Vor der Eröffnung war Norman Foster sehr zuversichtlich, was die Überleitungspläne vom veralteten Flughafen Kai Tak in der Innenstadt Hongkongs zum Neubau anging, der in der Hongkonger Bucht im wesentlichen auf neugewonnenem Land errichtet wurde. Alles sollte in einer einzigen Nacht reibungslos vonstatten gehen. Natürlich ging der Übergang nicht so glatt vor sich wie geplant; der Flughafen ist jedoch nach wie vor ein Symbol der wirtschaftlichen Macht Hongkongs, auch jetzt, unter chinesischer Verwaltung. Fosters Architektur schafft Räume, in denen sich Menschen wohl fühlen, in vieler Hinsicht ist sie aber auch ein Loblied auf die Technologie – jene Technologie, die den Bau eines so gewaltigen Flughafens fast termingerecht und im gesteckten Budgetrahmen ermöglichte. Der zeitgenössischen Architektur eröffnen sich im Hinblick auf Materialien und Technologien Möglichkeiten, wie sie noch vor wenigen Jahren unvorstellbar waren.

Se développant sur près de 520 000 m², ce terminal a été qualifié de «plus vaste espace public couvert jamais construit». Mesurant 1,27 km, sa structure conçue pour traiter 35 millions de passagers par an remplace l'ancien et vieillissant aéroport de Kai Tak situé en pleine ville. Norman Foster participé activement au plan de transfert entre les deux installations. Tout devait se passer en une seule nuit. Si les opérations ne se sont pas déroulées aussi bien que prévu, cet immense aéroport reste un symbole de la puissance économique de Hongkong, maintenant sous administration chinoise. L'architecture de Foster peut créer des espaces dans lesquels l'homme se sent à l'aise, mais elle est aussi à de nombreux égards une ode à la technologie. C'est la technologie actuelle qui a permis la construction d'un aussi énorme aéroport à peu près dans les délais et dans le cadre du budget prévu. L'architecture contemporaine doit également beaucoup à la disponibilité de matériaux de construction et de technologies qui n'existaient tout simplement pas il y a quelques années encore.

PLACES OF EXHIBITION

AUSSTELLUNGS-RÄUME
DES LIEUX D'EXPOSITION

A worldwide fashion that stretched from the late 1970s into the early 1990s left almost every major, affluent city and many provincial towns with their own art museum. Often, as in Japan, these structures were designed by prestigious architects, but just as often were devoid of substantive collections. In the late 1990s facilities for art have still been built, but often without the kind of state-sponsored generosity that characterized the 1980s. Then, too, cultural facilities have more and more often been called on to fulfill several different functions simultaneously, like the Culture and Congress Center in Lucerne by Jean Nouvel, or to meet new needs, as is the case of Renzo Piano's Jean-Marie Tjibaou Cultural Center (Nouméa, New Caledonia, 1992-98, see P 406-411). A history of separatist violence in this distant French overseas territory led the government of François Mitterrand to plan for a cultural center devoted to local traditions. It is a measure of the talent of Renzo Piano that he was able to create a remarkable, efficient facility while calling largely on local village tradition as a source for his forms. Within this framework, he of course makes use of advanced technology, but the result is a building, or rather a series of buildings, unlike

Aufgrund eines weltweiten Trends, der vom Ende der 70er bis in die frühen 90er Jahre anhielt, erhielten fast alle größeren wohlhabenden Städte und viele Orte in der Provinz eigene Kunstmuseen. Wie in Japan wurden diese Bauten häufig von renommierten Architekten errichtet, ebenso häufig fehlten ihnen jedoch eigenständige Sammlungen. Auch in den späten 90er Jahren wurden immer noch Häuser für die Kunst errichtet, häufig jedoch ohne die großzügige öffentliche Förderung, die sie noch in den 80er Jahren erfahren hatten. Darüber hinaus wird von Kultureinrichtungen immer häufiger erwartet, daß sie mehrere verschiedene Funktionen zugleich erfüllen, wie das Kultur- und Kongreßzentrum in Luzern von Jean Nouvel, oder daß sie neuen Bedürfnissen entsprechen, wie Renzo Pianos Kulturzentrum Jean-Marie Tjibaou (Nouméa, Neukaledonien, 1992-98, siehe P 406-411). Die Geschichte separatistischer Gewalt in diesem entlegenen Überseegebiet unter französischer Hoheit veranlaßte die Regierung François Mitterrand, ein Kulturzentrum zu errichten, das sich den lokalen Traditionen widmet. Daß es Renzo Piano gelang, einerseits eine bemerkenswerte und effiziente Einrichtung zu schaffen, während er sich andererseits am Formenschatz

Une mode universelle qui s'est répandue de la fin des années 70 au début des années 90 a doté presque chaque grande capitale et de nombreuses villes de province d'un nouveau musée d'art. Souvent, comme dans le cas du Japon, ces structures conçues par de prestigieux architectes, péchent par manque de collections substantielles. À la fin des années 1990, de nouveaux projets continuent à voir le jour, mais sans bénéficier de la même générosité publique que celle des années 80. Par ailleurs, les équipements culturels sont de plus en plus appelés à remplir plusieurs fonctions à la fois, comme le Centre de congrès et de la culture de Lucerne de Jean Nouvel, ou à répondre à de nouveaux besoins, comme dans le cas du Centre culturel Jean-Marie Tjibaou par Renzo Piano (Nouméa, Nouvelle Calédonie, 1992-98, voir P 406-411). Un sombre passé de violence dans ce lointain territoire d'outre-mer français a incité le gouvernement de François Mitterrand à projeter un centre culturel consacré aux traditions locales. Que Renzo Piano se soit montré capable de créer ce bâtiment aussi remarquable qu'efficace en s'appuyant largement sur les traditions tribales locales pour déterminer ses formes donne la mesure de son talent d'architecte. Il ne

any other seen in contemporary architecture. This is not an adaptation of indigenous forms by a local architect, but a renewal of existing ideas by an observant European.

Limited funds have encouraged adaptive reuse of existing buildings in many sectors, including the arts. One of the more interesting efforts of this type was carried out by the California architect Frederick Fisher in a former elementary school near Manhattan (P.S.1, Long Island City, New York, United States, 1995-97, see P 160-163). The original structure was built in two phases, the south wing in 1892 and the north wing in 1905, in a "Romanesque Revival" style. Abandoned by the City of New York, P.S.1 was converted into a center for contemporary art in 1976 by Alanna Heiss and her associates. With an $8.5 million budget, Frederick Fisher provided a total of 11,000 m² of space, including unusual exterior exhibition "rooms" formed by concrete walls in front of the entrance. Most of this space is however made up of lightly renovated former schoolrooms, showing that a low-budget conversion can make an ideal space for contemporary art. Far from insisting on the kind of all-over white space pioneered by New York's Museum of

der traditionellen Dorfarchitektur Neukaledoniens orientierte, darf als Indiz seines Talents gelten. Es entstand ein Gebäude oder vielmehr eine Gruppe von Gebäuden, die sich von allen anderen zeitgenössischen Bauten unterscheidet. Es ist keine Adaption einheimischer Formen durch einen ortsansässigen Architekten, sondern die Erneuerung vorhandener Ideen durch einen aufmerksam beobachtenden Europäer.

Die Verschlechterung der wirtschaftlichen Situation hat die Umwidmung bestehender Bauten in vielen Bereichen gefördert, darunter auch für Zwecke der Kunst. Eines der interessantesten Vorhaben dieser Art wurde von dem kalifornischen Architekten Frederick Fisher in einer ehemaligen Grundschule bei Manhattan realisiert (P.S.1, Long Island City, New York, 1995-97, siehe P 160-163). Der alte Bau war in zwei Phasen entstanden: 1892 der Südflügel und 1905 der nördliche, beide in neoromanischem Stil. Die von der Stadt New York aufgegebene Schule wurde 1976 von Alanna Heiss und Partnern in ein Zentrum für zeitgenössische Kunst umgewandelt. Mit einem Budget von 8,5 Millionen US$ schuf Frederick Fisher eine Ausstellungsfläche von insgesamt 11 000 m², darunter sehr ungewöhnliche, durch

s'agit pas ici de l'adaptation de formes indigènes par un architecte local, mais du renouvellement d'idées existantes par un Européen observateur.

La limitation des financements a encouragé la réutilisation et l'adaptation de bâtiments existants dans de nombreux domaines, y compris celui des arts. L'un des plus intéressants efforts manifestés dans cette direction est dû à l'architecte californien Frederick Fisher qui est intervenu sur une ancienne école élémentaire près de Manhattan (P.S.1, Long Island City, New York, États-Unis, 1995-97, voir P 160-163). Construite dans un style néo-roman en deux phases, l'aile sud en 1892 et l'aile nord en 1905, puis abandonnée par la ville de New York, P.S.1 fut transformée en un centre d'art contemporain en 1976 par Alanna Heiss et ses associés. Pour un budget de $8,5 millions, Frederick Fisher a créé environ 11 000 m² d'espace dont plusieurs curieuses «salles» d'exposition extérieures délimitées par des murs de béton montés devant l'entrée. L'essentiel de ces espaces est cependant constitué par les anciennes salles de classe rénovées, qui montrent qu'un budget de reconversion limité peut donner naissance à un espace idéal pour l'art contemporain. Loin de se contenter du type d'espace intégralement

PLACES OF EXHIBITION

Modern Art, Fisher has incorporated the varied and rich materials of a late 19th-century building. Curiously, the new modernity is far more tolerant of the past than was Modernism.

Another example of innovative renovation is the ZKM Center for Art and Media Technology (Karlsruhe, Germany, 1993-97, see P 436-441). Dedicated to the study and exhibition of the most advanced forms of media-related arts, the ZKM was inserted into a 1918 landmark munitions plant, after the city decided in 1992 to abandon the idea of a proposed new building to be designed by Rem Koolhaas. Surprisingly undamaged during the war, the 312 m long structure was one of the first concrete skeleton designs built in Germany. It was left largely intact by architect Peter Schweger, who placed a priority on maintaining its industrial character. Both the ZKM and P.S.1 are projects sure to be imitated in the future. Many industrial or administrative buildings outlive their usefulness, leaving vast amounts of space for culturally oriented programs. Again, where the aesthetics of Modernism demanded new space, current thinking finds great interest in older buildings, whose construction may indeed be much more solid than anything being

Betonwände im Freien vor dem Eingang gebildete Ausstellungs-»Räume«. Der größte Teil der Ausstellungsfläche besteht aus nur geringfügig umgestalteten Klassenräumen, was beweist, daß ein altes Gebäude mit geringem Aufwand zu einem idealen Domizil für zeitgenössische Kunst werden kann. Fisher hat, ohne auf dem vom New Yorker Museum of Modern Art vorgegebenen weißen Einheitsraum zu bestehen, die vielfältigen Baumaterialien vom Ende des 19. Jahrhunderts integriert. Seltsamerweise zeigt sich die neue Moderne weitaus toleranter gegenüber der Vergangenheit, als es die klassische Moderne war.

Ein weiteres Beispiel für einen innovativen Umbau ist das ZKM – Zentrum für Kunst und Medientechnologie (Karlsruhe, 1993-97, siehe P 436-441). Nachdem die Stadt Karlsruhe 1992 beschlossen hatte, den Plan eines neuen, von Rem Koolhaas entworfenen Gebäudes aufzugeben, wurde das dem Studium und der Ausstellung modernster Medienkunst gewidmete ZKM in einer denkmalgeschützten Munitionsfabrik von 1918 untergebracht. Das 312 m lange, im Krieg erstaunlicherweise unbeschädigt gebliebene Gebäude war einer der ersten Betonskelettbauten in Deutschland. Der Architekt

blanc dont la mode fut lancée par le Museum of Modern Art de New York, Fisher a intégré les matériaux riches et variés d'un bâtiment de la fin du XIXe siècle. Curieusement, cette nouvelle modernité est beaucoup plus respectueuse du passé que ne l'a été le modernisme.

Autre exemple de rénovation novatrice, le Centre ZKM pour les arts et les technologies des médias (Karlsruhe, Allemagne, 1993-97, voir P 436-441). Le ZKM qui se consacre à l'étude et à l'exposition des formes les plus avancées d'art lié aux médias, s'est installé dans une usine de munitions datant de 1918, après que la ville ait décidé, en 1992, d'abandonner l'idée d'un bâtiment neuf qui devait être réalisé par Rem Koolhaas. Ayant échappé aux destructions de la guerre, cette structure de 312 m de long est l'une des premières ossatures de béton édifiées en Allemagne. Elle fut en grande partie respectée par l'architecte Peter Schweger, qui a cherché en priorité à maintenir son caractère industriel. Le ZKM et le P.S.1 sont des projets qui feront certainement des émules. De nombreux bâtiments industriels ou administratifs vivent plus longtemps que leur fonction, et ouvrent de vastes perspectives aux projets d'orientation culturelle. Alors que l'esthé-

built today. Much as they are in the case of green architecture, aesthetics seem here to grow out of or be influenced by economic or technical constraints. Despite the slower rate of construction of new museums, some astonishing new buildings have been completed recently. One of the most frequently published of these is the first major project built by the New York architect Steven Holl. The Kiasma Museum of Contemporary Art (Helsinki, Finland, 1993-98, see P 234-243) was originally named "chiasma," signifying "an intersection or a crossing over," related to the crossing of optical nerves at the base of the brain. Measuring about 12,000 m², the building was built for a budget of $41 million, and is located in the heart of Helsinki, near the Parliament building, Eliel Saarinen's Helsinki Station and Alvar Aalto's Finlandia Hall. A prominent feature of the structure is its curved wall and roof, which gives a liveliness to the interior space while facilitating the admission of natural light to upper and lower level exhibitions. As Holl says, "this curved unfolding sequence provides elements of both mystery and surprise – which do not exist in a typical single or double loaded orthogonal arrangement of space." While respecting his prestigious architectural

Peter Schweger beließ die Fabrik weitgehend unverändert und entschied sich so für die Erhaltung ihres industriellen Charakters. Sowohl beim ZKM als auch bei der ehemaligen New Yorker Grundschule handelt es sich um Vorbilder, die in Zukunft sicherlich Nachahmung finden werden. Viele Industrie- oder Verwaltungsbauten überdauern ihre frühere Nutzung und bieten ein großes Potential für kulturelle Zwecke. Auch hier zeigt sich – im Gegensatz zum ästhetischen Anspruch der Moderne, die neue Räume forderte –, daß ein großes Interesse an älteren Gebäuden besteht, deren Konstruktion meist viel stabiler ist als die heutzutage errichteter Bauten. Wie bei der ökologischen Architektur ist auch hier die Gestaltung wirtschaftlichen oder technischen Faktoren unterworfen oder zumindest von ihnen beeinflußt.
Obgleich insgesamt weniger Museen gebaut werden, sind in letzter Zeit einige überraschende Neubauten entstanden. Einer der meistdiskutierten ist das erste Großprojekt des New Yorker Architekten Steven Holl. Das Kiasma-Museum für Gegenwartskunst (Helsinki, Finnland, 1993-98, siehe P 234-243) hieß ursprünglich »Chiasma« und bezeichnete damit »einen Schnittpunkt oder eine Kreuzung« – in

tique moderniste militait en faveur d'espaces nouveaux, la pensée actuelle trouve beaucoup d'intérêt à des bâtiments anciens, dont la construction peut se révéler, en fait, beaucoup plus solide que tout ce que l'on peut construire aujourd'hui. En grande partie comme dans le cas de l'architecture «verte», l'esthétique semble ici liée à des contraintes économiques ou techniques quand elle n'est pas influencée par elles.
Malgré le ralentissement de la construction de nouveaux musées, quelques étonnants bâtiments ont récemment vu le jour. L'un des plus souvent publiés est le premier grand projet de l'architecte newyorkais Steven Holl. Le Musée d'art contemporain Kiasma (Helsinki, Finlande, 1993-98, voir P 234-243) tire son nom de «chiasme» qui signifie, entre autres, «intersection ou croisement» des nerfs optiques à la base du cerveau. De 12 000 m² environ, il a été édifié pour un budget de $41 millions et se trouve au centre d'Helsinki, près du Parlement, de la gare d'Helsinki d'Eliel Saarinen, et du Finlandia Hall d'Aalto. Une des caractéristiques majeures de ce projet est son mur et son toit en courbes qui animent l'espace intérieur tout en facilitant l'éclairage naturel des niveaux d'exposition supérieurs

PLACES OF EXHIBITION

neighbors, Holl has managed to create a sculptural presence that carries out its primary function very well. This is no small feat, and it does once again underline the great variety of approaches open to contemporary architects. While it remains very personal, the Kiasma Museum is nonetheless clearly linked to the history of modern architecture and to its urban setting. This is a freedom that accepts the enriching constraints of space and time.

Although Steven Holl did receive substantial press coverage for his museum in Helsinki, far more attention was given to the first completed project of Daniel Libeskind. Born in Poland in 1946 and now a US citizen, Daniel Libeskind studied music in Israel and New York before taking up architecture at the Cooper Union in New York. Although he has had a substantial influence on the architectural profession through teaching, the Felix Nussbaum Museum (Osnabrück, Germany, 1996-98, see P 312-317) is in fact his first built, completed work. Built to commemorate the work of the painter Felix Nussbaum, who died in Auschwitz in 1944 at the age of 40, the $8.2 million structure is intended to evoke a "Museum without Exit." Its three intersecting volumes are clad in oak, zinc, and concrete.

Anspielung auf die Kreuzung der Sehnerven an der Gehirnbasis. Das Gebäude mit etwa 12 000 m² Gesamtfläche wurde mit einem Budget von 41 Millionen US$ errichtet und liegt im Zentrum Helsinkis, in der Nähe von Parlamentsgebäude, Eliel Saarinens Hauptbahnhof und Alvar Aaltos Finlandia-Halle. Wichtige Charakteristika des Baus sind die gebogene Wand und das gekrümmte Dach, die den Innenraum beleben und zugleich natürliches Licht in das obere und untere Ausstellungsgeschoß einlassen. Holl äußerte sich dazu so: »Diese sich entfaltende Folge von Krümmungen erzeugt geheimnisvolle und überraschende Elemente, die sich bei einer gewöhnlichen einfachen oder doppelten orthogonalen Aufteilung nicht ergeben.« Unter Berücksichtigung der renommierten Nachbarbauten ist es Holl gelungen, eine skulpturale Gestalt zu schaffen, die zugleich ihren funktionalen Anforderungen vollkommen entspricht. Dies ist keine geringe Leistung; und sie unterstreicht einmal mehr, wie vielfältig die Möglichkeiten sind, die zeitgenössischen Architekten bei der Lösung ihrer Aufgaben zu Gebote stehen. Obwohl das Kiasma-Museum ein sehr individuelles Erscheinungsbild aufweist, ist es dennoch deutlich der Geschichte der modernen Architektur und seiner Ein-

et inférieurs. Comme l'explique Holl: «Cette séquence en courbe offre à la fois des éléments de surprise et de mystère, qui n'existent pas dans une disposition classique orthogonale de l'espace». Tout en respectant ses prestigieux voisins, Holl a réussi à créer une présence sculpturale qui répond parfaitement à sa fonction de base. Cet exercice n'était pas forcément facile, et ce projet souligne une fois de plus la grande variété d'approches offertes aux architectes contemporains. Tout en demeurant une œuvre très personnelle, le Kiasma Museum n'en est pas moins lié à l'histoire de l'architecture moderne et à son environnement urbain. C'est une liberté qui accepte les contraintes enrichissantes de l'espace et du temps.

Si la presse a beaucoup parlé du musée de Steven Holl, il est certain que le premier projet achevé de Daniel Libeskind a encore davantage attiré son attention. Né en Pologne en 1946 et aujourd'hui citoyen américain, Libeskind a étudié la musique en Israël et à New York avant d'apprendre l'architecture à Cooper Union, à New York. Bien qu'il exerce depuis un certain temps une influence profonde par son enseignement, le Felix Nussbaum Museum (Osnabrück, Allemagne, 1996-98, voir

The idea of the "museum without exit" undoubtedly originated in the more ambitious Jewish Museum (Berlin, Germany, 1989-99, see P 318-327). This project was launched in 1988 as an addition to the Berlin Museum, originally intended to contain a "Jewish Department," as well as theater, fashion and toy displays. Daniel Libeskind's design won first prize in a competition held in 1989. The fall of the Berlin Wall and the decision to return the capital to the now unified city affected plans – the Jewish Museum now is an independent institution, and the Berlin Museum serves as the entrance-area. Its form, that of a fractured Star of David, or perhaps a variant on the lightning bolts of the SS, does not make for easy museum display. A decision to include "the entire history of the relationship between German Jews and non-Jews from Roman times to the present," in the words of the museum's director W. Michael Blumenthal, a former US Secretary of the Treasury, has left the structure at least temporarily without any exhibition or contents. Many sections of the building will in any case remain intentionally empty, symbolizing the void left by the absence of Jews who died in the wake of the Holocaust. Though W. Michael Blumenthal's connections

ordnung in das Stadtgefüge verpflichtet. Es steht für eine Freiheit, die Zwänge von Raum und Zeit als Herausforderung annimmt.
Das Presseecho auf Steven Holls Museum in Helsinki war beachtlich, weit mehr Aufmerksamkeit jedoch wurde dem ersten ausgeführten Projekt von Daniel Libeskind zuteil. Der 1946 in Polen geborene Libeskind, der heute amerikanischer Staatsbürger ist, studierte Musik in Israel und New York, bevor er das Studium der Architektur an der New Yorker Cooper Union aufnahm. Obgleich er durch seine Lehre erheblichen Einfluß auf die Architektur ausgeübt hat, ist das Felix-Nußbaum-Haus (Osnabrück, 1996-98, siehe P 312-317) Libeskinds erstes realisiertes Bauwerk. Es wurde mit einem Budget von etwa 14 Millionen DM zum Gedächtnis des Malers Felix Nußbaum errichtet, der 1944 im Alter von 40 Jahren in Auschwitz umkam. Es soll ein »Museum ohne Ausgang« darstellen. Seine drei sich überschneidenden Baukörper sind mit Eichenholz, Zink und Beton verkleidet.
Die Idee des »Museums ohne Ausgang« entstand zweifellos im Zusammenhang mit dem weitaus ambitionierteren Jüdischen Museum in Berlin (1989-99, siehe P 318-327). Das Projekt wurde 1988 als

P 312-317) est en réalité sa première œuvre achevée. Construit pour célébrer l'œuvre du peintre Nussbaum mort à Auschwitz en 1944 à 40 ans, ce bâtiment de $8,2 millions se veut un «musée sans issue.» Ses trois volumes qui se coupent sont recouverts de chêne, de zinc et de béton.
L'idée d'un «musée sans issue» vient certainement d'un projet plus ambitieux encore, celui du Musée juif de Berlin (1989-99, voir P 318-327). Ce projet lancé en 1988 comme une extension du Berlin Museum était chargé à l'origine de contenir un «département juif», ainsi qu'un théâtre et des expositions sur la mode et les jouets. La proposition de Daniel Libeskind remporta le premier prix du concours organisé en 1989. La chute du mur de Berlin et la décision de réinstaller le siège du gouvernement dans la ville réunifiée affecta le calendrier des travaux. Aujourd'hui, le Musée juif est une institution indépendante et le Berlin Museum est utilisée comme entrée. La forme – une étoile de David brisée, ou une variante des éclairs du symbole des SS – ne facilite pas l'installation des expositions. La décision de retracer «la totalité de la relation entre les juifs allemands et les non-juifs de l'époque romaine à nos jours», selon les termes du directeur du musée,

in the business world will undoubtedly give this museum the contents it seems to lack, there might be something to be said for leaving it empty. It seems that Daniel Libeskind was profoundly affected by Arnold Schoenberg's incomplete opera Moses and Aaron. Its missing third act, like the absence of those lost during the war, inspired the powerful emptiness of Libeskind's troubling masterpiece. Although the commemoration of the Holocaust is not to be viewed as a specifically political act, it does have political and historic connotations. As Daniel Libeskind says, "it is the responsibility of architecture and culture to address events and history." Once again, the belief that architecture can somehow "improve" men, an idea that may have last seriously been envisaged at the time of the rise of the Bauhaus, returns in a contemporary form. Lars Spuybroek from NOX in Rotterdam do not seek to make political statement. Rather they choose to address the problem of the changing comprehension of architectural space. His Water Pavilion – H$_2$0 Expo (Neeltje Jans, Netherlands, 1994-97, see P 396-399) is built on an artificial island near the famous Delta Works to the south of Rotterdam. Both inside and out it is an exercise in indeterminate form. From

Erweiterung des Berlin-Museums ins Leben gerufen und sollte ursprünglich eine »Jüdische Abteilung« sowie eine Theater-, Mode- und Spielzeugausstellung enthalten. Daniel Libeskinds Entwurf erhielt 1989 den ersten Preis im Wettbewerb. Der Fall der Mauer und der Entschluß, Berlin zur Hauptstadt des wiedervereinigten Deutschland zu machen, hatten eine Veränderung der Pläne zur Folge. Heute ist das Jüdische Museum einen eigenständige Institution; das Berlin-Museum dient nun als Eingangsbereich. Die Form eines gebrochenen Davidsterns – oder möglicherweise einer Variante der SS-Runen – erschwert die Nutzung des Baus als Museum. Die Entscheidung des früheren amerikanischen Finanzministers und jetzigen Museumsdirektors W. Michael Blumenthal, »die gesamte Geschichte der Beziehungen zwischen deutschen Juden und Nichtjuden von der Römerzeit bis zur Gegenwart« darzustellen, hat dazu geführt, daß das Museum zumindest vorerst ohne Exponate geblieben ist. Viele Gebäudeteile werden bewußt leer bleiben, um mit ihrer Leere die schmerzliche Lücke zu symbolisieren, die die Ermordung der Juden im Holocaust gerissen hat. Obgleich Blumenthal über gute Verbindungen zur Geschäftswelt verfügt, um den

W. Michael Blumenthal, ancien Ministre des Finances aux États-Unis, laisse pour l'instant le bâtiment sans exposition ni contenu précis. De nombreuses parties du bâtiment resteront de toute façon volontairement vides, pour symboliser celui créé par l'absence des juifs victimes de l'Holocauste. Si les relations dont dispose M. Blumenthal vont certainement aider à donner à ce musée le contenu dont il semble manquer, ce vide mérite aussi une explication. Il semble que Daniel Libeskind ait été profondément impressionné par l'opéra inachevé d'Arnold Schönberg, Moïse et Aaron. Son troisième acte manquant, comme l'absence des disparus victimes du nazisme, inspirent le vide puissant du troublant chef-d'œuvre de Libeskind. Si la commémoration de l'Holocauste ne doit pas être considérée comme un acte politique spécifique, elle ne manque pas de connotations politiques et historiques. Comme le fait remarquer Libeskind: «Il est de la responsabilité de l'architecture et de la culture de traiter des événements et de l'histoire.» Une fois encore, la croyance que l'architecture peut en quelque sorte «améliorer» l'homme, idée abordée pour la dernière fois lors de la montée en puissance du Bauhaus, reprend forme.

the outside, it resembles a giant silver slug, or perhaps an extravagant beached sea monster. In any case, it contains no straight lines, no right angles. The interior takes this concept even further – the visitor is plunged into a dimly lit atmosphere with no truly horizontal or vertical surface. Various surprising displays on water make up the contents of this pavilion, whose interior is directly related to the computer-generated environments of games for example. Although many architects, like the ever-present Peter Eisenman, have tried to make a case for architectural forms unlike those of the past, the young Dutch architect of NOX has let his design speak for him. His is the first generation to be able to take computer-aided design seriously, not only as a tool for churning out drawings, but as an element in the design process. This is truly a place of exhibition of a new type.

The Malaysian architect Ken Yeang, whose ideas for "bio-climatic" towers have been frequently published, has also sought to renew the idea of a place intended for exhibitions. His surprising idea, the Nagoya Expo 2005 Tower (Seto, Nagoya, Japan, 1997, project, see P 530.531), is to put an entire World's Fair into a 150 story, 600 m high sky-

fehlenden Inhalt für sein Museum zu beschaffen, spricht einiges dafür, es leer zu belassen. Es hat den Anschein, als sei Daniel Libeskind stark von Arnold Schönbergs unvollendeter Oper »Moses und Aaron« beeinflußt. Die kraftvolle Leere von Libeskinds aufwühlendem Meisterwerk leitet sich vom Fehlen des dritten Akts dieser Oper ebenso her wie von der schmerzlichen Abwesenheit derer, die Krieg und Naziherrschaft zum Opfer fielen.

Obgleich das Gedenken an den Holocaust nicht als spezifisch politischer Akt zu betrachten ist, hat es politische und historische Beiklänge. Wie Daniel Libeskind sagt, »liegt es in der Verantwortung von Architektur und Kultur, historische Ereignisse anzusprechen.« Hierin kommt einmal mehr die Überzeugung zum Ausdruck, Architektur könne zur »Besserung« des Menschen beitragen, – jene Idee, die zuletzt in der Zeit des frühen Bauhauses ernsthaft vertreten wurde.

Lars Spuybroek von der Gruppe NOX in Rotterdam ist nicht auf der Suche nach einer politischen Aussage. Das Ziel seiner Arbeit ist eher, sich mit dem Verständniswandel vom architektonischen Raum auseinanderzusetzen. Sein Wasserpavillon – H_2O Expo (Neeltje Jans, Niederlande, 1994-97, siehe

Lars Spuybroek du NOX de Rotterdam ne cherche sans doute pas à prendre une position politique. Il est plutôt choisi de traiter le problème de l'évolution de la compréhension de l'espace architectural. Son Pavillon aquatique – H_2O Expo (Neeltje Jans, Pays-Bas, 1994-97, voir P 396-399) est construit sur une île artificielle près du fameux chantier du Delta, au sud de Rotterdam. À la fois intérieur et extérieur, il représente un véritable exercice sur l'indétermination des formes. Vu de l'extérieur, il ressemble à une limace argentée géante, ou à quelque monstre de fantaisie échoué sur la plage. Il ne contient en fait ni lignes droites, ni angles droits. L'intérieur pousse le concept encore plus loin: le visiteur est plongé dans une atmosphère faiblement éclairée où l'on ne voit aucune surface vraiment horizontale ou verticale. Le pavillon se compose de diverses mises en scène surprenantes sur l'eau, dans un environnement de jeux électroniques. Si de nombreux architectes comme le toujours présent Peter Eisenman ont essayé de défendre des formes architecturales différentes de celles du passé, le jeune architecte néerlandais de NOX laisse son projet parler de lui-même. Il fait partie de la première génération à prendre réellement

PLACES OF EXHIBITION

scraper. This would avoid the deforestation of some 160 hectares of land. Estimated costs for the project, which would be the world's tallest skyscraper, approach $1.5 billion. Although unexpected, this concept does appeal to a Japanese passion for very large buildings, just as it brings forward new arguments in the rising tide of ecologically oriented architecture. Like many of Yeang's built towers, this huge building would have a complex form to facilitate natural ventilation or solar heating. Though it is unlikely that this tower will be built in its current version, Yeang's project is indicative of the world-wide impact of "green" design on both form and function.

P 396-399) wurde auf einer künstlichen Insel bei den berühmten Delta-Deichen südlich von Rotterdam erbaut. Innen wie außen ist dies der Versuch einer nicht festgelegten Form. Von außen ähnelt das Gebäude einer riesigen silbernen Schnecke – oder vielleicht einem gestrandeten Seeungeheuer. Auf jeden Fall hat es weder gerade Linien noch rechte Winkel. Im Innern setzt sich dieses Konzept fort – der Besucher gelangt in eine halbdunkle Atmosphäre, in der es keine horizontale oder vertikale Fläche gibt. Verschiedene überraschende Ausstellungsstücke zum Thema Wasser bilden den Inhalt dieses Pavillons. Sein Innenraum erinnert unmittelbar an digital generierte Räume aus Computerspielen. Während viele Architekten – unter ihnen der allgegenwärtige Peter Eisenman – versucht haben, alle Argumente für Architekturformen vorzubringen, die sich von denen der Vergangenheit bewußt absetzen, läßt der junge holländische Architekt von NOX seinen Entwurf für sich sprechen. Er gehört zur ersten Generation, die in der Lage ist, computergestütztes Entwerfen ernst zu nehmen: nicht nur, um Zeichnungen in schneller Folge herzustellen, sondern als Element im Planungsprozeß. Dies ist wirklich ein Ausstellungsraum neuen Typs.

au sérieux les possibilités de la C.A.O. qui n'est plus un simple outil de production de dessins, mais un élément du processus de conception. Ce pavillon préfigure réellement un nouveau type d'espace d'exposition.
L'architecte malais Ken Yeang dont les projets de tours «bioclimatiques» ont été fréquemment publiés, a également cherché à renouveler l'idée de lieu d'exposition. Son surprenant projet de tour pour l'exposition mondiale de 2005 (Seto, Nagoya, Japon, 1997, projet, voir P 530.531) consiste à regrouper la totalité des participations à cette foire internationale dans un gratte-ciel de 150 étages et 600 m de haut, ce qui permettrait d'éviter la déforestation de 160 hectares de terres. Le coût estimé de ce qui serait le plus haut gratte-ciel du monde, approche $1,5 milliard. Inattendu, ce concept répond à la passion très japonaise pour les très grands immeubles, tout en illustrant de nouveaux arguments dans la marée montante de l'architecture de sensibilité écologique. Comme beaucoup des tours que l'architecte a construites, cet énorme bâtiment présenterait une forme complexe pour faciliter la ventilation naturelle ou le chauffage solaire. Même s'il est peu probable

Der malayische Architekt Ken Yeang, dessen Entwürfe für »bioklimatische« Hochhäuser oft publiziert worden sind, hat ebenfalls versucht, unsere
Vorstellung von Ausstellungsräumen zu erneuern.
Seine innovative Idee ist, die gesamte Weltausstellung 2005 in einem Wolkenkratzer von 600 m
Höhe mit 150 Geschossen unterzubringen (Seto,
Nagoya, Japan, 1997, Projekt, siehe P 530.531).
So könnte die Rodung von etwa 160 ha Wald vermieden werden. Die geschätzten Kosten des Projekts,
des dann höchsten Gebäudes der Welt, betragen
etwa 1,5 Milliarden US$. Wenn auch unerwartet,
kommt dieses Konzept der japanischen Vorliebe für
sehr große Bauten entgegen, und es liefert neue Argumente für die Verbreitung ökologisch orientierter
Architektur. Wie viele andere von Yeang ausgeführte Hochhäuser würde auch dieses riesige Gebäude
eine gegliederte Form zur Nutzung natürlicher Belüftung und Solarheizung haben. Auch wenn dieser
Turm vermutlich nie in seiner vorliegenden Version
realisiert werden wird, ist Yeangs Entwurf ein Indikator für den weltweiten Einfluß »grüner« Konzepte auf Form und Funktion.

que ce projet voie le jour dans sa version actuelle,
il est révélateur de l'impact universel de la conception «verte» appliquée à la fois à la forme et à la
fonction.

PLACES FOR STUDY

STUDIEN-RÄUME
DES LIEUX POUR ÉTUDIER

University buildings have long been a source of potential work for talented architects all over the world. Recent years have been no exception to this rule. Libraries in particular have taken up where art-related facilities may have reached saturation point. Hiroshi Hara's Miyagi Prefectural Library (Sendai, Miyagi, Japan, 1993-98, see P 198-201) might be said to symbolize the futuristic inclinations of the Japanese in this area. Seen from a distance, the library resembles a space vehicle of some kind. It is interesting to note that while Western architects have at least temporarily moved away from this kind of design, there is a playfulness and futuristic side to the Japanese that makes it entirely acceptable for them. Then, too, Hara's library, which also takes on the aspect of an inhabited bridge, is not entirely unlike the work of European groups such as the English architects Future Systems. Local influences still shape contemporary architecture no matter how sophisticated international communication becomes.

The Netherlands remain a fertile land for contemporary architecture, partly because of the presence of such world-renowned figures as Rem Koolhaas. Koolhaas and his Office for Metropolitan Architec-

Seit jeher sind Universitätsbauten eine Herausforderung für talentierte Architekten aus aller Welt. Die vergangenen Jahre bildeten hier keine Ausnahme. Vor allem Bibliotheken sind an die Stelle von Bauaufträgen getreten, die mit Kunst zu tun haben; dieser Bedarf scheint gedeckt zu sein. Man könnte in Hiroshi Haras Bibliothek für die Präfektur Miyagi (Sendai, Miyagi, Japan, 1993-98, siehe P 198-201) ein Symbol für die futuristischen Neigungen der Japaner auf diesem Gebiet sehen. Aus der Entfernung betrachtet, ähnelt die Bibliothek einem Raumschiff. Es ist interessant zu beobachten, daß die Japaner zu einer Verspieltheit und Zukunftsgläubigkeit neigen, die ihnen eine solche Lösung akzeptabel macht, während westliche Architekten sich zumindest vorübergehend von dieser Art der Gestaltung entfernt haben. Haras Bibliothek hat etwas von einer bewohnten Brücke – ein Aspekt, der sie nicht völlig von Arbeiten europäischer Gruppen, wie der englischen Architekten Future Systems, trennt. Immer noch bestimmen regionale Einflüsse die zeitgenössische Architektur, unabhängig davon, wie raffiniert die internationale Kommunikation sich auch entwickelt.

Die Niederlande sind nach wie vor ein produktives Land, was die Architektur betrifft, nicht zuletzt

Dans le monde entier, les bâtiments universitaires sont depuis longtemps une importante source de commande pour les architectes de talent. Les années récentes n'ont pas fait exception à cette tradition. Les bibliothèques semblent être dans le vent alors que les équipements liés à l'art ont peut-être atteint un point de saturation. La Bibliothèque de la préfecture de Miyagi (Sendai, Miyagi, Japon, 1993-98, voir P 198-201) de Hiroshi Hara symbolise assez bien les penchants futuristes des Japonais dans ce secteur. Vue de loin, elle ressemble à une sorte de vaisseau spatial. Il est intéressant de remarquer que tandis que les architectes occidentaux ont au moins pour l'instant abandonné ce type de conception, il paraît correspondre au goût pour le ludique et l'anticipation que l'on observe chez les Japonais. Mais par ailleurs, cette réalisation à l'aspect de pont habité n'est pas à l'opposé des travaux de groupes européens comme les architectes britanniques de Future Systems par exemple. Les influences locales continuent à nourrir l'architecture contemporaine quel que soit le niveau atteint par la sophistication de la communication internationale.

Les Pays-Bas restent un terrain propice à l'architecture contemporaine, en partie grâce à la présen-

ture (OMA) recently completed one of his few large buildings, the Educatorium at the University of Utrecht (Netherlands, 1995-97, see P 294-303). The Educatorium contains a campus cafeteria with seating for 1,000, as well as two large lecture halls, seating respectively 400 and 500 persons. The skewed design of the lecture halls is clearly related to Koolhaas's Kunsthal Rotterdam. There is also a kind of "rough and ready" approach to the detailing seen in Lille's Grand Palais that is beginning to be a signature element of this architect's work. A strictly limited budget is at the origin of the choice of materials. Another group of Dutch architects, Mecanoo, completed one of their first major projects since the departure of one of the firm's founders Erick van Egeraat at the Delft Technical University, its Central Library (Netherlands, 1993-98, see P 342-349). With a total floor area of approximately 15,000 m², this building costs 60 million florins to build. As the architects say about the unusual structure of the new library: "It has a grass roof that rises at an angle from ground level, like a sheet of paper lifted at one corner." The grass roof provides excellent insulation for a large, 1,000 seat reading room, equipped with 300 computers. Participating in the

wegen der Präsenz so berühmter Vertreter des Fachs wie Rem Koolhaas. Er und sein Office for Metropolitan Architecture (OMA) haben kürzlich eines ihrer wenigen Großprojekte realisiert, das Educatorium der Universität Utrecht (Niederlande, 1995-97, siehe P 294-303). Es beherbergt eine Campus-Cafeteria mit 1 000 Plätzen und zwei große Hörsäle für 400 bzw. 500 Personen. Die schräge Form der Hörsäle geht eindeutig auf Koolhaas' Entwurf für die Kunsthal Rotterdam zurück. Die Detailgestaltung im »Rough-and-Ready«-Stil kennt man auch von derjenigen des Grand Palais in Lille; sie entwickelt sich zu einem Erkennnungsmerkmal dieses Architekten. Ein knappes Budget bestimmt die Wahl der Materialien. Mecanoo, eine andere Gruppe niederländischer Architekten, realisierte eines ihrer ersten Großprojekte nach dem Weggang eines der Gründer, Erick van Egeraat: die Zentralbibliothek der Universität Delft (Niederlande, 1993-98, siehe P 342-349). Bei einer Gesamtfläche von ca. 15 000 m² betrugen die Baukosten 60 Millionen Gulden. Die Architekten erläutern die ungewöhnliche Form der neuen Bibliothek so: »Sie hat ein Grasdach, das sich auf einer Seite vom Bodenniveau erhebt wie ein an einer

ce de créateurs aussi renommés que Rem Koolhaas. Celui-ci et son Office for Metropolitan Architecture (OMA), viennent d'achever l'un de leurs rares bâtiments de grandes dimensions, l'Educatorium de l'Université d'Utrecht (Pays-Bas, 1995-97, voir P 294-303). Ce nouvel équipement contient une cafétéria de 1 000 places, deux grandes salles de conférence contenant respectivement quatre et cinq cents places. La conception en coin des salles de conférence rappelle clairement le Kunsthal Rotterdam de Koolhaas. On y observe également une approche «brute de décoffrage» déjà observée dans le Grand Palais de Lille, et qui devient peu à peu la «signature» de l'architecte. Les strictes limites du budget expliquent le choix des matériaux. Une autre agence d'architectes néerlandais, Mecanoo, vient d'achever son premier grand projet depuis le départ de l'un de ses fondateurs, Erick van Egeraat, la Bibliothèque centrale de l'Université technique de Delft (Pays-Bas, 1993-98, voir P 342-349). Développant une surface utile totale de 15 000 m² environ, ce bâtiment a coûté 60 millions de florins. Les architectes expliquent ainsi la forme exceptionnelle de la nouvelle bibliothèque: «Son toit planté d'herbe s'élève à partir du sol,

rising tide of ecologically oriented designs, this library is marked by a high stucco-clad concrete cone with a metal point that projects above the reading room. It may be this element that has caused a Vancouver-based architect, Peter Cardew, to say that a building he designed, the Stone Band School, has a remarkable similarity to the design of Mecanoo. Claims of plagiarism are nothing new in architecture, but it is certain that the increasing availability of documentation, through the Internet for example, may make this kind of incident more and more frequent. Peter Cardew wrote to the magazine *Architecture* (January 1999) asking what a building in Delft might have to do with "the traditional underground structures of the Chilcotin Indians in a remote and rugged region of British Columbia." When asked about this problem, Francine Houben responded that she was not aware of Mr. Cardew's project, nor could she have been in any way inspired by his work. Grass-covered buildings are even older than claims of plagiarism in architecture, and their ecological benefits may be just as apparent in The Netherlands as in Canada. Just as the increasing availability of information about architecture makes possible a controversy in-

Ecke angehobenes Blatt Papier.« Das Grasdach bildet eine ausgezeichnete Isolierung für den großen, 1 000 Personen fassenden Lesesaal, der mit 300 Computern ausgestattet ist. Kennzeichen dieses Gebäudes im Trend ökologisch orientierter Architektur ist ein hoher, verputzter Betonkegel mit Metallspitze, der über dem Lesesaal aufragt. Möglicherweise hat dieses Element den in Vancouver ansässigen Architekten Peter Cardew zu der Aussage veranlaßt, das Mecanoo-Projekt ähnele erstaunlich der von ihm entworfenen Stone Band School. Vorwürfe des Plagiats hat es in der Architekturgeschichte immer gegeben, doch werden solche Vorfälle aufgrund der zunehmenden Verfügbarkeit von Dokumentationen, zum Beispiel im Internet, sicherlich immer häufiger werden. Peter Cardew richtete seine Anfrage, was ein Gebäude in Delft mit »den traditionellen unterirdischen Bauten der Chilcotin-Indianer in einer entfernten, rauhen Region von British Columbia« zu tun habe, an die Zeitschrift »Architecture« (Januar 1999). Mit diesem Problem konfrontiert, sagte Francine Houben, sie habe Cardews Projekt nicht gekannt und sei auch keinesfalls von seiner Arbeit beeinflußt. Grasgedeckte Gebäude sind sogar noch älter als Plagiatsvorwürfe in der

comme une feuille de papier soulevée par l'un de ses angles.» Cette couverture offre une excellente isolation à la vaste salle de lecture de 1 000 places, équipée de 300 ordinateurs. Dans la mouvance de l'architecture d'inspiration écologique, cette bibliothèque se signale par un cône de béton revêtu de stuc à pointe de métal qui se projette au-dessus de la salle de lecture. C'est peut-être cet élément qui a poussé un architecte de Vancouver, Peter Cardew à affirmer que le projet de Mecanoo était remarquablement semblable à sa Stone Band School. Les accusations de plagiat ne sont certes pas nouvelles en architecture, mais il est certain que la disponibilité de plus en plus grande de la documentation, par l'intermédiaire de l'internet par exemple, risque de rendre ce type d'incident de plus en plus fréquent. Peter Cardew a écrit au magazine «Architecture» (janvier 1999) pour demander ce qu'un bâtiment de Delft pouvait avoir à faire avec les «constructions souterraines traditionnelles des Indiens chilcotin d'une région perdue et sauvage de Colombie britannique». Interrogée, Francine Houben a répondu qu'elle n'avait aucune connaissance du projet de M. Cardew, et qu'elle n'avait pu en rien s'inspirer de son travail. Les bâtiments couverts d'herbe sont

volving an architect in Vancouver and another one in Rotterdam, so buildings designed in locations that might be considered as remote by some are now widely published. The Sunshine Coast University Club (Sippy Downs, Queensland, Australia, 1996, see P 138-141) by Clare Design is not at all on the scale of the Dutch university buildings described above. In fact, university officials considered using an industrial shed to house this sports pavilion and staff club. The architects were faced with the daunting task of putting up a building within six months for a modest A$600,000 budget. With three open, glazed sides, this structure required substantial bracing against potentially severe wind conditions. The use of plywood on visible surfaces, and hardwood floors, was inspired by knowledge of local building types. "We wanted the guts and ruggedness of the farm shed and the lightness and openness of a surf club," say the architects. Budgetary constraints have made the use of industrial materials and design elements frequent all over the world. What is new is that many architects have discovered that the "rough and ready" aspect of the forms generated in factory environments can be used in an aesthetically pleasing way.

Architektur, und ihre ökologischen Vorzüge mögen in den Niederlanden genauso einleuchten wie in Kanada.
Ebenso wie die zunehmende Verfügbarkeit von Informationen über Architektur eine Kontroverse zwischen einem Architekten in Vancouver und einem in Rotterdam ermöglicht, werden heute Bauwerke bekannt, die sich eigentlich an recht entlegenen Orten befinden. Der Sunshine Coast University Club (Sippy Downs, Queensland, Australien, 1996, siehe P 138-141) von Clare Design erreicht bei weitem nicht die Größenordnung der oben beschriebenen niederländischen Universitätsbauten. Tatsächlich erwog die Universitätsverwaltung in Sippy Downs ernsthaft die Nutzung einer Industriehalle, um eine Sport- und Klubanlage für ihre Mitarbeiter unterzubringen. Die Architekten standen vor der schwierigen Aufgabe, innerhalb von sechs Monaten ein Gebäude mit dem bescheidenen Budget von 600 000 A$ zu erstellen. Die Konstruktion mit drei offenen, verglasten Seiten erforderte erhebliche Aussteifungen gegen starke Windböen. Die Verwendung von Sperrholz und Hartholzböden ist von der regionalen Bauweise inspiriert. »Wir strebten das Kraftvolle und Robuste eines Schuppens und die

encore plus anciens que les accusations de plagiat en architecture et leurs bénéfices écologiques sont aussi apparents en Hollande qu'au Canada.
De même que la disponibilité grandissante de l'information sur l'architecture peut amener à une controverse entre un architecte de Vancouver et une agence de Rotterdam, des bâtiments construits dans des lieux qui peuvent sembler inaccessibles à certains sont aujourd'hui largement publiés. Le Sunshine Coast University Club (Sippy Downs, Queensland, Australie, 1996, voir P 138-141) de Clare Design n'est pas du tout à l'échelle des bâtiments néerlandais décrits plus haut. En fait, l'administration universitaire avait étudié la possibilité d'utiliser un hangar industriel pour ce pavillon de sports et club du personnel. Les architectes furent donc confrontés à la tâche ardue de construire un bâtiment en six mois pour un modeste budget de A$600 000. Avec ses trois façades ouvertes et vitrées, cette structure demandait un entretoisement structurel particulier pour résister à la force des vents particulièrement vive dans cette région. Le recours au contreplaqué sur les surfaces visibles et les sols en bois vient d'une pratique locale. «Nous voulions retrouver la nature brute d'un bâtiment agricole

PLACES FOR STUDY

The question of design is naturally very much on the mind of the Frenchman Philippe Starck. He is known all over the world for the objects and interiors he has created. He has also completed three buildings in Japan. Starck has often said that architecture should resemble objects, and indeed his Japanese projects carried that idea to its limit. In his extension to the National School of Decorative Arts (with Luc Arsène-Henry, Paris, France, 1995-98, see P 474.475) he has created one of the more surprising façades in contemporary architecture. Entirely blank, the white marble slab surface of the building has drawn considerable criticism. Although local residents staunchly opposed the project, it is not so much outsiders as insiders who feel that the opaque marble they see from their desks is oppressive or funerary. In fact, the inside of the building, and its glazed garden-side facade, are far less unexpected than this "gesture" in marble. Starck's Japanese buildings are not necessarily easy to use because of their unusual interior forms. Here he was joined by a talented Bordeaux architect, but the result of their work shows how an essentially decorative element can make a building somewhat less successful than had been hoped.

Leichtigkeit und Offenheit eines Klubhauses an«, erläutern die Architekten. Enge Budgetgrenzen haben die Verwendung industrieller Materialien und Bauelemente verbreitet. Neu ist die Entdeckung vieler Architekten, daß die im Industriebau entstandene »Rough-and-Ready«-Gestaltung in ästhetisch ansprechender Weise angewendet werden kann.
Design ist natürlich ein Thema für den Franzosen Philippe Starck. Mit seinen Objekten und Innenausstattungen ist er weltweit bekannt geworden. Starck hat jedoch auch drei Bauwerke in Japan realisiert. Er hat oft betont, daß Gebäude Objekten ähneln sollen, und in der Tat führen seine japanischen Projekte diesen Gedanken bis an die Grenze des Möglichen. An seinem Neubau für die École nationale des arts décoratifs (mit Luc Arsène-Henry, Paris, 1995-98, siehe P 474.475) hat Starck eine der besonders verblüffenden Fassaden zeitgenössischer Architektur geschaffen. Die vollkommen ungegliederte Außenhaut des Bauwerks aus weißen Marmor ist heftig kritisiert worden. Obgleich die Anwohner massiv gegen das Projekt protestierten, sind es weniger die Betrachter als seine Benutzer, die den lichtundurchlässigen Marmor an ihren Arbeitsplätzen als bedrückend oder friedhofsähnlich

ainsi que l'ouverture et la luminosité d'un club de surf», précisent les architectes. Dans le monde entier, les contraintes budgétaires poussent de plus en plus fréquemment à utiliser des éléments et des matériaux industriels. Mais de nombreux architectes ont découvert que l'aspect «brut de décoffrage» des formes générées par ces environnements peuvent donner des résultats esthétiques satisfaisants.
Le français Philippe Starck réfléchit évidemment beaucoup au design. Il est connu dans le monde entier pour ses objets et ses aménagements intérieurs, et a également construit trois bâtiments au Japon. Il a souvent déclaré que l'architecture devait ressembler à des objets, et ses projets japonais ont été l'occasion de pousser ce concept à ses extrêmes limites. Dans son extension de l'École nationale des arts décoratifs (avec Luc Arsène-Henry, Paris, 1995-98, voir P 474.475), il a créé l'une des plus surprenantes façades de l'architecture contemporaine. Entièrement aveugle, sa surface en plaques de marbre blanc s'est attirée de multiples critiques. Si les habitants du voisinage s'y sont fortement opposés, ce sont surtout ses usagers qui trouvent que ce marbre opaque donnent à leurs bureaux une

PLACES FOR WORK AND PLAY

ARBEITS- UND SPIEL-RÄUME
DES LIEUX DE TRAVAIL ET DE DÉTENTE

Housing, gathering, travel, or exhibition are sources of commissions, but places for work and play are also an essential element in the development of contemporary architecture. The projects selected here are for the most part on a relatively small scale. This is the case of Tadao Ando's spectacular Toto Seminar House (Tsuna-gun, Hyogo, Japan, 1994-97, see P 066-069). Located near the epicenter of the earthquake that devastated Kobe in 1995, the site provides a 180° ocean view towards the Kansai International Airport, which is located to the east, across Osaka Bay. "I had the image," Ando says, "of a building that is at one with the sea." The structure is designed as a seminar center with capacity for 60 persons. Through both the selected views from this spectacular location, and the walkway that leads to it, Ando seeks here to "make you feel as though you are immersed in the ocean itself." Ando has long since proven his ability to give great dignity to buildings, whether they be chapels, or in this case a building for Japan's largest manufacturer of toilets. This is undoubtedly what separates a great architect from lesser practitioners – a fact that holds just as true for the most contemporary architecture as for that of the past.

Wohnungen, Versammlungs- und Ausstellungsräume sind wesentliche Bauaufgaben. Aber auch Orte, die der Arbeit oder der Freizeitgestaltung dienen, sind ein wichtiges Element in der zeitgenössischen Architektur. Die hier ausgewählten Projekte sind überwiegend in kleinem Maßstab gehalten, etwa Tadao Andos Toto Seminar House (Tsuna-gun, Hyogo, Japan, 1994-97, siehe P 066-069). Der Bauplatz liegt nahe dem Epizentrum des Erdbebens, das 1995 die Stadt Kobe zerstörte. Er bietet einen Panoramablick über das Meer und den internationalen Flughafen Kansai in der Bucht von Osaka. »Ich hatte«, erläutert Ando, »die Vorstellung von einem Bauwerk, das eins ist mit dem Meer.« Das Seminargebäude ist für 60 Personen geplant. Sowohl durch die spektakulären Ausblicke als auch durch den Fußweg, der zu ihm führt, sucht der Architekt »das Gefühl zu vermitteln, man tauche in den Ozean ein«. Ando hat bereits früh seine Fähigkeit bewiesen, Gebäuden Würde zu verleihen – seien es Kapellen oder, wie hier, ein Gebäude für Japans größten Toiletten-Hersteller. Diese Fähigkeit unterscheidet einen großen Architekten von weniger begabten – ein Kriterium, das sowohl für die meisten Architekten der Gegenwart als auch für die der Vergangenheit gilt.

Se loger, se réunir, voyager ou exposer sont autant de sources de commandes architecturales, mais les lieux de travail et de détente forment aussi aujourd'hui l'un des plus importants domaines de l'architecture contemporaine. Les projets sélectionnés ici sont pour leur plus grand nombre à échelle relativement réduite. C'est le cas du spectaculaire centre de séminaires Toto de Tadao Ando (Tsuna-gun, Hyogo, Japon, 1994-97, voir P 066-069). Situé non loin de l'épicentre du tremblement de terre qui a ravagé Kobé en 1995, le site offre une vue panoramique sur l'océan et l'aéroport international de Kansai. «J'avais l'image d'un bâtiment qui ne fasse qu'un avec la mer», a déclaré l'architecte. La structure présente une capacité de 60 participants. À la fois par les vues soigneusement cadrées et la passerelle d'accès, Ando cherche ici «à vous faire sentir comme si vous étiez immergé dans l'océan lui-même». Il a depuis longtemps fait preuve de son talent à conférer une grande dignité à ses réalisations, que ce soit des chapelles ou comme ici pour le plus important fabricant de toilettes du Japon. C'est ce qui distingue un grand architecte de concurrents de moindre niveau, et qui est aussi vrai pour l'architecture contemporaine que celle du passé.

Joseph Menswear (London, 1997, see P 134.135), designed by David Chipperfield, is on an even smaller scale. Chipperfield is well known for his minimalist approach to shop design and architecture. This clothing shop was inserted into the ground and first floors of a four story 1960s office block at number 74 Sloane Avenue, just around the corner from the landmark Michelin "Bibendum" building. 6 m high glass panels mark the front of the shop, while stainless steel mesh envelops a second-floor showroom. Heavy dark metal doors are left open with a forced air "curtain" replacing the glass that might have been anticipated. Dark gray Pietra Serena floors and white walls give an impression of a certain austerity. A steel and wood spiral white staircase links the ground and first floors. Floor to ceiling windows give visitors an unexpected view of the street from the first floor. Undoubtedly convinced of the commercial viability of the work of recognized architects like David Chipperfield, the owner of this store, Joseph Ettedgui, has previously called not only on Chipperfield himself, but also on Norman Foster and Eva Jiricna.
The Dominus Winery (Yountville, Napa Valley, California, 1995-98, see P 216-221) by the Swiss

Joseph Menswear (London, 1997, siehe P 134.135) von David Chipperfield hat noch kleinere Dimensionen. Chipperfield ist bekannt für seine eher minimalistischen Ladengestaltungen. Das Londoner Bekleidungsgeschäft wurde in das Erd- und erste Obergeschoß eines viergeschossigen Bürogebäudes aus dem Jahre 1960 in der Sloane Avenue 74, nahe dem Michelin-Haus, eingefügt. 6 m hohe Glasplatten markieren die Ladenfront, während ein Edelstahlgeflecht den Ausstellungsraum im zweiten Obergeschoß einfaßt. Schwere, dunkle Metalltüren werden durch einen Druckluft-»Vorhang« offen gehalten, der das übliche Glas ersetzt. Dunkelgraue Böden aus Pietra Serena-Sandstein und weiße Wände lassen das Interieur streng wirken. Eine weiße Wendeltreppe aus Stahl und Holz verbindet das Erdgeschoß mit der oberen Etage. Geschoßhohe Fenster bieten Besuchern einen unerwarteten Ausblick auf die Straße. Der Geschäftsinhaber, Joseph Ettedgui, war vom kommerziellen Nutzen der Arbeit renommierter Architekten überzeugt und hatte zuvor nicht nur Chipperfield, sondern auch Norman Foster und Eva Jiricna angesprochen.
Die Weinkellerei Dominus (Yountville, Napa Valley, Kalifornien, 1995-98, siehe P 216-221) der Schwei-

La boutique pour hommes, Joseph Menswear (Londres, 1997, voir P 134.135), conçue par David Chipperfield est de dimensions encore plus réduites. L'architecte est très connu pour son approche minimaliste de l'aménagements de magasins et de l'architecture. Ce point de vente de vêtements occupe le rez-de-chaussée et le premier étage d'un immeuble de bureaux des années 60, au 74 Sloane Avenue, tout près du bâtiment classé de Michelin. Des panneaux de verre de 6 m de haut signalent sa façade, tandis qu'un treillage d'acier entoure le showroom du second étage. Les lourdes portes de métal sombre sont laissées ouvertes et un rideau d'air pulsé remplace les panneaux de verre que l'on s'attend à trouver à cet emplacement. Les sols en pietra serena gris foncé et les murs blancs donnent une certaine impression d'austérité, bien adaptée en fait au style de vêtements proposés. Un escalier en spirale blanc, en bois et acier, relie les deux niveaux. À l'étage, les baies en hauteur donnent aux visiteurs une vue surprenante sur la rue. Certainement convaincu de la viabilité commerciale des interventions d'architectes célèbres, le propriétaire du magasin, Joseph Ettedgui, a déjà fait appel à Chipperfield, mais aussi à Norman Foster et à Eva Jiricna.

PLACES FOR WORK AND PLAY

architects Herzog & de Meuron is one of the more unexpected places of work to have been completed in recent years. Chosen for this job by the owners of France's Château Petrus, the architects have opted for an extreme austerity and a very unusual cladding material – loose pieces of locally mined gray-green basalt held in place by wire containers. Currently completing the renovation of London's Bankside Power Station, which is becoming the Tate Gallery of Modern Art, Herzog & de Meuron have a taste for industrial forms whose aspect can be transfigured by a subtle handling of light and materials. This is also the case in California, where they have opted for the shape of shed or warehouse, while using both light and materials to create an exceptional work of art.

For different reasons, Toyo Ito's Odate Jukai Dome Park (Japan, 1995-97, see P 260-265) is equally unexpected in its almost rural setting in the northernmost reaches of the island of Honshu. This remarkable covered sports facility is used mostly for baseball. The off-center or semi-egg-shaped dome is made essentially with laminated Akita cedar, covered with a translucent Fluor-ethylene-resin coated fiberglass. The entire dome is raised above

zer Architekten Herzog & de Meuron ist eine der ausgefallensten Arbeitsstätten, die in den vergangenen Jahren entstanden sind. Die von den Besitzern des französischen Château Petrus beauftragten Architekten entschieden sich für extreme Strenge und ungewöhnliches Verkleidungsmaterial – locker zusammengefügte Brocken eines örtlichen graugrünen Basalts, die von Drahtkörben zusammengehalten werden. Herzog & de Meuron, die gegenwärtig den Umbau des Londoner Bankside-Kraftwerks für die Tate Gallery of Modern Art durchführen, haben eine Vorliebe für industrielle Formen, deren Wirkung sich durch den raffinierten Einsatz von Licht und Materialien verändern läßt. So sind sie auch bei ihrem Bau in Kalifornien vorgegangen, wo sie sich für die Form eines Lagerhauses entschieden und sowohl das Licht als auch die Baustoffe zur Gestaltung eines außergewöhnlichen Kunstwerks nutzten.

Ebenso ausgefallen, wenn auch aus anderen Gründen, ist Toyo Itos Jukai Dome Park (Japan, 1995-97, siehe P 260-265), in fast ländlicher Lage am nördlichsten Ende der Insel Honshu gelegen. Die bemerkenswerte Sporthalle wird vorwiegend für Baseball genutzt. Die asymmetrische, wie ein längs

La Dominus Winery (Yountville, Napa Valley, Californie, 1995-98, voir P 261-221) due aux architectes suisses Herzog & de Meuron est l'un des plus étonnants lieux de travail réalisés au cours de ces dernières années. Choisis par les propriétaires français de Château Petrus, les architectes ont opté pour une austérité extrême et des matériaux très peu courants: des morceaux de basalte gris-vert exploité localement, retenus dans des conteneurs en fil de fer. Achevant actuellement la rénovation de la centrale thermique de Bankside à Londres, future Tate Gallery of Modern Art, Herzog & de Meuron se signalent par un goût marqué pour les formes industrielles dont l'aspect peut être modifié par une manipulation subtile de la lumière et des matériaux. C'est le cas, ici, en Californie, où ils se sont déterminés pour une forme d'entrepôt ou de hangar, tout en se servant des matériaux et de la lumière pour donner naissance à une exceptionnelle œuvre d'art. Pour différentes raisons, le parc du dôme Jukai d'Odate (Japon, 1995-97, voir P 260-265) réalisé par Toyo Ito est tout aussi inattendu dans son cadre presque rural à l'extrémité la plus septentrionale de l'île d'Honshu. Cette remarquable installation sportive couverte sert essentiellement au base-ball. Le

the ground to admit light through glazed walls. Standing near a field, this dome assumes an unreal, almost extraterrestrial appearance, particularly when it is lit from within at night. This strange, again rather futuristic appearance, coupled with an indisputable mastery of design and building materials, ties this structure to its specific location even though it is not specifically Japanese in any traditional sense.

Sports facilities tend to be designed by anonymous architectural offices. French authorities were determined that the main stadium planned for the 1998 World Cup soccer events would not fall into this category. The competition they organized proved to be highly controversial, with architect Jean Nouvel bitterly contesting the results. The winning team MZRC (Michel Macary/ Aymeric Zublena and Michel Regembal/Claude Costantini) was in fact made up of two architectural offices that had not worked together before. Their Stade de France (Saint-Denis, 1994-97, see P 376-381) was built for about 2.6 billion French francs, on time and on budget. By all accounts the building was a substantial success with its suspended oval roof serving as a symbol for the World Cup. More sophisticated, and

halbiertes Ei geformte Kuppel besteht im wesentlichen aus laminierter Akita-Zeder und ist mit lichtdurchlässiger, kunstharzbeschichteter Glasfaser verkleidet. Die Kuppel ist vom Erdboden abgehoben, so daß Licht durch die verglasten Wände einfallen kann. Von außen wirkt sie unwirklich, fast außerirdisch, vor allem wenn sie nachts von innen erleuchtet ist. Dieses seltsame und wiederum eher futuristische Erscheinungsbild sowie die unstrittig meisterhafte Beherrschung von Gestaltung und Materialien binden das Bauwerk in seine Umgebung ein, auch wenn es der japanischen Tradition nicht in besonderer Weise verpflichtet ist.

Sportanlagen werden meist von anonymen Architekturbüros geplant. Beim Stadion für die Fußball-Weltmeisterschaft 1998 waren die französischen Behörden entschlossen, anders vorzugehen. Der Wettbewerb erwies sich als höchst widersprüchlich; die Ergebnisse wurden vom Architekten Jean Nouvel heftig angefochten. Die Preisträger MZRC (Michel Macary/Aymeric Zublena und Michel Regembal/Claude Costantini) kamen eigentlich aus zwei Architekturbüros, die zuvor nicht zusammengearbeitet hatten. Ihr Entwurf für das Stade de France (Saint-Denis, 1994-97, siehe P 376-381) wurde für

dôme elliptique ou en forme de demi-œuf est essentiellement édifié en cèdre d'Akita lamellé, recouvert de fibre de verre enduite de résine de fluoro-éthylène. En bordure de champs, ce dôme prend une apparence irréelle, presque extra-terrestre, en particulier lorsqu'il est éclairé de l'intérieur pendant la nuit. Cet aspect étrange et la maîtrise incontestable du projet et de ses matériaux ancre cette structure à son site même si elle n'est en rien japonaise au sens traditionnel du terme.

Les équipements sportifs sont souvent conçus par des agences d'architecture plus ou moins anonymes. Les autorités françaises souhaitaient que le grand stade projeté pour la Coupe du monde de football de 1998 échappe à ce destin. Le concours organisé provoqua une vive controverse, en particulier lorsqu'un des candidats évincés, Jean Nouvel, en contesta les résultats. L'équipe retenue MZRC (Michel Macary/Aymeric Zublena et Michel Regembal/Claude Costantini) était en fait composée de deux agences qui n'avaient jamais travaillé ensemble auparavant. Leur Stade de France (Saint-Denis, 1994-97, voir P 376-381) a été construit dans les délais prévus pour un budget respecté de 2,6 milliard de francs. Il a connu un grand succès et son

more complex, Nouvel's design might well have
adapted less well to this function.

It seems fitting to end this overview of recent architecture with two buildings erected in architecturally
less prominent countries, Mexico and Malaysia. The
first of these, the Televisa Services Building (Mexico City, Mexico, 1993-95, see P 496-499) by TEN
Arquitectos was the recipient of the 1998 Mies van
der Rohe Award for Latin American Architecture,
given at the Museum of Modern Art in New York.
A 7,500 m² facility including parking, offices, an
employee dining room, conference rooms and meeting space was built using concrete seismic walls and
concrete slab supported by steel framing at a cost
of $24 million. As the architects say, the "soaring
aluminum-paneled shell alludes to an industrial vernacular but also represents a technically expedient
method of construction." Constrained again by economic factors Enrique Norten from TEN Arquitectos
has used what he calls "an industrial vernacular."
Very specifically related to its site and multiple functions, the Televisa Building could not really exist
anywhere else, but it is the result of a growing international awareness of the ways and means to create
interesting buildings within tight budgets.

2,6 Milliarden Franc termingerecht und im Budgetrahmen fertiggestellt. Allen Berichten zufolge wurde das Bauwerk mit großer Begeisterung aufgenom-
men, und wurde mit seinem hängenden ovalen Dach
zum Symbol der Weltmeisterschaft. Nouvels intel-
lektuellerer und komplexerer Entwurf hätte dieser
Funktion wohl weniger entsprochen.

Es scheint angemessen, diesen Überblick über die
jüngste Architektur mit zwei Bauwerken aus den in
architektonischer Hinsicht unbekannteren Ländern
Mexiko und Malaysia zu beschließen. Das Televisa
Services Building (Mexico City, Mexiko, 1993-95,
siehe P 496-499) von TEN Arquitectos erhielt 1998
den Mies van der Rohe Award for Latin American
Architecture, den das Museum of Modern Art in New
York verleiht. Die 7 500 m² große Anlage, bestehend
aus Parkhaus, Büros, Kantine, Konferenz- und Be-
sprechungsräumen, wurde mit erdbebensicheren
Wänden und von einem Stahlskelett getragenen Betondecken für 24 Millionen US$ errichtet. Die Ar-
chitekten erklären: »Die aufragende, aluminiumverkleidete Schale spielt auf regionale Industriebauten
an und repräsentiert zugleich eine technisch ausgereifte Baumethode.« Wiederum von wirtschaftlichen
Faktoren bestimmt, hat Enrique Norten von TEN

toit ovale suspendu a servi de symbole à la Coupe.
Plus sophistiqué et plus complexe, le projet de
Nouvel aurait peut-être été moins bien adapté à sa
fonction.

Il pourrait sembler pertinent de terminer ce survol
de l'architecture récente par deux constructions éri-
gées dans le Mexique et la Malaisie. La première,
l'immeuble des services de Televisa (Mexico City,
Mexique, 1993-95, voir P 496-499), par TEN Arquitectos a été couronnée en 1998 par le Prix Mies
van der Rohe pour l'architecture latino-américaine,
remis au Museum of Modern Art de New York. Ce
bâtiment de 7 500 m² qui comprend des parkings,
des bureaux, un restaurant pour le personnel, des
salles de conférences et un espace de rencontre met
en œuvre des murs antisismiques et une dalle de
béton soutenue par une ossature en acier. Le budget
de construction a représenté $24 millions. Comme
l'ont écrit les architectes: «La coquille recouverte
de panneaux d'aluminium rappelle le vernaculaire
industriel mais représente aussi une méthode de
construction techniquement fiable. » Ce «vernaculaire industriel», comme l'appelait Enrique Norten
de TEN Arquitectos, est également dicté par des
contraintes économiques fortes. Particulièrement

Ken Yeang's Guthrie Pavilion (Shah Alam, Selangor, Malaysia, 1995-98, see P 524-529) shows how buildings that are essentially quite normal can be made remarkable through a combination of architectural imagination and technical ingenuity. The most striking feature of the building is its 2,500 m² wing-shaped air-inflated fabric canopy. Made from glass fabric on steel frames suspended from three 40 m masts by zinc-dipped spiral strand steel cables, the irregular canopy is designed to resist 125 km/h winds. The client, a property developer, wanted a recognizable form to mark this site, and Ken Yeang provided a design that makes sense both in terms of this request and the local climatic condition. Fashion will always play a role in the development of contemporary architecture. Modernism was after all a kind of fashion, driven first by sociological needs and then by style. The neo-minimalist architects who hold sway in Switzerland or Japan (some of them are present in this book) obviously are following or creating a trend. Succinctly put, they redefine Modernism with an innovative use of new or unexpected materials. Still, architects like Herzog & de Meuron find it "ideologically" acceptable to invest great energy in the renovation of an

Arquitectos sich auf die von ihm so bezeichneten »regionalen Industriebauten« bezogen. Das unmittelbar von seiner Lage und seinen vielfältigen Funktionen bestimmte Televisa Building könnte tatsächlich nirgendwo anders stehen, und es ist dennoch Ergebnis eines zunehmenden Bewußtseins, Mittel und Wege zu finden, um interessante Gebäude innerhalb enggesteckter finanzieller Grenzen zu realisieren. Ken Yeangs Guthrie-Pavillon (Shah Alam, Selangor, Malaysia, 1995-98, siehe P 524-529) zeigt, wie sich durchschnittliche Bauaufgaben mit architektonischer Phantasie und technischer Erfindungsgabe beachtlich gestalten lassen. Das auffälligste Merkmal des Bauwerks ist ein 2 500 m² großes flügelförmiges, luftgefülltes Schutzdach aus Glasfasergewebe. Es ist mit verzinkten, gedrehten Stahlseilen an drei 40 m hohen Masten aufgehängt, und kann aufgrund seiner ungewöhnlichen Form Windstärken von bis zu 125 km/h standhalten. Der Auftraggeber, ein Grundstücksmakler, wünschte eine einprägsame Form, die das Gelände dominieren sollte. Ken Yeang lieferte einen Entwurf, der darüber hinaus auch dem heißen Klima Malaysias gerecht wird. Moden werden immer eine Rolle in der zeitgenössischen Architektur spielen. Auch die Moderne war

bien adapté à son site et à ses multiples fonctions, cet immeuble ne pourrait exister en fait nulle part ailleurs, mais traduit une tendance internationale à la prise de conscience de méthodes et de moyens de constructions choisis en fonction de budgets étroitement limités. Le Pavillon Guthrie de Ken Yeang (Shah Alam, Selangor, Malaisie, 1995-98, voir P 524-529) illustre à quel point des immeubles essentiellement classiques peuvent être rendus remarquables lorsque l'imagination architecturale et l'invention technique s'en mêlent. La caractéristique la plus frappante de ce bâtiment est son auvent en tissu gonflé en forme d'aile de 2 500 m². Réalisé en tissu de verre sur un cadre métallique suspendu à trois mâts de 40 m par des câbles spiralés gainés de zinc, il est conçu pour résister à des vents de 125 km/h. Le promoteur immobilier qui avait passé la commande souhaitait une forme qui identifie son terrain, et Ken Yeang lui a apporté une solution qui allait largement au devant de ses souhaits tout en prenant en compte les conditions climatiques. La mode joue toujours un rôle dans le développement de l'architecture d'une époque. Le modernisme a lui aussi été une sorte de mode, nourrie au départ

PLACES FOR WORK AND PLAY

old power station in London. Living with the past is a hallmark of today's architecture, both for practical reasons, and because old buildings, particularly industrial ones, have been found to have a certain charm and power. The "Deconstructivist" movement with whom Daniel Libeskind, Zaha Hadid and Coop Himmelb(l)au have been identified are also dealing with fashion, despite their claims to the contrary. Skewed forms, odd angles and unexpected materials make up their palette, even if they are obliged at the end of the day to erect buildings that actually stand up and function. The 1980s were a time of large numbers of what Arata Isozaki calls "crazy little buildings." In Japan, for example, the "Bubble Economy" made even the most extravagant architecture seem cheap as compared with the land it was sitting on. This time is now over, even if work like that of Makoto Sei Watanabe does seem to come to us straight out of those heady times. The latest fashion trend might be considered the use of the computer as a real design tool. It is too early to tell if there will really be a lasting change in the built environment as a result of the computer. As of today, the potential is there, however, for something that will prove to be much more than a passing

letztlich eine Art Mode, die eher von soziologischen Bedürfnissen als von stilistischen Fragen bestimmt wurde. Die neo-minimalistischen Architekten, die das Bauen in der Schweiz oder in Japan bestimmen (einige von ihnen sind in diesem Band vertreten), folgen offensichtlich einem Trend oder kreieren ihn. Sie definieren die Moderne neu, indem sie neuartige oder ungewöhnliche Baustoffe verwenden. Andererseits finden es Architekten wie Herzog & de Meuron »ideologisch« akzeptabel, viel Energie in den Umbau eines alten Kraftwerks in London zu investieren. Es ist ein Charakteristikum heutiger Architektur, daß sie mit der Tradition lebt. Dabei spielen sowohl praktische Erwägungen eine Rolle als auch die Erkenntnis, daß alte Gebäude, besonders Industriebauten, Charme und Kraft ausstrahlen. Dekonstruktivisten wie Daniel Libeskind, Zaha Hadid und Coop Himmelb(l)au unterliegen ebenfalls Moden, auch wenn sie das Gegenteil behaupten. Ihr Formenschatz besteht aus schrägen Formen, ausgefallenen Winkeln und ungewöhnlichen Materialien; und doch sind auch sie letzten Endes gezwungen, Bauten zu errichten, die standfest sind und funktionieren. In den 80er Jahren entstand eine große Zahl von Projekten, die Arata Isozaki als »verrück-

d'une réflexion plus sociologique que stylistique. Les architectes néo-minimalistes très en pointe en Suisse ou au Japon, et dont certains sont présentés dans cet ouvrage, créent ou suivent à l'évidence une tendance. Ils redéfinissent le modernisme par une utilisation novatrice de matériaux nouveaux ou inhabituels. Ceci n'empêche pas des praticiens comme Herzog & de Meuron de trouver «idéologiquement» acceptable de consacrer une énorme énergie à la rénovation d'une vieille centrale thermique londonienne. Vivre avec le passé est une des caractéristiques marquantes de l'architecture d'aujourd'hui, à la fois pour des raisons pratiques et parce que l'on a découvert que les bâtiments anciens, en particulier industriels, pouvaient avoir beaucoup de charme et de force. Le mouvement déconstructiviste, avec lequel Daniel Libeskind, Zaha Hadid et Coop Himmelb(l)au se sont identifiés, se développe aussi dans un contexte de mode, même s'il prétend le contraire. Les formes en coin, les angles bizarres et les matériaux curieux constituent leur palette, même s'ils sont toujours obligés d'édifier des bâtiments qui tiennent debout et fonctionnent. Les années 1980 ont été une grande période pour ce qu'Arata Isozaki appelle les «petits immeubles

fashion. As always, the buildings that remain, and those that have a great influence, are not necessarily the most photogenic; they are the ones that function properly and age well. They are the ones that bring something more than a fashionable appearance – the ones that make the heart sing.

te kleine Gebäude« bezeichnete. In Japan zum Beispiel ließ die »Seifenblasenwirtschaft« noch die extravaganteste Architektur billig erscheinen im Vergleich zu den Grundstücken, auf denen sie stand. Diese Zeit ist nun vorüber, selbst wenn Arbeiten wie die von Makoto Sei Watanabe auf uns wirken, als stammten sie aus jenen ungestümen Tagen. Als neuesten Modetrend kann man die Verwendung des Computers als vollwertiges Entwurfswerkzeug bezeichnen. Es ist noch zu früh, um erkennen zu können, ob der Computer wirklich zu einem dauerhaften Wandel der gebauten Umwelt führen wird. Schon heute läßt sich aber sagen: Das Potential für weit mehr als eine vorübergehende Mode ist da. Die Bauwerke, die Bestand haben werden und großen Einfluß ausüben, sind nicht unbedingt die fotogensten – es sind diejenigen, welche zuverlässig funktionieren und auf gute Weise altern. Es sind jene Bauten, die mehr zu bieten haben als ein modernes Erscheinungsbild. Sie erreichen unser Herz.

fous». Au Japon, par exemple, l'économie de la bulle financière faisait que n'importe quelle réalisation pouvait sembler bon marché par rapport au prix du terrain sur laquelle elle se trouvait. Cette période est bien finie, même si des architectes comme Makoto Sei Watanabe semblent encore en faire partie. La dernière tendance à la mode pourrait être l'utilisation de l'ordinateur comme outil de conception. Il est trop tôt pour dire si cette évolution apportera un changement durable de l'environnement architectural, mais il semble qu'elle contienne en germe beaucoup plus qu'une mode éphémère. Comme toujours, les bâtiments qui restent, et ceux qui exercent l'influence la plus grande, ne sont pas nécessairement les plus photogéniques. Ce sont ceux qui remplissent correctement leur fonction et vieillissent bien; ceux qui apportent quelque chose de plus qu'une apparence aussi élégante soit-elle, ceux qui parlent au cœur.

TADAO ANDO

Born in Osaka in 1941, Tadao Ando is a self-educated architect, largely through his travels in the United States, Europe and Africa (1962-69). He founded Tadao Ando Architect & Associates in Osaka in 1969. He has received the Alvar Aalto Medal, Finnish Association of Architects (1985), Medaille d'or, French Academy of Architecture (1989), the 1992 Carlsberg Prize and the 1995 Pritzker Prize. He has taught at Yale (1987), Columbia (1988), and Harvard (1990). Notable

Tadao Ando, geboren 1941 in Osaka, erlernte den Beruf des Architekten als Autodidakt, vorwiegend auf Reisen durch Nordamerika, Europa und Afrika (1962-69). 1969 gründete er das Büro Tadao Ando Architect & Associates in Osaka. Er wurde mit der Alvar-Aalto-Medaille des Finnischen Architektenverbands (1985), der Medaille d'or der Académie Française d'Architecture (1989), dem Carlsberg-Preis (1992) und dem Pritzker Prize (1995) ausgezeichnet. Ando lehrte an den Universitäten Yale

Né à Osaka en 1941, Tadao Ando est un architecte autodidacte, qui s'est formé en grande partie au cours de ses voyages aux États-Unis, en Europe et en Afrique (1962-69). Il crée Tadao Ando Architects & Associates à Osaka en 1969. Titulaire de la Médaille Alvar Aalto de l'Association finlandaise des architectes (1985), de la Médaille d'or de l'Académie Française d'Architecture (1989), du Prix Carlsberg (1992) et du Pritzker Prize (1995). Il a enseigné à Yale (1987), Columbia (1988) et Har-

»ICH BIN AN EINEM DIALOG MIT DER ARCHI-
TEKTUR DER VERGANGENHEIT INTERESSIERT;
ER MUß JEDOCH DURCH MEINE EIGENE SICHT
UND ERFAHRUNG GEFILTERT WERDEN. ZWAR
BIN ICH LE CORBUSIER ODER MIES VAN DER
ROHE VERPFLICHTET, ABER ICH EIGNE MIR
IHR WERK AN UND INTERPRETIERE ES AUF
MEINE WEISE.« TADAO ANDO

«JE M'INTÉRESSE À UN DIALOGUE AVEC L'AR-
CHITECTURE DU PASSÉ, MAIS QUI DOIT PASSER
AU FILTRE DE MA VISION ET DE MON EXPÉ-
RIENCE. JE DOIS BEAUCOUP À LE CORBUSIER
OU À MIES VAN DER ROHE, MAIS JE PRENDS
CE QU'ILS ONT FAIT ET L'INTERPRÈTE À MA
FAÇON.» TADAO ANDO

TADAO ANDO ARCHITECT & ASSOCIATES
5-23, TOYOSAKI 2-CHOME
KITA-KU, OSAKA 531-0072
JAPAN

TEL: + 81 6 6375 1148
FAX: + 81 6 6374 6240

buildings include Rokko Housing (Kobe, Japan, 1981-93), Church on the Water (Hokkaido, 1988), Japan Pavilion Expo '92 (Seville, Spain, 1992), Forest of Tombs Museum (Kumamoto, Japan, 1992), and the Suntory Museum (Osaka, 1994). Current projects include new housing for Kobe and a large complex on the island of Awaji, and the new Museum of Modern Art in Fort Worth, Texas.

(1987), Columbia (1988) und Harvard (1990). Zu seinen bekanntesten Bauten zählen die Rokko-Wohnanlage (Kobe, Japan, 1981-93), die Kirche auf dem Wasser (Hokkaido, 1988), der japanische Pavillon für die Expo '92 in Sevilla (1992), das Forest of Tombs Museum (Kumamoto, Japan, 1992) und das Suntory Museum (Osaka, 1994). Neuere Projekte sind Wohnbauten in Kobe, ein großer Komplex auf der Insel Awaji und das neue Museum of Modern Art in Fort Worth, Texas.

vard (1990). Parmi ses réalisations les plus notables: immeuble de logements Rokko (Kobe, Japon, 1981-93), église sur l'eau (Hokkaido, 1988), Pavillon japonais pour Expo '92 (Séville, Espagne, 1992), Musée de la forêt des tombes (Kumamoto, Japon, 1992), et Musée Suntory (Osaka 1994). Parmi ses projets actuels: des logements à Kobe, un important complexe sur l'île d'Awaji et le nouveau Museum of Modern Art de Fort Worth, Texas.

PLANNING / PLANUNG: 10/94-2/96
CONSTRUCTION / BAU: 2/96-12/97
CLIENT / BAUHERR: TOTO, LTD
FLOOR AREA / NUTZFLÄCHE /
SURFACE UTILE: 3 192 M²
LANDSCAPE DESIGN / LANDSCHAFTS-
GESTALTUNG / ARCHITECTE PAYSAGISTE:
TADAO ANDO

TADAO ANDO
TOTO SEMINAR HOUSE
TSUNA-GUN, HYOGO, JAPAN, 1994-97

AS HE DID IN HIS PROJECT ON THE ISLAND OF NAOSHIMA, TADAO ANDO USES THE SLOPED SITE TO FRAME AND DIRECT THE VIEWS OF VISITORS TOWARD THE SEA.

WIE BEI SEINEM PROJEKT AUF DER INSEL NAOSHIMA NUTZT TADAO ANDO HIER DIE HANGLAGE DES GRUNDSTÜCKS, UM DEN BLICK AUFS MEER ZU LENKEN UND DIE AUSSICHT ZU RAHMEN.

COMME DANS SON PROJET POUR L'ÎLE DE NAOSHIMA, TADAO ANDO A MIS À PROFIT LA PENTE DU TERRAIN POUR CADRER ET ORIENTER LA VUE DES VISITEURS SUR LA MER.

Tadao Ando points out that he personally selected the site for this structure, near the epicenter of the earthquake that devastated Kobe in 1995. Tadao Ando was of course directly involved in numerous disaster efforts after that event. "I had the image," he says, "of a building that is at one with the sea." The site provides a 180° ocean view towards the Kansai International Airport, which is located to the east, across Osaka Bay. The structure is designed as a seminar center with a capacity of 60 persons. Set on a 45° slope facing southeast that drops 100 m, the building is divided into eight levels with a total floor area of 3,191 m², "to meld with the contours of the site." Both through the selected views from this spectacular location, and the walkway that leads to it, Ando seeks here to "make you feel as though you are immersed in the ocean itself."

Tadao Ando hat selbst das Grundstück ausgewählt, das nahe dem Epizentrum des Erdbebens liegt, welches 1995 die Stadt Kobe verwüstete. Er war nach dieser Katastrophe an zahlreichen Rettungseinsätzen unmittelbar beteiligt. »Mir schwebte ein Bauwerk vor,« erläutert Ando, »das eins ist mit dem Meer.« Das Gelände bietet einen Panoramablick auf das Meer und zum internationalen Flughafen Kansai im Osten, über die Bucht von Osaka. Das Seminarzentrum ist für 60 Personen ausgelegt. Es liegt an einem um 45° ansteigenden Südosthang, der sich bis auf 100 m über dem Meeresspiegel erhebt. Die Gesamtgeschoßfläche von 3 191 m² ist auf acht Ebenen verteilt, »damit das Gebäude mit dem Terrain verschmilzt.« Ando versucht durch die spektakulären Ausblicke, die der Standort ermöglicht und durch den Fußweg »das Gefühl zu vermitteln, man tauche ins Meer ein.«

Tadao Ando précise qu'il a personnellement choisi le site de cette construction, proche de l'épicentre du tremblement de terre qui a ravagé Kobe en 1995. Il a bien entendu participé aux efforts de reconstruction qui ont succédé au séisme. «J'avais l'image,» dit-il, «d'un bâtiment qui ne ferait qu'un avec la mer». Le site offre une vue à 180° sur l'océan vers l'est et l'aéroport international de Kansai, de l'autre côté de la baie d'Osaka. La structure abrite un centre de séminaires d'une capacité de 60 participants. Accroché à une pente à 45° orientée au sud-est sur un surplomb d'une centaine de mètres, le bâtiment se développe sur huit niveaux pour une surface totale de 3 191 m². Par les vues qu'il cadre à partir de cette implantation spectaculaire, et les cheminements qui y mènent, Ando a cherché ici à «vous faire sentir comme si vous étiez immergé dans l'océan lui-même».

TAKING ITS SITE AND THE NATURAL SUR-
ROUNDINGS INTO ACCOUNT, THE TOTO SEMI-
NAR HOUSE ALSO STANDS OUT CLEARLY AS
A MAN-MADE OBJECT.

DAS TOTO SEMINAR HOUSE NIMMT RÜCKSICHT
AUF STANDORT UND UMGEBUNG, UND BEHÄLT
DENNOCH DEN CHARAKTER EINES ARTEFAKTS.

TOUT EN PRENANT EN COMPTE SON SITE ET
SON ENVIRONNEMENT NATUREL, LA MAISON DE
SÉMINAIRES TOTO S'AFFIRME À L'ÉVIDENCE
COMME UNE CRÉATION RATIONNELLE.

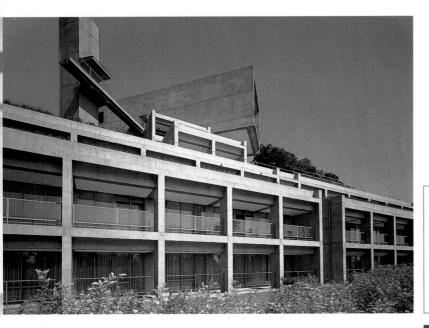

DESPITE THE IRREGULAR HILLSIDE, ANDO
RETAINS THE GEOMETRIC RIGOR THAT IS SO
CHARACTERISTIC OF HIS WORK.

AUCH AUF DEM UNREGELMÄSSIGEN HANG-
GRUNDSTÜCK WAHRT ANDO DIE FÜR SEIN
WERK CHARAKTERISTISCHE GEOMETRISCHE
STRENGE.

MALGRÉ LA PENTE IRRÉGULIÈRE DU TERRAIN,
ANDO A CONSERVÉ LA RIGUEUR GÉOMÉTRIQUE
CARACTÉRISTIQUE DE SON ŒUVRE.

TADAO ANDO
DAYLIGHT MUSEUM
GAMO-GUN, SHIGA, JAPAN, 1997-98

PLANNING / PLANUNG: 2/97-8/97
CONSTRUCTION / BAU: 10/97-5/98
CLIENT / BAUHERR: PRIVATE FARM CO, LTD
FLOOR AREA / NUTZFLÄCHE / SURFACE
UTILE: 196 M²

The most unusual feature of this single-story 196 m² museum is that it has absolutely no artificial lights. As Tadao Ando says, "this museum is probably out of tune with the current of these modern times, but as it allows visitors to experience these works of art under the same conditions and light as when the artist painted them, it just might bring them a step closer to the world of creating art." Built, as is most often the case in the work of Ando, of exposed concrete, the Daylight Museum closes at sunset. The exhibit room is lit by a skylight in the form of a portion of a circular arc. A frosted glass curtain wall provides the light for the corridor along the west side of the exhibit room. "I have come to be reminded of the fact that paintings are not to be suspended in time," says Ando, "sealed and worshipped once the artist applies the final brush stroke, but are rather our close friends and companions – living amongst us naturally and giving us passion and courage."

Dieser eingeschossige Bau mit 196 m² Nutzfläche verfügt über keinerlei künstliche Beleuchtung. Wie Tadao Ando sagt, »steht dieses Museum vermutlich im Widerspruch zum Trend unserer Zeit. Da es jedoch dem Besucher erlaubt, die Kunstwerke unter den gleichen Bedingungen und Lichtverhältnissen zu betrachten, wie sie bei ihrer Entstehung herrschten, kann es ihn auch einen Schritt näher an die Welt der Kunst heranführen.« Das in Sichtbeton ausgeführte Daylight Museum schließt bei Sonnenuntergang. Der Ausstellungsraum wird über einen bogenförmigen Obergaden belichtet. Eine Zwischenwand aus Mattglas läßt Licht in den Korridor fallen. »Ich habe mich daran erinnert, daß Bilder nicht auf ihre Entstehungszeit festgelegt werden sollten«, sagt Ando, »gesiegelt und bewundert, nachdem der Künstler den letzten Pinselstrich getan hat, daß sie vielmehr unsere engen Freunde und Begleiter sind – daß sie mit uns leben, uns Leidenschaft vermitteln und Mut machen.«

La plus étonnante caractéristique de ce musée de 196 m² sur un seul plan, est le refus absolu de tout éclairage artificiel. Comme le précise Tadao Ando: «Ce musée n'est probablement pas dans l'air du temps, mais il permet aux visiteurs de découvrir ces œuvres d'art dans les mêmes conditions et la même lumière que lorsque l'artiste les peignit, ce qui les fait peut-être progresser d'un pas dans l'univers de la création.» Construit en béton brut, comme souvent chez Ando, le musée ferme ses portes au coucher du soleil. La salle d'exposition est éclairée par une verrière en forme de section de cercle. Un mur-rideau en verre translucide éclaire le corridor tout le long du mur ouest de la salle d'exposition. «J'ai fini par me rappeler que les peintures ne sont pas suspendues dans le temps», explique Ando, «figées et adorées une fois le dernier coup de pinceau appliqué, mais qu'elles sont plutôt des amies proches, des compagnes qui vivent naturellement parmi nous et nous donnent courage et passion.»

SITTING LIGHTLY ON THE SITE, THE BUILDING'S GLASS WALL ADMITS AMPLE NATURAL LIGHT TO THE EXHIBITION AREA.

DIE GLASWAND DES LEICHT AUF DEN BODEN GESTELLTEN GEBÄUDES LÄSST REICHLICH TAGESLICHT IN DEN AUSSTELLUNGSBEREICH EINFALLEN.

POSÉ AVEC LÉGÈRETÉ SUR SON TERRAIN, L'ESPACE D'EXPOSITION BÉNÉFICIE D'UN ABONDANT ÉCLAIRAGE NATUREL GRÂCE À UN MUR DE VERRE.

ARCHITECTURE STUDIO

ARCHITECTURE STUDIO HAS EXPERIMENTED
SUCCESSFULLY WITH BRINGING POWERFUL
MODERN FORMS TO THE AREA OF PUBLIC OR
OFFICIAL CONSTRUCTION. THEIR STYLE IS MORE
ONE OF SURPRISE AND INNOVATION THAN OF
A SET VOCABULARY.

ARCHITECTURE STUDIO HAT ERFOLGREICH MIT
MODERNEN FORMEN IM ÖFFENTLICHEN BAUEN
EXPERIMENTIERT. IHR STIL IST EHER ÜBER-

Created in 1973, Architecture Studio has seven principals: Rodo Tisnado, Martin Robain, Alain Bretagnolle, René-Henri Arnaud, Jean-François Bonne, Laurent-Marc Fischer (from left to right) and Marc Lehmann. Their first major building was the Institut du Monde Arabe (Paris, 1981-87) with Nouvel, Soria and Lezènes. Others include the Embassy of France (Muscat, Oman, 1987-89), the

Architecture Studio wurde 1973 gegründet und besteht aus sieben Architekten: Rodo Tisnado, Martin Robain, Alain Bretagnolle, René-Henri Arnaud, Jean-François Bonne, Laurent-Marc Fischer (von links nach rechts) und Marc Lehmann. Ihr erster größerer Bau war das mit Nouvel, Soria und Lezènes geplante Institut du Monde Arabe in Paris (1981-87). Weitere bedeutende Werke sind die

Fondé en 1973, Architecture Studio compte sept associés: Rodo Tisnado, Martin Robain, Alain Bretagnolle, René-Henri Arnaud, Jean-François Bonne, Laurent-Marc Fischer (de gauche à droite) et Marc Lehmann. Leur première grande réalisation est l'Institut du Monde Arabe (Paris, 1981-87) conçu avec Nouvel, Soria et Lezènes. Parmi leurs autres réalisations importantes: l'ambassade de France (Masca-

ARCHITECTURE STUDIO
10, RUE LACUÉE
75012 PARIS
FRANCE

TEL: + 33 1 43 45 18 00
FAX: + 33 1 43 43 81 43
E-MAIL: as@architecture-studio.fr
WEB: www.architecture-studio.fr

Lycée du Futur (Jaunay Clan, France, 1986-87), and the University Restaurant (Dunkerque, France, 1991-93). Aside from Our Lady of the Ark of the Covenant (Paris, 1996-97), recent work includes: the Institut national du Judo (Paris, 1988-2000), the extension of the Exhibition Park at Paris-Nord Villepinte (2000), and the 220,000 m² European Parliament (Strasbourg, 1994-98).

Französische Botschaft in Muscat, Oman (1987-89), das Lycée du Futur in Jaunay Clan, Frankreich (1986-87) und die Mensa der Universität Dünkirchen (1991-93). Neuere Projekte sind das Institut national du Judo in Paris (1988-2000), die Erweiterung des Ausstellungsparks Villepinte in Paris-Nord (2000) und das Europäische Parlament in Straßburg (1994-98).

te, Oman, 1987-89), le lycée du Futur (Jaunay Clan, 1986-87), le restaurant universitaire (Dunkerque, 1991-93). Ils ont récemment entrepris l'église Notre-Dame de l'arche d'Alliance (Paris, 1996-97), l'Institut national du Judo (Paris, 1988-2000), l'extension du Parc d'exposition de Paris-Nord Villepinte (2000) et surtout le bâtiment du Parlement européen (220 000 m², Strasbourg, 1994-98).

OUR LADY OF THE ARK OF THE COVENANT

PARIS, FRANCE, 1996-97

THE GRID STRUCTURE THAT DEFINES THE
EXTERIOR OF THE BUILDING IS CARRIED INTO
ITS INTERIOR, CONFIRMING THE UNUSUAL
GEOMETRIC CONFIGURATION.

DIE GITTERKONSTRUKTION, DIE DAS GEBÄUDE
EINFASST, WIRD INS INNERE GEFÜHRT UND
BETONT DIE UNGEWÖHNLICHE GEOMETRISCHE
KONFIGURATION.

LA TRAME D'ACIER QUI DÉLIMITE L'EXTÉRIEUR
DU BÂTIMENT SE RETROUVE À L'INTÉRIEUR,
RAPPEL ET CONFIRMATION DE CETTE ÉTON-
NANTE CONFIGURATION GÉOMÉTRIQUE.

CLIENT / BAUHERR: ASSOCIATION DIOCÉSAINE
DE PARIS
FLOOR AREA / NUTZFLÄCHE / SURFACE UTILE:
1611 M²
COSTS / KOSTEN / COÛTS: 23 000 000 FF
FUNCTION / FUNKTION / FONCTION: CATHOLIC
SERVICES

THE SCAFFOLDING-LIKE EXTERNAL GRID
EVOKES THE CONTINUITY OF THE RELIGIOUS
FUNCTION WITH ITS ENVIRONMENT, ITS
CONTACT WITH THE COMMUNITY.

DAS GERÜSTÄHNLICHE AUSSENGITTER VER-
WEIST AUF DIE KONTINUITÄT DER RELIGIÖSEN
FUNKTION ZUR UMGEBUNG, AUF IHRE VER-
BINDUNG ZUR GEMEINSCHAFT.

LA TRAME EXTÉRIEURE, QUI POURRAIT FAIRE
PENSER À UN ÉCHAFAUDAGE, SYMBOLISE LA
CONTINUITÉ DE LA FONCTION RELIGIEUSE
DANS SON ENVIRONNEMENT, LE CONTACT AVEC
LA COMMUNAUTÉ.

Situated on the rue d'Alleray in the 15th arrondissement of Paris, this 350 seat-church was built with a budget of 23 million francs. A further 4 million francs were spent on works of art and furniture. It is surrounded by an unusual 24 m high metallic grid, which highlights the cubic central volume, intended to evoke the Ark of the Covenant. The main body of the church is set up on twelve 3 m high pilotis, which represent the Tribes of Israel as well as the twelve Apostles. Within, dark wood and black slate floors contrast with elements of the external metallic grid, which are symbolically intended to take their origin in the cross at the entrance to the choir. The white Thassos marble altar was conceived by the architects and made by Michael Prentice. Intended as a rigorous, modernist rendering of the power of the Scriptures, the work of Architecture Studio certainly shows that contemporary architecture and a certain spirituality are by no means incompatible.

Die in der rue d'Alleray im 15. Arrondissement von Paris gelegene Kirche mit 350 Plätzen wurde mit einem Budget von 23 Millionen Francs erbaut. Weitere vier Millionen Francs wurden für Kunstwerke und Möblierung ausgegeben. Der Bau ist von einem ungewöhnlichen, 24 m hohen Metallgitter umfangen, das den kubischen Mittelteil betont, der an die Bundeslade erinnern soll. Der zentrale Baukörper erhebt sich über zwölf 3 m hohen Piloti, die für die Stämme Israels und die zwölf Apostel stehen. Im Innern kontrastieren dunkles Holz und schwarze Schieferböden mit den Elementen des metallischen Außengitters, die dem Kreuz am Eingang zum Chor symbolisch entsprechen sollen. Der Altar aus weißem Thassos-Marmor wurde von den Architekten entworfen und von Michael Prentice ausgeführt. Die Kirche, von Architecture Studio als konsequent moderne Darstellung der Kraft der Heiligen Schrift entworfen, zeigt deutlich, daß zeitgenössische Architektur keineswegs unvereinbar ist mit einer gewissen Spiritualität.

Située rue d'Alleray dans le 15ème arrondissement de Paris, cette église de 350 places a été construite pour un budget de 23 millions de francs. Quatre millions supplémentaires ont été consacrés aux œuvres d'art et au mobilier. Elle est entourée d'une curieuse grille métallique de 24 m de haut, qui met en valeur son volume cubique censé évoquer l'arche d'Alliance. Le corps principal est surélevé sur douze pilotis de 3 m de haut, qui représentent les tribus d'Israël ou les douze Apôtres. À l'intérieur, des panneaux de bois sombre et un sol d'ardoise contrastent avec les éléments de la grille métallique extérieure qui prend symboliquement naissance dans la croix située à l'entrée du chœur. L'autel en marbre banc de Thassos a été dessiné par les architectes et réalisé par Michael Prentice. Traduction rigoureuse et moderniste de la puissance des Ecritures, ce travail d'Architecture Studio montre à l'évidence que l'architecture contemporaine et une certaine spiritualité ne sont pas incompatibles.

USING UNUSUAL MATERIALS SUCH AS PAPER, SHIGERU BAN EXPANDS AND REDEFINES THE LIMITS OF AN ARCHITECTURE INSPIRED BY MODERNISM. HE TAKES THE ICONIC MINIMA-LISM OF PRECURSORS SUCH AS MIES A STEP FURTHER.

DURCH DIE VERWENDUNG UNTYPISCHER MATE-RIALIEN WIE PAPIER ERWEITERT SHIGERU BAN DIE GRENZEN EINER VON DER MODERNE

SHIGERU BAN

Born in 1957 in Tokyo, Shigeru Ban studied at the Southern California Institute of Architecture from 1977 to 1980. He attended the Cooper Union School of Architecture, where he studied under John Hejduk (1980-82). He worked in the office of Arata Isozaki (1982-83) before founding his own firm in Tokyo in 1985. His work includes numerous exhibition designs (Alvar Aalto show at the Axis Gallery, Tokyo, 1986). Among his buildings are

Shigeru Ban, geboren 1957 in Tokio, studierte von 1977 bis 1980 am Southern California Institute of Architecture (SCI-Arc) und von 1980 bis 1982 bei John Hejduk an der Cooper Union School of Architecture in New York. 1982-83 arbeitete er im Büro von Arata Isozaki, bevor er 1985 seine eigene Firma in Tokio gründete. Er gestaltete zahlreiche Ausstellungen, so die Alvar-Aalto-Schau in der Axis Gallery in Tokio 1986. Zu seinen Bauten gehören

Né en 1957 à Tokyo, Shigeru Ban fait ses études au Southern California Institute of Architecture (SCI-Arc) de 1977 à 1980, puis à la Cooper Union School of Architecture, où il suit l'enseignement de John Hejduk (1980-82). Il travaille pour Arata Isozaki (1982-83), avant de créer sa propre agence à Tokyo en 1985. Il a conçu de nombreuses exposi-tions (dont l'exposition Alvar Aalto, Axis Gallery, Tokyo, 1986). Parmi ses réalisations architectu-

INSPIRIERTEN ARCHITEKTUR. ER FÜHRT DEN
MINIMALISMUS VON VORGÄNGERN WIE MIES
VAN DER ROHE EINEN SCHRITT WEITER.

À PARTIR DE MATÉRIAUX INHABITUELS COMME
LE PAPIER, SHIGERU BAN REPOUSSE ET REDÉ-
FINIT LES LIMITES D'UNE ARCHITECTURE INS-
PIRÉE DU MODERNISME. IL FAIT FRANCHIR UN
NOUVEAU PAS AU MINIMALISME.

SHIGERU BAN, ARCHITECTS
5-2-4 MATSUBARA BAN BLDG, 1ST FL.
SETAGAYA, TOKYO 156-0043
JAPAN

TEL: + 81 3 3324 6760
FAX: + 81 3 3324 6789
WEB: www.dnp-sp.co.jp/millennium/SB/VAN.html

the Odawara Pavilion (Kanagawa, 1990), the
Paper Gallery (Tokyo, 1994), the Paper House
(Lake Yamanaka, 1994-95), and the Paper Church
(Takatori, Hyogo, 1995), all in Japan. He has also
designed ephemeral structures such as his Paper
Refugee Shelter, made with plastic sheets and paper
tubes, for the United Nations High Commissioner
for Refugees (UNHCR). He was chosen to design
the Japanese Pavilion at Expo 2000, Hanover.

der Odawara-Pavillon (Kanagawa, 1990), die Paper
Gallery (Tokio, 1994), das Paper House am Yamanaka-See (1994-95) und die Paper Church (Takatori, Hyogo, 1995), alle in Japan. Shigeru Ban hat
auch Behelfsbauten aus Plastikfolie und Pappröhren
für den Hohen Flüchtlingskommissar der Vereinten
Nationen (UNHCR) geplant. Zur Zeit arbeitet er
am Japanischen Pavillon für die Expo 2000 in
Hannover.

rales au Japon: le Pavillon Odawara (Kanagawa,
1990), la Paper Gallery (Tokyo, 1994), la Maison
de papier (Lac Yamanaka, 1994-95), et l'Église de
papier, (Takatori, Hyogo, 1995). Il conçoit également des structures éphémères comme son abri
pour réfugiés en feuilles de plastique et tubes de
papier pour le Haut Commissariat aux Réfugiés
(HCRNU). Il a été choisi pour concevoir le pavillon
japonais à Expo 2000, Hanovre.

SHIGERU BAN
PAPER HOUSE
LAKE YAMANAKA, YAMANASHI, JAPAN, 1994-95

COMPLETION / FERTIGSTELLUNG / FIN DE LA
CONSTRUCTION: 7/95
CLIENT / BAUHERR: WITHHELD / UNGENANNT /
NON COMMUNIQUÉ
FLOOR AREA / NUTZFLÄCHE / SURFACE UTILE:
100 M²
COSTS / KOSTEN / COÛTS: WITHHELD / UNGE-
NANNT / NON COMMUNIQUÉS
STRUCTURE / BAUWEISE: PAPER TUBES /
PAPIERROHRE / TUYAUX EN PAPIER

This 100 m² house is one of three built by the architect near Lake Yamanaka. It was the first project in Japan to use recycled paper tubes as a structural material in a permanent building. Naturally, paper has frequently been used in partitions in Japanese architecture, and Shigeru Ban had previously built such structures as the Odawara Festival Main Hall (1990) with the same material. He also designed a Paper Church and Paper Log

Das 100 m² große Wohnhaus ist eines von dreien, die der Architekt am Yamanaka-See errichtete. Zum ersten Mal in Japan werden hier recycelte Pappröhren als Konstruktionsmaterial für ein dauerhaftes Gebäude verwendet. Papier wird in der japanischen Architektur natürlich häufig für Trennwände benutzt, und Shigeru Ban hat schon früher Bauten mit diesem Material errichtet, wie die Festival-Halle in Odawara (1990). Er entwarf auch eine Kirche

Cette maison de 100 m² fait partie d'une série de trois construites par l'architecte près du lac Yamanaka. C'est le premier projet réalisé au Japon à partir de tubes en papier recyclé pour un bâtiment à vocation permanente. Le papier est traditionnellement utilisé pour les cloisons des maisons japonaises, et Shigeru Ban avait déjà construit des structures de ce type avec le même matériau, dans le Grand Hall du Festival d'Odawara (1990) par

A RADICALLY SIMPLE PLAN DEFINES FLEXIBLE INTERIOR SPACE ADAPTED TO THE JAPANESE LIFE-STYLE.

P 082.083

EIN RADIKAL EINFACHER GRUNDRISS BE-STIMMT DEN FLEXIBLEN, DEM JAPANISCHEN LEBENSSTIL ANGEPASSTEN INNENRAUM.

LE PLAN D'UNE SIMPLICITÉ RADICALE DÉFINIT UN ESPACE INTÉRIEUR SOUPLE, ADAPTÉ AU STYLE DE VIE JAPONAIS.

Houses for refugees from the 1995 Kobe earthquake. The 110 tubes of the Paper House are set on a 10 x 10 m platform in a looping "S" shaped pattern. Each tube is 280 mm in diameter and 2.7 m high. The larger loop of the "S," made with 80 tubes, defines a large, open living area, looking out onto the surrounding forest, while a bathroom is located in the smaller loop.

und »Blockhütten« aus Pappe und Papier für die Überlebenden des Erdbebens in Kobe von 1995. Die 110 Röhren des Papierhauses sind in geschwungener S-Form auf eine 10 x 10 m große Plattform gestellt. Der Durchmesser der Röhren beträgt 280 mm, die Höhe 2,7 m. Die größere Schleife des S umfaßt mit 80 Röhren einen großen, offenen Wohnbereich mit Blick auf den umgebenden Wald, die kleinere ein Badezimmer.

exemple. Il a aussi conçu une église en papier et des maisons en bûches de papier pour les réfugiés du tremblement de terre de Kobe en 1995. Les 110 tubes de la maison se dressent sur une plate-forme de 10 x 10 m selon un tracé en S. Chaque tube mesure 280 mm de diamètre et 2,7 m de haut. La boucle la plus large du S, formée de 80 tubes, définit un vaste espace de séjour, tandis que la salle de bains est située dans la petite boucle.

**ONLY THE BATHROOM IS SEPARATED FROM THE
FREE-PLAN OPEN INTERIOR SPACE.**

NUR DAS BAD IST VOM DURCHGEHEND
OFFENEN INNENRAUM ABGETRENNT.

DANS LE PLAN LIBRE DE L'ESPACE INTÉRIEUR
OUVERT, SEULE LA SALLE DE BAINS EST
ISÓLÉE.

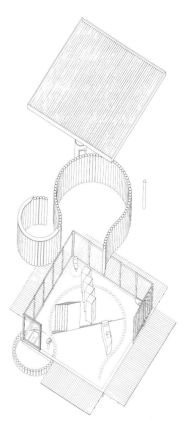

SHIGERU BAN
WALL-LESS HOUSE
KARUIZAWA, NAGANO, JAPAN, 1997

COMPLETION / FERTIGSTELLUNG / FIN DE
LA CONSTRUCTION: 8/97
CLIENT / BAUHERR: WITHHELD / UNGENANNT /
NON COMMUNIQUÉ
FLOOR AREA / NUTZFLÄCHE / SURFACE
UTILE: 60 M²
COSTS / KOSTEN / COÛTS: WITHHELD / UNGE-
NANNT / NON COMMUNIQUÉS

**ONLY VERY FINE COLUMNS AND RAILS PER-
MITTING THE DIVISION OF THE SPACE INTER-
RUPT THE PRISTINE SIMPLICITY OF THIS
HOUSE.**

DIE KONSEQUENTE SCHLICHTHEIT DIESES
WOHNHAUSES WIRD NUR VON SEHR SCHLAN-
KEN STÜTZEN AUFGELOCKERT, DIE DEN RAUM
GLIEDERN.

SEULES DE TRÈS MINCES COLONNES ET DES
MAINS COURANTES DIVISENT L'ESPACE ET
INTERROMPENT LA LUMINEUSE SIMPLICITÉ
DE CETTE MAISON.

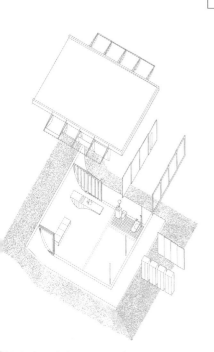

This is the eighth in a series of so-called Case Study Houses designed by Shigeru Ban. The idea of the Case Study Houses comes naturally from the California designs of the late 1940s and 1950s. Built on a steeply sloped, wooded site, the house consists of a 60 m² slab that is embedded into the hillside, curving up at the rear to support the light steel roof. This design permitted the architect to create an open living surface with just three 55 mm thick columns. Although the kitchen, bathroom and toilet are situated without any enclosure, sliding panels can be used to partition the space. Shigeru Ban calls this the "universal floor" concept. Movable glass panels can protect the interior space, but the net result of the design effort was to literally create a wall-less house.

Dies ist das achte einer Serie sogenannter »Case Study Houses« Shigeru Bans. Die Idee zu solchen »Fallstudien« geht auf kalifornische Entwürfe vom Ende der 40er und 50er Jahre zurück. Das an einem steilen, bewaldeten Hang errichtete Haus besteht aus einer 60 m² großen Platte, die in den Hügel eingebettet und an der Rückseite aufwärts gebogen ist, um das leichte Stahldach zu tragen. So entstand ein offener Wohnbereich mit nur drei 55 mm starken Stützen. Zwar sind Küche, Bad und Toilette nicht durch Wände getrennt, doch dienen Schiebewände als Raumteiler. Shigeru Ban nennt dies das »Universalgeschoß«-Konzept. Mit Hilfe verschiebbarer Glastafeln kann der Innenraum geschlossen werden. Das Ergebnis ist jedoch im wörtlichen Sinne ein Haus ohne Wände.

Cette maison est la huitième d'une série de « Case Study Houses » conçues par l'architecte. Ces études de cas spécifiques s'inspirent de la série de projets californiens de la fin des années 40 et des années 50. Construite sur un terrain boisé en pente raide, la maison est constituée d'une dalle de béton de 60 m², encastrée dans le flanc de la colline et recourbée à l'arrière pour soutenir un toit en acier léger. Ce principe de conception a permis de créer une surface ouverte à peine interrompue par des colonnes de 55 mm d'épaisseur. Bien que la cuisine, la salle de bains et les toilettes ne soient pas fermées, des panneaux coulissants peuvent servir à diviser l'espace. Des panneaux mobiles en verre peuvent protéger l'espace intérieur, mais le résultat essentiel est – littéralement – une maison sans murs.

BDM

Two of the principals of BDM are Jean-Louis Ducerf (left), born in 1948, who received his degree in architecture (DPLG, atelier Jean Bossu) in 1975 before studying the restoration of historic monuments (CESMA, Chaillot, 1977), and Jean-Louis Marc (right), born in 1950, who obtained his DPLG in 1981 (UP 6) and a "Licence d'urbanisme" in 1982 (Paris VIII). Giada Ricci, who received her diploma from the Florence Faculty of Architecture

Leiter von BDM sind der 1948 geborene Jean-Louis Ducerf (links), der 1975 sein Diplom in Architektur am DPLG, Atelier Jean Bossu, erwarb und 1977 Denkmalpflege am CESMA in Chaillot studierte, sowie der 1950 geborene Jean-Louis Marc (rechts), der 1981 sein Diplom (DPLG, UP 6) und 1982 die »Licence d'Urbanisme« (Paris VIII) bekam. Giada Ricci, die 1974 ihr Studium an der Florentiner Architekturfakultät abschloß, war

Jean-Louis Ducerf (à gauche), né en 1948, architecte DPLG (1975, atelier Jean Bossu), qui s'est spécialisé par la suite dans la restauration des monuments historiques (CESMA, Chaillot, 1977) et Jean-Louis Marc (à droite), né en 1950, DPLG en 1981 (UP 6) et licencié en urbanisme en 1982 (Paris VIII) sont deux des principaux associés de BDM. Giada Ricci, diplômée de la faculté d'architecture de Florence en 1974, a été architecte-assis-

WORKING WITH FORMS INSPIRED BY ABAN-DONED MINING FACILITIES, THE FRENCH TEAM OF BDM HAS CREATED A STRUCTURE THAT IS BOTH MODERN AND ROOTED IN 19TH-CENTURY INDUSTRY.

IN FORMEN, DIE SICH VON STILLGELEGTEN BERGWERKSBAUTEN ABLEITEN, SCHUF BDM EIN GEBÄUDE, DAS MODERN UND DENNOCH

VOM INDUSTRIEBAU DES 19. JAHRHUNDERTS BEEINFLUSST IST.

TRAVAILLANT À PARTIR DE FORMES INSPIRÉES D'INSTALLATIONS MINIÈRES ABANDONNÉES, L'ÉQUIPE FRANÇAISE DE BDM A CRÉÉ UNE STRUCTURE À LA FOIS MODERNE ET ENRACI-NÉE DANS L'INDUSTRIE LOCALE DU SIÈCLE DERNIER.

BDM ARCHITECTES
51, RUE DES PETITES ÉCURIES
75010 PARIS
FRANCE

TEL: + 33 1 47 70 24 69
FAX: + 33 1 48 00 98 41

in 1974, was an assistant architect for the Jean Moulin Residence project published here. BDM has worked on the rehabilitation of student residences for the University of Burgundy, Le Creusot (1991-93), elementary schools for the towns of Soignolles en Brie and Ciry le Noble (1992-95), and psychiatric facilities for Ville Evrard (1995-96).

Mitarbeiterin beim hier vorgestellten Studenten-wohnheim Jean Moulin. BDM hat die Sanierung von Wohnheimen der Universität von Burgund in Le Creusot (1991-93) durchgeführt, Grundschulen für die Städte Soignolles en Brie und Ciry le Noble (1992-95) und Bauten für die psychiatrischen Kliniken von Ville-Evrard (1995-96) geplant.

tante sur le projet de la résidence Jean Moulin publié ici. BDM est déjà intervenu sur la réhabilita-tion de résidences étudiantes pour l'Université de Bourgogne, Le Creusot (1991-1993), des écoles élémentaires pour les villes de Soignolles-en-Brie et Ciry-le-Noble (1992-95), et des équipements psychiatriques pour Ville-Evrard (1995-96).

BDM

JEAN MOULIN STUDENT RESIDENCE

LE CREUSOT, FRANCE, 1993

CLIENT / BAUHERR: COMMUNAUTÉ URBAINE CUCM + S.C.I.C.
FLOOR AREA / NUTZFLÄCHE / SURFACE UTILE: 2 476 M²
FUNCTION / FUNKTION / FONCTION: 80 STUDIOS
COSTS / KOSTEN / COÛTS: 14 000 000 FF

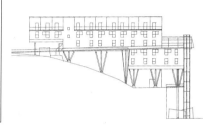

P 090.091

BECAUSE OF THE STEEP DROP IN THE SITE, THE BUILDING RESTS PARTIALLY ON PILOTIS, ACCENTUATING ITS TEMPORARY OR INDUSTRIAL CHARACTER.

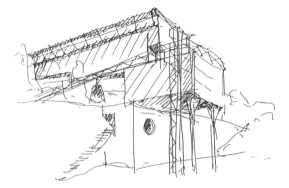

WEGEN DER STEILEN HANGLAGE STEHT DAS GEBÄUDE ZUM TEIL AUF STÜTZEN, WAS SEINEN TEMPORÄREN ODER INDUSTRIELLEN CHARAKTER BETONT.

POUR COMPENSER LE DÉCROCHEMENT ABRUPT DU TERRAIN, LE BÂTIMENT REPOSE EN PARTIE SUR PILOTIS, CE QUI ACCENTUE SON ASPECT TEMPORAIRE OU INDUSTRIEL.

This five-level metal-frame building contains 80 rooms for students, and a cafeteria. Built in Le Creusot in Burgundy on the site of a former iron and steel works, the student residence adopts the typology of the industrial buildings that are typical of the region. The 2,476 m² of floor space is cantilevered over heavy stone walls, originally built around 1880, and is surrounded by what the architects call a "garden of relics." Access is from a public footbridge at the third level or from an elevator. All of the facades are covered in gray lacquered steel, and the pilotis and structural frame are made of galvanized steel. Located near the city of Le Creusot, the building sits over a ravine, which originally dropped 30 m before being progressively leveled by operations related to the mining facilities. Because the elevator and footbridge are open to the public the building also serves as a link between the lower and upper areas.

Der fünfgeschossige Metallskelettbau enthält 80 Wohnräume für Studenten und eine Cafeteria. Auf dem Gelände eines früheren Stahlwerks in Le Creusot (Burgund) errichtet, greift der Bau die Typologie örtlicher Industriebauten auf. 2 476 m² Geschoßfläche kragen auf Trägern über Natursteinwänden von 1880 aus. Ein von den Architekten sogenannter »Reliquiengarten« umgibt das Studentenwohnheim. Der Zugang erfolgt über eine Fußgängerbrücke oder mit dem Aufzug. Alle Fassaden sind in grau lackiertem Stahl verkleidet, Stützen und Tragwerk bestehen aus verzinktem Stahl. Das nahe der Innenstadt von Le Creusot gelegene Gebäude steht über einer ursprünglich 30 m tiefen Schlucht, die jedoch durch Aushub aus dem Bergbau allmählich nivelliert wurde. Weil Aufzug und Fußgängerbrücke öffentlich zugänglich sind, verbindet der Bau auch die unteren mit den oberen Stadtbereichen.

Ce bâtiment à ossature métallique de cinq niveaux contient 80 chambres pour étudiants et une cafétéria. Construit au Creusot (Bourgogne) sur le site d'une ancienne aciérie, il a adopté la typologie des bâtiments industriels typiques de cette région. Les 2 476 m² de surface se déploient en porte-à-faux au-dessus d'épais murs de pierre édifiés vers 1880 et sont entourés de ce que les architectes appellent un «jardin de reliques». L'accès se fait au troisième niveau par une passerelle publique ou un ascenseur. La totalité de la façade est recouverte d'acier laqué gris, tandis que les pilotis et la structure sont en acier galvanisé. Situé près de la ville du Creusot, le bâtiment donne sur un ravin, jadis profond d'une trentaine de mètres, mais peu à peu comblé par des rejets de mines. Comme sa passerelle et son ascenseur sont publics, il fait également office de lien entre la crête et le fond du ravin.

BEN VAN BERKEL IS ONE OF THE FIRST AND MOST SIGNIFICANT DUTCH ARCHITECTS TO EMERGE WITH A SENSIBILITY SPECIFICALLY IN TUNE WITH COMPUTER DESIGN. HE HAS CONSISTENTLY SHOWN AN ABILITY TO CREATE UNEXPECTED FORMS, WHETHER FOR A BRIDGE OR FOR A PRIVATE HOUSE.

BEN VAN BERKEL, EINER DER BEDEUTENDSTEN NIEDERLÄNDISCHEN ARCHITEKTEN, HAT EIN BESONDERES GESPÜR FÜR DIE GESTALTUNG MIT DEM COMPUTER. SEINE ENTWÜRFE SIND STETS ÜBERRASCHEND, SEI ES BEI EINER BRÜCKE ODER EINEM WOHNHAUS.

BEN VAN BERKEL

Ben van Berkel was born in Utrecht in 1957, and studied at the Rietveld Academie in Amsterdam and at the Architectural Association (AA) in London, receiving the AA Diploma with honors in 1987. After working briefly in the office of Santiago Calatrava, in 1988 he set up his practice in Amsterdam with Caroline Bos. He was visiting professor at Columbia, and visiting critic at Harvard (1994), Diploma Unit Master, AA, London (1994-95). As well as the Erasmus Bridge in Rotterdam (inaugurated in 1996), Van Berkel & Bos Archi-

Ben van Berkel, geboren 1957 in Utrecht, studierte an der Rietveld-Akademie in Amsterdam und an der Architectural Association (AA) in London, wo er 1987 sein Diplom mit Auszeichnung erwarb. Nach kurzer Tätigkeit bei Santiago Calatrava gründete er 1988 mit Caroline Bos ein eigenes Büro in Amsterdam. 1994 war van Berkel Gastprofessor an der Columbia University in New York und Gastkritiker in Harvard, von 1994 bis 1995 Diploma Unit Master an der AA in London. Außer der 1996 eröffneten Erasmus-Brücke in Rotterdam hat das

Ben van Berkel naît à Utrecht en 1957 et étudie à la Rietveld Academie à Amsterdam et à l'Architectural Association (AA) à Londres, dont il sort diplômé avec honneurs en 1987. Après avoir brièvement travaillé dans l'agence de Santiago Calatrava en 1988, il ouvre son cabinet à Amsterdam, en association avec Caroline Bos. Professeur invité à Columbia, New York, et critique invité à Harvard en 1994, Diploma Unit Master à l'AA, Londres en 1994-95. En dehors du pont Erasme à Rotterdam (inauguré en 1996), Van Berkel & Bos Archi-

BEN VAN BERKEL EST L'UN DES PREMIERS
ET DES PLUS IMPORTANTS ARCHITECTES
NÉERLANDAIS À SE MONTRER RÉELLEMENT
SENSIBLE À L'INTÉRÊT DE LA CRÉATION PAR
ORDINATEUR. IL SAIT DEPUIS LONGTEMPS
CRÉER DES FORMES INATTENDUES, AUSSI
BIEN POUR UN PONT QUE POUR UNE RÉSI-
DENCE PARTICULIÈRE.

UN STUDIO VAN BERKEL & BOS BV
STADHOUDERSKADE 113
1073 AX AMSTERDAM
THE NETHERLANDS

TEL: + 31 20 570 2040
FAX: + 31 20 570 2041
E-MAIL: info@unstudio.com
WEB: www.unstudio.com

tectural Bureau has built the Karbouw (1990-92) and ACOM office buildings (1989-93), and the REMU electricity station (1989-93), all in Amersfoort, housing projects and the Aedes East gallery for Kristin Feireiss (now Director of the Netherlands Architecture Institute, Rotterdam) in Berlin. More recent projects in The Netherlands include a new museum for Nijmegen and an extension for the Rijksmuseum Twente in Enschede (1992-96), and the Piet Hein Tunnel Buildings in Amsterdam (1997).

Architekturbüro Van Berkel & Bos die Büro-gebäude Karbouw und ACOM (1989-93) und das Elektrizitätswerk REMU (1989-93), alle in Amersfoort, ausgeführt. In Berlin entstanden Wohnbauten und die Galerie Aedes East für Kristin Feireiss (die jetzt Leiterin des Niederländischen Architektur-instituts in Rotterdam ist). Zu den jüngsten Projekten in den Niederlanden gehören ein neues Museum in Nijmegen, die Erweiterung des Rijksmuseum Twente in Enschede (1992-96) und die Piet-Hein-Tunnelbauten in Amsterdam (1997).

tectural Bureau a construit à Amersfoort les immeubles de bureaux Karbouw et ACOM (1989-93) et la centrale électrique REMU (1989-93), ainsi que des projets de logements et la galerie Aedes East à Berlin pour Kristin Feireiss (actuellement directrice de l'Institut néerlandais d'architecture à Rotterdam). Parmi les projets les plus récents, dans les Pays-Bas, un nouveau musée à Nimègue et une extension du Rijksmuseum Twente à Enschede (1992-96), ainsi que les bâtiments du Piet Hein Tunnel à Amsterdam (1997).

BEN VAN BERKEL
MÖBIUS HOUSE
'T GOOI, THE NETHERLANDS, 1993-97

PLANNING / PLANUNG: 1993
COMPLETION / FERTIGSTELLUNG / FIN DE LA
CONSTRUCTION: 1997
CLIENT / BAUHERR: WITHHELD / UNGENANNT /
NON COMMUNIQUÉ
FLOOR AREA / NUTZFLÄCHE / SURFACE UTILE:
550 M²
COSTS / KOSTEN / COÛTS: WITHHELD / UNGE-
NANNT / NON COMMUNIQUÉS

**THE CONCEPT OF THE MÖBIUS STRIP, AT THE
ORIGIN OF THE DESIGN OF THIS HOUSE, HAS
BEEN SUBLIMATED WHILE RETAINING THE
IDEA OF A CONTINUITY BETWEEN NIGHT AND
DAY, WORK AND REST.**

DER ARCHITEKT HAT DAS MÖBIUSSCHE BAND
ALS AUSGANGSPUNKT FÜR SEINEN ENTWURF
GENOMMEN UND IHM DIE IDEE DER KONTI-

NUITÄT VON TAG UND NACHT, ARBEIT UND
ERHOLUNG ZUGRUNDE GELEGT.

L'IDÉE DE L'ANNEAU DE MÖBIUS, À L'ORIGINE
DU DESSIN DE CETTE MAISON, A ÉTÉ SUBLIMÉE
POUR ILLUSTRER LE CONCEPT DE CONTINUITÉ
ENTRE LE JOUR ET LA NUIT, LE TRAVAIL ET LE
REPOS.

Designed to take in as much as possible of the natural surroundings because of its stretched out form, this 550 m² house has been compared by the architect to the effect that visitors of the Kröller-Müller may experience. One end of the house is cantilevered out over a sandy pit. The continuous band or Möbius strip that is at the origin of Ben van Berkel's spatial concept, is realized through unexpected shifts of materials, such as the use of glazed facades over concrete surfaces, or furniture made of concrete. The architect's intention was not to translate the mathematical formula for the Möbius strip into built form, but to "conceptualize or thematize" it through "architectural ingredients such as the light, the staircases, and the way in which people move through the house." The Möbius House is a manifestation of the continuing interest that Ben van Berkel has shown in computer-generated environments and forms, as evidenced in his offices for Karbouw in Amersfoort (1990-92). The whole of the house is intended to convey the idea of a continuous, 24-hour cycle of life and sleep.

Der Architekt hat für dieses 550 m² große Wohnhaus eine gestreckte Form gewählt, um möglichst viel von der natürlichen Umgebung einzubeziehen – er vergleicht die Wirkung des Gebäudes mit der des Kröller-Müller-Museums in Otterlo. Eine Seite des Hauses ragt über eine Sandgrube. Das Möbiussche Band, das dem räumlichen Konzept zugrunde liegt, wird durch unerwartete Materialkontraste konkretisiert – etwa durch Glasfassaden auf Betonflächen oder Möbel aus Beton. Die Absicht des Architekten bestand nicht in der Übersetzung der mathematischen Formel für das Möbiussche Band in gebaute Form, sondern darin, es durch »architektonische Bestandteile, etwa Licht, Treppen oder die Art, wie die Menschen sich in dem Haus bewegen, zu konzeptionalisieren oder zu thematisieren.« Das Möbius-Haus manifestiert erneut Ben van Berkels Interesse an computergenerierten Räumen und Formen, das sich bereits im Bürogebäude Karbouw in Amersfoort (1990-92) niedergeschlagen hat. Das Haus soll die Vorstellung eines ununterbrochenen, 24 Stunden umfassenden Zyklus aus Wachen und Schlafen vermitteln.

Avec son plan étalé, conçu pour respecter autant que faire se peut son environnement naturel, l'effet produit par cette maison de 550 m² a pu être comparé par son auteur à celui que ressentent les visiteurs du musée Kröller-Müller. Une des parties de la maison est en porte-à-faux au-dessus d'une fosse de sable. La bande continue ou anneau de Möbius à l'origine de ce concept spatial se matérialise dans des utilisations décalées de matériaux comme des façades vitrées devant un mur de béton ou des meubles en béton. L'intention de l'architecte était non pas de transcrire architecturalement la formule mathématique de l'anneau de Möbius, mais de la «conceptualiser ou thématiser» à travers des «composantes architecturales comme la lumière, les escaliers et la manière dont les occupants se déplacent dans la maison.» La maison Möbius est une manifestation de l'intérêt constant porté par Ben van Berkel dans les environnements et formes générés par ordinateur, comme le montrent les bureaux qu'il a réalisés pour Karbouw à Amersfoort (1990-92). L'ensemble de la maison veut véhiculer l'idée du cycle vital des 24 heures de vie et de sommeil.

EXTERIOR AND INTERIOR SURFACES SEEM
ALMOST INTERCHANGEABLE AND THE HOUSE
MOVES IN AN UNINTERRUPTED SERIES OF
SPACES BETWEEN ITS PUBLIC AND PRIVATE
AREAS.

AUSSEN- UND INNENFLÄCHEN WIRKEN FAST
AUSTAUSCHBAR – DAS HAUS IST IN UNUNTER-
BROCHENER BEWEGUNG ZWISCHEN DEN RÄU-
MEN ÖFFENTLICHER UND PRIVATER NATUR.

LES SURFACES INTÉRIEURES ET EXTÉRIEURES
SEMBLENT PRESQUE INTERCHANGEABLES, ET
LA MAISON CRÉE D'ELLE-MÊME UNE CIRCULA-
TION ININTERROMPUE DE L'ESPACE ENTRE LES
PARTIES DE RÉCEPTION ET PRIVÉES.

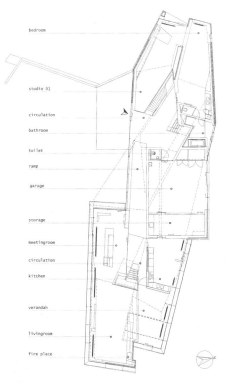

bedroom
studio 01
circulation
bathroom
toilet
ramp
garage
storage
meetingroom
circulation
kitchen
verandah
livingroom
fire place

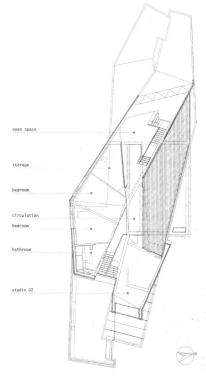

open space
storage
bedroom
circulation
bedroom
bathroom
studio 02

DIE MASSIVITÄT DES BETONS WECHSELT AB MIT OFFENEN, VERGLASTEN VOLUMEN – EINE GEWICHTIGE ARCHITEKTUR, DIE DENNOCH LEICHT ERSCHEINT.

LA MASSIVITÉ DU BÉTON ALTERNE AVEC DES VOLUMES DE VERRE: ARCHITECTURE DE POIDS ET LÉGÈRETÉ APPARENTE.

P 098.099

THE SOLIDITY OF CONCRETE ALTERNATES WITH OPEN GLASS VOLUMES, SHIFTING FROM A WEIGHTY ARCHITECTURE TO ONE OF APPARENT LIGHTNESS.

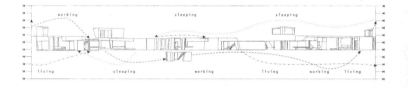

BOLLES + WILSON

Peter Wilson was born in Melbourne in 1950. He studied at the University of Melbourne (1968-70), and at the Architectural Association (AA) in London (1972-74). Julia Bolles Wilson was born in 1948 in Münster, and studied at the University of Karlsruhe (1968-76) and at the AA (1978-79) while Wilson was Unit Master (1978-88). They formed the Wilson Partnership in London in 1980,

Peter Wilson, geboren 1950 in Melbourne, studierte an der University of Melbourne und an der Architectural Association (AA) in London (1972-74). Julia Bolles Wilson wurde 1948 in Münster geboren und studierte an der Universität Karlsruhe (1968-76) sowie an der AA (1978-79), als Peter Wilson dort Unit Master war (1978-88). 1980 gründeten sie in London die Wilson Partnership

Peter Wilson naît à Melbourne en 1950. Il étudie à l'Université de Melbourne (1968-70) et à l'Architectural Association (AA) de Londres (1972-74). Julia Bolles Wilson, née en 1948 à Münster, fait ses études à l'Université de Karlsruhe (1968-76), et à l'AA (1978-79), lorsque Wilson y exerce comme Unit master (1978-88). Ils créent le Wilson Partnership à Londres en 1980, et l'Architekturbüro

ARCHITECTURAL PRACTICES THAT MIX THE BEST OF THE ANGLO-SAXON WORLD WITH A GERMAN SIDE ARE RARE. EDUCATED AT THE AA IN LONDON, LIKE BEN VAN BERKEL, BOLLES + WILSON ARE CLOSELY INVOLVED WITH ROTTERDAM'S KOP VAN ZUID AREA.

ARCHITEKTURBÜROS, DIE BESTE TRADITIONEN DER ANGELSÄCHSISCHEN WELT MIT DEUTSCHEN EINFLÜSSEN VERBINDEN, SIND SELTEN. DIE AN

DER AA IN LONDON AUSGEBILDETEN BOLLES + WILSON SIND INTENSIV AM AUSBAU DES ROTTERDAMER BEZIRKS KOP VAN ZUID BETEILIGT.

LES AGENCES D'ARCHITECTURE QUI ASSOCIENT LE MEILLEUR DE L'UNIVERS ANGLO-SAXON À UNE CULTURE ALLEMANDE SONT RARES. BOLLES + WILSON SONT PARTICULIÈREMENT IMPLIQUÉS DANS LE PROJET DE KOP VAN ZUID À ROTTERDAM.

ARCHITEKTURBÜRO BOLLES + WILSON
ALTER STEINWEG 17
48143 MÜNSTER
GERMANY

TEL: + 49 251 48272-0
FAX: + 49 251 48272-24
E-MAIL: info@bolles-wilson.com

and Architekturbüro Bolles + Wilson in 1987. The office moved to Münster, Germany, in 1988. Their projects include a "Garden folly" at International Garden and Greenery Exposition in Osaka. Peter Wilson built the Suzuki House (Tokyo, 1993). Other recent projects include the WLV Office Building in Münster, and the Kop van Zuid in Rotterdam.

und 1987 das Architekturbüro Bolles + Wilson, das sie 1988 nach Münster verlegten. Zu ihren Projekten gehören ein »Garden Folly« auf der International Garden and Greenery Exposition in Osaka und das von Peter Wilson geplante Suzuki House (Tokio, 1993) sowie das Bürogebäude der WLV in Münster und die Kaianlagen Kop van Zuid in Rotterdam.

Bolles + Wilson en 1987, qui s'installe à Münster, en Allemagne, en 1988. Parmi leurs réalisations: une «folie de jardin» pour l'International Garden and Greenery Exposition à Osaka et la Suzuki House (Tokyo, 1993), ainsi que, plus récemment, l'immeuble de bureaux W. L. V. à Münster et le Kop van Zuid à Rotterdam.

BOLLES + WILSON
QUAY BUILDINGS
KOP VAN ZUID, ROTTERDAM, THE NETHERLANDS, 1991-96

CLIENT / BAUHERR: CITY OF ROTTERDAM /
ROTTERDAM HARBOUR COMPANY
FLOOR AREA / NUTZFLÄCHE / SURFACE UTILE:
4 000 M² (QUAY), 200 M² (BRIDGEWATCHER'S
HOUSE)
COSTS / KOSTEN / COÛTS: 6 000 000 NLG (QUAY),
1 200 000 NLG (QUAY BUILDINGS)

Located near the Erasmus Bridge designed by Ben van Berkel, the quay buildings designed by Bolles + Wilson signal the amplitude of the future development of the Kop van Zuid area, the former docks of Rotterdam. The main building is the Bridgewatcher's House, which controls the movable section of the Erasmus Bridge as well as other lifting bridges on the Maas. The three facades of this structure are each clad in a different material – glazed brick on the street side, flat metal sheet facing the harbor, and baked enamel panels on the Quay. An elevated promenade leads to this tower along the waterside, while surface finishing such as the rough granite paving below was also designed by the architects. "Electronic Rocks" lit from below, and a "Tower of Electronic Numbers" complete this ensemble, which assumes its own artistic form.

Die Gestaltung der Kaianlagen von Bolles + Wilson, die nahe Ben van Berkels Erasmus-Brücke liegen, ist charakteristisch für den Maßstab der künftigen Entwicklung des Gebiets Kop van Zuid, der früheren Docks von Rotterdam. Größtes Bauwerk ist das Gebäude der Brückenwacht, die den beweglichen Teil der Erasmus-Brücke sowie der anderen Hebebrücken der Maas kontrolliert. Die drei Fassaden des Baus sind in unterschiedlichen Materialien verkleidet – glasierter Backstein an der Straßenseite, Flachblech an der zum Hafen gerichteten Seite und gebrannte Emailplatten am Kai. Eine höher gelegene Promenade, deren Belag mit rauhem Granit ebenfalls von den Architekten gestaltet wurde, führt zu diesem Hochhaus am Ufer. Von unten beleuchtete »elektronische Felsen« und ein »Turm der elektronischen Zahlen« geben dem Ensemble sein künstlerisches Gepräge.

Non loin du pont Erasme de Ben van Berkel, ces «bâtiments du quai» conçus par Bolles + Wilson fonctionnent comme un signal qui annonce le développement de la zone de Kop van Zuid, d'anciens docks de Rotterdam. Le bâtiment principal est la Maison de surveillance du pont qui contrôle la partie mobile du pont Erasme ainsi que d'autres ponts levants sur la Meuse. Ses trois façades sont revêtues chacune d'un matériau différent – brique vernissée côté rue, tôle métallique blanche face au port, et panneaux émaillés noir sur le quai. Une promenade surélevée conduit à cette tour en bordure de rive. Les surfaces, y compris le pavement de granit, ont également été conçues par les architectes. Des «rochers électroniques», éclairés par en dessous, et une «Tour des nombres électroniques» complètent cet ensemble qui assume parfaitement son aspect artistique.

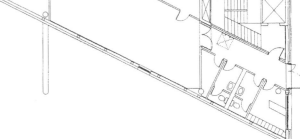

WITH ITS SIMPLE TRIANGULAR DESIGN, THE
BRIDGEWATCHER'S HOUSE MANAGES TO LOOK
RADICALLY DIFFERENT ON EACH SIDE.

IN SEINER SCHLICHTEN, DREIECKIGEN FORM
SIEHT DAS GEBÄUDE DER BRÜCKENWACHT
VON JEDER SEITE VÖLLIG ANDERS AUS.

AU MOYEN D'UN SIMPLE PLAN TRIANGULAIRE,
LE CENTRE DE SURVEILLANCE DES PONTS
RÉUSSIT À PARAÎTRE RADICALEMENT DIFFÉ-
RENT SUR TOUTES SES FAÇADES.

BOLLES + WILSON
NEW LUXOR THEATER
ROTTERDAM, THE NETHERLANDS, 1998-2000

Although office buildings are now under construction in the still rather desolate area of the Kop van Zuid, aside from the nearby Hotel New York there was no center of night-time activity. The 1,500 seat New Luxor Theater will truly announce the creation of a new area of the city. A "giant red zebra crossing" in front of the theater will announce the presence of the tomato-red spiral wrapping facades of the structure itself. One unusual feature of the site

Obwohl in dem immer noch ziemlich trostlosen Rotterdamer Gebiet Kop van Zuid neue Bürogebäude im Bau sind, gab es dort bisher (abgesehen vom nahegelegenen Hotel New York) keinerlei Nachtleben. Das 1500 Plätze fassende New Luxor Theater kündigt die Entstehung eines neuen Stadtteils an. Ein »riesiger roter Zebrastreifen« vor dem Theater wirkt wie ein Echo der tomatenroten, spiralförmig umlaufenden Fassade des Baus. Zu den

Bien que de nombreux immeubles de bureaux soient en construction dans le quartier encore vide de Kop van Zuid, aucun centre de vie nocturne n'avait été prévu en dehors d'un hôtel. Le New Luxor de 1500 places concrétise la naissance de ce nouveau quartier urbain. «Un passage protégé rouge géant» devant le théâtre fait écho à la spirale rouge tomate qui enveloppe la structure elle-même. Une des contraintes du site et du bâtiment était de prévoir

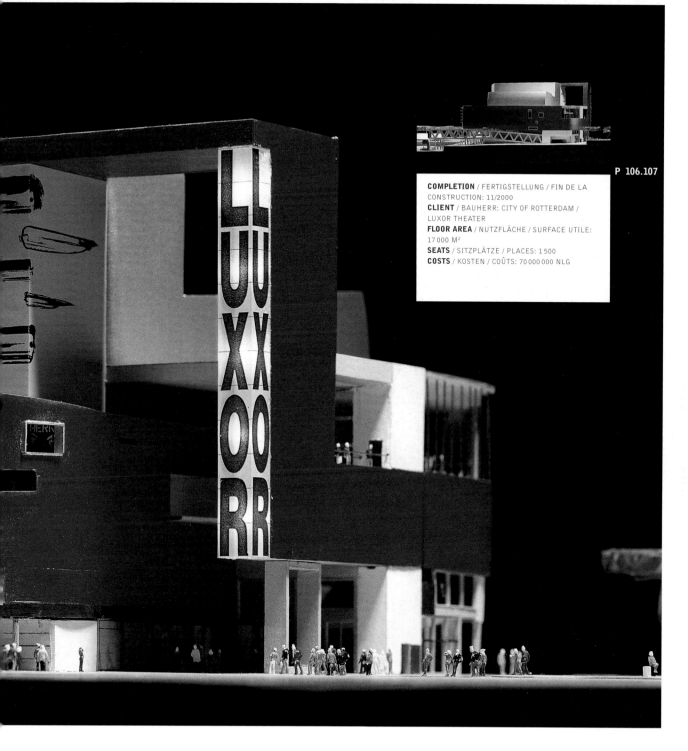

COMPLETION / FERTIGSTELLUNG / FIN DE LA CONSTRUCTION: 11/2000
CLIENT / BAUHERR: CITY OF ROTTERDAM / LUXOR THEATER
FLOOR AREA / NUTZFLÄCHE / SURFACE UTILE: 17 000 M²
SEATS / SITZPLÄTZE / PLACES: 1 500
COSTS / KOSTEN / COÛTS: 70 000 000 NLG

and the building was that 18 m trucks had to be able to gain access to the upper-level stage. Taking into account the optimal turning radius of these large vehicles, the architects decided to use the roof of the truck ramp as a promenade through the building. The site of the theater is quite close to the Erasmus Bridge and the architects' own Quay Buildings.

ungewöhnlichen Bedingungen von Bauplatz und Gebäude gehörte, daß 18 m lange Lastwagen die Bühnenebene im Obergeschoß anfahren können mußten. Unter Berücksichtigung des Wendekreises dieser Fahrzeuge beschlossen die Architekten, das Dach der Anlieferungsrampe als Durchgang durch das Gebäude zu nutzen. Das Theater liegt nahe der Erasmus-Brücke und den ebenfalls von Bolles + Wilson gestalteten Kaianlagen.

l'accès à des camions de 18 m de long au niveau supérieur de la scène. À partir du rayon de braquage de ces grands véhicules, les architectes ont décidé de faire du toit de la rampe des camions une sorte de promenade autour du bâtiment. Le site est assez proche du pont Erasme et des Quay Buildings.

MARIO BOTTA

Born in Mendrisio, Switzerland (1943), Mario Botta left school at 15 to become apprentice in a Lugano architectural office. He designed his first house the following year. After studies in Milan and Venice, he worked briefly in the entourage of Le Corbusier, Louis Kahn and Luigi Snozzi. He built private houses in Ticino (in Cadenazzo, 1970-71, Riva San Vitale, 1971-73, and Ligornetto, 1975-76). Major buildings include Médiathèque (Villeur-

Mario Botta, geboren 1943 in Mendrisio, Schweiz, verließ 15jährig die Schule und begann eine Lehre in einem Architekturbüro in Lugano. Dort entwarf er 1959 sein erstes Wohnhaus. Nach Studien in Mailand und Venedig arbeitete er zeitweilig bei Le Corbusier, Louis Kahn und Luigi Snozzi. Danach baute er Einfamilienhäuser im Tessin (in Cade-nazzo, 1970-71, Riva San Vitale, 1971-73 und Ligornetto, 1975-76). Zu Bottas Großprojekten

Né à Mendrisio, Suisse, en 1943, Mario Botta quit-te l'école à 15 ans pour devenir apprenti dans une agence d'architecture de Lugano. Il dessine sa pre-mière maison l'année suivante. Après avoir étudié à Milan et à Venise, et brièvement travaillé dans l'entourage de Le Corbusier, Louis Kahn et Luigi Snozzi, il construit des villas dans le Tessin: à Cadenazzo (1970-71), Riva San Vitale (1971-73), ou Ligornetto (1975-76). Parmi ses principales

"THE HISTORY OF ARCHITECTURE, WHICH I KNOW, IS THAT OF CHURCHES FROM THE ROMANESQUE TO RONCHAMP. WHEN YOU THINK ABOUT IT, YOU REALIZE THAT MEDITERRANEAN CULTURE IS VERY MUCH ONE OF CHURCHES." MARIO BOTTA

»DIE ARCHITEKTURGESCHICHTE, WIE ICH SIE KENNE, IST DIE DER KIRCHEN VON DER ROMANIK BIS RONCHAMP. BEIM NACHDENKEN DAR-

ÜBER ERKENNT MAN, DASS DIE MEDITERRANE KULTUR VORWIEGEND EINE DER KIRCHEN IST.« MARIO BOTTA

« L'HISTOIRE DE L'ARCHITECTURE, QUE JE CONNAIS, EST CELLE DES ÉGLISES, DU ROMAN À RONCHAMP. LORSQUE VOUS Y RÉFLÉCHISSEZ, VOUS RÉALISEZ QUE LA CULTURE MÉDITERRANÉENNE EST ESSENTIELLEMENT MARQUÉE PAR DES LIEUX DE CULTE.» MARIO BOTTA

STUDIO MARIO BOTTA
VIA CIANI 16
6904 LUGANO
SWITZERLAND

TEL: + 41 91 972 8625
FAX: + 41 91 970 1454
E-MAIL: botta@tinet.ch

banne, 1984-88), Cultural Center (Chambéry, 1982-87), Evry Cathedral (1988-95), all in France, San Francisco Museum of Modern Art (1992-95), Chapel (Monte Tamaro, Switzerland, 1992-96), Museum Jean Tinguely (Basel, 1993-96), Church of Saint John the Baptist (Mogno, Switzerland, 1986-98), and a design for the renovation of the Presbytery of the Cathedral of Santa Maria del Fiore (Florence, 1997).

gehören die Médiathèque in Villeurbanne (1984-88), das Kulturzentrum in Chambéry (1982-87) und die Kathedrale in Evry, (1988-95), alle in Frankreich; das San Francisco Museum of Modern Art (1992-95), eine Kapelle (Monte Tamaro, Schweiz, 1992-96), das Museum Jean Tinguely in Basel (1993-96) und ein Entwurf für die Sanierung des Presbyteriums des Florentiner Doms Santa Maria del Fiore (1997).

réalisations: la médiathèque de Villeurbanne (1984-88), le Centre culturel André Malraux (Chambéry, 1982-87), la cathédrale d'Evry (1988-95), le San Francisco Museum of Modern Art (1992-95), une chapelle (Monte Tamaro, Suisse, 1992-96), le Musée Jean Tinguely (Bâle, 1993-96), l'église de Mogno (Suisse, 1986-98) et un projet pour la rénovation du presbytère de la cathédrale de Santa Maria del Fiore à Florence (1997).

MARIO BOTTA

CHURCH OF SAINT JOHN THE BAPTIST

MOGNO, TICINO, SWITZERLAND, 1986/92-98

PLANNING / PLANUNG: 1986/90-92
CONSTRUCTION / BAU: 1992-96/98
CLIENT / BAUHERR: SOCIETY FOR THE
RESTORATION OF MOGNO CHURCH
FLOOR AREA / NUTZFLÄCHE / SURFACE UTILE:
123 M²
COSTS / KOSTEN / COÛTS: 1 500 000 SFR

OVAL IN PLAN, THE CHURCH HAS A CIRCULAR
OCULUS THAT BRINGS AMPLE DAYLIGHT INTO
ITS SMALL INTERIOR.

DIE KIRCHE AUF OVALEM GRUNDRISS HAT
EINEN KREISFÖRMIGEN OKULUS, DURCH DEN
AUSREICHEND TAGESLICHT IN DEN KLEINEN
INNENRAUM FÄLLT.

DE PLAN OVALE, L'ÉGLISE POSSÈDE UN OCU-
LUS CIRCULAIRE QUI FOURNIT UN AMPLE
ÉCLAIRAGE NATUREL À SA NEF DE DIMEN-
SIONS RELATIVEMENT RÉDUITES.

Following a catastrophic double avalanche that swept away most of the village of Mogno in the remote Maggia valley near Locarno, Switzerland, in April 1986, the mayor of the town, Giovan Luigi Dazio, called on Mario Botta to design a replacement for the 17th-century church that had stood there. Botta's response for the 178 m² site was an unusual oval plan that resembles a truncated cylinder in elevation. The design drew substantial criticism, which delayed the construction and coincidentally led to Botta receiving another commission for a chapel on the Monte Tamaro, near Bellinzona. Clad in white Peccia marble and Riveo gray granite, both of which are locally mined, the completed chapel in Mogno is a defiant symbol of architectural solidity, affirmed in opposition to the power of nature. The alternating bands of white and gray together with the density of the stone evoke Romanesque architecture, of which Botta is admittedly quite fond, while the strict use of a modern geometric vocabulary makes it clear that this is no pastiche.

Nach einem Lawinenunglück, das im April 1986 den Großteil des Dorfs Mogno im Maggia-Tal bei Locarno zerstört hatte, erteilte der Bürgermeister Giovan Luigi Dazio Mario Botta den Auftrag, einen Ersatz für die Kirche aus dem 17. Jahrhundert zu planen. Bottas Antwort auf das 178 m² große Baugrundstück war ein ungewöhnlicher ovaler Grundriß. Über diesem erhebt sich abgeschrägter Zylinder. Der Entwurf stieß auf harsche Kritik, die eine Verzögerung der Realisierung zur Folge hatte – und Botta den Auftrag für eine Kapelle auf dem Monte Tamaro bei Bellinzona eintrug. Die mit örtlichem weißen Peccia-Marmor und grauem Riveo-Granit verkleidete Kirche Johannes der Täufer ist ein trutziges Symbol architektonischer Standhaftigkeit gegenüber den Kräften der Natur. Der Wechsel von weißen und grauen Bändern und die Dichte des Werksteins erinnern an die romanische Architektur, die Botta bewundert. Die strikte Verwendung einer modernen Formensprache macht indes deutlich, daß es sich nicht um ein Pasticcio handelt.

À la suite de la catastrophique double-avalanche qui a rayé de la carte la plus grande partie du village de Mogno dans la lointaine vallée de Maggia près de Locarno, en Suisse, en avril 1986, le maire de la ville, Giovan Luigi Dazio, fit appel à Mario Botta pour remplacer l'église du XVIIe siècle. La réponse de l'architecte pour le terrain de 178 m² prit la forme d'un curieux plan ovale qui fait penser à un cylindre tronqué en élévation. De vives critiques ont retardé la construction, mais ont suscité une nouvelle commande passée à Botta pour une chapelle près du Monte Tamaro, près de Bellinzona. Recouverte de marbre blanc de Peccia et de granit gris de Riveo, deux pierres locales, l'église Saint-Jean-Baptiste à Mogno symbolise la résistance du construit face à la puissance de la nature. Les bandes alternées de gris et de blanc et la densité de la pierre évoquent l'architecture romane que Botta admire particulièrement, mais le vocabulaire géométrique moderne éloigne toute idée de pastiche.

WITH ITS REFERENCES TO THE FLYING BUT-
TRESSES OF GOTHIC ARCHITECTURE OR ITS
HEAVY BANDS OF GRANITE AND MARBLE, THE
CHURCH HEARKENS BACK TO THE PAST.

THE ARCHITECT DESIGNED THE ALTAR AND
OTHER CHURCH FURNITURE. LOCALLY QUAR-
RIED STONE WAS USED FOR THE BUILDING.

IHR BEZUG AUF DEN GOTISCHEN STREBE-
BOGEN UND DIE SCHWEREN BÄNDER AUS
GRANIT UND MARMOR VERBINDET DIE KIRCHE
MIT DER VERGANGENHEIT.

DER ARCHITEKT SELBST GESTALTETE DEN
ALTAR UND ANDERE AUSSTATTUNGSSTÜCKE.
FÜR DEN BAU WURDE VOR ORT GEBROCHENER
NATURSTEIN VERWENDET.

DANS SES RÉFÉRENCES AUX CONTREFORTS
DE L'ARCHITECTURE GOTHIQUE, OU À SES
BANDEAUX ALTERNÉS DE GRANIT ET DE
MARBRE, L'ÉGLISE PREND RACINE DANS LE
PASSÉ.

L'ARCHITECTE A DESSINÉ L'AUTEL ET
D'AUTRES ÉLÉMENTS DE MOBILIER. LA PIERRE
DE CONSTRUCTION EST D'ORIGINE LOCALE.

BRANSON COATES

Doug Branson (left), born in 1951, and Nigel Coates (right), born in 1949, formed Branson Coates in 1983. Both were educated at the Architectural Association (AA) in London. Coates taught at the AA for many years, first as an assistant to Bernard Tschumi and then as Unit Master of Unit 10 (1977-89). The work of Branson Coates includes Bohemia Jazz Club (1986), Caffé Bongo

Doug Branson (links), geboren 1951, und Nigel Coates (rechts), geboren 1949, die 1983 das Büro Branson Coates gründeten, studierten beide an der Architectural Association (AA) in London. Coates hat viele Jahre an der AA gelehrt, zunächst als Assistent von Bernard Tschumi und danach als Unit Master der Unit 10 (1977-89). Zu ihren ausgeführten Bauten gehören der Bohemia Jazz Club (1986),

Doug Branson (à gauche), né en 1951, et Nigel Coates (à droite), né en 1949, créent Branson Coates en 1983, après avoir fait, tous deux, leurs études à l'Architectural Association (AA) de Londres. Coates enseigne à l'AA pendant de nombreuses années, d'abord comme assistant de Bernard Tschumi, puis comme Unit Master de l'Unit 10 (1977-89). Parmi leurs travaux: le Bohemia Jazz

EDUCATED AT THE AA IN LONDON, BRANSON AND COATES BECAME KNOWN IN THE 1980'S FOR THEIR ESTHETICALLY SURPRISING TOKYO RESTAURANTS AND CLUBS. TODAY THEY ARE EMBLEMATIC OF THE ARCHITECTURE OF "COOL BRITANNIA."

BRANSON UND COATES, AN DER AA IN LONDON AUSGEBILDET, WURDEN IN DEN 80ER JAHREN MIT IHREN ÄSTHETISCH ÜBERRASCHENDEN

RESTAURANTS UND KLUBS IN TOKIO BEKANNT. HEUTE STEHEN SIE FÜR DIE ARCHITEKTUR DES »COOL BRITANNIA«.

FORMÉS À L'A.A. DE LONDRES, BRANSON ET COATES SE SONT FAIT CONNAÎTRE DANS LES ANNÉES 1980 PAR D'ÉTONNANTS RESTAURANTS ET CLUBS CONSTRUITS À TOKYO. ILS REPRÉSENTENT AUJOURD'HUI L'ARCHITECTURE DE LA «COOL BRITANNIA».

BRANSON COATES ARCHITECTURE
23 OLD STREET
LONDON EC1V 9RR
ENGLAND

TEL: + 44 20 7 490 0343
FAX: + 44 20 7 490 0320
E-MAIL: ecstacity@dial.pipex.com

(1986), the Nishi Azubu Wall (1990), all in Tokyo, and the Nautilus Bar and Seafood Restaurant at Schiphol Airport, Netherlands (1993). One of their most recent buildings is the National Centre for Popular Music in Sheffield (1996-98), whose quatrefoil form inspired that of the Powerhouse::UK structure published here.

das Caffé Bongo (1986) und Nishi Azubu Wall (1990), alle in Tokio, außerdem die Nautilus-Bar und das Fischrestaurant auf dem Flughafen Schiphol bei Amsterdam (1993). Eines ihrer jüngsten Projekte ist das National Centre for Popular Music in Sheffield (1996-98), von dessen Kleeblattform auch das hier vorgestellte Powerhouse::UK inspiriert ist.

Club (1996), le Caffé Bongo (1986) et le Nishi Azubu Wall (1990), tous à Tokyo, et le Nautilus Bar et Seafood Restaurant de l'aéroport de Schiphol, Pays-Bas (1993). L'une de leurs plus récentes réalisations est le National Centre for Popular Music à Sheffield (1996-98), dont la forme en trèfle à inspiré celle de la Powerhouse::UK publiée ici.

BRANSON COATES

BRANSON COATES
POWERHOUSE::UK
LONDON, ENGLAND, 1997-98

START OF PLANNING / PLANUNGSBEGINN /
COMMENCEMENT DU PLANNING: 8/97
CONSTRUCTION / BAU: 3/98-4/98
CLIENT / BAUHERR: DEPARTMENT OF TRADE
AND INDUSTRY
FLOOR AREA / NUTZFLÄCHE / SURFACE UTILE:
1 225 M²

THE QUATREFOIL STRUCTURE OF POWER-
HOUSE::UK IS DIRECTLY RELATED IN ITS DESIGN
TO BRANSON COATES' NATIONAL CENTRE FOR
POPULAR MUSIC IN SHEFFIELD.

DER KLEEBLATTFÖRMIGE GRUNDRISS DES
POWERHOUSE::UK GEHT AUF BRANSON COATES'
NATIONAL CENTRE FOR POPULAR MUSIC IN
SHEFFIELD ZURÜCK.

LA STRUCTURE EN TRÈFLE DE POWER-
HOUSE::UK EST DIRECTEMENT INSPIRÉE
DANS SA CONCEPTION DU NATIONAL CENTRE
FOR POPULAR MUSIC ÉDIFIÉ PAR BRANSON
COATES À SHEFFIELD.

Erected temporarily in Horse Guards Parade in the spring of 1998 in order to highlight "the dynamic atmosphere of Britain's creative industries," Powerhouse::UK consisted of four 15 m pods, each containing a focus on different areas of creativity: "Lifestyle," "Communicating," "Networking," and "Learning." Access to each of these pods was from a central reception area. The design of the complex is based on Branson Coates' own National Centre for Popular Music in Sheffield, whose four stainless steel-clad drums "rotate in response to changes in wind direction." Colored silver, the inflatable pods contained a sampling of all the best of what Tony Blair called "Cool Britannia," from popular music to motorcycle design. Despite its direct relation in form to the Sheffield structure, the intention of Powerhouse::UK was to demonstrate that temporary architecture can be far more interesting and effective than the type of "off-the-shelf" structures that are more frequently used in such circumstances.

Powerhouse::UK wurde im Frühjahr 1998 vorübergehend auf Horse Guards Parade errichtet, dem Platz in London, auf dem die Queen ihre jährliche Geburtstagsparade abnimmt. Es sollte »die dynamische Atmosphäre von Englands kreativer Industrie« vorstellen und bestand aus vier 15 m langen »Kokons«, die je ein Thema zum Gegenstand hatten: »Lifestyle«, »Kommunikation«, »Vernetzung« und »Wissen«. Der Entwurf basiert auf Branson Coates' National Centre for Popular Music in Sheffield, dessen vier mit Edelstahl verkleidete Trommeln »rotieren, wenn der Wind sich dreht«. Die silberfarbenen, aufblasbaren Kokons zeigten das Beste von dem, was Tony Blair als »Cool Britannia« bezeichnet hat – von Volksmusik bis Motorraddesign. Auch wenn Powerhouse::UK sich auf den Bau in Sheffield bezieht, sollte es zeigen, daß zeitgenössische Architektur viel interessanter sein kann als die Fertigbauten, die meist für solche Zwecke verwendet werden.

Construction éphémère édifiée à l'occasion de la Horse Guards Parade du printemps 1998 pour mettre en valeur «le dynamisme des industries de la création en Grande-Bretagne», Powerhouse::UK se composait de quatre éléments de 15 m de diamètre contenant chacun l'illustration d'un thème sur les différents domaines de la créativité «Style de vie», «Communiquer», «Etre en réseau» et «Apprendre». La conception s'inspirait de celle du National Centre for Popular Music construit à Sheffield par Branson Coates, dont les quatre «tambours» revêtus d'acier inoxydable «pivotent pour répondre aux changements de direction des vents». De couleur argent, ces éléments gonflables contenaient un échantillonnage du meilleur de la production de ce que Tony Blair avait appelé «Cool Britannia», de la musique populaire aux motos. L'intérêt de Powerhouse::UK était de monter qu'une architecture éphémère pouvait être beaucoup plus intéressante et efficace que les structures industrielles habituellement utilisées dans ces circonstances.

WILL BRUDER

Born in Milwaukee, Wisconsin, in 1946, Will Bruder has a B.F.A. degree in sculpture from the University of Wisconsin-Milwaukee, and is self-trained as an architect. He apprenticed under Paolo Soleri and Gunnar Birkerts. He obtained his architecture license in 1974, and created his own studio the same year. He was a fellow at the American Academy in Rome for six months in 1987. He has taught and lectured at MIT, ASU and the "cable works"

Will Bruder, geboren 1946 in Milwaukee, Wisconsin, erwarb den B.F.A. in Bildhauerei, als Architekt ist er Autodidakt. Er ging bei Paolo Soleri und Gunnar Birkerts in die Lehre, bevor er 1974 die Zulassung als Architekt erhielt und sein eigenes Büro gründete. 1987 war er ein halbes Jahr an der American Academy in Rom tätig. Gelehrt hat Bruder unter anderem am Massachusetts Institute of Technology. Sein bedeutendster Bau ist die Phoenix

Né à Milwaukee, Wisconsin, en 1946, Will Bruder est diplômé en sculpture de l'Université de Wisconsin-Milwaukee et architecte autodidacte. Il fait son apprentissage auprès de Paolo Soleri et de Gunnar Birkerts. Licencié en architecture en 1974, il crée son propre studio la même année, puis reste à l'American Academy de Rome pendant six mois en 1987. Il enseigne et donne des conférences entres autres au Massachusetts Institute of Technology.

ALS AUTODIDAKT IST WILL BRUDER EINER DER
ORIGINELLSTEN AMERIKANISCHEN ARCHITEK-
TEN. AUS DEM SÜDWESTEN DES KONTINENTS
STAMMEND, WEISS ER EBENSO DIE LOKALEN
TRADITIONEN ZU NUTZEN WIE NEUE WEGE ZU
GEHEN.

ARCHITECTE AUTODIDACTE, WILL BRUDER
EST L'UN CRÉATEURS AMÉRICAINS LES PLUS
ORIGINAUX. IL RÉUSSIT À SE SERVIR DE SES
ORIGINES DU SUD-OUEST ET DES TRADITIONS
LOCALES, MÊME LORSQU'IL OUVRE DE NOU-
VELLES PERSPECTIVES ESTHÉTIQUES ET
TECHNIQUES.

william p. bruder-architect, ltd
1314 WEST CIRCLE MOUNTAIN ROAD
NEW RIVER, ARIZONA 85027
UNITED STATES

TEL: + 1 602 465 7399
FAX: + 1 602 465 0109
E-MAIL: bruder@netwest.com

in Helsinki. His most important built work is
the Phoenix Central Library in Phoenix, Arizona
(1989-95). Recent projects include Teton County
Library and Riddell Advertising, Jackson, Wyoming, Temple Kol Ami, Scottsdale, Arizona, Deer
Vallery Rock Art Center, Phoenix, Arizona, and
residences in Boston, Colorado, Arizona, Canada
and Australia, as well as a restaurant in
Manhattan.

Central Library in Phoenix, Arizona (1989-95).
Zu Bruders neueren Projekten gehören die Teton
County Library und Riddell Advertising in Jackson,
Wyoming, die Kol Ami-Synagoge in Scottsdale,
Arizona, das Deer Vallery Rock Art Center in
Phoenix, Arizona, ein Restaurant in Manhattan
sowie Wohnhäuser in Boston, Colorado, Arizona,
Kanada und Australien.

Ses œuvres les plus importantes sont la Phoenix
Central Library à Phoenix, Arizona (1989-95), la
Teton County Library et l'agence Riddell Advertising à Jackson, Wyoming, la synagogue Kol Ami
à Scottsdale, Arizona, le Valley Rock Art Center à
Phoenix, Arizona, et des résidences à Boston, dans
le Colorado, l'Arizona, au Canada et en Australie,
ainsi qu'un restaurant à Manhattan.

WILL BRUDER

TEMPLE KOL AMI

SCOTTSDALE, ARIZONA, UNITED STATES, 1992-94

CLIENT / BAUHERR: JEWISH CONGREGATION
TEMPLE KOL AMI
FLOOR AREA / NUTZFLÄCHE / SURFACE UTILE:
13 750 SQ FT
COSTS / KOSTEN / COÛTS: US$ 1 100 000

**BRUDER HAS MADE HIS LIMITED BUDGET INTO
AN ADVANTAGE BY CALLING ON AN AUSTERITY
THAT SUITS BOTH THE SITE AND THE FUNC-
TION OF THIS BUILDING.**

BRUDER HAT DAS BESCHEIDENE BUDGET ZUM
VORTEIL GEWENDET, INDEM ER SICH FÜR EINE
NÜCHTERNHEIT ENTSCHIED, DIE DEM STAND-
ORT UND DER FUNKTION DES GEBÄUDES
ENTSPRICHT.

BRUDER A FAIT DES CONTRAINTES BUDGÉTAI-
RES UN AVANTAGE EN CHOISISSANT UNE
APPROCHE AUSTÈRE QUI CONVIENT AUSSI
BIEN AU SITE QU'À LA FONCTION DU TEMPLE.

According to the architect, the original concept for this "worship and learning center" was to "create a metaphorical village in the spirit of the ancient desert communities of Masada and Jerusalem." Built with standard sandblasted concrete blocks, the building reflects the modest construction budget, yet the architect has enriched the design through such devices as the gently curving east wall, which leans up to 7° off the vertical toward the interior. The sand aggregate modules are left exposed, with no covering, both inside and out. It is through the play of light on these surfaces, filtered in through the ceilings, that Will Bruder succeeds in introducing power and life into rooms that otherwise would be qualified as Spartan. He also relies on the presence of children to bring color and movement to the spaces.

Nach dem Architekten bestand das ursprüngliche Konzept dieses »Zentrums für Gebet und Gelehr-samkeit« darin, »die Metapher eines Dorfs im Geist der alten Wüstengemeinden von Masada und Jerusalem zu schaffen.« Die aus genormten, sandgestrahlten Betonsteinen errichtete Kol Ami-Synagoge verrät ihr bescheidenes Budget. Der Architekt hat den Bau jedoch durch besondere Gestaltungsmittel bereichert. So ist die Ostwand sanft gekrümmt und neigt sich im Winkel von 7° nach innen. Mit dem Spiel des von den Decken re-flektierten Lichts auf den unverputzten Wänden ist es Bruder gelungen, das andernfalls als spartanisch zu bezeichnende Innere mit Kraft und Leben zu erfüllen. Auch geht er davon aus, daß Kinder den Räumen Farbe und Lebendigkeit geben werden.

Selon l'architecte, le concept original de ce « lieu de prière et d'enseignement » était de « créer un village métaphorique dans l'esprit des anciennes commu-nautés du désert de Masada et de Jérusalem. » Edifié en parpaings de ciment sablé, le bâtiment exprime la modestie du budget de construction, mais l'architecte a su l'enrichir par des interven-tions comme le mur est délicatement incurvé qui penche de 7° vers l'intérieur. Les modules en agré-gat de sable sont laissés bruts, sans parement, aussi bien à l'extérieur qu'à l'intérieur. C'est par le jeu de la lumière sur les surfaces, filtrée par les pla-fonds, que Bruder réussit à introduire la vie et la présence dans ces pièces qui auraient pu autrement être jugées spartiates. Il compte également sur la présence des enfants pour introduire la couleur et le mouvement dans ces espaces.

CLIENT / BAUHERR: BRECK AND CARLA O'NEILL
FLOOR AREA / NUTZFLÄCHE / SURFACE UTILE:
7 800 SQ FT
COSTS / KOSTEN / COÛTS: WITHHELD / UNGE-
NANNT / NON COMMUNIQUÉS
LANDSCAPE DESIGN / LANDSCHAFTS-
GESTALTUNG / ARCHITECTE PAYSAGISTE:
VERDONE LANDSCAPE ARCHITECTURE

mad river

WILL BRUDER
MAD RIVER BOAT TRIPS
JACKSON, WYOMING, UNITED STATES, 1995-97

LOCAL RANCH BUILDINGS BUT ALSO THE MOUNTAINOUS SCENERY ARE AT THE ORIGIN OF THIS UNEXPECTED, YET MODERN FORM.

ÖRTLICHE FARMBAUTEN UND DIE GEBIRGS-LANDSCHAFT HABEN DIE UNGEWÖHNLICHE, ABER MODERNE FORM ANGEREGT.

FORMES INATTENDUES ET MODERNES IN-SPIRÉES DE L'ARCHITECTURE LOCALE DE RANCHS ET DU PAYSAGE DE MONTAGNES.

This 730 m² structure is intended as a "functionally organized warehouse for staging whitewater rafting adventures, a departure facility energized by an illuminated sculptural blue translucent fiberglass reception counter arcing through space with the energy of a wave on the river, a commercial retail space to acquire physical trappings, souvenirs and video documentation, a river runners' museum documenting the history of the region's river lore, a bunkhouse with rooms for four river guides and bus drivers, and a sophisticated living loft suspended above the shop and museum …" The building is set on an 11 x 40 m "footprint." Its east elevation rises to the maximum allowed height of 10.5 m. A wood frame structure, Mad River Boat Trips is "wrapped in a taut skin of corrugated 'black iron' or rust patina." Set on a highway (US89A), the building brings to mind many local ranch or service facilities, and is intended as a "metaphorical extension of Snow King Mountain to the East."

Der Bau mit 730 m² Geschoßfläche soll als »funktionales Lagerhaus für die Inszenierung von Wildwasserfahrten dienen: die Abfahrtszone, hervorgehoben durch eine beleuchtete, skulptural geformte Empfangstheke aus blauer, durchscheinender Glasfaser, die mit der Kraft einer Flußwelle in den Raum schwingt, ein Verkaufsbereich, um verschiedene Kleinigkeiten, Souvenirs und Videos zu erstehen, ein Fluß-Museum, das die regionale Geschichte und Überlieferung dokumentiert, eine Unterkunft mit Schlafräumen für vier Flußwärter und Busfahrer, sowie ein über dem Laden und dem Museum aufgehängtes Loft …« Der Bau steht auf einem 11 x 40 m großen »Fußabdruck« und seine Ostfassade erhebt sich bis zur zulässigen Höhe von 10,5 m. Die Holzkonstruktion ist »eingehüllt in eine gespannte Haut aus gewelltem ›Schwarzblech‹ oder Rostpatina.« Das am Highway US 89A gelegene Haus erinnert an Ranch- oder Dienstleistungsbauten und ist als »symbolische Erweiterung des Snow King Mountain nach Osten« gedacht.

Cette structure de 730 m² est un «hangar fonctionnellement organisé pour la mise en scène d'expéditions en radeau, un point de départ énergisé par un comptoir de réception sculptural en fibre de verre bleu translucide qui décrit un arc dans le volume avec toute l'énergie d'une vague sur la rivière, un espace de vente qui propose des équipements, des souvenirs et des documents vidéo, un refuge avec des chambres pour quatre guides et chauffeurs de cars, et un loft sophistiqué suspendu au-dessus de la boutique et du musée …» Pour une empreinte au sol de 11 x 40 m, le bâtiment atteint à l'est les 10,5 m de haut autorisés. Faisant appel à une ossature de bois, il est «enveloppé d'une peau tendue de ‹fer noir› ondulé ou de patine rouillée». Situé en bordure d'une route nationale (US89A), il rappelle les ranchs de la région ou certains bâtiments fonctionnels, et se veut une «extension métaphorique de la Snow King Mountain, vers l'Est».

SANTIAGO CALATRAVA

Born in Valencia in 1951, Santiago Calatrava studied art and architecture at the Escuela Técnica Superior de Arquitectura in Valencia (1968-73), and engineering at the ETH in Zurich (doctorate in technical science, 1981). He opened his own architecture and civil engineering office the same year. His built work includes Gallery and Heritage Square, BCE Place (Toronto, 1987), the Bach de

Santiago Calatrava, geboren 1951 in Valencia, studierte dort Kunst und Architektur (1968-73) und Ingenieurbau an der ETH in Zürich, wo er 1981 promovierte. Im gleichen Jahr gründete er dort sein eigenes Büro für Architektur und Bauingenieurwesen. Zu Calatravas Bauten gehören Gallery und Heritage Square, BCE Place (Toronto, 1987), die Bach de Roda-Brücke (1985-87) und die Torre de

Né à Valence en Espagne en 1951, Santiago Calatrava étudie l'art et l'architecture à la Escuela Técnica Superior de Arquitectura de Valencia (1968-73), et l'ingénierie à l'ETH, à Zurich, dont il est docteur en sciences techniques, en 1981, date à laquelle il ouvre son agence d'architecture et d'ingénierie. Parmi ses réalisations: Gallery and Heritage Square, BCE Place (Toronto, 1987), le

"I WANTED TO ACCENTUATE THE TRANSPAREN-
CY OF THE STATION. IN AN URBAN ENVIRON-
MENT, WHICH WILL UNDOUBTEDLY BECOME
EVEN DENSER, THE ORIENTE STATION WILL
RESEMBLE AN OASIS. IT WILL BE A PLACE
WHERE PEOPLE WILL COME TO REST!"
SANTIAGO CALATRAVA

»ICH WOLLTE DIE TRANSPARENZ DES BAHN-
HOFS BETONEN. IN EINER STÄDTISCHEN BE-
BAUUNG, DIE SICH ZWEIFELLOS NOCH VER-
DICHTET, WIRD DER BAHNHOF EINER OASE
ÄHNELN. ER WIRD EIN ORT SEIN, ZU DEM DIE
LEUTE KOMMEN, UM RUHE ZU FINDEN.«
SANTIAGO CALATRAVA

«JE VOULAIS ACCENTUER LA TRANSPARENCE
DE LA GARE. DANS UN ENVIRONNEMENT
URBAIN QUI SE DENSIFIERA CERTAINEMENT,
LA GARE DE L'ORIENT RESSEMBLERA À UNE
OASIS. CE SERA UN LIEU OÙ L'ON VIENDRA
SE REPOSER!» SANTIAGO CALATRAVA

CALATRAVA VALLS EURL
5 RUE D'ARGOUT
75002 PARIS
FRANCE

TEL: + 33 1 53 00 92 92
FAX: + 33 1 42 33 19 81

Roda Bridge (Barcelona, 1985-87), the Torre de
Montjuic (Barcelona, 1989-92), the Kuwait Pavilion and the Alamillo Bridge at Expo '92, Seville,
and the Lyon-Satolas TGV Station (1989-94). He
recently completed the Oriente Station in Lisbon.
He was a finalist in the competition for the Reichstag in Berlin, and is building a museum of science
and a new bridge in Valencia.

Montjuic (1989-92) in Barcelona, der Kuwait-
Pavillon und die Alamillo-Brücke für die Expo '92
in Sevilla sowie der TGV-Bahnhof Lyon-Satolas
(1989-94). Calatravas Entwurf für den Reichstag
in Berlin kam in die Endauswahl. Gegenwärtig baut
er ein Wissenschaftsmuseum und eine neue Brücke
in Valencia.

pont Bach de Roda (Barcelone, 1985-87), la Torre
de Montjuic (Barcelone, 1989-92), le pavillon du
Koweit à Expo '92, Séville, et le pont Alamillo pour
la même manifestation, ainsi que la gare de TGV
de Lyon-Satolas (1989-94). Il a vient d'achever la
gare de l'Oriente à Lisbonne. Finaliste du concours
pour le Reichstag, à Berlin, il construit actuellement un musée des sciences et un pont à Valence.

SANTIAGO CALATRAVA
ORIENTE STATION
LISBON, PORTUGAL, 1993-98

COMPETITION / WETTBEWERB / CONCOURS: 1993
CLIENT / BAUHERR: G.I.L. (GARE INTERMODAL
DE LISBOA) / EXPO '98
FLOOR AREA / NUTZFLÄCHE / SURFACE UTILE:
175 000 M²
COSTS / KOSTEN / COÛTS: 37 000 000 000 ESC

OF THE STATION'S CANOPIES, CALATRAVA SAYS, "IT IS A GESTURE TOWARD THE PUBLIC, A WAY OF SAYING THAT THIS IS NOT ONLY A PLACE FOR THOSE WHO KNOW, BUT FOR EVERYONE."

ZU DEN VORDÄCHERN SAGT CALATRAVA: »SIE SIND EINE GESTE FÜR DAS PUBLIKUM UND SAGEN, DASS DIES NICHT NUR EIN ORT FÜR JENE IST, DIE SICH AUSKENNEN, SONDERN FÜR JEDEN.«

POUR CALATRAVA LES VASTES AUVENTS DE LA GARE SONT «UNE FAÇON DE DIRE QUE CE N'EST PAS SEULEMENT UN LIEU POUR CEUX QUI SAVENT, MAIS POUR TOUT LE MONDE».

Part of the development plan for Expo '98, the Oriente station is located about 5 km from the historic center of Lisbon, not far from the shores of the Tagus River. The most readily visible aspect of the project is undoubtedly the 78 x 238 m covering over the eight raised railway tracks, whose typology recalls that of "trees on a hillside," according to the architect. Rather than emphasizing the break between the city and the river implied by the station, and its elevated tracks, Calatrava has sought to open passageways and re-establish links. Pedestrians can walk through the ground level to gain access to the former Expo '98 fair grounds, for

Als Teil des ambitionierten Bebauungsplans für die Expo '98 liegt die Oriente Station etwa 5 km vom historischen Stadtkern Lissabons entfernt, nicht weit vom Ufer des breiten Tejo. Die ausladende Überdachung der acht erhöht geführten Bahngleise, die 78 x 238 m mißt, ist sicherlich der auffälligste Aspekt des Entwurfs. In Calatravas Worten erinnert die Gestaltung an »Bäume auf einem Hügel«. Anstatt den Einschnitt zu betonen, der durch den Bahnhof und die hochgelegten Gleise zwischen City und Fluß entstand, hat Calatrava versucht, Durchgänge zu öffnen und Verbindungen wiederherzustellen. Fußgänger können das Erdgeschoß durch-

Composante de l'important programme urbain lancé à l'occasion d'Expo '98 à Lisbonne, la gare de l'Orient se trouve à 5 km environ du centre historique de la capitale, non loin de la rive du Tage, très large à cet endroit. La caractéristique la plus immédiatement visible du projet est certainement la structure de couverture de 78 x 238 m des huit voies dont la typologie rappelle selon l'architecte «des arbres au flanc d'une colline». Plutôt que d'accentuer la rupture entre la ville et le fleuve qu'entraîne l'implantation de la gare et de ses voies surélevées, Calatrava a cherché à ouvrir des passages et à rétablir des lignes. Les piétons peuvent la tra-

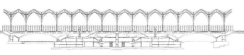

"THIS IS OBVIOUSLY NOT AN INTROVERTED TYPE OF ARCHITECTURE. I AM ON A HILLSIDE IN LISBON AND I LOOK AROUND ME. WHAT IS LACKING? SOME PROTECTION FROM THE SUN AND THE RAIN." SANTIAGO CALATRAVA

»DIES IST EINDEUTIG KEINE INTROVERTIERTE ARCHITEKTUR. ICH STEHE AUF EINEM HÜGEL IN LISSABON UND SCHAUE MICH UM. WAS

FEHLT? EIN SCHUTZ VOR SONNE UND REGEN.« SANTIAGO CALATRAVA

«CE N'EST MANIFESTEMENT PAS UN TYPE D'ARCHITECTURE INTROVERTI. JE SUIS SUR UNE COLLINE DE LISBONNE ET REGARDE AUTOUR DE MOI. QUE MANQUE-T-IL? QUELQUE CHOSE POUR PROTÉGER DU SOLEIL ET DE LA PLUIE.»

example. The complex includes two enormous glass and steel awnings over the openings, the larger of which, on the riverside, measures no less than 112 m in length and 11 m in width. Contrary to expectations, it is the opening on the riverside that is intended as the main access point. There are a bus station and car park, a metro station below (not designed by Calatrava), and a longitudinal gallery including commercial spaces. Ticketing and service facilities are located 5 m below the tracks, with an atrium marking the longitudinal gallery 5 m lower.

queren, um etwa das frühere Gelände der Expo '98 zu erreichen. Zur Anlage gehören zwei gewaltige Vordächer aus Glas und Stahl über den Eingängen; das größere am Flußufer ist 112 m lang und 11 m breit. Anders als man vermuten würde, liegt der Haupteingang auf dieser Seite. Hier befinden sich auch ein Omnibusbahnhof und ein Parkplatz darunter eine (nicht von Calatrava entworfene) U-Bahnstation und eine in Längsrichtung verlaufende Einkaufspassage. Fahrkartenverkauf und Service-einrichtungen sind 5 m unter den Gleisen angeordnet. Ein Atrium bildet den Eingang zu der weitere 5 m tiefer gelegenen Passage.

verser au niveau du sol pour accéder à l'enceinte d'Expo '98, par exemple. Le complexe comprend deux énormes auvents de verre et d'acier au-dessus des ouvertures, dont la plus large, donnant sur le fleuve ne mesure pas moins de 112 m de long et 11 m de large. L'ouverture vers le fleuve constitue le principal point d'accès. L'ensemble réunit par ailleurs une gare routière, une station de métro en sous-sol (dessinée par un autre architecte), et une galerie longitudinale pour espaces commerciaux. Vente de billets et services se trouvent à 5 m en dessous des voies, un atrium signalant la galerie longitudinale 5 m plus bas.

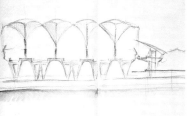

AS HE DID IN HIS STADELHOFEN STATION IN ZURICH, CALATRAVA SETS THE ORIENTE STATION DOWN ON A SOLID UNDERPINNING OF GALLERIES FORMED BY CONCRETE RIBS.

WIE DEN BAHNHOF STADELHOFEN IN ZÜRICH STELLT CALATRAVA DIE ORIENTE STATION AUF EINEN MASSIVEN UNTERBAU MIT PASSAGEN, DIE VON BETONRIPPEN GEGLIEDERT SIND.

COMME POUR LA GARE DE STADELHOFEN À ZURICH, CALATRAVA A PLACÉ LA GARE DE L'ORIENT AU-DESSUS D'UN SOCLE DE GALERIES.

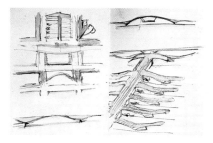

DAVID CHIPPERFIELD

Born in London in 1953, David Chipperfield obtained his Diploma in Architecture from the Architectural Association, London (1977). He worked in the offices of Norman Foster and Richard Rogers, before establishing David Chipperfield Architects (London, 1984). Built work includes Arnolfini Arts Centre (Bristol, 1987), Design Store (Kyoto, Japan, 1989), Matsumoto Headquarters Building (Oka-

David Chipperfield, geboren 1953 in London, erwarb 1977 dort sein Diplom in Architektur an der Architectural Association. Nach Tätigkeit in den Büros von Norman Foster und Richard Rogers gründete er 1984 in London David Chipperfield Architects. Er baute das Arnolfini Arts Centre in Bristol (1987), den Design Store in Kioto (1989) und den Sitz der Firma Matsumoto in Okayama

Né à Londres en 1953, David Chipperfield obtient son diplôme d'architecte de l'Architectural Association de Londres en 1977. Il travaille dans les agences de Norman Foster et de Richard Rogers, avant de fonder David Chipperfield Architects (Londres, 1984). Parmi ses réalisations: l'Arnolfini Arts Centre (Bristol, 1987), le Design Store (Kyoto, Japon, 1989), le siège social de Matsumoto (Oka-

BOTH FOR HIS WORK IN INTERIOR DESIGN AND FOR HIS OWN ARCHITECTURE, DAVID CHIPPERFIELD IS CONSIDERED ONE OF THE LEADING LIGHTS OF A "MINIMALIST" OR "NEO-MODERNIST" TREND IN BRITISH AND EUROPEAN ARCHITECTURE.

DURCH SEINE ARBEITEN IM BEREICH DER INNENARCHITEKTUR WIE DURCH SEINE EIGENEN BAUTEN IST DAVID CHIPPERFIELD ZU EINER FÜHRENDEN FIGUR DER MINIMALISTISCHEN ODER NEOMODERNISTISCHEN BRITISCHEN UND EUROPÄISCHEN ARCHITEKTUR GEWORDEN.

À LA FOIS PAR SON TRAVAIL D'AMÉNAGEMENTS INTÉRIEURS ET SON ARCHITECTURE, DAVID CHIPPERFIELD EST L'UNE DES PLUS IMPORTANTES PERSONNALITÉS DE LA TENDANCE MINIMALISTE OU NÉOMODERNISTE BRITANNIQUE ET EUROPÉENNE.

DAVID CHIPPERFIELD ARCHITECTS
COBHAM MEWS, AGAR GROVE
LONDON NW1 9SB
ENGLAND

TEL: + 44 20 7 267 9422
FAX: + 44 20 7 267 9347
E-MAIL: studio@dchipperfield.demon.co.uk

yama, Japan, 1990), Plant Gallery and Central Hall of the Natural History Museum (London, 1993), Wagamama Restaurant (London, 1996), River & Rowing Museum (Henley-on-Thames, 1996). His current work includes Landeszentralbank, Gera, Germany, Housing, Berlin-Spandau, office building, Düsseldorf, and reconstruction of the Neues Museum, Berlin (2000-06).

(1990), die Plant Gallery und Central Hall des Natural History Museum (1993), das Wagamama-Restaurant in London (1996) und das River & Rowing Museum in Henley-on-Thames (1996). Gegenwärtig arbeitet er an der Landeszentralbank in Gera, an Wohnbauten in Berlin-Spandau, einem Bürogebäude in Düsseldorf und der Rekonstruktion des Neuen Museums in Berlin (2000-06).

yama, Japon, 1990), la galerie des plantes et le hall central du Natural History Museum (Londres, 1993), le Wagamama Restaurant (Londres, 1996), le River & Rowing Museum (Henley-on-Thames, 1996). En cours: siège de la Landeszentralbank, Gera, Allemagne, logements à Berlin-Spandau, immeuble de bureaux à Düsseldorf, et reconstruction du Neues Museum à Berlin (2000-06).

DAVID CHIPPERFIELD
JOSEPH MENSWEAR
LONDON, ENGLAND, 1997

David Chipperfield had already designed the Issey Miyake shop on Sloane Street, as well as numerous other store interiors. This clothing shop was inserted into the ground and first floors of a four-story 1960s office block at number 74 Sloane Avenue, just around the corner from the landmark Michelin "Bibendum" building. 6 m high glass panels mark the front of the shop, while stainless steel mesh envelops a second-floor showroom. Heavy dark metal doors are left open with a forced air "curtain" replacing the glass that might have been anticipated. Dark gray *Pietra Serena*

David Chipperfield hatte bereits die Boutique für Issey Miyake in der Sloane Street und zahlreiche andere Ladeninterieurs entworfen, bevor er Joseph Menswear in London gestaltete. Das Bekleidungsgeschäft wurde ins Erd- und erste Obergeschoß eines viergeschossigen Bürogebäudes von 1960 in der Sloane Avenue 74 eingefügt, um die Ecke steht das bekannte Michelin Building. 6 m hohe Glastafeln markieren die Ladenfront, während Edelstahlgewebe den Ausstellungsraum im zweiten Obergeschoß umschließt. Die dunklen Metalltüren werden durch einen Druckluft-»Vorhang« offen-

David Chipperfield avait déjà conçu le magasin Issey Miyake de Sloane Street, ainsi que de nombreux autres aménagements de boutiques. Ce magasin de vêtements occupe le rez-de-chaussée et le premier étage d'un immeuble de bureaux des années 60, au 74 Sloane Avenue, tout près du bâtiment classé du Michelin Building. Des panneaux de verre de 6 m de haut signalent la façade tandis qu'un treillage d'acier masque le showroom du second étage. Les lourdes portes de métal sombre sont laissées ouvertes et un rideau d'air pulsé remplace les panneaux de verre que l'on s'attend à trouver à

ALTHOUGH CHIPPERFIELD'S REFITTING OF
THE BUILDING'S FACADE DOES NOT EXTEND TO
THE TOP LEVEL, HE SUCCEEDS IN GIVING AN
ESTHETIC UNITY TO THE WHOLE.

OBWOHL ER DAS OBERGESCHOSS NICHT
KOMPLETT NEUGESTALTETE, GELINGT ES
CHIPPERFIELD, DEM GANZEN ÄSTHETISCHE
EINHEITLICHKEIT ZU VERLEIHEN.

BIEN QUE L'INTERVENTION DE CHIPPERFIELD
SUR LA FAÇADE NE CONCERNE PAS L'ÉTAGE
SUPÉRIEUR, IL A RÉUSSI À DONNER UNE
UNITÉ ESTHÉTIQUE À L'ENSEMBLE.

COMPLETION / FERTIGSTELLUNG /
FIN DE LA CONSTRUCTION: 10/97
CLIENT / BAUHERR: JOSEPH, LTD
FLOOR AREA / NUTZFLÄCHE / SURFACE
UTILE: 400 M²
COSTS / KOSTEN / COÛTS: WITHHELD /
UNGENANNT / NON COMMUNIQUÉS

loors and white walls give an impression of a
ertain austerity that is indeed well suited to the
menswear sold here. A steel and wood spiral white
taircase links the ground and first floors. Floor
o ceiling windows give visitors an unexpected
iew of the street from the first floor. Undoubtedly
onvinced of the commercial viability of the work
f recognized architects like David Chipperfield,
he owner of this store, Joseph Ettedgui, has previ-
usly called not only on Chipperfield himself, but
lso on Norman Foster and Eva Jiricna.

gehalten, der das übliche Glas ersetzt. Böden aus
dunkelgrauem Pietra Serena-Sandstein und weiße
Wände strahlen eine Strenge aus, die der hier an-
gebotenen Herrenbekleidung durchaus entspricht.
Eine weiße Wendeltreppe aus Stahl und Holz verbindet Erd- und Obergeschoß. Geschoßhohe Fenster
bieten den Kunden einen unerwarteten Blick vom
Obergeschoß auf die Straße. Der Geschäftsinhaber,
Joseph Ettedgui, ist vom kommerziellen Nutzen
der Arbeit renommierter Architekten überzeugt: Er
hatte zuvor nicht nur Chipperfield, sondern auch
Norman Foster und Eva Jiricna angesprochen.

cet emplacement. Les sols en *pietra serena* gris
foncé et les murs blancs donnent une certaine
impression d'austérité, bien adaptée au style de
vêtements proposés. Un escalier en spirale blanc,
construit en bois et acier, relie les deux niveaux.
A l'étage, les baies toute hauteur donnent aux visiteurs une vue surprenante sur la rue. Convaincu
de l'intérêt commercial des interventions d'architectes célèbres, le propriétaire du magasin, Joseph
Ettedgui a déjà fait appel à Chipperfield, mais
aussi à Norman Foster et Eva Jiricna.

CLARE DESIGN

Lindsay Clare (left) was born in Brisbane in 1952, and Kerry Clare (right) was born in Sydney in 1957. They both obtained their degrees in architecture from the Queensland University of Technology, and set up their practice in Mooloolaba in 1980. Their built work includes more than 100 projects such as the McWilliam Residence (1990), Clare Residence (1991), Hammond Residence (1994), and Cotton Tree Pilot Housing (1995), all on Sunshine Coast. They have attempted to "combine principles of modernism and traditional Queensland architec-

Lindsay Clare (links), geboren 1952 in Brisbane, und Kerry Clare (rechts), geboren 1957 in Sydney, erwarben beide ihr Architektur-Diplom an der Queensland University of Technology und gründeten 1980 ein Büro in Mooloolaba. Sie haben über 100 Projekte ausgeführt, darunter die Wohnhäuser McWilliam (1990), Clare (1991) und Hammond (1994), sowie die Siedlung Cotton Tree Pilot Housing (1995), alle an der Sunshine Coast. In ihren Bauten versuchen Clare Design, »Prinzipien der Moderne mit dem traditionellen Baustil von

Lindsay Clare (à gauche) naît en 1952 à Brisbane, et Kerry Clare (à droite) à Sydney en 1954. Tous deux obtiennent leur diplôme d'architecture à la Queensland University of Technology et créent leur agence à Mooloolaba en 1980. Ils ont réalisé plus de cent projets comme la McWilliam Residence (1990), la Clare Residence (1991), la Hammond Residence (1994) et le Cotton Tree Pilot Housing (1995), toutes à la Sunshine Coast. Ils tentent de combiner «les principes du modernisme et de l'architecture traditionnelle du Queensland pour géné-

THE WORK OF LINDSAY AND KERRY CLARE IS INDICATIVE OF THE RICH POSSIBILITIES THAT EXIST IN AUSTRALIA TO CREATE A TYPE OF MODERN ARCHITECTURE, WHICH IS AT ONCE RELATED TO THE LOCAL SITUATION, AND TO INTERNATIONAL TRENDS.

DIE ARCHITEKTEN LINDSAY UND KERRY CLARE SCHAFFEN MIT IHRER ARBEIT EINEN BAU-TYPUS, DER DIE AUSTRALISCHE ARCHITEKTUR

MIT MODERNEN INTERNATIONALEN TENDEN-ZEN VERBINDET.

L'ŒUVRE DE LINDSAY ET KERRY CLARE ILLUS-TRE LES MULTIPLES POSSIBILITÉS OFFERTES EN AUSTRALIE POUR LA CRÉATION D'UN TYPE D'ARCHITECTURE À LA FOIS LIÉ À LA SITUATION LOCALE ET AUX TENDANCES INTERNATIONALES.

CLARE DESIGN
LV 18 MCKELL BLDG   P.O. BOX 5010
2-24 RAWSON PLACE   MAROOCHYDORE SOUTH
SYDNEY 2000 NSW   4458 QUEENSLAND
AUSTRALIA   AUSTRALIA

TEL: + 61 2 9372 8357
FAX: + 61 2 9372 8344

ture in order to generate solutions that respond to environment, contemporary culture and community needs." Lindsay and Kerry Clare are currently working as design directors for the New South Wales Government Architect. Current projects include the Sydney Cove Waterfront Strategy, the Royal Botanic Gardens Exhibition Center, the Olympic Village School and the Environment Center for the Riverina Institute of TAFE (Technical and Further Education).

Queensland zu verbinden, um Lösungen zu finden, die der Umwelt, der zeitgenössischen Kultur und den Bedürfnissen der Gemeinschaft gerecht werden.« Gegenwärtig arbeiten Lindsay und Kerry Clare als Planungsleiter für den Regierungsarchitekten von Neusüdwales. Ihre jüngsten Projekte sind die Sydney Cove Waterfront Strategy, das Ausstellungszentrum der Royal Botanic Gardens, die Schule im Olympischen Dorf und das Umweltzentrum des Riverina Institute of TAFE (Technical and Further Education).

rer des solutions qui répondent aux besoins de l'environnement de la culture contemporaine et de la communauté». Ils travaillent actuellement comme directeurs des projets pour le bureau d'architecture du gouvernement de la Nouvelle-Galles du Sud. Parmi leurs récents projets: le plan directeur pour le front de mer de Sydney Cove, le centre d'exposition des Royal Botanic Gardens, l'école du Village olympique et le Environment Centre pour le Riverina Institute of TAFE (Technical and Further Education).

CLARE DESIGN

SUNSHINE COAST UNIVERSITY CLUB

SIPPY DOWNS, QUEENSLAND, AUSTRALIA, 1996

RETAINING THE FEELING OF AN INDUSTRIAL SHED, THE STRUCTURE IS ALSO RELATED TO THE OPENNESS OF BEACHSIDE ARCHITECTURE.

OBGLEICH DER CHARAKTER EINER INDUSTRIE-HALLE BEIBEHALTEN WIRD, HAT DAS GEBÄUDE DIE OFFENHEIT EINER STRANDBEBAUUNG.

TOUT EN GARDANT CERTAINS TRAITS D'UN BÂTIMENT INDUSTRIEL, LA STRUCTURE N'EST PAS SANS RELATIONS AVEC L'ARCHITECTURE DE PLAGE.

CLIENT / BAUHERR: THE UNIVERSITY OF THE
SUNSHINE COAST
FLOOR AREA / NUTZFLÄCHE / SURFACE
UTILE: 685 M²
COSTS / KOSTEN / COÛTS: A$ 600 000

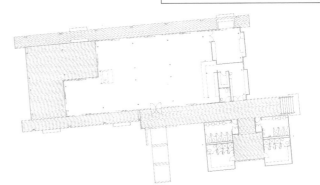

Because University officials seriously considered using an industrial shed to house this sports pavilion and staff club, the architects were faced with the daunting task of putting up a building within six months for a modest A$ 600,000 budget. With three open, glazed sides, this structure required substantial bracing against potentially severe wind conditions. The use of plywood on visible surfaces, and hardwood floors, was inspired by knowledge of local building types. "We wanted the guts and ruggedness of the farm shed and the lightness and openness of a surf club," say the architects. The 5 m height of the roof was in part determined by the need to create efficient passive ventilation, while the extended, horizontal design took into account the possibility of future extensions. Set on an "insistently horizontal," treeless plain, the University Club has become "one of the major social centers" in this new campus, in which Clare Design has been involved since its creation.

Nachdem die Universität erwogen hatte, eine Industriehalle als Sportpavillon und Klubhaus zu nutzen, wurden die Architekten vor die Aufgabe gestellt, in sechs Monaten ein Gebäude zum knappen Budget von 600 000 A$ zu erstellen. Mit drei verglasten Seiten benötigte der Bau starke Aussteifungen. Regionale Bauweisen regten zur Verwendung von Sperrholz und von Hartholzböden an. »Wir wollten das Robuste eines Schuppens mit der Leichtigkeit eines Surfklubhauses verbinden«, sagen die Architekten. Die Deckenhöhe von 5 m ermöglicht ausreichend passive Ventilation; die horizontale Ausbreitung berücksichtigt eventuelle Erweiterungen. Der in einer »streng horizontalen«, baumlosen Ebene stehende Klub ist zu einem »der bedeutendsten sozialen Zentren« des neuen Campus geworden, für den Clare Design seit seiner Gründung gebaut haben.

L'administration de l'Université ayant pensé un temps se servir d'un hangar industriel pour abriter des activités sportives et le club du personnel, les architectes se sont vus confrontés à la tâche délicate de créer un bâtiment en six mois pour le modeste budget de A$ 600 000. Avec ses trois façades ouvertes et vitrées, cette structure a exigé un entretoisement particulier pour résister à la force des vents particulièrement vive dans cette région. Le recours au contreplaqué sur les surfaces visibles et les sols en plancher de bois dur sont une tradition locale. «Nous voulions retrouver la nature brute d'un bâtiment agricole, ainsi que l'ouverture et la luminosité d'un club de surf», précisent les architectes. La hauteur du toit – 5 m – tient à la nécessité de créer une ventilation passive, et la conception très horizontale anticipe une extension future. Edifié dans une plaine dénuée d'arbres «puissamment horizontale», l'University Club est devenu l'un des «centres majeurs de la vie sociale» de ce nouveau campus.

LEADING LIGHTS OF THE SO-CALLED DECON-
STRUVIST MOVEMENT IN THE 1980'S, THE
FOUNDING PARTNERS OF COOP HIMMELB(L)AU,
WOLF PRIX AND HELMUT SWICZINSKY ARE
TODAY BEGINNING TO PUT THEIR RADICAL
ARCHITECTURAL IDEAS INTO PRACTICE.

COOP HIMMELB(L)AU

Wolf Prix (right) and Helmut Swiczinsky (left) founded Coop Himmelb(l)au in 1968 in Vienna, Austria. In 1988 they opened a second office in Los Angeles. Wolf Prix was born in 1942 in Vienna, and educated at the Technische Universität, Vienna, the Southern California Institute of Architecture (SCI-Arc), and the Architectural Association (AA), London. He has been a professor of the masterclass of architecture at the University of Applied Arts, Vienna, and an adjunct professor at SCI-Arc. Swiczinsky was born in 1944 in Poznań, Poland,

Wolf Prix (rechts) und Helmut Swiczinsky (links) gründeten Coop Himmelb(l)au 1968 in Wien. 1988 eröffneten sie ein Büro in Los Angeles. Der 1942 in Wien geborene Wolf Prix studierte an der TU Wien, dem Southern California Institute of Architecture (SCI-Arc) und der Architectural Association (AA) in London. Er ist Professor der Meisterklasse für Architektur an der Hochschule für Angewandte Kunst in Wien und außerordentlicher Professor am SCI-Arc. Helmut Swiczinsky wurde 1944 in Posen (heute Poznań, Polen) geboren, wuchs in Wien auf

Wolf Prix (à droite) et Helmut Swiczinsky (à gauche) ont fondé Coop Himmelb(l)au à Vienne, Autriche, en 1968 et ouvert une seconde agence à Los Angeles en 1988. Wolf Prix, né à Vienne en 1942, étudie à la Technische Universität de Vienne, au Southern California Institute of Architecture (SCI-Arc) et à l'Architectural Association de Londres. Il est professeur d'architecture de l'Université des arts appliqués de Vienne, et professeur adjoint à SCI-Arc. Helmut Swiczinsky naît en 1944 à Poznań, Pologne, mais est élévé à Vienne où il

COOP HIMMELB(L)AU
PRIX & SWICZINSKY GMBH
SEILERSTÄTTE 16/11
1010 VIENNA
AUSTRIA

TEL: + 43 1 512 0284
FAX: + 43 1 513 4754

ALS FÜHRENDE VERTRETER DES SOGENANN-
TEN DEKONSTRUKTIVISMUS IN DEN 80ER
JAHREN BEGINNEN WOLF PRIX UND HELMUT
SWICZINSKY HEUTE, IHRE RADIKALEN ARCHI-
TEKTURVORSTELLUNGEN IN DIE PRAXIS UM-
ZUSETZEN.

PRINCIPAUX REPRÉSENTANTS DU MOUVEMENT
DÉCONSTRUCTIVISTE DES ANNÉES 1980, LES
FONDATEURS DE COOP HIMMELB(L)AU, WOLF
PRIX ET HELMUT SWICZINSKY COMMENCENT
AUJOURD'HUI À METTRE LEURS CONCEPTIONS
RADICALES EN PRATIQUE.

ised in Vienna, and educated at the Technische
niversität, Vienna, and at the AA, London.
mpleted projects of the group include the Roof-
o Remodeling in Vienna, masterplan for Melun-
nart, France, and the east pavilion of the Gro-
nger Museum (Groningen, Netherlands, 1990-94).
ey also remodeled the Austrian Pavilion in the
ardini, Venice, Italy. Recent work includes the
ademy of Fine Arts, Munich, the UFA Cinema
nter, Dresden, and the SEG Apartment Tower,
enna.

und studierte an der dortigen TU sowie an der AA
in London. Zu den Bauten der Gruppe gehören ein
Dachausbau in Wien, der Masterplan für Melun-
Sénart in Frankreich und der Ostpavillon des
Groninger Museum (Groningen, Niederlande, 1990-
94), außerdem der Umbau des Österreichischen
Pavillons in den Giardini in Venedig, die Erweite-
rung der Kunstakademie in München, der UFA-
Palast in Dresden und das SEG-Appartementhoch-
haus in Wien.

étudie à la Technische Universität et à l'AA, à
Londres. Parmi leurs réalisations figurent la restructuration du sommet d'un immeuble viennois, le
plan directeur de Melun-Sénart, France, le pavillon
Est du Groninger Museum (Groningue, Pays-Bas,
1990-94). Ils ont également remodelé le pavillon
autrichien des Giardini à Venise, Italie. Parmi
leurs réalisations les plus récentes: l'Académie des
Beaux-Arts de Munich, le UFA-Palast, Dresde,
et la tour d'appartements, Vienne.

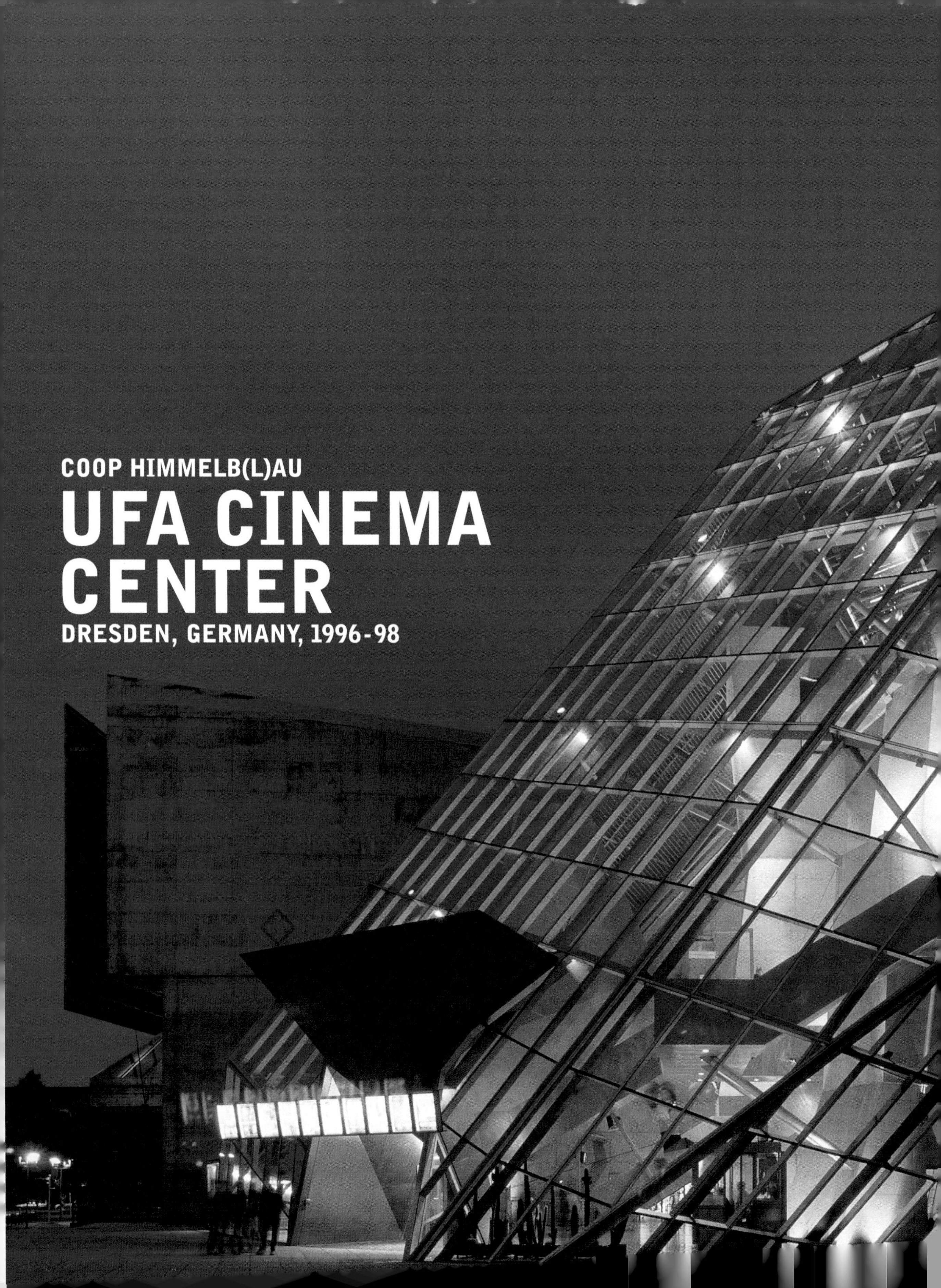

COOP HIMMELB(L)AU

UFA CINEMA CENTER

DRESDEN, GERMANY, 1996-98

COMPETITION / WETTBEWERB / CONCOURS: 1993
PLANNING / PLANUNG: 2/96-97
CONSTRUCTION / BAU: 3/97-3/98
CLIENT / BAUHERR: UFA-THEATER GMBH & CO.
KG, DÜSSELDORF, GERMANY
FLOOR AREA / NUTZFLÄCHE / SURFACE
UTILE: 6 174 M²
SEATS / SITZPLÄTZE / PLACES: 2 600
COSTS / KOSTEN / COÛTS: 32 000 000 DM

THE UNEXPECTED, CRYSTALLINE FORM OF THE CINEMA IS IN SHARP CONTRAST TO ITS URBAN ENVIRONMENT.

MENACING AND SCULPTURAL, THE CINEMA IS TRUE TO THE ANGULAR DESIGNS FAVORED BY COOP HIMMELB(L)AU.

DIE UNGEWÖHNLICHE KRISTALLINE FORM DES KINOS STEHT IN STARKEM KONTRAST ZU SEINER UMGEBUNG.

DER BEDROHLICHE UND SKULPTURALE BAU IST DIE UMSETZUNG DER VON COOP HIMMEL-B(L)AU FAVORISIERTEN SCHRÄGEN ENTWÜRFE.

INATTENDUE, LA FORME CRISTALLINE DE CE COMPLEXE DE SALLES CONTRASTE FORTEMENT AVEC SON ENVIRONNEMENT URBAIN.

MENAÇANT ET SCULPTURAL, LE CINÉMA EST BIEN DANS L'ESPRIT DES FORMES ANGULEUSES QUI SONT LA MARQUE DE COOP HIMMEL-B(L)AU.

Built for UFA Theater GmbH for a relatively limited budget of 12,000 DM per seat, this structure contains eight theaters and a total of 2,600 seats. The theaters are inscribed in a five-story concrete block, which is partially enclosed in a crystalline glass box that serves as a foyer. Four of the small theaters are situated below ground level. Contrasting in a marked way with the neighboring Stalinist architecture, the unusual forms of this theater are intended to give new vitality to the city center, linking two avenues – St. Petersburger strasse and Prager Strasse. 30 years after the creation of their firm, Wolf Prix and Helmut Swiczinsky are beginning with structures such as this one to accumulate a more sizable body of built work. Identified in a specific way with the so-called Deconstructivist movement, their work in Dresden might well bring to mind designs of the German Expressionist architects. According to Wolf Prix, the building is "designed like a video-clip and seeks to do away with centralized perspective."

Das für die UFA-Theater GmbH mit dem relativ geringen Budget von 12 000 DM je Platz errichtete Multiplex-Kino enthält acht Säle mit insgesamt 2 600 Plätzen. Die Säle sind in einen fünfgeschossigen Betonblock eingefügt, der teilweise von einer kristallinen Glashülle umgeben ist, welche als Foyer dient. Mit seinen Formen, die in deutlichem Gegensatz zur benachbarten Monumentalarchitektur stehen, soll der Komplex dem Stadtzentrum neue Vitalität geben, indem er zwei Hauptstraßen verbindet: die St. Petersburger und die Prager Straße. 30 Jahre nach der Gründung ihres Büros können Wolf Prix und Helmut Swiczinsky auf eine beachtliche Anzahl ähnlich ausgeführter Bauten zurückblicken. Auch wenn die Architekten meist als Dekonstruktivisten bezeichnet werden, erinnert der UFA-Palast an Entwürfe der deutschen Expressionisten. Wie Wolf Prix erläuterte, wurde das Gebäude »wie ein Videoclip geplant. Es versucht, die Zentralperspektive zu überwinden.«

Construit pour UFA-Theater GmbH avec un budget relativement limité de 12 000 DM par place, ce complexe contient huit salles d'un total de 2 600 sièges qui s'insèrent dans un bloc de béton de cinq niveaux en partie enfermé dans une boîte de verre qui fait office de foyer. Quatre des plus petites salles se trouvent en sous-sol. En opposition marquée avec les témoignages de l'architecture stalinienne qui l'entourent, ce complexe de forme surprenante se propose de revivifier le centre ville et de relier deux grands axes, la St. Petersburger Strasse et la Prager Strasse. Wolf Prix et Helmut Swiczinsky ont fondé Coop Himmelb(l)au en 1968 à Vienne, et 30 ans plus tard, accumulent les réalisations importantes dont celle-ci. S'ils sont souvent identifiés au mouvement déconstructiviste, leur projet pour Dresde rappelle surtout ceux d'architectes expressionnistes allemands. Selon Wolf Prix, ce bâtiment est «conçu comme un vidéo-clip et cherche à rompre avec le principe de perspective centralisée».

INTERIOR PERSPECTIVES ARE ARRESTING AND
EVEN DIZZYING, AN UNEXPECTED COMBINATION
FOR A MOVIE THEATER COMPLEX.

DIE INNENANSICHTEN SIND FASZINIEREND
UND VERWIRREND – EINE ERSTAUNLICHE
KOMBINATION FÜR EIN KINO.

LES PERSPECTIVES INTÉRIEURES SONT SUR-
PRENANTES QUAND ELLES NE METTENT PAS
MAL À L'AISE, CE QUI PEUT SURPRENDRE POUR
UN COMPLEXE CINÉMATOGRAPHIQUE.

ALMOST GEOLOGICAL IN ITS ABRUPT ANGULARITY, THE UFA CINEMA LOOKS ALSO TO A STUDIED IMBALANCE, A KIND OF FROZEN ERUPTION.

FAST GEOLOGISCH IN SEINER ABRUPTEN SPITZWINKLIGKEIT DEUTET DER UFA-PALAST AUCH EIN BEABSICHTIGTES UNGLEICHGEWICHT, EINE ART ERSTARRTER ERUPTION AN.

PRESQUE GÉOLOGIQUE DANS LA BRUTALITÉ DE SON TRAITEMENT ANGULEUX, LE UFA-PALAST DONNE UNE IMPRESSION DE DÉSÉQUILIBRE ÉTUDIÉ, D'UNE SORTE D'ÉRUPTION FIGÉE.

STEVEN EHRLICH

Born in New York in 1946, Steven Ehrlich received his B. Arch. degree from the Rensselaer Polytechnic Institute, Troy, New York in 1969. He studied indigenous vernacular architecture in North and West Africa from 1969 to 1977. He has completed numerous private residences, including the Friedman Residence (1986), the Ehrman-Coombs Residence (Santa Monica, 1989-91), and the Schulman Residence (Brentwood, 1989-92), all in the Los Angeles area. Other built work includes the Shatto Recreation Center (Los Angeles, 1991), Sony Music

Steven Ehrlich, geboren 1946 in New York, erwarb 1969 den Bachelor of Architecture am Rensselaer Polytechnic Institute in Troy, New York. Von 1969 bis 1977 studierte er die Architektur der Eingeborenen Nord- und Westafrikas. Ausgeführt hat er zahlreiche Privathäuser, darunter das Haus Friedman (1986), das Haus Ehrman-Coombs in Santa Monica (1989-91) und das Haus Schulman in Brentwood (1989-92), die alle in der Region Los Angeles liegen. Zu seinen weiteren realisierten Bauwerken gehören das Shatto Recreation Center

Né à New York en 1946, Steven Ehrlich est diplômé en architecture du Rensselaer Polytechnic Institute de Troy, New York en 1969. Il étudie l'architecture vernaculaire indigène en Afrique du Nord et de l'Ouest de 1969 à 1977. Il a réalisé de nombreuses résidences privées dont la Friedman Residence (1986), la Ehrman-Coombs Residence (Santa Monica, 1989-91), et la Schulman Residence (Brentwood, 1989-92) toutes situées dans la région de Los Angeles. Il a également signé le Shatto Recreation Center (Los Angeles, 1991), le

COMBINING AN EAST COAST EDUCATION WITH
EXTENSIVE TRAVEL EXPERIENCE, STEVEN
EHRLICH HAS BEEN ONE OF THE MOST CON-
SISTENTLY INVENTIVE CALIFORNIAN
ARCHITECTS.

STEVEN EHRLICH, DER SEINE AUSBILDUNG AN
DER OSTKÜSTE MIT AUSGEDEHNTER REISE-
ERFAHRUNG VERBINDET, IST EINER DER PHAN-
TASIEVOLLSTEN KALIFORNISCHEN
ARCHITEKTEN.

FORMÉ SUR LA CÔTE EST ET GRAND VOYAGEUR,
STEVEN EHRLICH EST DEPUIS LONGTEMPS L'UN
DES ARCHITECTES CALIFORNIENS LES PLUS
INVENTIFS.

STEVEN EHRLICH ARCHITECTS
10865 WASHINGTON BLVD
CULVER CITY, CALIFORNIA 90232
UNITED STATES

TEL: + 1 310 838 9700
FAX: + 1 310 838 9737
E-MAIL: inquire@s-ehrlich.com
WEB: www.s-ehrlich.com

Entertainment Campus (Santa Monica, 1993),
Child Care Center for Sony Pictures (1993-95) and
Game Show Network (1995), Culver City, and the
Robertson Branch Library (Los Angeles, 1996).
More recently, he has worked on the Dream-
Works SKG Animation Studios (Glendale, Califor-
nia, 1998), the Orange Coast Collage Art Center
(Costa Mesa, 2000), and the Biblioteca Latino-
americana & Washington Youth Center (San Jose,
1999).

(Los Angeles, 1991), der Sony Music Entertainment Campus in Santa Monica (1993), das Child
Care Center für Sony Pictures (1993-95) und das
Game Show Network (1995), beide in Culver City,
sowie die Robertson Branch Library in Los Angeles
(1996). Neueste Arbeiten sind die DreamWorks
SKG Animation Studios (Glendale, Kalifornien,
1998), das Orange Coast College Art Center (Costa
Mesa, 2000) und die Biblioteca Latinoamericana
und das Washington Youth Center in San Jose
(1999).

Sony Music Entertainment Campus (Santa Monica,
1993), le Child Care Center Sony Pictures (1993-
95) et le Game Show Network (1995) à Culver
City, et la Robertson Branch Library (Los Angeles,
1996). Plus récemment encore il a travaillé sur les
DreamWorks SKG Animation Studios (Glendale,
Californie, 1998), l'Orange Coast Collage Art
Center (Costa Mesa, 2000) et la Biblioteca Latinoamericana & Washington Youth Center (San Jose,
1999).

STEVEN EHRLICH
HOUSE EXTENSION
SANTA MONICA, CALIFORNIA, UNITED STATES, 1996-98

This extension to Richard Neutra's 1938 Lewin House is approximately 300 m² in size and contains an entertainment area and pool, garage and parking areas as well as servants' quarters. The garage and servants' quarters are set in such a way as to block some of the noise of the nearby Pacific Coast Highway, for this house set on the beach in Santa Monica looks directly, via a steel gate that can be lowered into the ground, towards the Pacific. Given the exalted status of Neutra in California, Ehrlich's

Die Erweiterung von Richard Neutras Haus Lewin (1938) umfaßt eine Fläche von etwa 300 m² und besteht aus Freizeitbereich mit Schwimmbad, Garage, Parkplätzen und Räumen für Personal. Diese und die Garage dienen als Lärmschutz gegen den Pacific Coast Highway. Das Haus liegt am Strand von Santa Monica mit Blick – durch ein versenkbares Stahltor – auf den Pazifik. Angesichts des Renommees, das Neutra in Kalifornien genießt, stand Ehrlich vor keiner einfachen Aufgabe. »Der

Cette extension de la Lewin House de Richard Neutra (1938) de 300 m² environ contient une piscine et un espace de loisirs, un garage et des emplacement de parkings ainsi que des logements de domestiques. Le garage et les logements sont disposés de façon à bloquer en partie le bruit de la Pacific Coast Highway, puisque la maison se trouve sur la plage de Santa Monica avec une vue directe sur l'océan, via des grilles d'acier qui peuvent disparaître dans le sol. Etant donné le statut dont jouit

IN CALIFORNIA, RICHARD NEUTRA IS RIGHT-
FULLY CONSIDERED ONE OF THE GREAT FIGURES
OF MODERNISM. ADDING TO ONE OF HIS HOUSES
WAS A PARTICULARLY DAUNTING ASSIGNMENT.

IN KALIFORNIEN WIRD RICHARD NEUTRA ZU
RECHT ALS GROSSER VERTRETER DER MODER-
NE BETRACHTET. DIE ERWEITERUNG EINES
SEINER HÄUSER WAR DAHER EINE BESON-
DERS HEIKLE AUFGABE.

EN CALIFORNIE, RICHARD NEUTRA EST À JUSTE
TITRE CONSIDÉRÉ COMME L'UNE DES GRANDES
FIGURES DU MODERNISME. AGRANDIR L'UNE
DE SES MAISONS ÉTAIT UNE TÂCHE DÉLICATE.

CLIENT / BAUHERR: WITHHELD / UNGENANNT /
NON COMMUNIQUÉ
TOTAL FLOOR AREA / GESAMTFLÄCHE / SURFACE
TOTALE: 5 800 SQ FT
EXTENSION / ERWEITERUNGSBAU / AGRANDIS-
SEMENT: 2 600 SQ FT
COSTS / KOSTEN / COÛTS: WITHHELD / UNGE-
NANNT / NON COMMUNIQUÉS
LANDSCAPE DESIGN / LANDSCHAFTSARCHITEK-
TUR / ARCHITECTE PAYSAGISTE: BARRY BEER,
BEER & ASSOCIATES

task was not a simple one. "I'd like to think the pavilion, with the new materials and the evaporating glass walls, takes Neutra's ideas a step further," says Ehrlich. "It's much more minimal than he was ever able to achieve in those days." The pavilion is designed with a barrel-vaulted form and retractable glass walls that indeed fit the minimalist description, but mark the extension as not being in any sense an imitation of Neutra's work.

Pavillon aus modernen Materialien mit seinen transparenten Glaswänden führt Neutras Ideen fort,« sagt er: »Das Gebäude ist viel minimaler, als Neutra es zu seiner Zeit erreichen konnte.« Der Pavillon hat ein Tonnengewölbe und einziehbare Glaswände. Dies entspricht in der Tat der Beschreibung als minimalistisch, macht jedoch zugleich deutlich, daß der Anbau keine Imitation von Neutras Architektur anstrebt.

tout ce qui touche à Neutra en Californie, la tâche de Ehrlich n'était pas des plus aisées. «J'ai voulu penser le pavillon avec de nouveaux matériaux et des murs de verres éclipsables pour pousser encore plus loin les idées de Neutra», précise-t-il. «L'ensemble est beaucoup plus minimaliste que ce que l'on pouvait faire à cette époque.» Le pavillon à voûte en berceau correspond bien à cette description minimaliste, même si cette extension n'est en rien un pastiche du travail de Neutra.

WITH THE PALISADES AND THEIR ROWS OF TALL PALMS ABOVE, THE HOUSE SITS DIRECTLY ON THE BEACH.

DAS HAUS STEHT UNMITTELBAR AM STRAND; DARÜBER DIE PACIFIC PALISADES MIT IHREN HOHEN PALMEN.

BORDÉE DE PALISSADES ET DE PALMIERS GÉANTS, LA MAISON EST DIRECTEMENT SITUÉE SUR LA PLAGE.

P 156.157

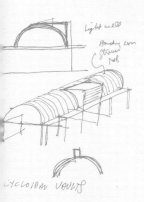

FREDERICK FISHER

Born in Cleveland, Ohio, in 1949, Frederick Fisher attended Oberlin College, graduating in 1971, and entered the UCLA Graduate School of Architecture and Urban Planning the same year. He worked in the office of Frank O. Gehry in Santa Monica from 1978 to 1980. He created the firm Fisher/Roberts with UCLA classmate Thane Roberts before setting up his own independent practice. His work includes

Frederick Fisher, geboren 1949 in Cleveland, Ohio, studierte bis 1971 am Oberlin College und setzte seine Ausbildung im gleichen Jahr an der Graduate School of Architecture and Urban Planning der University of California Los Angeles (UCLA) fort. Von 1978 bis 1980 arbeitete er im Büro von Frank O. Gehry in Santa Monica. Mit seinem Studienfreund Thane Roberts gründete er das Büro Fisher/

Né à Cleveland, Ohio, en 1949, Frederick Fisher étudie à l'Oberlin College dont il sort diplômé en 1971, pour entrer à la UCLA Graduate School of Architecture and Urban Planning la même année. Il travaille pour Frank O. Gehry à Santa Monica de 1978 à 1980, puis crée l'agence Fisher/Roberts avec son condisciple d'UCLA, Thane Roberts, et enfin sa propre structure. Parmi ses réalisations: la

THOUGH NOT ORIGINALLY A CALIFORNIAN, FRED FISHER DISPLAYS AN ABILITY TO REUSE AND ADAPT AN EXISTING BUILDING THAT SEEMS VERY MUCH IN TUNE WITH THE EPHEMERAL ARCHITECTURE OF THE WEST COAST.

OBWOHL ER NICHT AUS KALIFORNIEN STAMMT, HAT FISHER HIER EINEN UMBAU GESCHAFFEN, DER AN DIE EPHEMERE ARCHITEKTUR DER WESTKÜSTE ERINNERT.

BIEN QU'IL NE SOIT PAS D'ORIGINE CALIFORNIENNE, FRED FISHER FAIT PREUVE D'UNE HABILETÉ CERTAINE DANS LA RÉUTILISATION ET L'ADAPTATION DE BÂTIMENTS EXISTANTS DANS LE TON DES ARCHITECTURES ÉPHÉMÈRES DE LA CÔTE OUEST.

FREDERICK FISHER & PARTNERS, ARCHITECTS
12248 SANTA MONICA BLVD
LOS ANGELES, CALIFORNIA 90025-2518
UNITED STATES

TEL: + 1 310 820 6680
FAX: + 1 310 820 6118
EMAIL: fredf@ff-p.com

the Eli Broad Family Foundation, a renovation of a 1927 structure in Santa Monica (1989), the L. A. Louver Gallery in Venice, California (1994), P. S.1 in Long Island City, New York (1995-97), and a number of private residences in California, as well as the West Shinjuku Studio Apartments, Tokyo (1990).

Roberts, bevor er sich mit einer eigenen Firma selbständig machte. Zu seinen realisierten Projekten gehören die Eli Broad Family Foundation, der Umbau eines Gebäudes von 1927 in Santa Monica (1989), die Louver Gallery in Venice, Kalifornien (1994), P. S.1 in Long Island City, New York (1995-97), mehrere Villen in Kalifornien und die West Shinjuku Studio Apartments in Tokio (1990).

Eli Broad Family Foundation, rénovation d'un bâtiment de 1927 à Santa Monica (1989), la L. A. Louver Gallery (Venice, Californie, 1994), P. S.1 (Long Island City, New York, 1995-97), et un certain nombre de résidences privées en Californie ainsi que les West Shinjuku Studio Apartments (Tokyo, 1990).

FREDERICK FISHER

P.S.1

LONG ISLAND CITY, NEW YORK, NEW YORK, UNITED STATES, 1995-97

CLIENT / BAUHERR: P.S.1
FLOOR AREA / NUTZFLÄCHE / SURFACE UTILE:
125 000 SQ FT
COSTS / KOSTEN / COÛTS: US$ 8 500 000

P.S.1 is a former elementary school located in Long Island City, just across the river from Manhattan. The structure was built in two phases, the south wing in 1892 and the north wing in 1905, in a "Romanesque Revival" style. Abandoned by the City of New York, it was converted into a center for contemporary art in 1976 by Alanna Heiss and her associates. For budgetary reasons, they engaged in minimal construction work despite the fact that the building was in good part dilapidated. In the 1990s renovation became inevitable, and Alanna Heiss called on the Californian architect Frederick Fisher. With an $8.5 million budget, he provided a total of about 11,000 m² of space, including unusual exterior exhibition "rooms" formed by concrete walls in front of the entrance. In fact, one of Fisher's most radical gestures was to place the entrance where the rear of the school had been, using the former parking lot and playground for the concrete "rooms." Although some new, large exhibition spaces were created, Fisher's basic plan was to make the best use of the existing volumes.

P.S.1 ist eine ehemalige Volksschule in Long Island City. Das Gebäude wurde in zwei Phasen errichtet: der Südflügel 1892 und der Nordflügel 1905, beide im neoromanischen Stil. Die Schule wurde 1976 von Alanna Heiss und Mitarbeitern zu einem Zentrum für Gegenwartskunst umfunktioniert. Aus finanziellen Gründen wurden damals nur geringfügige Umbauarbeiten durchgeführt. In den 90er Jahren wurde eine Renovierung unvermeidlich, mit der Heiss Frederick Fisher beauftragte. Zu einem Budget von 8,5 Millionen US $ lieferte dieser eine Gesamtnutzfläche von etwa 11 000 m². Dazu zählen Ausstellungs-»Räume« unter freiem Himmel vor dem Eingang, die von Betonwänden begrenzt werden. Der radikalste Eingriff bestand darin, den Eingang an die Rückseite zu verlegen und den früheren Parkplatz und Pausenhof für die Beton-»Räume« zu nutzen. Auch wenn er so viele neue, große Räume schuf, war es Fishers eigentliches Ziel, den vorhandenen Bau optimal zu nutzen.

P.S.1 est une ancienne école maternelle de Long Island City, juste en face de Manhattan. Construite en deux phases – l'aile sud en 1892 et l'aile nord en 1905 en style néo-roman – elle a été abandonnée par la ville de New York avant d'être reconvertie en centre d'art contemporain en 1976 par Alanna Heiss et ses associés. Pour des raisons budgétaires, ils choisirent de limiter au maximum la reconstruction, malgré le mauvais état des lieux. Dans les années 90, des travaux de rénovation s'imposèrent et Alanna Heiss fit appel à l'architecte californien Frederick Fisher. Pour un budget de $8,5 millions, il réussit à rénover et créer environ 11 000 m², dont des «salles» d'exposition extérieures délimitées par des murs de béton face à l'entrée. L'une de ses décisions les plus radicales fut d'implanter l'entrée à l'arrière de l'école, ce qui permettait d'utiliser l'ancien parking et les terrains de jeux pour ses «pièces» de béton. En dehors de quelques généreux espaces nouveaux, Fisher a réutilisé au maximum les volumes existants.

FISHER TURNED THE BACK OF THE SCHOOL
BUILDING INTO ITS ENTRANCE AND ADDED A
SERIES OF CONCRETE WALLS TO MAKE OUT-
DOOR GALLERIES (SEE ALSO P 160.161).

FISHER VERLEGTE DEN EINGANG AN DIE
RÜCKSEITE DER SCHULE UND FÜGTE EINE
REIHE VON BETONWÄNDEN AN, DIE FREILICHT-
GALERIEN BILDEN (S. AUCH P 160.161).

FISHER A REPORTÉ L'ENTRÉE DE L'ÉCOLE
SUR L'ARRIÈRE ET CRÉÉ UNE SUCCESSION DE
MURS EN BÉTON QUI DÉLIMITE DES GALERIES
D'EXPOSITION EXTÉRIEURES (VOIR AUSSI
P 160.161).

WINNER OF THE 1999 PRITZKER PRIZE, LORD NORMAN FOSTER IS ONE OF THE MOST PROLIFIC AND TALENTED ARCHITECTS WORKING IN THE WORLD TODAY. HIS BUILDINGS COMBINE A KNOWLEDGE OF INDUSTRIAL TECHNIQUES WITH BREATHTAKING FORMS.

NORMAN FOSTER

Born in Manchester in 1935, Norman Foster studied architecture and city planning at Manchester University (1961). Awarded the Henry Fellowship to Yale University, he received the M. Arch. degree, and met Richard Rogers, with whom he created Team 4. He received the Royal Gold Medal for Architecture (1983), and the American Institute of Architects Gold Medal for Architecture (1994). He was knighted in 1990 and made a life peer in 1999. Lord Norman Foster has built the IBM Pilot Head Office (Cosham, 1970-71), Sainsbury Centre

Norman Foster, geboren 1935 in Manchester, studierte bis 1961 Architektur und Stadtplanung an der Manchester University. Er wurde mit dem Henry Fellowship der Yale University ausgezeichnet und schloß dort seine Studien mit dem Master of Architecture ab. In Yale lernte er Richard Rogers kennen, mit dem er Team 4 gründete. 1983 wurde Foster mit der Royal Gold Medal for Architecture ausgezeichnet und 1990 geadelt. 1994 wurde ihm die Gold Medal for Architecture des American Institute of Architects verliehen, 1999 wurde er zum

Né à Manchester en 1935, Norman Foster a étudié l'architecture et l'urbanisme à Manchester University (1961). Titulaire d'un Henry Fellowship de Yale University dont il est Master of Architecture, il rencontre Richard Rogers avec lequel il fonde Team 4. Il reçoit la Royal Gold Medal of Architecture en 1983, est anobli en 1990 et se voit décerner la Médaille d'or d'architecture de l'American Institute of Architects en 1994. Il a été fait lord en 1999. Norman Foster a construit en particulier: le siège pilote d'IBM (Cosham, 1970-71), le Sainsbury

LORD NORMAN FOSTER, DEM 1999 DER
PRITZKER-PREIS VERLIEHEN WURDE, IST
GEGENWÄRTIG EINER DER PRODUKTIVSTEN
UND TALENTIERTESTEN ARCHITEKTEN DER
WELT. ER VERBINDET DIE BEHERRSCHUNG
INDUSTRIELLER TECHNIKEN MIT ATEMBE-
RAUBENDEN FORMEN.

TITULAIRE DU PRIS PRITZKER 1999, NORMAN
FOSTER EST L'UN DES ARCHITECTES LES PLUS
TALENTUEUX ET DES PLUS PROLIFIQUES
ACTUELLEMENT À L'ŒUVRE DANS LE MONDE.
SES RÉALISATIONS ASSOCIENT UNE MAÎTRISE
APPROFONDIE DES TECHNIQUES DE CONSTRUC-
TION INDUSTRIELLE À DES FORMES HORS DE
L'ORDINAIRE.

P 164.165

FOSTER AND PARTNERS
RIVERSIDE THREE
22 HESTER ROAD
LONDON SW11 4AN
ENGLAND

TEL: + 44 20 7 738 04 55
FAX: + 44 20 7 738 11 07/08
E-MAIL: enquiries@fosterandpartners.com
WEB: www.fosterandpartners.com

for Visual Arts and Crescent Wing, University of East Anglia (Norwich, 1976-77; 1989-91), Hong Kong and Shanghai Banking Corporation Headquarters (Hong Kong, 1981-86), London's third airport, Stansted (1987-91), Faculty of Law (Cambridge, 1993-95), and the Commerzbank Headquarters (Frankfurt, Germany, 1994-97). Recent projects include Hong Kong International Airport (1995-98), New German Parliament, Reichstag (Berlin, 1993-99), and British Museum Redevelopment (London, 1997-2000).

Lord ernannt. Zu seinen Bauten zählen das IBM Pilot Head Office in Cosham (1970-71), das Sainsbury Centre for Visual Arts und der Crescent Wing der University of East Anglia in Norwich (1976-77, 1989-91), der Sitz der Hong Kong and Shanghai Bank in Hongkong (1981-86), Londons dritter Flughafen, Stansted (1987-91), die Juristische Fakultät der University of Cambridge (1993-95) und die Commerzbank-Zentrale in Frankfurt a. M. (1994-97). Gegenwärtig führt er die Modernisierung des British Museum in London (1997-2000) durch.

Centre for Visual Arts et la Crescent Wing pour l'University of East Anglia (Norwich, 1976-77; 1989-91), le siège de la Hong Kong and Shanghai Banking Corporation (1981-86), le troisième aéroport de Londres, Stansted (1987-91), la faculté de droit, University of Cambridge, (1993-95), le siège de la Commerzbank (Francfort-sur-le-Main, Allemagne, 1994-97). Ses récents chantiers comprennent l'aéroport Hongkong International, le nouveau Reichstag et le remaniement du British Museum (Londres, 1997-2000).

NORMAN FOSTER

HONG KONG
INTERNATIONAL AIRPORT

HONG KONG, CHINA, 1995-98

CLIENT / BAUHERR: HONG KONG AIRPORT
AUTHORITY
FLOOR AREA / NUTZFLÄCHE / SURFACE UTILE:
516 000 M²
COSTS / KOSTEN / COÛTS: US$ 20 000 000 000
CAPACITY / KAPAZITÄT / CAPACITÉ:
87 000 000 PASSENGERS P.A. (IN 2040)

**BUILT ON AN ARTIFICIAL ISLAND, THE AIRPORT
IS PART OF ONE OF THE LARGEST CIVIL
CONSTRUCTION PROJECTS IN THE WORLD IN
THE LAST QUARTER CENTURY.**

DER AUF EINER KÜNSTLICHEN INSEL ERRICH-
TETE FLUGHAFEN IST EINES DER GRÖSSTEN
BAUPROJEKTE DER WELT IM LETZTEN VIERTEL
DIESES JAHRHUNDERTS.

EDIFIÉ SUR UNE ÎLE ARTIFICIELLE, CE NOUVEL
AÉROPORT EST L'UN DES PLUS VASTES PROJETS
CIVILS DE CE DERNIER QUART DE SIÈCLE.

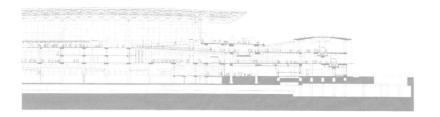

At nearly 520,000 m², the terminal building of Hong Kong International Airport has been called "the largest enclosed public space ever made." The structure, 1.27 km long, is designed to handle 35 million passengers a year, and was designed around a 36 m module. The lightweight steel roof was assembled on site into 129 units each weighing 132 tons. Nor are these the only superlatives associated with the new airport. It is part of the $20 billion Airport Core Program, whose intention was to permit the rapid movement of passengers from Hong Kong to Chek Lap Kok, 34 km away. As many as 21,000 persons worked on the construction of the

Mit fast 520 000 m² Nutzfläche gilt das Abfertigungsgebäude des Internationalen Flughafens Hongkong als »größter je umbauter öffentlicher Raum«. Das 1,27 km lange Gebäude soll zunächst jährlich 35 Millionen Passagiere abfertigen und wurde auf Basis eines 36 m-Moduls geplant. Das leichte Stahldach wurde vor Ort aus 129 Elementen zusammengefügt, die jeweils 132 t wiegen. Dies sind jedoch nicht die einzigen Superlative des neuen Flughafens. Er ist Teil des mit 20 Milliarden US$ ausgestatteten Airport Core Program, das zum Ziel hat, Passagiere schnellstmöglich von Hongkong zum 34 km entfernten Chek Lap Kok zu befördern.

Mesurant près de 520 000 m² et 1,27 km de long, ce terminal qualifié de «plus vaste espace public couvert jamais réalisé», est prévu pour traiter 35 millions de passagers par an. Sa conception fait appel à un module de 36 m. Le toit léger en acier assemblé sur place se compose de 129 éléments de 132 tonnes chacun. Ce projet superlatif fait partie du programme «Airport Core» de $20 milliards qu inclut le transport rapide de passagers de Hong Kong au site de Chek Lap Kok, éloigné de 34 km. À un certain moment, 21 000 personnes ont travaillé à la construction de l'aéroport dont le chantier a duré six ans, de la sélection des architectes à

P 168.169

airport at one time, and the project was finished in six years from the selection of the architects to completion. Foster was also responsible for the HACTL Superterminal and Express Center, whose seven-story cargo-handling building measuring 260,000 m² is the largest single cargo terminal in the world, and the Ground Transportation Center, which concentrates train platforms and facilities for all "landside" transportation. Working with the Hong Kong firm Mott Connell, the so-called Mott Consortium, including Foster's group, totaled 230 persons including 72 architects.

Zeitweise arbeiteten 21 000 Menschen am Bau des Flughafens; das Projekt wurde innerhalb von sechs Jahren nach dem Bauauftrag fertiggestellt. Foster war auch für den HACTL Superterminal mit Express Center verantwortlich; das siebenschossige Luftfrachtgebäude ist mit 260 000 m² Gesamtnutzfläche das weltweit größte Frachtterminal mit Transportzentrum. Er umfaßt auch Bahnrampen und Einrichtungen für jede Art des Warenverkehrs zu Lande. An der Arbeit mit der Hongkonger Firma Mott Connell, die mit Fosters Gruppe das Mott Consortium bildete, waren insgesamt 230 Personen beteiligt, darunter 72 Architekten.

son achèvement. Foster a également été responsable du Super Terminal et Centre Express HACTL, terminal de fret de sept niveaux de 260 000 m² – le plus vaste du monde – ainsi que du Centre des transports au sol qui regroupe des voies ferrées et des services divers pour tous les transports terrestres. Le Mott Consortium qui réunissait le groupe de Foster et l'agence de Hongkong, Mott Connell, a compté par un moment 230 collaborateurs, dont 72 architectes.

NORMAN FOSTER
REICHSTAG
BERLIN, GERMANY, 1993-99

COMPETITION / WETTBEWERB / CONCOURS: 1992/93
CONSTRUCTION / BAU: 7/95-4/99
1. FULL PLENARY SESSION / 1. PLENAR SITZUNG / 1. SÉANCE PLÉNIÈRE: 19.04.1999
CLIENT / BAUHERR: BUNDESREPUBLIK DEUTSCHLAND
FLOOR AREA / NUTZFLÄCHE / SURFACE UTILE: 11 500 M²
COSTS / KOSTEN / COÛTS: 600 000 000 DM

THE REICHSTAG BUILDING MEASURES 135 X 90 M WITH 11,500 M² OF PRIMARY NET USABLE AREA. THE ORIGINAL DOME, DESIGNED BY PAUL WALLOT, WAS DEMOLISHED IN 1954.

FOSTER'S INTERVENTION IS VISIBLE FROM THE EXTERIOR MAINLY THROUGH THE GLASS DOME THAT SERVES TO BRING LIGHT INTO THE CHAMBER AND TO PERMIT VISITORS TO SEE THE PROCEEDINGS.

DAS GEBÄUDE MISST 135 X 90 M MIT EINER NUTZFLÄCHE VON 11 500 M². DIE URSPRÜNG-LICHE KUPPEL VON PAUL WALLOT WURDE 1954 ABGERISSEN.

FOSTERS EINGRIFF ZEIGT SICH NACH AUSSEN IN ERSTER LINIE DURCH DIE GLÄSERNE HALB-KUPPEL, DIE LICHT IN DEN PARLAMENTSSAAL LÄSST UND BESUCHERN ERLAUBT, DIE DEBATTEN ZU VERFOLGEN.

LE REICHSTAG MESURE 135 X 90 M AVEC UNE SURFACE UTILE DE 11 500 M². LE DÔME DESSINÉ PAR PAUL WALLOT ÉTAIT DÉMOLIS EN 1954.

DE L'EXTÉRIEUR L'INTERVENTION DE FOSTER EST PRINCIPALEMENT VISIBLE PAR LA COUPO-LE DE VERRE QUI LAISSE ENTRER LA LUMIÈRE ET PERMET AUX VISITEURS DE POURSUIVRE LES SÉANCES.

The German Bundestag approved Norman Foster's final scheme for the renovation of the Reichstag on June 29, 1994, having announced the intention to reuse the building as the seat of German parliament on October 31, 1991. Foster was the winner of an international competition whose other finalists were Santiago Calatrava and the Dutch architect Pi De Bruijn. Having originally called for 34,000 m² of space, the final plan took into account about 11,500 m². Foster removed much of the 1960s interiors and replaced the original dome designed

Der Deutsche Bundestag billigte am 29. Juni 1994 Norman Fosters endgültigen Entwurf für den Umbau des Reichstags, nachdem am 31. Oktober 1991 beschlossen worden war, das Gebäude wieder als Sitz des deutschen Parlaments zu nutzen. Foster hatte den internationalen Wettbewerb gewonnen, in dem außer ihm Santiago Calatrava und Pi De Bruijn ausgezeichnet worden waren. Ursprünglich war eine Nutzfläche von 34 000 m² gefordert worden, der Ausführungsplan beschränkte sich jedoch auf 11 500 m². Foster entfernte die meisten Ein-

Le Bundestag a approuvé le 29 juin 1994 le projet final de Norman Foster pour la rénovation du Reichstag, après avoir décidé que ce bâtiment redevienne le siège du parlement allemand le 31 octobre 1991. Foster avait remporté le concours international face aux finalistes Santiago Calatrava et l'architecte néerlandais Pi De Bruijn. Prévu au départ pour 34 000 m², le plan définitif n'en a traité que 11 500. Foster a supprimé la plus grande partie des aménagements des années 1960 et remplacé d'une certaine façon le dôme dessiné par Paul Wal-

THE THEMES OF TRANSPARENCY AND LIGHT-
NESS HAVE BEEN BROUGHT TO THE FORE BY
NORMAN FOSTER, CONTRASTING WITH THE
WEIGHTY ARCHITECTURE OF WALLOT, AND THE
HISTORY OF THE BUILDING ITSELF.

FOSTER HAT TRANSPARENZ UND LEICHTIGKEIT
IN DEN SAAL GEBRACHT, WAS MIT DER SCHWE-
RE VON WALLOTS ARCHITEKTUR UND DER
GESCHICHTE DES GEBÄUDES KONTRASTIERT.

FOSTER A APPORTÉ TRANSPARENCE ET
LÉGÈRETÉ À LA SALLE, QUI CONTRASTE AVEC
L'ARCHITECTURE DE WALLOT ET L'HISTOIRE
DE CE BÂTIMENT.

y Paul Wallot with a glass hemisphere that brings
atural light into the main chamber. Visitors' galeries are also placed on helical ramps in the dome.
s Foster says, "aside from having the best views,
he public are symbolically above the politicians
ho are answerable to them." The architect placed
 great deal of importance on the extensive use of
atural ventilation and light, bringing transparency
o a building that carries with it as no other the
istory of Germany.

bauten der 60er Jahre und ersetzte die Kuppel
von Paul Wallot durch eine gläserne Halbkugel,
die Tageslicht in den Parlamentssaal einläßt und
Besuchergalerien auf umlaufenden Rampen enthält.
Foster erklärte: »Abgesehen davon, daß den Zuschauern die beste Sicht geboten wird, sitzen sie
symbolisch über den Politikern, die sich ihnen gegenüber verantworten müssen.« Der Architekt legte
großen Wert auf ausreichend natürliche Belüftung
und Belichtung und gab dem geschichtsträchtigen
Gebäude besondere Transparenz.

lot par une demi-sphère de verre qui permet
l'éclairage naturel de la salle des séances. Les
galeries des visiteurs sont en rampes hélicoïdales à
l'intérieure du dôme. « En plus de bénéficier de la
meilleure vue, le public se trouve symboliquement
au-dessus des hommes politiques qui répondent
devant lui », a commenté Foster. L'architecte a
beaucoup insisté sur la ventilation et la lumière
naturelles, afin d'apporter le maximum de transparence à un bâtiment qui symbolise comme nul
autre une partie de l'histoire allemande.

NICHOLAS GRIMSHAW

A 1965 graduate of the Architectural Association, Nicholas Grimshaw was born in 1939 in London. He created his present firm, Nicholas Grimshaw and Partners Ltd, in 1980. His numerous factory structures include those built for Herman Miller in Bath (1976), BMW at Bracknell (1980), the furniture maker Vitra at Weil am Rhein, Germany

Nicholas Grimshaw, geboren 1939 in London, schloß 1965 sein Studium an der Architectural Association in London ab. 1980 gründete er sein Büro Nicholas Grimshaw and Partners Ltd. Zu seinen zahlreichen Werken gehören Industriebauten für die Firmen Herman Miller in Bath, England (1976), BMW in Bracknell (1980) und Vitra in

Diplômé en 1965 de l'Architectural Association, Nicholas Grimshaw est né en 1939 à Londres. Il crée son agence actuelle, Nicholas Grimshaw and Partners Ltd., en 1980. Il conçoit de nombreuses usines dont celle de Herman Miller à Bath (1976), BMW à Bracknell (1980), Vitra à Weil am Rhein, Allemagne (1981) ou l'imprimerie du Financial

ONE OF THE OUTSTANDING FIGURES OF BRITISH ARCHITECTURE, NICHOLAS GRIMSHAW WAS RESPONSIBLE FOR THE WATERLOO INTERNATIONAL TERMINAL IN LONDON FOR THE EUROSTAR TRAINS.

NICHOLAS GRIMSHAW, EINER DER FÜHRENDEN BRITISCHEN ARCHITEKTEN, ENTWARF DEN INTERNATIONAL TERMINAL FÜR DIE EUROSTARZÜGE IM LONDONER BAHNHOF WATERLOO.

L'UNE DES PLUS REMARQUABLES PERSONNALITÉS DE L'ARCHITECTURE BRITANNIQUE, NICHOLAS GRIMSHAW EST L'AUTEUR DU TERMINAL INTERNATIONAL DU TRAIN EUROSTAR À WATERLOO STATION.

NICHOLAS GRIMSHAW & PARTNERS LTD
1 CONWAY STREET
FITZROY SQUARE
LONDON W1P 6LR
ENGLAND

TEL: + 44 20 7 631 0869
FAX: + 44 20 7 636 4866
E-MAIL: npg@easynet.co.uk

(1981), and the Financial Times, London (1988). He also built houses associated with the Sainsbury Supermarket Development in Camden Town, London (1989), and the British Pavilion at the Expo '92 in Seville. One of his most visible works is the Waterloo International Terminal, London (1988-93).

Weil am Rhein (1981), ferner das Gebäude der »Financial Times« in London (1988), Bauten für die Sainsbury Supermarket Development in Camden Town, London (1989) und der Britische Pavillon auf der Expo '92 in Sevilla. Eines seiner spektakulärsten Bauwerke ist der Waterloo International Terminal in London (1988-93).

Times à Londres en 1988. Il construit également des maisons dans le cadre du Sainsbury Supermarket Development à Camden Town, Londres (1989), ainsi que le pavillon britannique de l'Expo '92 à Séville. L'une de ses œuvres les plus connues est le terminal international de la gare de Waterloo, Londres (1988-93).

NICHOLAS GRIMSHAW
THE EDEN PROJECT
ST. AUSTELL, CORNWALL, ENGLAND, 1996-2001

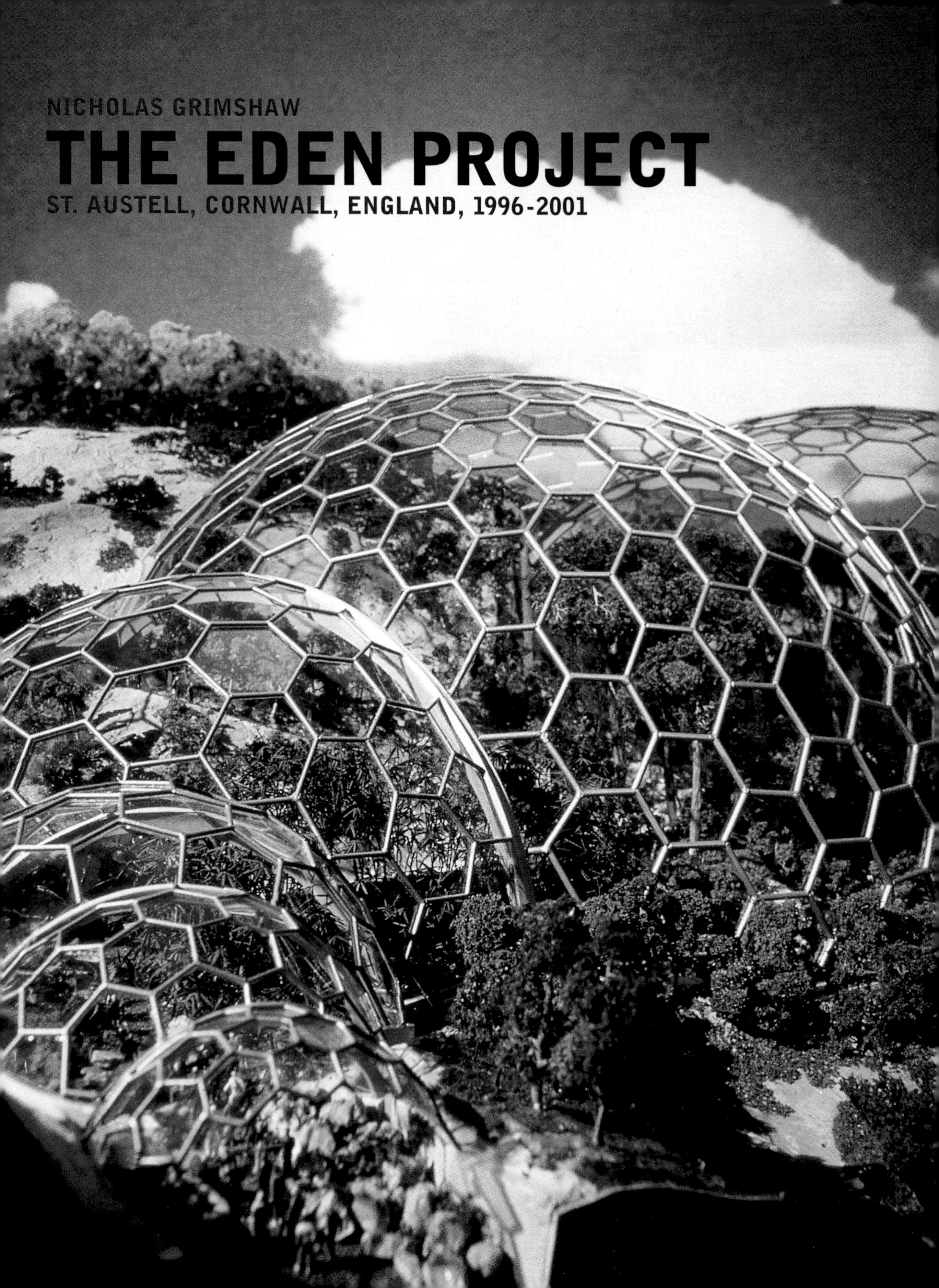

COMPLETION / FERTIGSTELLUNG / FIN
DE LA CONSTRUCTION: 4/2000 (PHASE 1)-4/2001
CLIENT / BAUHERR: EDEN PROJECT, LTD
FLOOR AREA / NUTZFLÄCHE / SURFACE UTILE:
23 000 M²
COSTS / KOSTEN / COÛTS: £53 000 000
FUNCTION / FUNKTION / FONCTION: BOTANICAL
INSTITUTE FOR EDUCATION, RESEARCH AND
PUBLIC ATTRACTION

THE PRESENCE OF NATURE IN A CONTROLLED, ENCLOSED ENVIRONMENT IS REMINISCENT OF SCIENCE FICTION ARCHITECTURE.

DIE PRÄSENZ DER NATUR IN EINEM GESCHLOS-SENEN GEBÄUDE ERINNERT AN SCIENCE-FICTION-ARCHITEKTUR.

LA PRÉSENCE DE LA NATURE DANS UN ENVIRONNEMENT CLOS ÉVOQUE PRESQUE UNE ARCHITECTURE DE SCIENCE-FICTION.

This very unusual project is intended as a "showcase for global biodiversity and human dependence upon plants." It will be made up of 23,000 m² of "linked, climate-controlled transparent capsules (biomes) set in a design landscape." The budget for this project, which makes use of the same consultants who worked on Grimshaw's very successful Waterloo International Terminal, is £53 million. Although its objectives might be considered as more far-reaching, it calls to mind the Yamanashi Museum of Fruit designed by Itsuko Hasegawa in Japan, which is also made up of a series of greenhouse structures. The domes in St. Austell are to be based on lightweight structures with the highest possible volume in relation to their surface. The cladding is made up of "optically clear air inflated foil (ETFE) pillows." The whole will "give the impression of a biomorphic organism." Other buildings will be added to the complex, such as a visitor center utilizing "earth construction techniques."

Dieses ungewöhnliche Projekt soll ein »Schaukasten für die globale Bio-Vielfalt und die Abhängigkeit des Menschen von Pflanzen« sein. Bestehen wird es aus »miteinander verbundenen, klimatisierten, transparenten Kapseln (Biomen) in einer gestalteten Landschaft« auf einer Fläche von 23 000 m². Das Budget für das Projekt, an dem dieselben Berater wie an Grimshaws höchst erfolgreichem Waterloo International Terminal beteiligt sind, beträgt 53 Millionen £. Auch wenn es sich ambitioniertere Ziele setzt, erinnert es an das von Itsuko Hasegawa gestaltete Obstmuseum in Yamanashi, Japan. Die Kuppeln in St. Austell sollen Leichtbaukonstruktionen mit höchstmöglichem Volumen im Verhältnis zur Oberfläche sein. Die Verkleidung besteht aus »optisch klaren, Luftkissen aus ETFE-Folie«, und der gesamte Komplex wird »den Eindruck eines biomorphen Organismus« vermitteln. Weitere Gebäude werden hinzukommen, so etwa ein Besucherzentrum, das in »Erdbautechnik« errichtet werden soll.

Ce très curieux projet se veut «une vitrine de la biodiversité globale et de la dépendance humaine des plantes». Il sera constitué de 23 000 m² de «capsules transparentes en réseau activées par les changements climatiques (biomes) intégrées en un paysage aménagé». Le budget de ce projet, qui fait appel aux mêmes consultants que ceux du remarquable terminal international de Waterloo Station, s'élève à £53 millions. Bien que ses objectifs semblent plus ambitieux, il ne va pas sans rappeler le Musée du fruit Yamanashi (Japon), conçu par Itsuko Hasegawa, qui se compose également d'une série de serres. Les dômes de St. Austell feront appel à des structures légères pour offrir le plus grand volume possible par rapport à leur surface. Le parement est en «coussins gonflés en feuilles de plastique (ETFE) optiquement clair». L'ensemble donnera l'impression d'un «organisme biomorphe». D'autres bâtiments complèteront l'ensemble, dont un centre d'accueil des visiteurs qui fera appel à des «techniques de construction en terre».

THE INTERNATIONAL INTEREST IN A RETURN
TO MINIMALISM IN CONTEMPORARY ARCHITEC-
TURE IS ABLY REPRESENTED BY THE PROJECT
OF GROSE BRADLEY PUBLISHED HERE.

GROSE BRADLEY

James Grose was born in 1954 in Brisbane. He is a Chartered Architect in Queensland and New South Wales. He was Director of Grose Bradley PL from 1988 to 1998, and is currently a Principal of Bligh Voller Nield. His Australian work includes numerous private houses such as the McMullen House (Toowoon Bay, 1989), the A3 House (Sydney, 1991), the Myer House (Rocky Point, 1992), the

James Grose, geboren 1954 in Brisbane, ist niedergelassener Architekt in Queensland und Neusüdwales. Von 1988 bis 1998 leitete er das Büro Grose Bradley PL, gegenwärtig ist er Chef der Firma Bligh Voller Nield. Unter seinen Bauten in Australien sind zahlreiche Wohnhäuser, so das House McMullen in Toowoon Bay (1989), das A3 House in Sydney (1991), House Myer in Rocky

James Grose, né en 1954 à Brisbane, est architecte diplômé du Queensland et de la Nouvelle-Galles du Sud (New South Wales). Il a dirigé Grose Bradley PL de 1988 à 1998, et est actuellement l'un des associés de l'agence Bligh Voller Nield. Il a construit de nombreuses maisons privées en Australie dont la McMullen House (Toowoon Bay, 1989), la A3 House (Sydney, 1991), la Myer House (Rocky

DAS HIER VORGESTELLTE PROJEKT VON GROSE
BRADLEY IST AUSDRUCK DES INTERNATIONA-
LEN INTERESSES AN DER RÜCKKEHR ZUM
MINIMALISMUS IN DER ZEITGENÖSSISCHEN
ARCHITEKTUR.

L'INTÉRÉT PORTÉ DANS LE MONDE AU RETOUR
DU MINIMALISME EN ARCHITECTURE S'ILLUS-
TRE EN PARTICULIER DANS LE PROJET DE
GROSE BRADLEY PRÉSENTÉ ICI.

JAMES GROSE
LEVEL 2
189 KENT STREET
SYDNEY 2000 NSW
AUSTRALIA

TEL: + 61 2 9252 1222
FAX: + 61 2 9252 1776
E-MAIL: sydney@bvn.com.au

Granger House (Oxford Falls, 1996), and the Steel House (Mooball, 1997), for which he received a 1998 Award for Outstanding Architecture. He is working on facility buildings for the Sydney 2000 Olympic Games. A monograph on the work of Grose Bradley was published in 1998 by L'Arcaedizioni, Milan, under the title *The Poetics of Materiality*.

Point (1992), Granger House in Oxford Falls (1996) und das Steel House in Mooball (1997), für das er 1998 den Award for Outstanding Architecture er-hielt. Gegenwärtig plant Grose Sportstätten für die Olympischen Spiele 2000 in Sydney. 1998 erschien unter dem Titel »The Poetics of Materiality« eine Monographie über Grose Bradley im Mailänder Verlag L'Arcaedizioni.

Point, 1992), la Granger House (Oxford Falls, 1996) et la Steel House (Mooball, 1997), pour la-quelle il a reçu un Award for Outstanding Archi-tecture en 1998. Il travaille actuellement à des bâ-timents prévus pour les Jeux Olympiques de Sydney en l'an 2000. Une monographie sur son œuvre a été publiée en 1998 par L'Arcaedizioni, Milan, sous le titre « La poétique de la matérialité ».

GROSE BRADLEY
STEEL HOUSE
MOOBALL, NEW SOUTH WALES, AUSTRALIA, 1996-97

This minimalist design stands out clearly from its spectacular natural setting. Facing directly toward the east, it is set on a ridge with a 50 km view toward Byron Bay, the point farthest to the east in Australia, and also up the Gold Coast, to the south of Brisbane. Set on a platform, the house features retractable blinds for protection against the rising sun. Clad largely in glass in order to permit the owner to fully enjoy the view, the house sits on a platform, highlighting the architects' desire not to

Sein minimalistischer Entwurf hebt das Haus deutlich von der spektakulären natürlichen Umgebung ab. Nach Osten ausgerichtet, liegt es auf einem Bergrücken mit 50 km weit reichender Aussicht zur Byron Bay, dem östlichsten Punkt Australiens, und zur Gold Coast im Süden von Brisbane. Das auf eine Plattform gestellte Haus ist mit einziehbaren Sonnenblenden ausgestattet und überwiegend mit Glas verkleidet, um den ungehinderten Genuß des Ausblicks zu ermöglichen. Das Steel House, das wie

Cette maison minimaliste se détache avec vigueur de son spectaculaire cadre naturel. Orientée à l'est, au sommet d'une crête, sa vue porte à 50 km dans la direction de Byron Bay, le point le plus oriental de l'Australie, et jusqu'à la Gold Coast au sud de Brisbane. Elle repose sur une plate-forme, créée par l'architecte pour ne pas porter atteinte à l'environnement. Ses volets rétractables la protégent du soleil levant. Les vastes baies vitrées de sa façade permettent de pleinement admirer la vue. Comme

disturb the natural environment. Sitting above the ground, like a temporary dwelling, the Steel House could quite easily be removed without leaving any trace of its existence. This impermanent appearance is an intentional objective of the architects. The design of the house has also been related to the horizontality and the openness of the Australian landscape.

eine Behelfskonstruktion vom Boden abgehoben ist, könnte leicht entfernt werden, ohne eine Spur zu hinterlassen. Ein solches, nicht auf Dauer angelegtes Erscheinungsbild war das erklärte Ziel der Architekten. Die Gestaltung lehnt sich außerdem an die Horizontalität und Offenheit der australischen Landschaft an.

un campement temporaire, elle pourrait être déplacée sans laisser la moindre trace de son passage. Ce caractère «éphémère» répond à une des intentions de Grose Bradley, qui s'est également inspiré de l'horizontalité et de l'ouverture du paysage australien.

CLIENT / BAUHERR: WITHHELD / UNGENANNT /
NON COMMUNIQUÉ
FLOOR AREA / NUTZFLÄCHE / SURFACE UTILE:
200 M²
COSTS / KOSTEN / COÛTS: A$ 150 000

**BOTH IN ITS RADICALLY SIMPLE PLAN, AND
IN ITS DESIRE TO LEAVE THE SITE INTACT,
THIS HOUSE IS CLOSELY RELATED TO EARLY
MODERNIST DESIGNS.**

MIT SEINEM RADIKAL EINFACHEN GRUNDRISS
UND DEM BEMÜHEN, UMGEBUNG UND AUS-
SICHT NICHT ZU BEEINTRÄCHTIGEN, IST DAS
HAUS BAUTEN DER FRÜHEN MODERNE
VERWANDT.

PAR LA SIMPLICITÉ DE SON PLAN ET LA VOLON-
TÉ DE L'ARCHITECTE DE NE PAS PORTER AT-
TEINTE AU SITE, CETTE MAISON SE RAPPROCHE
DES PREMIERS PROJETS DES MODERNISTES.

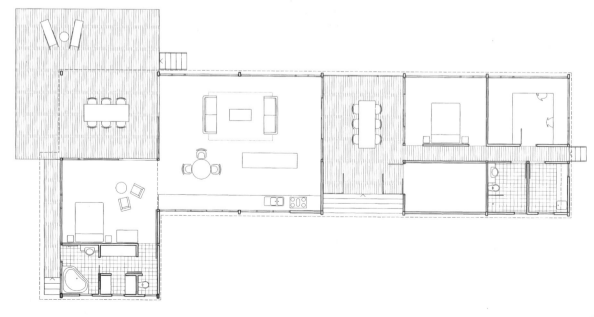

ZAHA HADID

Zaha M Hadid, born in Baghdad 1950, studied architecture at the Architectural Association in London beginning in 1972, and was awarded the Diploma Prize in 1977. She then became a partner of Rem Koolhaas in the Office for Metropolitan Architecture and taught at the AA, at Harvard, the University of Chicago, in Hamburg and at Columbia University in New York. Well-known for her paintings and drawings she has had a substantial influ-

Zaha M Hadid, 1950 in Bagdad geboren, studierte ab 1972 an der Architectural Association (AA) in London und erhielt 1977 den Diploma Prize. Danach wurde sie Partnerin von Rem Koolhaas im Office for Metropolitan Architecture und lehrte an der AA und in Harvard, der University of Chicago, in Hamburg und an der Columbia University. Hadid ist durch ihre Gemälde und Zeichnungen bekannt geworden. Obwohl nur wenige ihrer Entwürfe reali-

Zaha M Hadid, née à Bagdad en 1950, étudie à l'Architectural Association (AA) de Londres en 1972 dont elle reçoit le Diploma Prize en 1977. Elle s'associe ensuite avec Rem Koolhaas dans l'Office for Metropolitan Architecture (OMA), et enseigne à l'AA, à Harvard, à l'Université de Chicago, à Hambourg et Columbia University. Connue pour ses peintures et ses dessins, elle exerce une réelle influence, bien qu'elle ait relativement peu

ZAHA HADID, DIE WOHL BEKANNTESTE
ARCHITEKTIN DER WELT, UNTERNIMMT DEN
ÜBERGANG ZUR PRAXIS DES BAUENS MIT DER
GLEICHEN ENERGIE UND INNOVATIVEN KRAFT,
DIE IHRE ENTWÜRFE CHARAKTERISIEREN.

PERHAPS THE BEST-KNOWN WOMAN ARCHITECT
IN THE WORLD, ZAHA HADID IS MAKING THE
TRANSITION TO BUILT WORK WITH ALL OF THE
ENERGY AND INNOVATION THAT CHARACTERIZE
HER DRAWINGS.

SANS DOUTE LA FEMME ARCHITECTE LA PLUS
CÉLÈBRE DU MONDE, ZAHA HADID A AUJOUR-
D'HUI ATTEINT LE POINT OÙ ELLE VA TRADUIRE
SOUS FORME CONSTRUITE L'ÉNERGIE ET LA
CRÉATIVITÉ QUI CARACTÉRISENT SES DESSINS
D'ARCHITECTURE.

ZAHA M HADID
STUDIO9
10 BOWLING GREEN LANE
LONDON EC1R 0BD
ENGLAND

TEL: + 44 20 7 253 5147
FAX: + 44 20 7 251 8322
E-MAIL: zaha@hadid.u-net.com

ence, despite having built relatively few buildings. She has completed the Vitra Fire Station (Weil am Rhein, Germany, 1990-94) and exhibition designs such as that for "The Great Utopia", Solomon R. Guggenheim Museum (New York, 1992). Significant competition entries include her design for the Cardiff Bay Opera House (Wales, 1994-96), the Habitable Bridge (London, 1996), and the Luxembourg Philharmonic Hall (1997).

siert wurden, so das Vitra-Feuerwehrhaus in Weil am Rhein (1990-94), hat sie großen Einfluß ausgeübt. 1992 entwarf sie das Ausstellungsdesign »The Great Utopia« im New Yorker Guggenheim Museum. Zu ihren Wettbewerbsbeiträgen gehören Entwürfe für das Cardiff Bay Opera House (Wales, 1994-96), für die Habitable Bridge in London (1996) und die Luxemburger Philharmonie (1997).

construit. Elle a cependant réalisé le poste des pompiers de l'usine Vitra (Weil am Rhein, Allemagne, 1990-94), et a conçu des expositions comme «The Great Utopia» du Solomon R. Guggenheim Museum (New York, 1992). Parmi ses participation à des concours: le projet du Cardiff Bay Opera House (Pays de Galles, 1994-96), le Pont habitable (Londres, 1996) ou la Salle philarmonique de Luxembourg (1997).

ZAHA HADID
CONTEMPORARY ARTS CENTER
CINCINNATI, OHIO, UNITED STATES, 1998-2001

CLIENT / BAUHERR: CONTEMPORARY AR⁻
CENTER, CINCINNATI
FLOOR AREA / NUTZFLÄCHE / SURFACE U⁻
8000 M²
COSTS / KOSTEN / COÛTS: US$ 27 500 000

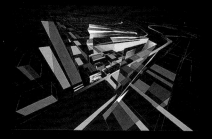

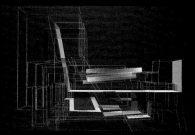

Despite its relatively provincial reputation.
Cincinnati boasts recent buildings by Michael
Graves, Cesar Pelli, Harry Cobb (Pei Cobb Freed),
Peter Eisenman, and Frank O Gehry Thus the
choice of Zaha Hadid for the new 8,000 m²
Contemporary Arts Center (CAC) was not a total
surprise. Hadid was chosen over 96 other architects
n a worldwide search to design the $27,5 million
structure. Conceived like a German kunsthalle.
without any permanent collection, the new building
will feature gallery spaces that "appear to be
carved from a single block," hovering over the
obby. According to the office of Zaha Hadid, "the
building's exterior presents an animated skin a
collage of transparent elements that weave into the
galleries' mass and reveal a texture of activity and
art in constant flux, thus enlivening the building as
a whole." Ben Nicholson, a Chicago architect who
was a member of the selection committee, calls

Trotz seines eher provinziellen Rufs kann sich
Cincinnati neuer Bauten von Michael Graves, Cesar
Pelli, Harry Cobb, Peter Eisenman und Frank O
Gehry rühmen So kam die Vergabe des Auftrags
für das neue, 8.000 m² umfassende Contemporary
Arts Center an Zaha Hadid nicht völlig überra
schend Sie wurde nach einer Ausschreibung unter
96 Mitbewerbern ausgewählt, um das 27,5 Mio $
Projekt zu planen Der wie eine deutsche Kunsthalle
ohne ständige Sammlung konzipierte Neubau wird
Galerieraume enthalten, die, »wie aus einem Block
geschnitten«, über der Eingangshalle schweben
Laut Hadids Büro »gleicht das Außere des Gebau
des einer lebendigen Haut einer Collage aus
transparenten Elementen, die in die Masse des
Museums eingewoben sind und eine Textur aus
Aktivität und Kunst in bestandigem Wechsel bilden,
wodurch das Gebaude als Ganzes belebt wird «
Ben Nicholson, ein Architekt aus Chicago, nennt

Malgré sa reputation de provincialisme,
n'a pas hesite à faire appel au cours des
precedents a Michael Graves, Cesar Pe
Cobb, Peter Eisenman et Frank Gehry. L
Zaha Hadid pour son nouveau Contempo
Center de 8 000 m² n'est donc pas une s
totale. L'architecte a été choisie parmi 9
praticiens du monde entier, pour édifier
de $ 27,5 millions A l'image d'une Kuns
l'allemande, c'est-à-dire sans collection
le nouveau bâtiment offrira des galeries
bleront sculptées dans un seul bloc », sus
au dessus du hall. Selon l'agence de Had
térieur du bâtiment sera recouvert d'une
peau animée – collage d'éléments transp
s'insinueront dans les galeries – qui révé
et la matière des activités et des exposit
mant du coup l'ensemble du bâtiment.»
Nicholson, architecte de Chicago, a qua

HIROSHI HARA

UNLIKE OTHER JAPANESE ARCHITECTS OF HIS GENERATION LIKE ISOZAKI AND ANDO, HARA IS FASCINATED BY VISIONS OF THE FUTURE THAT INCLUDE INTERCONNECTED WEBS OF SKYSCRAPERS FOR EXAMPLE.

IM GEGENSATZ ZU ANDEREN JAPANISCHEN ARCHITEKTEN SEINER GENERATION WIE ISOZAKI UND ANDO IST HARA FASZINIERT VON ZUKUNFTSVISIONEN, ZU DENEN ETWA

Born in Kawasaki, Japan, in 1936, Hiroshi Hara received his BA from the University of Tokyo (1959), his MA in 1961, and his PhD from the same institution in 1964, before becoming an associate professor in the University's Faculty of Architecture. Though his first work dates from the early 1960s, he began his collaboration with Atelier Φ in 1970. Notable structures include numerous private houses, such as his own residence, Hara House

Hiroshi Hara, geboren 1936 in Kawasaki, erwarb 1959 den B.A., 1961 den M.A. und 1964 den Doktorgrad an der Universität Tokio und wurde zum außerordentlichen Professor an der dortigen Architekturfakultät berufen. Obwohl sein erster Bau aus den frühen 60er Jahren datiert, begann seine Zusammenarbeit mit Atelier Φ erst 1970. Zu Haras Bauten zählen zahlreiche Wohnhäuser, so sein eigenes Haus, Haus Hara in Machida, Tokio

Né à Kawasaki, Japon, en 1936, Hiroshi Hara est B.A. de l'Université de Tokyo (1959), M.A. en 1961 et Ph.D de la même institution en 1964, avant de devenir professeur associé de sa faculté d'architecture. Si ses premières réalisations remontent au début des années 1960, il débute sa collaboration avec l'Atelier Φ en 1970. Il réalise en particulier de nombreuses résidences privées, dont la sienne, à Machida (Tokyo, 1973-74). Il participe en

MITEINANDER VERBUNDENE WOLKENKRATZER
GEHÖREN.

A LA DIFFÉRENCE D'AUTRES ARCHITECTES
JAPONAIS DE SA GÉNÉRATION, COMME ISOZAKI
ET ANDO, HARA EST FASCINÉ PAR DES VISIONS
FUTURISTES, QU'ILLUSTRENT PAR EXEMPLE,
SES RÉSEAUX DE TOURS INTERCONNECTÉES.

HIROSHI HARA + ATELIER Φ
10-3, HACHIYAMA-CHO,
SHIBUYA-KU, TOKYO 150-0035
JAPAN

TEL: + 81 3 3464 8670
FAX: + 81 3 3464 8612
E-MAIL: atelier-phi@mvg.biglobe.ne.jp

(Machida, Tokyo, 1973-74). He participated in the 1982 International Competition for the Parc de la Villette, Paris, built the Yamato International Building (Ota-ku, Tokyo, 1985-86), the Ida City Museum (Nagano, 1986-88), and the Sotetsu Culture Center (Yokohama, Kanagawa, 1988-90). His recent work includes the Umeda Sky Building, Kita-ku, Osaka (1988-93), and the JR Kyoto Railway Station (Sakyo-ku, Kyoto, 1991-97).

(1973-74). 1982 nahm Hara am internationalen Wettbewerb für den Parc de la Villette in Paris teil. Unter seinen Bauten sind das Yamato International Building (Ota-ku, Tokio, 1985-86), das Ida City Museum (Nagano, 1986-88), das Sotetsu-Kulturzentrum (Yokohama, Kanagawa, 1988-90) und das Umeda Sky Building (Kita-ku, Osaka, 1988-93).

1982 au concours international pour le Parc de la Villette à Paris, construit le Yamato International Building (Ota-ku, Tokyo, 1985-86), l'Ida City Museum (Nagano, 1986-88) et le Centre culturel Sotetsu (Yokohama, Kanagawa, 1988-90). Il a récemment achevé l'Umeda Sky Building (Kita-ku, Osaka, 1988-93) et la gare JR de Kyoto (Sakyo-ku, Kyoto, 1991-97), toutes au Japon.

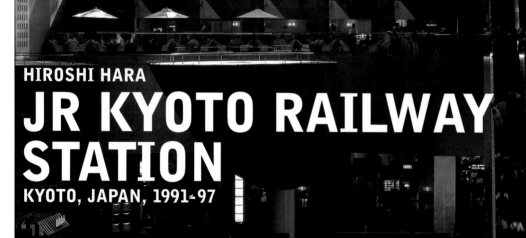

HIROSHI HARA

JR KYOTO RAILWAY STATION

KYOTO, JAPAN, 1991-97

THE MASSIVE FORM OF THE KYOTO JR STATION IS PIERCED BY AN ENORMOUS INTERIOR/EXTERIOR ATRIUM.

DIE MASSIVE FORM DES BAHNHOFS IN KIOTO WIRD VOM GEWALTIGEN INNEN- UND AUSSEN-ATRIUM AUFGELOCKERT.

LA FORME MASSIVE DE LA GARE DE KYOTO EST TRAVERSÉE PAR UN ÉNORME ATRIUM INTÉRIEUR/EXTÉRIEUR.

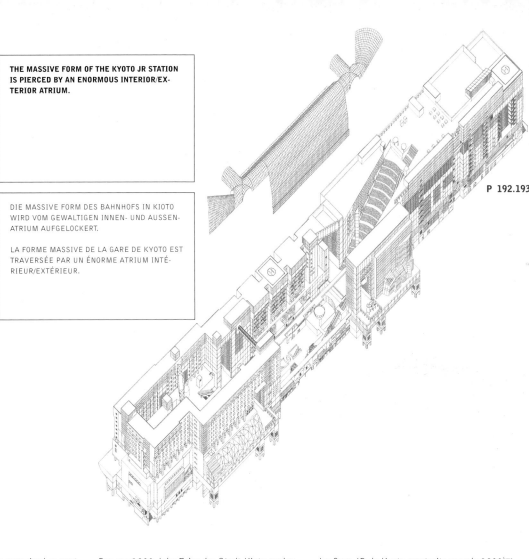

The JR Kyoto Railway Station, conceived as part of the 1200th anniversary of the city, assumes the shape of a massive wall, partly because the 3.8 hectare site is unusually narrow. Consisting of three basements, 16 stories and a one-story penthouse, this complex is no less than 470 m long and 59.5 m high, for a total floor area of 237,689 m². As Hiroshi Hara points out, "the station itself occupies only one tenth of the total area, the rest being occupied by hotels, stores and offices. It is designed so that the persons visiting the train station will not necessarily be aware of the other activities, or of the overall size of the building." Since its opening, the station has been the gathering place for thousands of Kyoto residents, who come for the stores, restaurants, and concerts in the huge open area in the middle of the building. Hara says, "in the Kyoto Station, the site itself and the nature of the project assume the existence of multiple levels of communication. The subway passes below, and there is the train above. This type of complexity naturally has an effect on the building since elevators cannot be placed just anywhere, for example."

Der zur 1200-Jahr-Feier der Stadt Kioto geplante Bahnhof der Japan Railway (JR) hat die Form einer massiven Mauer – nicht zuletzt aufgrund des ungewöhnlich schmalen Grundstücks von 3,8 ha. Der aus drei Untergeschossen, 16 Freigeschossen und einem Penthouse bestehende Komplex ist nicht weniger als 470 m lang und 59,5 m hoch bei einer Gesamtnutzfläche von 237 689 m². Hara erläutert dazu: »Der Bahnhof selbst nimmt nur ein Zehntel der Gesamtfläche ein, der Rest sind Hotels, Läden und Büros. Er ist so geplant, daß Reisende die anderen Bereiche und Aktivitäten oder die Ausmaße des Gebäudes nicht unbedingt wahrnehmen.« Seit seiner Eröffnung ist der Bahnhof Treffpunkt für die Bewohner Kiotos geworden, welche die Läden, Restaurants und Konzerte im riesigen Freibereich in der Mitte des Gebäudes besuchen. Laut Hara »deuten Gelände und Form der Anlage die verschiedenen Kommunikationsebenen an. Die U-Bahn führt unten hindurch, darüber verkehren Eisenbahnzüge. Diese Komplexität hat natürlich Auswirkungen auf das Gebäude, da etwa Fahrstühle nicht beliebig plaziert werden können.«

La Gare JR de Kyoto construite pour le 1200ème anniversaire de la ville a pris la forme d'un mur massif, pour répondre en partie à l'extrême étroitesse de son terrain de 3,8 hectares. Composée de trois niveaux de sous-sols, de 16 étages et d'une penthouse, elle ne mesure pas moins de 470 m de long pour 59,5 m de haut, et une surface utile de 237 689 m². Comme le fait remarquer l'architecte, «la gare en elle-même n'occupe qu'un dixième de la surface totale, le reste étant occupé par des hôtels, des magasins et des bureaux. Les voyageurs ne se rendront pas compte des autres activités, ou des dimensions du bâtiment.» Depuis son inauguration, la gare est le point de rencontre de milliers d'habitants de Kyoto, qui aiment y venir pour leurs courses, les restaurants et les concerts donnés dans l'énorme espace ouvert en partie centrale. Selon Hara, «le site lui-même et la nature du projet entraînent l'existence de multiples niveaux de communication. Le métro passe sous le bâtiment et le train au-dessus. Ce type de complexité exerce un effet sur la conception; par exemple, les ascenseurs ne pouvaient pas être implantés n'importe où.»

PLANNING / PLANUNG: 1991-94
COMPLETION / FERTIGSTELLUNG / FIN DE LA
CONSTRUCTION: 7/97
CLIENT / BAUHERR: WEST JAPAN RAILWAY
COMPANY / KYOTO STATION BUILDING
DEVELOPMENT CO, LTD
FLOOR AREA / NUTZFLÄCHE / SURFACE UTILE:
237 689 M²
COSTS / KOSTEN / COÛTS: 95 000 000 000 ¥

**ALTHOUGH CRITICS CLAIM THE ARCHITECT
DIVIDED THE CITY IN TWO, IT WAS THE RAILWAY
COMPANY THAT INSISTED ON ITS ELONGATED
FORM AND MASS.**

DIE GESTRECKTE FORM DES GEBÄUDES GEHT
AUF FORDERUNGEN DER EISENBAHNGESELL-
SCHAFT ZURÜCK, TRUG HARA ABER DIE KRITIK
EIN, DER BAU TEILE DIE STADT.

MÊME SI DES CRITIQUES REPROCHENT À HARA
D'AVOIR DIVISÉ LA VILLE EN DEUX, C'EST LA
COMPAGNIE FERROVIAIRE JR QUI A VOULU
CETTE FORME MASSIVE ET ALLONGÉE.

THE STATION IS LOCATED IN THE MODERN
AREA OF KYOTO, RELATIVELY FAR FROM THE
HISTORIC TEMPLES.

DER BAHNHOF LIEGT IM NEUEN TEIL KIOTOS,
RELATIV WEIT VON DEN ALTEN TEMPELN
ENTFERNT.

LA GARE EST SITUÉE DANS LA PARTIE MO-
DERNE DE KYOTO, ASSEZ LOIN DES TEMPLES
HISTORIQUES.

HIROSHI HARA
MIYAGI PREFECTURAL LIBRARY
SENDAI, MIYAGI, JAPAN, 1993-98

PLANNING / PLANUNG: 1993-95
CONSTRUCTION / BAU: 1995-3/98
CLIENT / BAUHERR: PREFECTURE OF MIYAGI
FLOOR AREA / NUTZFLÄCHE / SURFACE
UTILE: 18 227 M²
COSTS / KOSTEN / COÛTS: 10 060 000 000 ¥

Located toward the northeast of the island of Honshu in a suburb of the city of Sendai, this 200 m long structure is set near a university and a research facility. The bridge-like design is partially related to the desire to preserve the wooded natural environment, but the elongated form also brings to mind the horizontal "city" design of the JR Kyoto Railway Station. Hiroshi Hara is clearly interested in "mega-structures" with possible interconnections, as is the case in his recent tower in Osaka. Here,

Die in einem Vorort der Stadt Sendai im Nordosten der Insel Honshu errichtete, 200 m lange Bibliothek liegt nahe der Universität und einem Forschungsinstitut. Ihre Brückenform ist zum Teil auf den Wunsch zurückzuführen, die bewaldete Umgebung zu erhalten; die langgestreckte Gestalt erinnert aber auch an den horizontalen »Stadt«-Entwurf des Bahnhofs in Kioto. Hiroshi Hara setzt sich mit dem Problem auseinander, wie »Megastrukturen« miteinander zu verbinden sind. Dieses

Située au nord-est de l'île de Honshu, dans une banlieue de la ville de Sendai, cette structure de 200 m de long est implantée auprès d'une université et d'un centre de recherches. Sa conception en pont tient en partie au souhait de préserver l'environnement boisé naturel, mais l'allongement de la forme rappelle également la «ville» horizontale de la gare JR de Kyoto. Hiroshi Hara s'intéresse à l'évidence aux méga-structures aux multiples interconnections, comme dans le cas de la tour qu'il vient d'achever à

HARA'S TASTE FOR THE FORMS OF SCIENCE FICTION COMES FORWARD IN THIS LONG, ROUNDED SPACECRAFT OF A LIBRARY.

HARAS VORLIEBE FÜR SCIENCE-FICTION-FORMEN ZEIGT SICH IN DIESEM LANGEN, BRÜCKENÄHNLICHEN BAU, DER EINE BIBLIOTHEK BEHERBERGT.

LE GOÛT DE HARA POUR LES FORMES DE SCIENCE-FICTION SE RETROUVE DANS CETTE BIBLIOTHÈQUE EN FORME DE VAISSEAU SPATIAL.

spaces have been made on the first and second floors in anticipation of the modification of reading habits and the development of the computer-oriented environment. An open-stack reading room conceived like an extendable "mall" is located on the third floor. The horizontal, "aerodynamic" form of the structure certainly gives it a futuristic appearance, which is a hallmark of the style of Hara.

Bemühen prägt auch sein jüngstes Hochhaus in Osaka. In der Bibliothek von Sendai antizipieren Räume im ersten und zweiten Obergeschoß die veränderten künftigen Lesegewohnheiten und eine von Computern geprägte Umgebung. Das dritte Obergeschoß beherbergt einen Lesesaal mit Freihandbestand in Form einer erweiterbaren »Mall«. Die horizontale, »aerodynamische« Form des Bauwerks gibt ihm zweifellos ein futuristisches Gepräge, das charakteristisch für Haras Stil ist.

Osaka. Dans cette bibliothèque, des espaces ont été réservés au premier et second niveau pour anticiper les modifications attendues des habitudes de lecture et le développement d'un environnement informatisé. Une salle de lecture de plan ouvert, à la façon d'un «mail» extensible, se trouve au troisième niveau. La forme aérodynamique de la structure lui donne une apparence futuriste, qui est par ailleurs la marque du style de Hara.

THE ROUNDED EXTERIOR SHAPES OF THE BUILDING ARE CARRIED THROUGH INTO LARGE INTERIOR VOLUMES.

DIE GERUNDETEN AUSSENFORMEN DES GE-
BÄUDES SETZEN SICH IN DEN WEITLÄUFIGEN
INNENBEREICHEN FORT.

LES FORMES EXTÉRIEURES ARRONDIES SE
RÉPERCUTENT DANS LES VASTES VOLUMES
INTÉRIEURS.

ITSUKO HASEGAWA

Itsuko Hasegawa was born in Shizuoka Prefecture in 1941. She graduated from Kanto Gakuin University in Yokohama in 1964. After working in the atelier of Kiyonori Kikutake (1964-69), she was a research student in the Department of Architecture of the Tokyo Institute of Technology. She was subsequently an assistant of Kazuo Shinohara in the same school (1971-78) before creating Itsuko Hasegawa Atelier (1979) in Tokyo. Her built work includes houses in Nerima (1986), Kumamoto

Itsuko Hasegawa, 1941 in der Präfektur Shizuoka geboren, beendete 1964 ihr Studium an der Universität Kanto Gakuin in Yokohama. Nach fünfjähriger Tätigkeit im Atelier von Kiyonori Kikutake (1964-69) wurde sie Mitarbeiterin des Tokyo Institute of Technology, wo sie Assistentin von Kazuo Shinohara war (1971-78). 1979 gründete sie ihr eigenes Büro in Tokio. Zu ihren wichtigen Bauten gehören Privathäuser in Nerima (1986), Kumamoto (1986) und Higashi-Tamagawa (1987). In den

Itsuka Hasegawa est née dans la préfecture de Shizuoka en 1941. Diplômée de l'Université Kanto Gakuin à Yokohama en 1964, elle travaille auprès de Kiyonori Kikutake (1964-69), puis étudie en tant que chercheuse au département d'architecture de l'Institut de Technologie de Tokyo. Elles est ensuite assistante de Kazuo Shinohara dans la même institution (1971-78) avant de créer l'Atelier Itsuko Hasegawa à Tokyo (1979). Parmi ses réalisations: des maisons à Berima (1986), Kumamoto (1986) et

ITSUKO HASEGAWA ATELIER
ARCHITECTURAL LANDSCAPE DESIGN
1-9-7 YUSHIMA BUNKYO-KU
TOKYO 113-0034
JAPAN

TEL: + 81 3 3818 5470
FAX: + 81 3 3818 4381
E-MAIL: iha-sec@mx1.nisiq.net

FROM THE TIME OF HER EARLIEST DESIGNS, ITSUKO HASEGAWA HAS BEEN INTERESTED IN THE IDEA OF RECREATING NATURE IN AN ARTIFICIAL FORM IN HER WORK.

SEIT IHREN ERSTEN ENTWÜRFEN IST ITSUKO HASEGAWA AN EINER KÜNSTLICHEN NEU-ERSCHAFFUNG DER NATUR INTERESSIERT.

DÈS SES PREMIERS PROJETS, ITSUKO HASE-GAWA S'EST INTÉRESSÉE AU CONCEPT DE RECRÉATION ARTIFICIELLE DE LA NATURE.

1986), and Higashi-Tamagawa (1987), all in Japan. In more recent years she has built on a larger scale: Shonandai Cultural Center (Fujisawa, Kanagawa, 1987-90), Oshima-machi Picture Book Museum Imizu, Toyama, 1992-94), and the Sumida Culture Factory (Sumida, Tokyo, 1991-94). In 1995 she completed the University Gymnasium at Hikone, and the Museum of Fruit in Yamanashi. Itsuko Hasegawa was the runner-up in the 1993 competition for the new Cardiff Bay Opera House.

letzten Jahren hat Hasegawa größere Projekte realisiert, so etwa das Kulturzentrum Shonandai (Fujisawa, Kanagawa, 1987-90), das Bilderbuchmuseum Oshima-machi (Imizu, Toyama, 1992-94) und eine Kulturfabrik (Sumida, Tokio, 1991-94). 1995 wurden die Sporthalle der Universität in Hikone und das Obstmuseum in Yamanashi fertiggestellt. 1993 erhielt Itsuko Hasegawas Wettbewerbsentwurf für das neue Cardiff Bay Opera House den zweiten Preis.

Higashi-Tamagawa (1987), toutes au Japon. Récemment, elle a réalisé des projets de plus d'ampleur comme le Centre culturel Shonandai (Fujisawa, Kanagawa, 1987-90), le Musée du livre illustré Oshima-machi (Imizu, Toyama, 1992-94) et la Sumida Culture Factory (Sumida, Tokyo, 1991-94). En 1995, elle a achevé le gymnase de l'Université de Hikone et le Musée du fruit à Yamanashi. Elle a participé au concours pour le Cardiff Bay Opera House.

ITSUKO HASEGAWA

NIIGATA PERFORMING ARTS CENTER

NIIGATA CITY, NIIGATA, JAPAN, 1993-98

CLIENT / BAUHERR: NIIGATA CITY
FLOOR AREA / NUTZFLÄCHE / SURFACE
UTILE: 25 009 M²
COSTS / KOSTEN / COÛTS: 28 500 000 000 ¥

**THE PERFORMING ARTS CENTER IS SET IN AN
ENVIRONMENT DESIGNED BY HASEGAWA.**

DAS PERFORMING ARTS CENTER STEHT IN
EINER VON HASEGAWA GESTALTETEN
LANDSCHAFT.

LE CENTRE DES ARTS DU SPECTACLE EST
INSÉRÉ DANS UN ENVIRONNEMENT CONÇU
PAR L'ARCHITECTE.

City Performing Arts Center
Garden
Building
Park
River

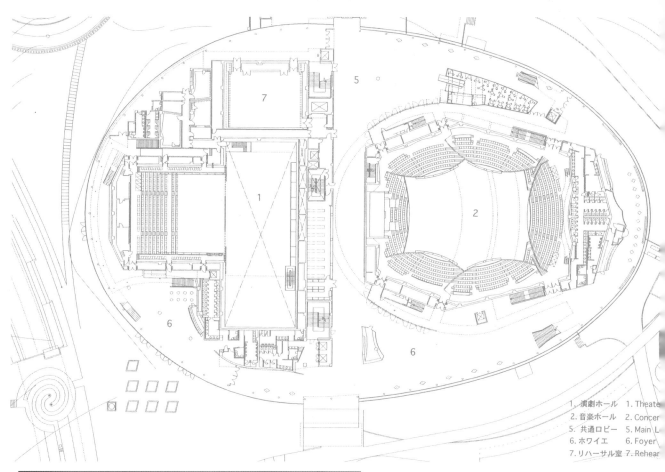

Itsuko Hasegawa won an open competition to build this facility in Niigata, a city of half a million people located on the western coast, near the Sea of Japan. The program called for a 1,900-seat concert hall, a 900-seat theater and a 375-seat Noh Theater, the whole surrounded by an 8 hectare park set on land reclaimed from the Shinano River, which crosses the city. The idea of this park was to create seven man-made islands linked by bridges. As Itsuko Hasegawa says, "the main building is

Itsuko Hasegawa gewann den Wettbewerb um den Bau dieses Kulturzentrums in Niigata. Das Projekt sollte eine Konzerthalle mit 1900, ein Theater mit 900 und ein Noh-Theater mit 375 Sitzen umfassen. Die Anlage steht in einem 8 ha großen Park, der dem Fluß Shinano abgewonnen wurde. Die Idee für diesen Park bestand darin, sieben künstliche, durch Brücken verbundene Inseln anzulegen. Itsuko Hasegawa sagt dazu: »Das Hauptgebäude ist als *man-maku* konzipiert (eine temporäre Wand, die zur

Itsuka Hasegawa a remporté l'appel d'offres sur concours pour cet équipement culturel, commande de Niigata, ville de 500 000 habitants de la côte ouest, en bordure de la mer du Japon. Le programme comportait une salle de concert de 1900 places, un théâtre de 900 places et un théâtre de Nô de 375 places, le tout entouré d'un parc de 8 hectares gagné sur le fleuve Shinano qui traverse la cité. Le concept de ce parc s'appuie sur la création de sept îles artificielles reliées par des ponts. Comme l'ex-

THE BASIC OVAL FORM HOUSES A VARIETY OF
FUNCTIONS INCLUDING A CONCERT HALL AND
TWO THEATERS.

DER BAU MIT OVALEM GRUNDRISS HAT VIELE
UNTERSCHIEDLICH GENUTZTE BEREICHE,
DARUNTER EINE KONZERTHALLE UND ZWEI
THEATER.

LE BÂTIMENT OVALE ABRITE UN CERTAIN
NOMBRE DE FONCTIONS, DONT UNE SALLE DE
CONCERTS ET DEUX SALLES DE SPECTACLE.

nceived as a *manmaku* (a temporary screen set
 at festivals to define spatial limits) – a kind of
ntral open space in the city, not unlike ... what
e Japanese term *harrapa* (empty field). The
anmaku ripples in the wind, allowing petals and
wer scents to float through, and enabling people
tside to know what is happening inside; this is an
teractive, tranquil, and meditative space, designed
r the enjoyment of both the citizens of Niigata
d visitors from around the world."

räumlichen Abgrenzung bei Festen aufgestellt wird)
– als eine Art zentraler Freiraum in der Stadt, ähnlich dem ..., was die Japaner *harrapa* (freies Feld)
nennen. Das *manmaku* schwankt im Wind, läßt
Blütenblätter und -düfte umherschweben, und die
Menschen draußen können wahrnehmen, was im
Innern passiert. Es ist ein interaktiver, ruhiger und
meditativer Raum, der geplant wurde, um die Bürger von Niigata und Besucher aus aller Welt zu
erfreuen.«

plique l'architecte: «Le bâtiment principal est
conçu comme un *manmaku* (écran tendu au cours
de festivités pour définir des limites), sorte d'espace
créé au cœur de la ville, pas très éloigné ... du
concept japonais de *harrapa* (champ vide). Le
manmaku ondule dans le vent ce qui permet aux
spectateurs extérieurs de savoir ce qui se passe
à l'intérieur. C'est un espace interactif, serein et
méditatif, conçu pour le plaisir des habitants de
Niigata et des visiteurs du monde entier.

KNOWN FOR THEIR MINIMALIST RIGOR, THE
SWISS ARCHITECTS HERZOG & DE MEURON ARE
COMPLETING THEIR MOST AMBITIOUS PROJECT,
THE NEW TATE GALLERY OF MODERN ART IN
LONDON.

DIE FÜR IHRE MINIMALISTISCHE STRENGE
BEKANNT GEWORDENEN SCHWEIZER ARCHI-
TEKTEN HERZOG & DE MEURON BAUEN GEGEN-
WÄRTIG IHR EHRGEIZIGSTES PROJEKT: DIE
NEUE TATE GALLERY OF MODERN ART IN
LONDON.

HERZOG & DE MEURON

Jacques Herzog and Pierre de Meuron were both
born in Basel in 1950. They received degrees in
architecture at the ETH in Zurich in 1975, after
studying with Aldo Rossi, and founded their firm
Herzog & de Meuron in Basel in 1978. Their built
work includes the Antipodes I Student Housing at
the Université de Bourgogne, Dijon (1991-92), the
Ricola Europe Factory and Storage Building in
Mulhouse (1993), and the Sammlung Goetz build-

Jacques Herzog und Pierre de Meuron wurden beide 1950 in Basel geboren. Sie studierten an der
ETH in Zürich bei Aldo Rossi, wo sie 1975 ihr Diplom machten. 1978 gründeten sie in Basel Herzog
& de Meuron. Zu ihren Bauten gehören das Studentenwohnheim Antipodes I der Université de
Bourgogne in Dijon (1991-92), das Fabrik- und
Lagergebäude der Firma Ricola in Mülhausen
(1993) und die Galerie der Sammlung Goetz in

Jacques Herzog et Pierre de Meuron sont tous deux
nés à Bâle en 1950. En 1975, ils reçoivent le diplôme d'architecture de l'ETH de Zurich, où ils ont
suivi l'enseignement d'Aldo Rossi, et, en 1978, fon-
dent à Bâle leur agence, Herzog & de Meuron. Ils
réalisent, entre autres, des logements pour étudiant
(Antipodes I, Université de Bourgogne, Dijon, 199
92), l'usine et entrepôt Ricola Europe à Mulhouse
(1993) et la galerie de la Sammlung Goetz

CONNUS POUR LEUR RIGUEUR MINIMALISTE,
LES ARCHITECTES SUISSES HERZOG & DE
MEURON METTENT ACTUELLEMENT À LONDRES
LA DERNIÈRE MAIN À LEUR PLUS AMBITIEUX
PROJET, LA NOUVELLE TATE GALLERY OF
MODERN ART.

HERZOG & DE MEURON ARCHITEKTEN
RHEINSCHANZE 6
4056 BASEL
SWITZERLAND

TEL: + 41 61 385 5757
FAX: + 41 61 385 5758
E-MAIL: hdmarch@access.ch

P 210.211

g (Munich, 1989-92). Most notably they were
hosen early in 1995 to design the new Tate
allery of Modern Art, to be situated in the
ankside Power Station on the Thames, opposite
t Paul's Cathedral (opening June 2000). They
ere also shortlisted in the competition for the new
esign of the Museum of Modern Art in New York
1997).

München (1989-92). 1995 erhielten sie ihren
bedeutendsten Auftrag: die Londoner Tate Gallery
of Modern Art, für die bis zum Jahr 2000 die
Bankside Power Station an der Themse (gegenüber
Saint Paul's Cathedral) umgebaut wird. Beim
Wettbewerb für die Umgestaltung des Museum of
Modern Art in New York (1997) kamen Herzog &
de Meuron in die engere Wahl.

(Munich, 1989-92). Ils sont sélectionnés en 1995
pour concevoir la nouvelle Tate Gallery of Modern
Art installée dans l'ancienne centrale thermique
de Bankside, sur la Tamise, face à la cathédrale
Saint-Paul (ouverture prévue en juin 2000), et font
partie de la sélection finale pour le concours du
remaniement du Museum of Modern Art à New
York (1997).

HERZOG & DE MEURON
STUDIO RÉMY ZAUGG
MULHOUSE, FRANCE, 1995-96

PLANNING / PLANUNG: 1995
CONSTRUCTION / BAU: 1995-96
CLIENT / BAUHERR: RÉMY ZAUGG, BASEL /
MULHOUSE
FLOOR AREA / NUTZFLÄCHE /
SURFACE UTILE: 263 M²
COSTS / KOSTEN / COÛTS: 400 000 SFR

**ASIDE FROM THE CONCRETE OVERHANGS,
THIS ATELIER COULD HARDLY BE SIMPLER.**

VOM AUSKRAGENDEN DACH ABGESEHEN,
KÖNNTE DIESES ATELIER KAUM SCHLICHTER
SEIN.

IL ÉTAIT DIFFICILE D'IMAGINER UNE FORME
PLUS SIMPLE POUR CET ATELIER.

CLOSED ON TWO SIDES, THE ATELIER IS
OPEN ON THE OTHER TWO FACADES TO ADMIT
NATURAL LIGHT AND THE VIEW OF THE SUR-
ROUNDINGS.

ZWEI FASSADEN SIND DURCH GLASFRONTEN
GEÖFFNET, DIE NATÜRLICHE BELICHTUNG UND
DEN AUSBLICK IN DIE UMGEBUNG ZULASSEN.

FERMÉ SUR DEUX CÔTÉS, L'ATELIER EST
OUVERT SUR SES DEUX AUTRES FAÇADES
POUR LAISSER ENTRER LA LUMIÉRE NATU-
RELLE ET BÉNÉFICIER DE LA VUE SUR SON
ENVIRONNEMENT.

A noted artist, Rémy Zaugg has had a long association with the architects. He was responsible for
the presentation of their exhibition in 1995 at the
Centre Pompidou in Paris, for example. They also
worked together on the master plan for the Dijon
campus, and for museum structures in Semur-en-
Auxois and Aarau. In this instance, they worked
together as well to produce a strict workplace and
exhibition area for the artist. It is essentially a
concrete box, with overhanging eaves whose only

Der Künstler Rémy Zaugg ist den Architekten seit
langem eng verbunden. Er war mitverantwortlich
für ihre Ausstellung im Centre Pompidou (Paris,
1995) und hat mit Herzog & de Meuron am Masterplan für den Campus von Dijon und den Museumsbauten in Semur-en-Auxois und Aarau zusammengearbeitet. Zauggs Atelier entstand als nüchterner
Arbeits- und Ausstellungsraum in Kooperation mit
den Architekten. Es besteht im wesentlichen aus
einer Betonkiste mit überhängenden Dachtraufen.

Artiste bien connu, Rémy Zaugg travaille depuis
longtemps avec les deux architectes. Il est l'auteur,
entre autres, de la présentation de leur exposition
au Centre Pompidou à Paris en 1995. Ils ont également collaboré au plan directeur du campus
de Dijon, et à des bâtiments pour les musées de
Semur-en-Auxois et Aarau. Dans ce cas précis, ils
ont conçu ensemble cet atelier-lieu d'exposition.
Essentiellement boîte de béton à vastes auvents, le
petit bâtiment ne possède pour seul décor que les

...xternal differentiation is due to natural, planned ...ater runoff marks. The atelier within resembles ...he artist's work in its strict, almost harsh minim-...lism. Overhead skylights provide ample natural ...ght, which is evenly distributed on the walls and ...vork areas. Because it is the product of the inter-...ction between Rémy Zaugg and Herzog & de ...Meuron, this atelier might almost be considered ... textbook example of contemporary minimalist ...r neo-minimalist architecture.

Die beabsichtigten Spuren des Regenwassers an den Wänden bilden die einzige Differenzierung des Äußeren. Im Innern entspricht das Atelier mit sei-nem fast schroffen Minimalismus dem Werk Rémy Zauggs. Oberlichter lassen reichlich Tageslicht ein. Das Atelier ist die Frucht gegenseitiger Einflüsse von Rémy Zaugg und Herzog & de Meuron und kann damit nahezu als Schulbeispiel zeitgenössischer minimalistischer oder neo-minimalistischer Archi-tektur gelten.

traces produites par l'écoulement calculé des eaux sur la façade. A l'intérieur, l'atelier rappelle l'œuvre de l'artiste dans son minimalisme strict, presque dur. Des verrières zénithales fournissent un géné-reux éclairage naturel, distribué de la même façon sur les murs et les zones de travail. Cet atelier est presque un exemple séminal de minimalisme con-temporain ou d'architecture néo-minimaliste.

HERZOG & DE MEURON
DOMINUS WINERY
YOUNTVILLE, NAPA VALLEY, CALIFORNIA, UNITED STATES, 1995-98

PLANNING / PLANUNG: 1995
CONSTRUCTION / BAU: 1996-98
CLIENT / BAUHERR: CHRISTIAN MOUEIX AND
CHERISE CHEN-MOUEIX
FLOOR AREA / NUTZFLÄCHE / SURFACE
UTILE: 4 100 M²
COSTS / KOSTEN / COÛTS: US$ 5 400 000

**WIRE BASKET STRUCTURES HOLD IN PLACE
THE SURPRISING GRAY-GREEN BASALT WALLS.**

DRAHTKÖRBE GEBEN DEN UNGEWÖHNLICHEN
MAUERN AUS GRAUGRÜNEM BASALT HALT.

LES ÉTONNANTS MURS DE BASALTE GRIS-VERT
SONT MAINTENUS PAR UNE STRUCTURE EN FIL
D'ACIER.

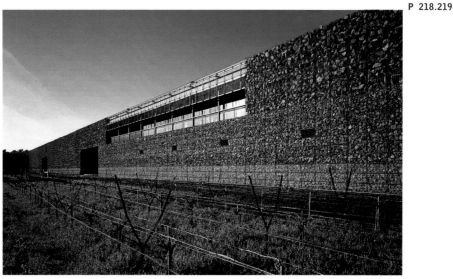

The very walls of the Dominus Winery are ingenious. They are made of "gabions," loose pieces of locally mined gray-green basalt held in place by wire containers. This unusual cladding material effectively shields the concrete walls from the sun, a positive factor in a business where the temperature of the wine must be strictly controlled. The clients of Swiss architects Herzog & de Meuron's first building in the Americas are the noted art collectors Christian and Cherise Moueix, whose Château Petrus is one of the most sought-after Bordeaux wines. The interest of the architects in contemporary art was one factor linking them to Cherise Moueix, an American who worked in a Paris art gallery before marrying. Seen from a distance, the 4,100 m² winemaking facility looks more like a dark wall with long, low openings for trucks than it does a traditional California winery in any sense. Within, it is strict, indeed minimal.

Schon die Wände der Kellerei Dominus sind genial. Sie bestehen aus »Schanzkörben«, losen Brocken eines örtlich abgebauten graugrünen Basalts in Drahtbehältern. Das ungewöhnliche Verkleidungsmaterial schützt die Betonwände vor der Sonne – ein wichtiger Faktor für die Winzer, muß die Temperatur des Weins doch stets kontrolliert werden. Die Bauherren der ersten Arbeit von Herzog & de Meuron in Amerika sind die Kunstsammler Christian und Cherise Moueix, deren Château Petrus zu den begehrtesten Bordeaux-Weinen gehört. Das Interesse der Architekten an zeitgenössischer Kunst verband sie mit Cherise Moueix, einer Amerikanerin, die vor ihrer Heirat in einer Pariser Galerie tätig war. Aus der Ferne ähnelt die 4 100 m² große Weinkellerei eher einer dunklen Mauer mit breiten Öffnungen für Lastwagen als einem herkömmlichen kalifornischen Weingut. Das Innere ist nüchtern, ja minimalistisch.

Même les murs du chais Dominus sont extraordinaires. Il sont en «gabions», un basalte gris-vert trouvé dans la région, empilé et tenu en place dans des conteneurs en fil d'acier. Ce matériau de parement plus qu'inhabituel protège les murs de béton du soleil, élément important quand on sait que la température du vin doit être strictement contrôlée. Les clients de cette première réalisation américaine des architectes suisses Herzog & de Meuron sont les grands collectionneurs d'art Christian et Cherise Moueix, dont le Château Petrus est l'un des Bordeaux les plus recherchés. L'intérêt des architectes pour l'art contemporain est un des éléments qui a incité Cherise Moueix, une Américaine qui a travaillé à Paris dans une galerie d'art, à les choisir. Vue de loin, ce chais de 4 100 m² fait davantage penser à un grand mur sombre percé d'ouvertures basses pour les camions qu'à un chais californien traditionnel. L'intérieur est strict, très minimaliste.

DESPITE THE RUGGED EXTERIOR, THE INTER-
IOR DISPLAYS THE KIND OF STRICT MINIMALISM
FOR WHICH THE ARCHITECTS ARE KNOWN.

TROTZ DES RAUHEN ÄUSSEREN IST DAS
INNERE DEM STRENGEN MINIMALISMUS VER-
PFLICHTET, FÜR DEN DIE ARCHITEKTEN
BEKANNT SIND.

EN DEHORS DE SES FAÇADES BRUTES, L'INTÉ-
RIEUR DU CHAIS EST TRAITÉ DANS L'ESPRIT
DE CE MINIMALISME STRICT QUI A FAIT LA
CÉLÉBRITÉ DES DEUX ARCHITECTES.

COMPETITION / WETTBEWERB / CONCOURS:
1994
PLANNING / PLANUNG: 1995-97
CONSTRUCTION / BAU: 1998-99
CLIENT / BAUHERR: TATE GALLERY, LONDON
FLOOR AREA / NUTZFLÄCHE / SURFACE
UTILE: 34 547 M²
COSTS / KOSTEN / COÛTS: £ 68 500 000

HERZOG & DE MEURON
TATE GALLERY
OF MODERN ART
LONDON, ENGLAND, 1995-99

P 222.223

THIS COMPUTER-GENERATED IMAGE SHOWS
THE TATE BANKSIDE BUILDING AS WELL AS
THE FOOTBRIDGE DESIGNED BY NORMAN
FOSTER AND ANTHONY CARO.

DAS COMPUTERBILD ZEIGT DAS GALERIE-
GEBÄUDE AN DER BANKSIDE UND DIE VON
NORMAN FOSTER UND ANTHONY CARO GE-
PLANTE FUSSGÄNGERBRÜCKE.

CETTE IMAGE DE SYNTHÈSE MONTRE LE
BÂTIMENT DE LA NOUVELLE TATE ET LA PAS-
SERELLE CONÇUE PAR NORMAN FOSTER ET
ANTHONY CARO.

COMPUTER-GENERATED IMAGES SHOW THE MAIN TURBINE HALL SPACE AS WELL AS EXHIBITION GALLERIES.

DIE GROSSE TURBINENHALLE DIENT ALS FOYER, AN DAS SICH DIE AUSSTELLUNGS-BEREICHE ANSCHLIESSEN.

IMAGES DE SYNTHÈSE MONTRANT LE HALL DES TURBINES ET LES GALERIES D'EXPOSITION.

Built in two phases (1947-63), Bankside Power Station was designed by Sir Giles Gilbert Scott, noted for Battersea Power Station and Waterloo Bridge as well as the famous red telephone booth. Located directly opposite St Paul's Cathedral, the building was decommissioned in 1981 because of its excessive pollution of the capital. The Tate Gallery acquired an option on the structure in 1994 and appointed Herzog & de Meuron architects the following year for a new gallery of contemporary and modern art following an international competition that attracted 148 entries. Their design for the building revolves around the use of the former Turbine hall (155 m long, 23 m wide and 35 m high) as the entry area for the public. The total floor area of the museum is 34,547 m², with the galleries concentrated on the Thames side of the structure – whose outside surfaces have been left largely intact. The intervention of Herzog & de Meuron is, as usual, minimalist, making the maximum possible use of the existing structure and adding only the simple volumes of the new galleries and related spaces.

Architekt des in zwei Phasen (1947-63) errichteten Bankside-Kraftwerks war Sir Giles Gilbert Scott. Die gegenüber von St. Paul's gelegene Anlage wurde 1981 aufgegeben, weil sie erheblich zur Umweltverschmutzung beitrug. Die Tate Gallery erwarb 1994 eine Option auf das Gebäude und beauftragte 1995, nach einem internationalen Wettbewerb mit 148 Teilnehmern, Herzog & de Meuron mit dem Bau eines neuen Museums für zeitgenössische und moderne Kunst. Zentraler Aspekt ihres Entwurfs ist die Nutzung der früheren Turbinenhalle (Länge 155 m, Breite 23 m, Höhe 35 m) als Eingangsbereich. Die Gesamtnutzfläche des Museums beträgt 34 547 m²; die Ausstellungsbereiche sind auf der Uferseite konzentriert, die Fassaden weitgehend unverändert belassen. Die Eingriffe von Herzog & de Meuron sind, wie üblich, minimal; sie erreichen die größtmögliche Nutzung des bestehenden Gebäudes und fügen nur die schlichten Volumina der neuen Ausstellungsbereiche mit Nebenräumen an.

Edifiée en deux phases (1947-63), la centrale thermique de Bankside a été conçue par Sir Giles Gilbert Scott, père de la Battersea Power Station, de Waterloo Bridge et de la fameuse cabine de téléphone rouge. Situé juste en face de la cathédrale Saint-Paul, le bâtiment avait été désaffecté en 1981 parce qu'il polluait de façon excessive l'air de la capitale. La Tate Gallery prit une option en 1994 et, à l'issue d'un concours international qui attira 148 participants, demanda en 1995 à Herzog & de Meuron d'aménager ses nouvelles galeries d'art moderne et contemporain. Leur projet repose sur la transformation de l'ancien hall des turbines (155 m de long, 23 de large et 35 de haut) en hall d'entrée. La surface totale du musée s'élève aujourd'hui à 34 547 m². Les galeries sont concentrées sur la façade côté Tamise du bâtiment dont l'extérieur n'a pratiquement pas été touché. L'intervention des deux architectes est, comme d'habitude, minimaliste, tire le maximum de la structure existante et se contente de créer des volumes simples pour les galeries et les espaces qui les desservent.

DAMIEN HIRST
AND MIKE RUNDELL

Mike Rundell & Associates was created in 1993 to produce architectural projects designed by Mike Rundell, who is best known as a sculptor and installation artist. Rundell was born in 1958 in London, and attended Oxford (1976-79) and the Camberwell School of Art (1986-89). He has completed 20 projects in the last three years, ranging from Tchaikovsky's flat in Saint Petersburg to a chain of hotels. Damien Hirst, born in 1965 in Bristol, is

Mike Rundell & Associates wurde 1993 zur Ausführung der von dem als Künstler bekannt gewordenen Mike Rundell entworfenen Bauten gegründet. Rundell, geboren 1958 in London, studierte in Oxford (1976-79) und an der Camberwell School of Art, London (1986-89). Er hat in den letzten drei Jahren 20 Projekte ausgeführt: von Tschaikowskys Wohnung in St. Petersburg bis zu Bauten für eine Hotelkette. Damien Hirst, geboren 1965 in Bristol,

L'agence Mike Rundell & Associates a été créée en 1993 pour réaliser les projets architecturaux de Mike Rundell, surtout connu comme sculpteur et artiste d'installations. Rundell est né en 1958 à Londres et à étudié à Oxford (1976-79) et à la Camberwell School of Art (1986-89). Il a réalisé 20 projets au cours de ces trois dernières années, de l'appartement de Tchaïkovsky à Saint-Pétersbourg à une chaîne d'hôtels. Damien Hirst, né à

DAMIEN HIRST, WINNER OF ENGLAND'S TURNER PRIZE, IS BEST KNOWN FOR HIS ART. HIS PARTNER IN THIS PROJECT, MIKE RUNDELL, IS ACTUALLY AN ARTIST AS WELL. TOGETHER THEY HAVE EXPERIMENTED WITH THE RESTAURANT AS AN ART FORM.

DAMIEN HIRST, TRÄGER DES ENGLISCHEN TURNER-PREISES, IST ALS KÜNSTLER BEKANNT GEWORDEN. MIKE RUNDELL, SEIN PARTNER BEI DIESEM PROJEKT, IST EIGENTLICH EBENFALLS KÜNSTLER. MIT DIESEM RESTAURANT HABEN SIE EIN »GESAMTKUNSTWERK« GESCHAFFEN.

P 226.227

DAMIEN HIRST, TITULAIRE DU TURNER PRIZE, EST SURTOUT CONNU POUR SON ŒUVRE ARTISTIQUE. SON ASSOCIÉ DANS CE PROJET, MIKE RUNDELL, EST ÉGALEMENT ARTISTE. ENSEMBLE ILS ONT FAIT DE LA CRÉATION DE RESTAURANT UNE FORME D'ART.

WHITE CUBE
44 DUKE STREET
ST. JAMES'S
LONDON SW1Y 6DD
ENGLAND

TEL: + 44 20 7 930 5373
FAX: + 44 20 7 930 9973

MIKE RUNDELL & ASSOCIATES LTD
CAMBERWELL HALL
45 GROVE LANE
LONDON SE5 8SP
ENGLAND

TEL; + 44 20 7 564 5252
FAX: + 44 20 7 708 3753

one of the best-known representatives of the socalled Young British Art. He lives and works in Devon. Winner of the 1995 Turner Prize, with his controversial work *Mother and Child, Divided*, he has often placed an emphasis on what he calls the "healing power of art." His "spot paintings" with their "pharmaceutical" aspect make it clear that the theme of the restaurant he designed with Mike Rundell was no accident.

ist einer der bekanntesten Vertreter der sogenannten Young British Art. Er lebt und arbeitet in Devon. 1995 erhielt er für sein umstrittenes Werk »Mother and Child, Divided« den Turner-Preis. Hirst betont immer wieder die »heilende Kraft der Kunst«. Seine »spot paintings« mit ihrem »pharmazeutischen« Aspekt machen deutlich, daß das Thema des von ihm und Mike Rundell gestalteten Restaurants kein Zufall war.

Bristol en 1965 est l'un des plus célèbre représentants du mouvement «Young British Art.» Il vit et travaille dans le Devon. Distingué par le Turner Prize 1995 avec une œuvre controversée «Mother and Child, Divided», il met souvent l'accent sur ce qu'il nomme «le pouvoir curatif de l'art.» Ses «spot paintings» d'aspect «pharmaceutique» expliquent le thème de ce restaurant conçu en collaboration avec Mike Rundell.

DAMIEN HIRST AND MIKE RUNDELL
PHARMACY RESTAURANT
LONDON, ENGLAND, 1997-98

HIRST'S WORK HAS FREQUENTLY DEALT WITH THE THEME OF THE PHARMACY, SO IT WAS A NATURAL SUBJECT FOR THE DECOR OF THIS RESTAURANT.

HIRST HAT SICH – WIE AUCH HIER – HÄUFIG MIT DEM THEMA »PHARMAZIE« AUSEINANDER-GESETZT.

L'ŒUVRE DE HIRST A SOUVENT TRAITÉ LE THÈME DES MÉDICAMENTS, D'OÙ LE CHOIX DU DÉCOR DE CE RESTAURANT.

REFURBISHMENT / UMBAU / RÉNOVATION: 9/97-1/98
CLIENT / BAUHERR: DAMIEN HIRST / BLUE LODGE LTD
FLOOR AREA / NUTZFLÄCHE / SURFACE UTILE: 475 M²
COSTS / KOSTEN / COÛTS: £ 626 000

The noted artist and Turner Prize winner Damien Hirst was the client for this restaurant project, and designed the works of art as well. He called on Rundell Associates to renovate an existing restaurant, reputed for its "difficult" location. Within, the two restaurant floors are meant to have entirely different atmospheres. Polished concrete floors and medical cabinets dominate on the ground floor, intended for a younger clientele, while the first floor is more restrained, as evidenced by the wood floors. Paintings representing butterflies in pastel tones are hung around this space. Unperturbed by criti-

Der bekannte Künstler und Turner-Preisträger Damien Hirst war Auftraggeber dieses Projekts und hat selbst die Kunstwerke gestaltet. Hirst beauftragte Rundell Associates mit dem Umbau eines Restaurants, das für seine »schwierige Lage« bekannt war. Im Innern sind die beiden Restaurantgeschosse bewußt in völlig unterschiedlicher Atmosphäre gehalten. Geschliffene Betonböden und Arzneischränke dominieren das für eine jüngere Klientel gedachte Erdgeschoß, während das Obergeschoß eher dezent gestaltet ist, wie schon der Holzboden deutlich macht. An den Wänden hängen

Le célèbre artiste et titulaire du Turner Prize, Damien Hirst est le propriétaire de ce restaurant, dont il a conçu les œuvres d'art exposées. Il a fait appel à Rundell Associates pour rénover cet établissement qui existait déjà, et était connu pour son implantation «difficile.» A l'intérieur, les deux niveaux offrent chacun une atmosphère entièrement différente. Les sols en béton poli et le mobilier d'hôpital dominent au rez-de-chaussée conçu pour une clientèle jeune, tandis que l'étage est plus sage, comme en témoignent ses sols en parquet. Des tableaux représentant des papillons dans des tons pastels

THE RESTAURANT AND BAR OFFER DECORS RELATED TO THE PHARMACY THEME IN DIFFERENT STYLES.

DIE AUSSTATTUNG VON RESTAURANT UND BAR VARIIERT DAS THEMA »APOTHEKE«.

LE RESTAURANT ET LE BAR DÉCLINENT LE THÈME DE LA PHARMACIE.

cism of this restaurant, Damien Hirst says, "first of all art is about life, and always has been, and the art world is about money, and always has been." Works of art are placed throughout, from the reception area to the urinal in the men's room. The floor of the restaurant is 475 m².

Bilder von Schmetterlingen in Pastelltönen. Von kritischen Äußerungen zum Pharmacy Restaurant unbeeindruckt, sagt Damien Hirst: »In der Kunst geht es vor allem um Leben, das war schon immer so; und in der Kunstwelt geht es vor allem um Geld, das war auch schon immer so.« Kunstwerke sind allgegenwärtig, vom Empfangsbereich bis zu den Pissoirs auf der Herrentoilette. Das Restaurant hat eine Gesamtfläche von 475 m².

sont accrochés tout autour de cet espace. Imperturbable face aux critiques, Damien Hirst a déclaré: «L'art traite de la vie, et l'a toujours fait, tandis que le monde de l'art traite de l'argent, et l'a toujours fait». Les œuvres d'art sont omniprésentes de la réception aux toilettes. La surface au sol est de 475 m².

STEVEN HOLL

ONE OF THE MOST INTELLECTUAL AND INFLU-
ENTIAL ARCHITECTS OF HIS GENERATION,
STEVEN HOLL HAS ATTAINED INTERNATIONAL
NOTORIETY WITH HIS FIRST MAJOR EUROPEAN
PROJECT.

Steven Holl, born in 1947 in Bremerton, Wa-
shington, gained his B. Arch. at the University of
Washington, Seattle (1970), then studied in Rome
and at the AA in London (1976). He began his
career in California and opened his own office in
New York in 1976. He taught at the University of
Washington, Syracuse University, and, since 1981,
at Columbia University. Notable buildings: Hybrid
Building (Seaside, Florida, 1984-88), Berlin AGB
Library (Berlin, competition entry, 1988), Void
Space/Hinged Space, Housing, Nexus World

Steven Holl, geboren 1947 in Bremerton, Washington, erwarb 1970 den Bachelor of Architecture der
University of Washington in Seattle und studierte
dann in Rom und an der Londoner Architectural
Association (1976). Er eröffnete 1976 in New York
ein eigenes Büro. Holl lehrte an der University of
Washington und der Syracuse University, seit 1981
an der Columbia University. Zu seinen Projekten
gehören das Hybrid Building in Seaside, Florida
(1984-88), der Wettbewerbsentwurf für die
Amerika-Gedenkbibliothek in Berlin, Void Space/

Né en 1947 à Bremerton, Washington, Bachelor
of Architecture University of Washington, 1970,
études à Rome et à l'Architectural Association de
Londres (1976). Il entame sa carrière en Californie
et ouvre sa propre agence à New York en 1976. Il
a enseigné à l'Université de Washington, Syracuse
University et, depuis 1981, à Columbia University.
Réalisations les plus importantes: Hybrid Building
(Seaside, Floride, 1984-88), participation au concours de la Bibliothèque AGB (Berlin, Allemagne,
1988), Void Space/Hinged Space, Logements,

STEVEN HOLL, EINER DER INTERESSANTESTEN UND EINFLUSSREICHSTEN ARCHITEKTEN SEINER GENERATION, HAT MIT SEINEM ERSTEN GROSSEN PROJEKT IN EUROPA INTERNATIONALE BERÜHMTHEIT ERLANGT.

L'UN DES ARCHITECTES LES PLUS INFLUENTS DE SA GÉNÉRATION, STEVEN HOLL EST AUSSI UN THÉORICIEN QUI A ATTEINT À LA NOTORIÉTÉ INTERNATIONALE PAR SON PREMIER GRAND PROJET EN EUROPE.

STEVEN HOLL ARCHITECTS
435 HUDSON STREET, 4TH FL.
NEW YORK, NEW YORK 10014
UNITED STATES

TEL: + 1 212 989 0918
FAX: + 1 212 463 9718
E-MAIL: mail@stevenholl.com
WEB: www.stevenholl.com

(Fukuoka, Japan, 1989-91), Stretto House (Dallas, Texas, 1989-92), Makuhari Housing (Chiba, Japan, 1992-97), Chapel of St. Ignatius, Seattle University (Seattle, Washington, 1994-97), and the Kiasma Museum of Contemporary Art (Helsinki, Finland, 1993-98). Current work also includes the Cranbrook Institute of Science (Bloomfield Hills, Michigan, 1996-99). Winner of the 1998 Alvar Aalto Medal, Holl is also working on the Bellevue Art Museum, Bellevue, Washington, and the Knut Hamsun Museum, Hamarøy, Norway.

Hinged Space, experimenteller Wohnungsbau Nexus World in Fukuoka, Japan (1989-91), das Haus Stretto in Dallas, Texas (1989-92), die Wohnsiedlung Makuhari in Chiba, Japan (1992-97), die Ignatius-Kapelle der Seattle University in Seattle, Washington (1994-97) und das Cranbrook Institute of Science in Bloomfield Hills, Michigan (1996-99). Gegenwärtig arbeitet Holl, der 1998 mit der Alvar-Aalto-Medaille ausgezeichnet wurde, am Art Museum in Bellevue, Washington und am Knut-Hamsun-Museum in Hamarøy, Norwegen.

Nexus World (Fukuoka, Japon, 1989-91), Stretto House (Dallas, Texas, 1989-92), immeuble de logements Makuhari, (Chiba, Japon, 1992-97), chapelle de Saint-Ignace, Seattle University, (1994-97), Kiasma Musée d'art contemporain (Helsinki, Finlande, 1993-98) et Cranbrook Institute of Science (Bloomfield Hills, Michigan, 1996-99). Titulaire de la Médaille Alvar Aalto 1998, il travaille actuellement sur le Bellevue Art Museum, Bellevue, Washington, et le Musée Knut Hamsun, Hamarøy, Norvège.

STEVEN HOLL

KIASMA MUSEUM
OF CONTEMPORARY ART

HELSINKI, FINLAND, 1993-98

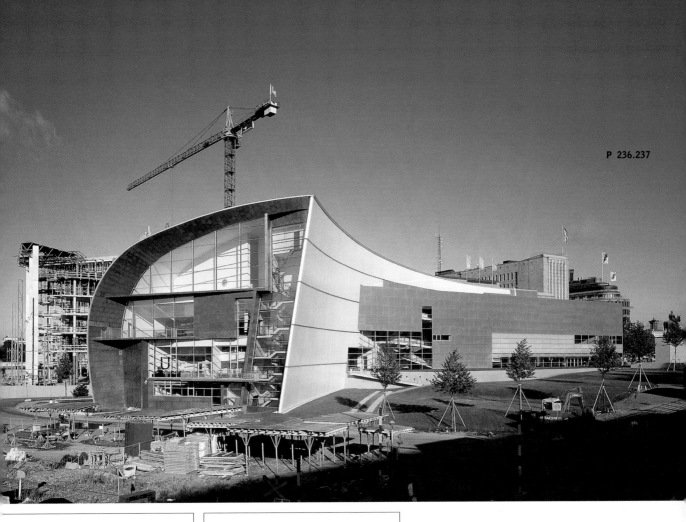

TWO VIEWS OF THE MUSEUM SEEN FROM
OPPOSITE SIDES AND A PLAN SHOW ITS
UNUSUAL CONFIGURATION.

DIE VERSCHIEDENEN ANSICHTEN UND
DER GRUNDRISS VERDEUTLICHEN DIE
UNGEWÖHNLICHEN FORMEN DES BAUS.

DEUX VUES DU MUSÉE, PRISES DE DEUX
CÔTÉS OPPOSÉS, ET PLAN.

COMPETITION / WETTBEWERB / CONCOURS: 1993
PLANNING / PLANUNG: 1993-96
CONSTRUCTION / BAU: 1996-98
CLIENT / BAUHERR: FINNISH MINISTRY OF
EDUCATION
FLOOR AREA / NUTZFLÄCHE / SURFACE
UTILE: 12 000 M²
EXHIBITION SPACE / AUSSTELLUNGSFLÄCHE /
SURFACE D'EXPOSITION: 3 600 M²
COSTS / KOSTEN / COÛTS: US$ 41 000 000

**A RELATIVELY STRAIGHTFORWARD FACADE
FACES A POOL AND AN EQUESTRIAN STATUE.**

VOR DER RELATIV NÜCHTERNEN FASSADE
SPIEGELT SICH EINE REITERSTATUE IM
WASSERBECKEN.

UNE FAÇADE CLASSIQUE DONNE SUR UN
BASSIN ET UNE STATUE ÉQUESTRE.

Steven Holl was chosen to design this project following a competition that included Coop Himmelb(l)au, Kazuo Shinohara, and Álvaro Siza as well as more than 500 entrants from Finland and neighboring countries. Compared to a "nuclear submarine" by its numerous opponents, Steven Holl's project was originally named "chiasma," signifying "an intersection or a crossing over," related to the crossing of optical nerves at the base of the brain. Measuring about 12,000 m², the building was built for a budget of $41 million, and is located in the heart of Helsinki, near the Parliament building,

Nach einem Wettbewerb, an dem neben Coop Himmelb(l)au, Kazuo Shinohara und Álvaro Siza über 500 Architekten aus Finnland und den Nachbarländern teilgenommen hatten, wurde Steven Holl mit der Planung dieses Museums beauftragt. Sein von vielen Gegnern als »Atom-U-Boot« bezeichneter Entwurf hieß ursprünglich »Chiasma«, was Schnittpunkt oder Kreuzung bedeutet, bezogen auf die Kreuzung der Sehnerven an der Gehirnbasis. Das Gebäude mit etwa 12 000 m² Gesamtnutzfläche wurde mit einem Budget von 41 Millionen US $ errichtet. Es liegt im Zentrum Helsinkis in der

Steven Holl a été choisi pour ce projet à l'issue d'un concours qui avait attiré plus de 500 participants scandinaves, sans compter Coop Himmelb(l)au, Kazuo Shinohara et Álvaro Siza. Comparé à un « sous-marin nucléaire » par ses nombreux adversaires, ce projet fut baptisé « chiasma », terme qui désigne le croisement des nerfs optiques dans le cerveau. D'une surface totale d'environ 12 000 m², le bâtiment situé en plein cœur d'Helsinki, près du Parlement, de la gare d'Eliel Saarinen et du Finlandia Hall d'Alvar Aalto, a coûté $41 millions. Parmi ses principales caractéristiques, son toit et

KIASMA OR "CHIASMA" SIGNIFIES AN INTER-
SECTION OR A CROSSING OVER.

KIASMA ODER »CHIASMA« BEDEUTET
SCHNITTPUNKT ODER KREUZUNG.

KIASMA OU «CHIASMA» SIGNIFIE INTER-
SECTION OU CROISEMENT.

Eliel Saarinen's Helsinki Station and Alvar Aalto's Finlandia Hall. A prominent feature of the structure is its curved wall and roof, which give a liveliness to the interior space while facilitating the admission of natural light to upper- and lower-level exhibitions. As Holl says, "this curved unfolding sequence provides elements of both mystery and surprise – which do not exist in a typical single- or double-loaded orthogonal arrangement of space." The exterior of the building is clad in polished zinc, aluminum, brass, and glass.

Nähe von Parlamentsgebäude, Eliel Saarinens Hauptbahnhof und Alvar Aaltos Finlandia-Halle. Auffällig sind die gebogene Wand und das gekrümmte Dach des Neubaus. Sie beleben den Innenraum und lassen Tageslicht ins obere und untere Ausstellungsgeschoß fallen. Holl sagt dazu: »Diese sich entfaltende Folge von Krümmungen erzeugt ebenso geheimnisvolle wie überraschende Elemente, die bei der sonst üblichen einfachen oder doppelten orthogonalen Aufteilung nicht entstehen.« Der Bau ist mit poliertem Zink, Aluminium, Messing und Glas verkleidet.

son mur incurvés qui animent l'espace intérieur tout en facilitant l'entrée de la lumière naturelle dans les salles d'exposition. Pour Holl: «Cette séquence de déploiement en courbe apporte des éléments à la fois de mystère et de surprise, qui ne pourraient exister dans un plan orthogonal classique.» Les façades sont recouvertes de zinc poli, d'aluminium, de laiton et de verre.

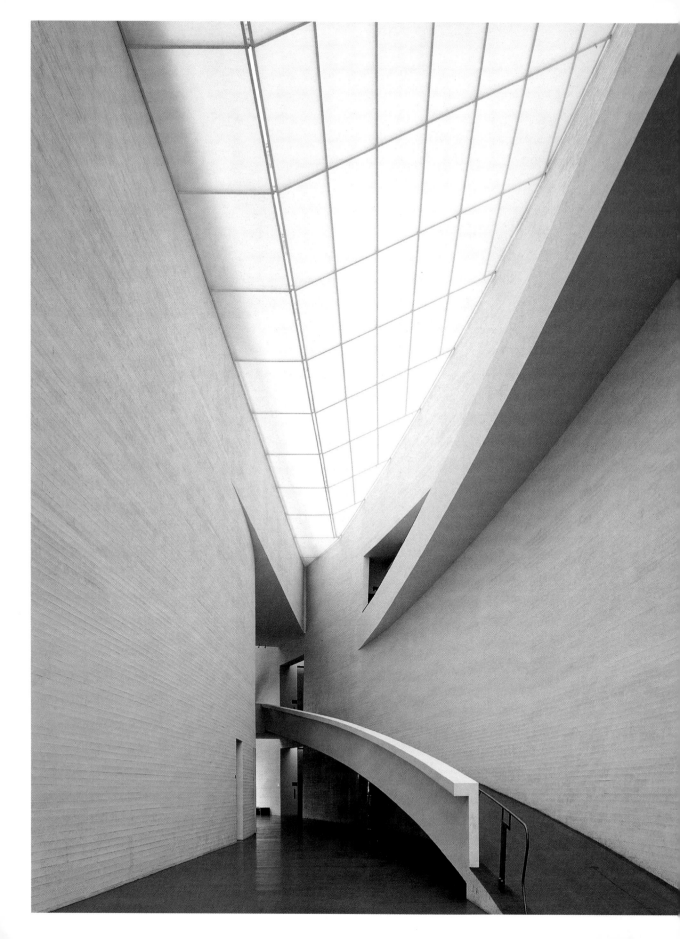

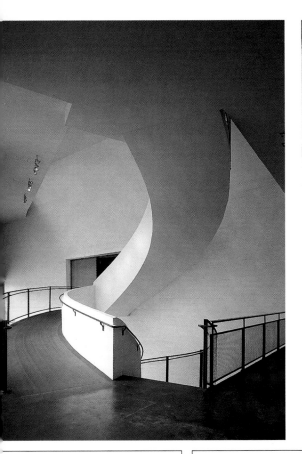

VIEWS OF INTERNAL STAIRWAYS GIVE AN IDEA
OF THE UNUSUAL COMBINATION OF SPACE AND
LIGHT IMAGINED BY STEVEN HOLL.

DIE INNENANSICHTEN DES TREPPENHAUSES
VERMITTELN EINE VORSTELLUNG VOM UNGE-
WÖHNLICHEN ZUSAMMENSPIEL VON RAUM
UND LICHT.

VUES DE L'ESCALIER INTÉRIEUR DONNANT
UNE IDÉE DE LA MANIÈRE ORIGINALE DONT
HOLL CONJUGUE L'ESPACE ET LA LUMIÈRE.

ARATA ISOZAKI

Born in Oita City on the Island of Kyushu in 1931, Arata Isozaki graduated from the Architectural Faculty of the University of Tokyo in 1954, and established Arata Isozaki & Associates in 1963, having worked in the office of Kenzo Tange. Winner of the 1986 Royal Institute of British Architects Gold Medal, he has been a juror of major competitions, such as that held in 1988 for the new Kansai International Airport. Notable buildings include Gunma Prefectural Museum of Fine Arts (Japan, 1971-74),

Arata Isozaki, geboren 1931 in Oita auf Kyushu, beendete 1954 sein Studium an der Tokioter Universität. Danach arbeitete er bei Kenzo Tange und gründete 1963 Arata Isozaki & Associates. 1986 wurde er mit der Gold Medal des Royal Institute of British Architects ausgezeichnet. Er war als Preisrichter in großen Wettbewerben tätig, so 1988 bei der Ausschreibung für den Internationalen Flughafen Kansai. Zu seinen Bauten zählen das Gunma Prefectural Museum of Fine Arts (Japan, 1971-74)

Né à Oita sur l'île de Kyushu en 1931, Arata Isozaki sort diplômé de la Faculté d'architecture de l'Université de Tokyo en 1654 et fonde Arata Isozaki & Associates en 1963, après avoir travaillé dans l'agence de Kenzo Tange. Titulaire de la Médaille d'or du Royal Institute of British Architects en 1986, il participe au jury de nombreux grands concours internationaux, dont celui du nouvel aéroport de Kansai en 1988. Parmi ses réalisations les plus remarquables: Musée d'art moderne (Gunma, Japon

ARATA ISOZAKI IS IN MANY WAYS THE MOST
IMPORTANT LIVING JAPANESE ARCHITECT.
THOUGH HIS STYLE HAS CHANGED OFTEN, HE
HAS REMAINED A SIGNIFICANT FORCE IN
JAPAN FOR PROGRESSIVE AND INTELLIGENT
USE OF ARCHITECTURE.

ARATA ISOZAKI IST EINER DER BEDEUTEND-
STEN JAPANISCHEN ARCHITEKTEN. OBGLEICH
ER SEINEN STIL HÄUFIG WANDELTE, STEHT ER

FÜR EINE PROGRESSIVE UND INTELLIGENTE
ARCHITEKTUR.

ARATA ISOZAKI EST À DE NOMBREUX ÉGARDS
LE PLUS IMPORTANT ARCHITECTE JAPONAIS
ACTUEL. MÊME SI SON STYLE A SOUVENT
CHANGÉ, SON APPORT PROGRESSISTE ET SON
UTILISATION INTELLIGENTE DES FORMES
EXERCENT UNE GRANDE INFLUENCE.

ARATA ISOZAKI & ASSOCIATES
NOGIZAKA ATELIER
9-6-17 AKASAKA, MINATO-KU
TOKYO 107-0052
JAPAN

TEL: + 81 3 3405 1526
FAX: + 81 3 3475 5265

he Tsukuba Center Building (Japan, 1978-83),
he Museum of Contemporary Art (Los Angeles,
981-86), Art Tower Mito (Japan, 1986-90), Team
Disney Building (near Orlando, Florida, 1990), the
Center of Japanese Art and Technology (Krakow,
Poland, 1991-94), and B-con Plaza (Oita, Japan,
1991-95). Current projects include Higashi Shi-
zuoka Plaza Cultural Complex, Shizuoka, and
Ohio's Center of Science and Industry (COSI),
Columbus, Ohio.

und das Tsukuba Center Building (Japan, 1978-83),
das Museum of Contemporary Art in Los Angeles
(1981-86), der Art Tower Mito (Japan, 1986-90),
das Team Disney Building bei Orlando, Florida
(1990), das Zentrum für japanische Kunst und
Technologie in Krakau, Polen (1991-94) und die
B-con Plaza in Oita, Japan (1991-95). Neueste
Projekte sind der Kulturkomplex Higashi Shizuoka
in Shizuoka und das Center of Science and Industry
(COSI) in Columbus, Ohio.

1971-74), le Tsukuba Center Building (Japon,
1978-83), le Museum of Contemporary Art (Los
Angeles, 1981-86), la Tour d'art Mito (Japon,
1986-90), le Team Disney Building (près d'Orlando,
Floride, 1990), le Centre japonais d'art et de tech-
nologie (Cracovie, Pologne, 1991-94) et B-con
Plaza (Oita, Japan, 1991-95). Parmi ses projets
actuels figurent le complexe culturel Higashi
Shizuoka Plaza, Shizuoka, et le Ohio's Center of
Science and Industry (COSI), Colombus, Ohio.

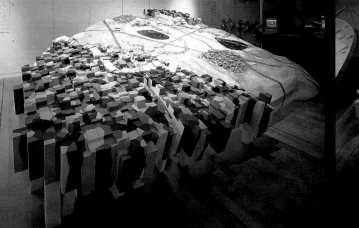

ARATA ISOZAKI'S IDEA WAS TO CREATE A VIRTUAL CITY WITH THE HELP OF OTHER ARCHITECTS, USING THE INTERNET.

ARATA ISOZAKIS IDEE WAR, MIT ANDEREN ARCHITEKTEN EINE VIRTUELLE STADT IM INTERNET ZU ERSCHAFFEN.

L'IDÉE D'ARATA ISOZAKI ÉTAIT DE CRÉER UNE CITÉ VIRTUELLE AVEC L'AIDE D'AUTRES ARCHITECTES ET DE L'INTERNET.

ARATA ISOZAKI
HAISHI "MIRAGE CITY"
ZHUHAI CITY, HENGQIN ISLAND, CHINA, 1996-97

FLOOR AREA / NUTZFLÄCHE / SURFACE UTILE:
400 HA (ISLAND PART), 200 HA (BAY PART)
EXHIBITION / AUSSTELLUNG / EXPOSITION:
"THE MIRAGE CITY – ANOTHER UTOPIA," NTT
COMMUNICATION CENTER, 19.04.-13.07.1997

P 246.247

1996, at the Venice Biennale, Arata Isozaki xhibited the first images of a project to build aishi "Mirage City" on an artificial island in the outh China Sea off the coasts of Macao and engqin Island. The special economic development one of Zhuhai on Hengqin Island sought to create international trade area with this project. A umber of "guests" such as Alejandro Zaera-Polo nd Farshid Moussavi, Elizabeth Diller and Ricardo cofidio and the artist Tadashi Kawamata were vited to participate in sessions that modified the rchitecture of the island progressively. He took his idea one step further when he was called on to rganize the first exhibition of the Tokyo ntercommunication Center, a multimedia space ponsored by NTT. Using computer technology, ree different forms were proposed for the "ideal" ty. One idea consisted in placing virtual projects esigned by such architects as Peter Eisenman, an Nouvel and Bernard Tschumi on this island. Internet site was set up to offer free access to e projects: www.ntticc.or.jp/special/utopia.

Auf der Biennale von Venedig 1996 stellte Arata Isozaki die ersten Bilder eines Projekts für die Stadt Haishi unter dem Titel »Mirage City« vor. Diese Stadt soll auf einer künstlichen Insel im Südchinesischen Meer zwischen Macao und der Insel Hengqin errichtet werden. Eine Anzahl von »Gästen« wie Alejandro Zaera-Polo und Farshid Moussavi, Elizabeth Diller, Ricardo Scofidio und Tadashi Kawamata wurden zur Teilnahme an Konferenzen aufgefordert, deren Ergebnis eine schrittweise Veränderung der Architektur auf der Insel war. Isozaki führte diesen Gedanken weiter, als er aufgefordert wurde, die erste Ausstellung des NTT Intercommunication Center in Tokio zu organisieren. Mithilfe digitaler Technik wurden drei verschiedene Formen für die »ideale« Stadt vorgeschlagen. Eine der Ideen bestand darin, virtuelle Projekte von Architekten wie Peter Eisenman, Jean Nouvel oder Bernard Tschumi auf der Insel aufzustellen. Um die Entwürfe zugänglich zu machen, wurde eine Internet-Seite eingerichtet: www.ntticc.or.jp/special/utopia.

En 1996, lors de la Biennale de Venise, Arata Isozaki a dévoilé les premières images de son projet pour la « Cité mirage » d'Haishi qui pourrait être édifiée sur une île artificielle de la Mer de Chine, entre Macao et l'île de Hengqin. Un certain nombre d'invités, comme Alejandro Zaera-Polo et Farshid Moussavi, Elizabeth Diller et Ricardo Scofidio, ou l'artiste Tadashi Kawamata ont été conviés à participer à des ateliers de réflexion sur la modification progressive de l'architecture de l'île. Isozaki poussa cette idée encore plus loin, lorsqu'il fut appelé par NTT pour organiser la première exposition de l'Intercommunication Center de Tokyo, un centre multi-média. Grâce à des technologies numériques, trois formes différentes furent proposées pour la cité « idéale ». Une des idées consistait à insérer dans l'île des projets virtuels conçus par des architectes comme Peter Eisenman, Jean Nouvel ou Bernard Tschumi. Un site Internet permettait d'accéder librement aux projets: www.ntticc.or.jp/special/utopia.

ARATA ISOZAKI

NARA
CENTENNIAL HALL

NARA, JAPAN, 1992-98

PLANNING / PLANUNG: 9/92-10/95
CONSTRUCTION / BAU: 4/96-10/98
CLIENT / BAUHERR: CITY OF NARA
FLOOR AREA / NUTZFLÄCHE / SURFACE
UTILE: 22 682 M²
COSTS / KOSTEN / COÛTS: WITHHELD /
UNGENANNT / NON COMMUNIQUÉS

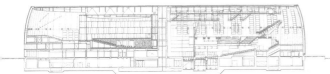

art of a municipal redevelopment scheme intend-
d to create a new urban area around the JR Nara
rain Station, Isozaki's project was chosen after an
nternational competition. Inspired by local temple
oofs, this oval plan structure measures 138 m on
he long axis, which is set along the north-south
ne of the ancient urban grid, and 42 m on the
hort axis. A large hall is intended as a convention
acility, a medium-sized hall for chamber music,
nd a small multipurpose hall in the basement.
he most remarkable aspect of the building, and
s most visible, is the enormous "conicoid" outer
hell, clad in pre-cast concrete panels and fired tiles
hosen to resemble traditional Japanese "smoked
les" (ibushi-gawara). By rotating the main oval
olume of the hall in the direction of the train
racks, the architect has created the entrance hall
f the structure in continuity with the spacious
utdoor plaza. The total floor area of the Hall
s 22,682 m².

Isozakis Entwurf wurde als Teil des Entwicklungs-
plans für einen neuen Stadtteil im Umkreis des
Bahnhofs in Nara in einem internationalen Wettbewerb ausgewählt. Das von japanischen Tempeldächern inspirierte Gebäude über ovalem Grundriß
hat eine Längsachse von 138 m, die auf der Linie
des alten Stadtrasters verläuft, und eine 42 m lange
Querachse. Ein großer Saal soll als Kongreßhalle,
ein mittelgroßer für Kammermusik und eine kleine-
rer verschiedenen Zwecken dienen. Der auffälligste
Aspekt des Gebäudes ist seine gewaltige kegelför-
mige Schale, die mit vorgefertigten Betonplatten
und gebrannten Fliesen verkleidet ist, die den
traditionellen japanischen »Rauchfliesen« (ibushi-
gawara) ähneln. Indem er das große Volumen der
Halle nach dem Verlauf der Bahngleise ausgerichtet
hat, verband Isozaki die Eingangshalle mit dem
weitläufigen Vorplatz. Die Gesamtnutzfläche der
Nara Centennial Hall beträgt 22 682 m².

C'est dans le contexte d'un concours international
pour le projet d'un nouveau quartier autour de la
gare JR de Nara que la proposition d'Isozaki a
été sélectionnée. Inspiré par les toits des temples
locaux, cette structure de plan ovale mesure 138 m
de long (sur l'axe nord-sud de l'ancienne trame
urbaine) et 42 m de large. Une grande salle est
prévue pour les congrès, une de taille moyenne
pour les concerts de musique de chambre et une
plus petite, mais polyvalente, en sous-sol. L'élément
le plus remarquable et le plus visible de ce bâtiment
est son énorme coquille extérieure cylindro-conique,
recouverte de panneaux de béton préfabriqués, et
de tuiles flammées choisies pour leur proximité
des «tuiles fumées» traditionnelles (ibushi-gawara).
En faisant pivoter le volume ovale principal vers
les voies ferrées, l'architecte a dégagé une entrée
dans la continuité de la vaste place extérieure. La
surface totale de l'ensemble est de 22 682 m².

IN A PRESTIGIOUS SITE, NEAR THE JR NARA STATION, ISOZAKI HAS CREATED A DISTANT ECHO OF THE NEARBY TEMPLES.

AN EINEM BEVORZUGTEN STANDORT, NAHE DEM BAHNHOF DER JAPAN RAILWAY IN NARA, HAT ISOZAKI EIN FERNES ECHO DER BENACHBARTEN TEMPEL GESCHAFFEN.

DANS UN SITE DE PRESTIGE, PRÈS DE LA GARE DE NARA, ISOZAKI A RÉUSSI À RÉVEILLER UN DISCRET ÉCHO À LA PRÉSENCE DES TEMPLES VOISINS.

BASED ON A SERIES OF THREE ROTATED OVALS, THE CURVING FACADES OF THE BUILDING BRING TO MIND THE GREAT WOODEN TEMPLES OF NARA.

AUF DER BASIS VON DREI VERSETZTEN OVALEN ERINNERN DIE GEKRÜMMTEN FASSADEN DES GEBÄUDES AN DIE GROSS-ARTIGEN HOLZTEMPEL IN NARA.

GÉNÉRÉES PAR LA ROTATION DE TROIS FORMES OVALES, LES FAÇADES EN COURBES RAPPELLENT LES GRANDS TEMPLES DE BOIS DE NARA.

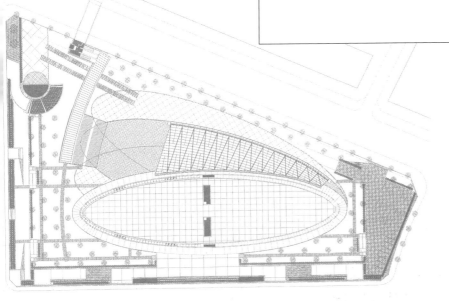

ARATA ISOZAKI

SHIZUOKA CONVENTION AND ARTS CENTER "GRANSHIP"

SHIZUOKA, JAPAN, 1993-98

SITUATED NEXT TO THE TOKYO-OSAKA
SHINKANSEN LINES AND NOT FAR FROM MOUNT
FUJI, THIS IS A HIGHLY VISIBLE STRUCTURE.

AN DER STRECKE DES HOCHGESCHWINDIG-
KEITSZUGS TOKIO-OSAKA, NICHT WEIT VOM
FUJIYAMA GELEGEN, IST DIESER BAU WEITHIN
SICHTBAR.

PRÈS DES VOIES DU SHINKANSEN TOKYO-
OSAKA ET NON LOIN DU FUJI YAMA, CE BÂTI-
MENT EST PARTICULIÈREMENT VISIBLE.

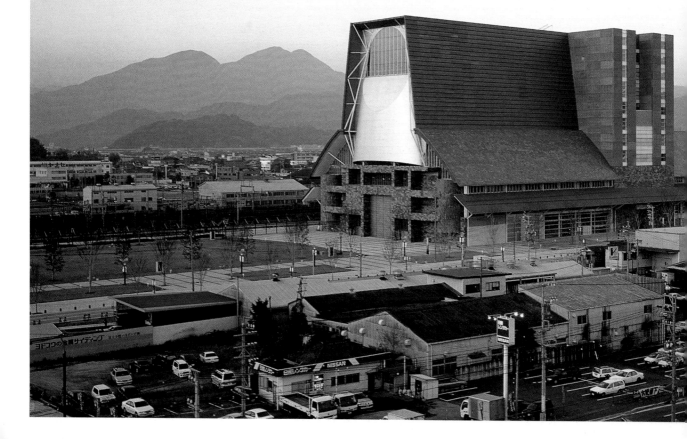

This 60,630 m² facility is set just next to the high-speed Shinkansen lines linking Tokyo to Osaka and other southern destinations. Formerly a Japan National Railway yard, the site is midway between the cities of Shimizu and Shizuoka in the so-called Higashi Shizuoka district. These two cities are scheduled to merge, meaning that Isozaki's building will be at the center of a new municipality. The timing of the construction was based on plans to hold international "Second Theater Olympics" in the building from April to June 1999. The program called for a large hall with a capacity of up to 5,000 persons and a medium one seating about

Die Anlage mit 60 630 m² Gesamtnutzfläche liegt an der Strecke des Hochgeschwindigkeitszugs Shinkansen, die Tokio mit Osaka und weiteren Städten im Süden Japans verbindet. Das einstige Gelände der Staatlichen Japanischen Eisenbahn befindet sich zwischen den Städten Shimizu und Shizuoka im sogenannten Distrikt Higashi Shizuoka. Die beiden Städte sollen zusammenwachsen, was bedeutet, daß Isozakis Bau im Zentrum einer neuen Stadt liegen wird. Er mußte rechtzeitig zur »Zweiten Theater-Olympiade« fertiggestellt werden, die von April bis Juni 1999 dort veranstaltet wurde. Die Ausschreibung forderte einen großen

Ce bâtiment de 60 630 m² est implanté en bordure des voies du train à grande vitesse, le Shinkansen, qui relie Tokyo à Osaka et d'autres villes méridionales, sur un ancien terrain des Chemins de fer nationaux du Japon du quartier d'Higashi Shizuoka, entre Shimizu et Shizuoka. Ces deux municipalités devraient bientôt fusionner, ce qui aura pour effet de placer le bâtiment au centre du nouvel ensemble. Le calendrier de la construction avait été établi en fonction de la volonté d'y organiser les Secondes Olympiades du théâtre (avril-juin 1999). Le programme prévoyait une grande salle pouvant accueillir jusqu'à 5 000 personnes, une salle moyenne

PLANNING / PLANUNG: 7/93-10/95
CONSTRUCTION / BAU: 12/95-8/98
CLIENT / BAUHERR: SHIZUOKA PREFECTURE
FLOOR AREA / NUTZFLÄCHE / SURFACE
UTILE: 60 630 M²
COSTS / KOSTEN / COÛTS: WITHHELD /
UNGENANNT / NON COMMUNIQUÉS

COMBINING ELEMENTS RELATED TO JAPANESE
TRADITION WITH THE LATEST COMPUTER
DESIGN TECHNIQUES, ISOZAKI CREATES AN
ORIGINAL FORM.

ISOZAKI SCHUF MIT MODERNSTEN ENTWURFS-
TECHNIKEN EINE EINPRÄGSAME FORM DURCH
DIE VERBINDUNG TRADITIONELLER JAPANI-
SCHER ELEMENTE.

ISOZAKI A CRÉÉ UNE FORME ORIGINALE À PAR-
TIR D'ÉLÉMENTS QUI RELÈVENT DE LA TRADI-
TION JAPONAISE ET DES PLUS RÉCENTES
TECHNIQUES DE C.A.O.

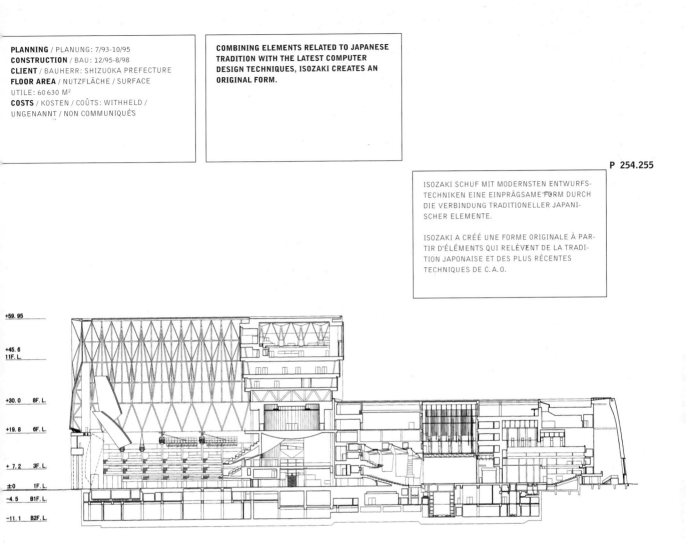

800, as well as the "Shizuoka Art Theater" with 400 seats. One of the most prominent features of the design is a very large curved exterior wall, which brings to mind the facade that Isozaki conceived for Domus, Casa del Hombre, in La Coruña, Spain (1993-95). In dealing with the large scale of this project, Arata Isozaki has called, for example, on his knowledge of cathedral or basilica architecture. He has stated that, in this respect, "An architectural form from the past is being used as a hidden basis for the design". This is visible for instance in the 60 m high main hall.

Saal für 5 000 Personen, einen mittleren mit etwa 800 Sitzen sowie das Shizuoka Art Theater mit 400 Sitzen. Eines der wichtigsten Merkmale des Entwurfs ist die sehr hohe, gekrümmte Außenwand, die an das von Isozaki 1993-95 geplante Domus, Casa del Hombre in La Coruña, Spanien, erinnert. Bei der Bewältigung des großen Maßstabs dieser Anlage sind Isozaki seine Kenntnisse der Kathedral-architektur von Nutzen gewesen. Er hat hierzu gesagt, daß »eine Architekturform der Vergangenheit als verborgene Grundlage für den Entwurf dient.« Dies ist etwa am 60 m hohen Hauptsaal ablesbar.

de 800 places et le Théâtre d'Art de Shizuoka, de 400. L'une des principales caractéristiques de ce projet est son immense mur extérieur incurvé qui rappelle la façade conçue par l'architecte pour Domus, Casa del Hombre à La Corogne, en Espagne (1993-95). Pour répondre à la gigantesque échelle du projet, Isozaki s'est appuyé sur sa connaissance des cathédrales et des basiliques, précisant même que «une forme architecturale du passé est la base cachée de ce projet». C'est particulièrement visible dans le hall principal de 60 m de haut.

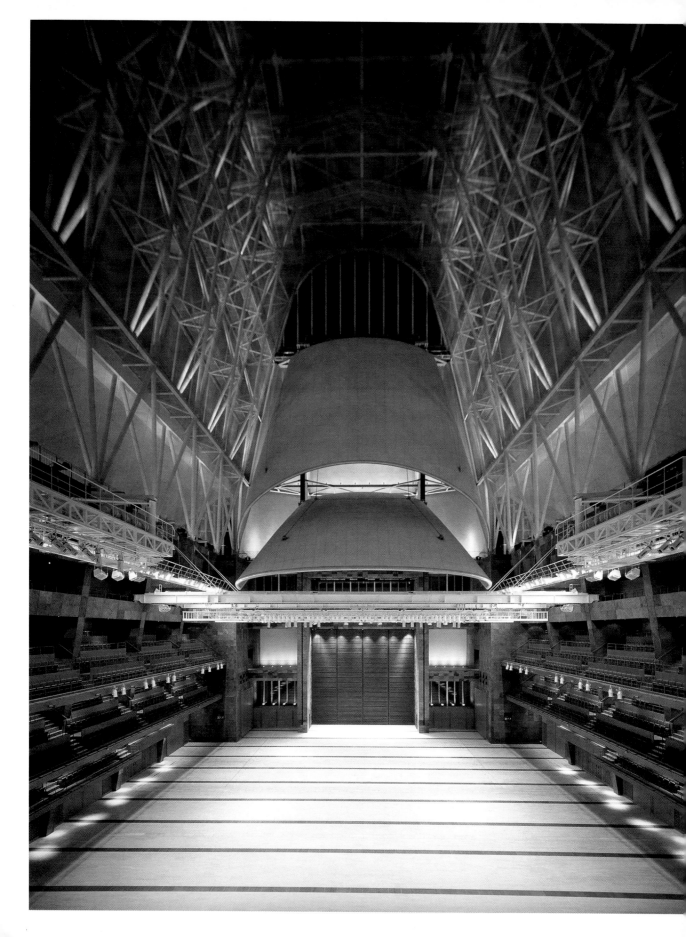

P 256.257

THE CONCEPT OF THE SAMURAI'S HELMET SEEMS TO BE AN ELEMENT IN THE ARCHITECT'S DESIGN.

DIE FORM DES SAMURAIHELMS SCHEINT DEN ENTWURF BEEINFLUSST ZU HABEN.

L'IDÉE DU HEAUME DE SAMOURAÏ NE SEMBLE PAS ÉTRANGÈRE AU PROJET DE L'ARCHITECTE.

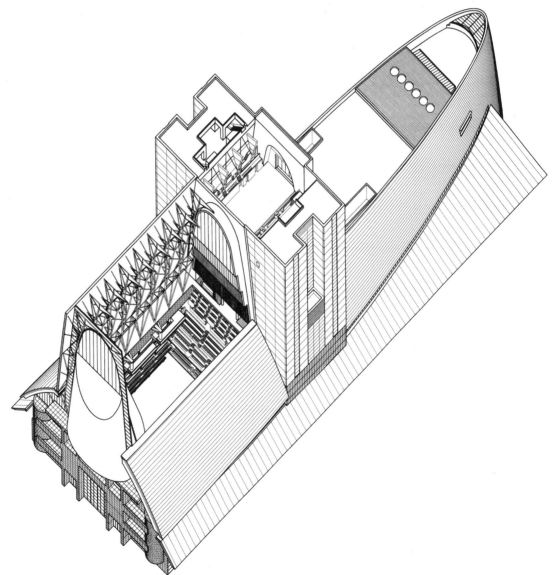

IF ANDO IS JAPAN'S MASTER OF CONCRETE
AND WEIGHTY ARCHITECTURE, ITO IS THE
LEADING FIGURE CREATING A LIGHT ARCHITEC-
TURE MADE OF ALUMINUM OR EVEN WOOD
AND FIBERGLASS.

WÄHREND ANDO ALS JAPANS MEISTER DER
BETONARCHITEKTUR GILT, KANN ITO ALS DER
FÜHRENDE ARCHITEKT EINER LEICHTEN
BAUWEISE AUS ALUMINIUM BZW. HOLZ UND
GLASFASER BEZEICHNET WERDEN.

TOYO ITO

Born in 1941 in Seoul, Korea, Toyo Ito graduated
from the University of Tokyo in 1965, and worked
in the office of Kiyonori Kikutake until 1969. He
created his own office in 1971, assuming the name
of Toyo Ito & Associates in 1979. His completed
work in Japan includes the Silver Hut Residence
(Tokyo, 1984), Tower of the Winds (Yokohama,
Kanagawa, 1986), Yatsushiro Municipal Museum
(Yatsushiro, Kumamoto, 1989-91), and the Elderly

Toyo Ito, 1941 in Seoul geboren, schloß 1965 sein
Studium an der Universität Tokio ab und arbeitete
bis 1969 im Büro von Kiyonori Kikutake. 1971
machte er sich selbständig; seit 1979 heißt sein
Büro Toyo Ito & Associates. Zu seinen herausragenden Bauten gehören die Silver Hut Residence
in Tokio (1984), der »Turm der Winde« in Yokohama, Kanagawa (1986), das städtische Museum
in Yatsushiro, Kumamoto auf der Insel Kyushu

Né en 1941 à Séoul, Corée, Toyo Ito est diplômé
de l'Université de Tokyo en 1965, et travaille pour
Kiyonori Kikutake jusqu'en 1969. Il crée sa propre
agence en 1971, qui prend le nom de Toyo Ito &
Associates en 1979. Parmi ses réalisations: la résidence Silver Hut (Tokyo, 1984), la Tour des vents
(Yokohama, Kanagawa, 1986), le Musée municipal
de Yatsushiro sur l'île de Kyushu (Yatsushiro,
Kumamoto, 1989-91), la maison pour personnes

SI ANDO EST LE MAÎTRE JAPONAIS DU BÉTON
ET DE L'ARCHITECTURE DES VOLUMES MAS-
SIFS, ITO EST LE PRINCIPAL DÉFENSEUR D'UNE
ARCHITECTURE LÉGÈRE RÉALISÉE EN ALUMI-
NIUM, VOIRE MÊME EN BOIS OU EN FIBRE DE
VERRE.

TOYO ITO & ASSOCIATES, ARCHITECTS
FUJIYA BLDG
19-4 1 CHOME, SHIBUYA, SHIBUYA-KU
TOKYO 150-0002
JAPAN

TEL: + 81 3 3409 5822
FAX: + 81 3 3409 5969
E-MAIL: nishimura@toyo-ito.co.jp

People's Home (1992-94) and Fire Station (1992-95), both located in the same city on the island of Kyushu. He participated in the Shanghai Luijiazui Center Area International Planning and Urban Design Consultation in 1992, and has built a Public Kindergarten at Eckenheim (Frankfurt, Germany, 1988-91). Recent projects include his Odate Jukai Dome Park in Odate, Akita (1995-97).

(1989-91) sowie ein Altersheim (1992-94) und eine Feuerwehrstation (1992-95) in derselben Stadt. Er beteiligte sich am internationalen Wettbewerb für den Bereich Luijiazui in Shanghai (1992) und baute einen städtischen Kindergarten im Frankfurter Stadtteil Eckenheim (1988-91). Itos jüngstes Projekt ist der Odate Jukai Dome Park in Odate, Akita, Japan (1995-97).

âgées (Yatsushiro, 1992-94) et la caserne de pompiers (Yatsushiro, 1992-95). Il participe au concours international d'urbanisme pour le quartier de Luijiazui à Shangai en 1992, et a dessiné un jardin d'enfants municipal (Eckenheim, Francfort-sur-le-Main, Allemagne, 1988-91). Il a récemment achevé le Odate Jukai Dome Park (Odate, Akita, 1995-97).

SET IN A TINY HOT SPRING VILLAGE IN THE FAR
NORTH OF THE ISLAND OF HONSHU, THE DOME
PARK STANDS OUT AS AN INCONGRUOUS OBJECT.

DER IN EINEM KLEINEN DORF IM ÄUSSERSTEN
NORDEN DER INSEL HONSHU GELEGENE DOME
PARK HEBT SICH MIT SEINER FUTURISTISCHEN
FORM STARK VON DER UMGEBUNG AB.

SITUÉ DANS UN PETIT VILLAGE THERMAL À
L'EXTRÊME NORD DE L'ÎLE DE HONSHU, LE
DOME PARK S'IMPOSE PAR SON APPARENCE
D'OBJET INCONGRU.

TOYO ITO

ODATE
JUKAI DOME PARK

ODATE, JAPAN, 1995-97

Located in a remote village in the far north of Honshu, this remarkable covered sports facility is used mostly for baseball. The off-center or semi-egg-shaped dome is made essentially with laminated Akita cedar, covered with a translucent fluor-ethylene-resin coated fiberglass. The entire dome is raised above the ground to admit light through glazed walls. Standing near a field in this largely

Die Sporthalle liegt in einem abgelegenen Dorf im Norden der Insel Honshu und wird vorwiegend für Baseball genutzt. Sie hat ein ungewöhnliches Dach: die asymmetrische Kuppel besteht im wesentlichen aus Akita-Zeder und ist mit kunstharzbeschichteter Glasfaser verkleidet. Die Kuppel wurde vom Erdboden abgehoben, so daß Licht durch die verglasten Wände fallen kann. Der Bau, der zwischen Feldern

Situé dans une petite ville éloignée à l'extrême nord de Honshu, cette remarquable installation sportive sert essentiellement au base-ball. De forme légèrement elliptique ou en demi-œuf, le dôme est en lamellé de cèdre d'Akita, recouvert de fibre de verre armée d'une résine de fluoréthylène. Le dôme est en totalité soulevé du sol pour laisser entrer la lumière parois de verre. Au milieu des champs, il prend une

P 262.263

**IN REALITY, ITS STRANGE FORM IS RELATED
TO THAT OF NEARBY SNOW-CAPPED MOUNTAINS.**

DIE SELTSAME FORM BEZIEHT SICH AUF DIE
SCHNEEBEDECKTEN BERGE DER UMGEBUNG.

CETTE FORME QUI SEMBLE ÉTRANGE RAPPEL-
LE EN FAIT LES SOMMETS ENNEIGÉS DES
MONTAGNES PROCHES.

CLIENT / BAUHERR: AKITA PREFECTURE AND
ODATE CITY
FLOOR AREA / NUTZFLÄCHE / SURFACE UTILE:
21 914 M²
COSTS / KOSTEN / COÛTS: 8 600 000 000 ¥

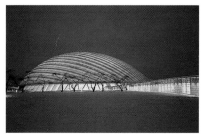

agricultural area, the dome assumes an unreal,
almost extraterrestrial appearance, particularly
when it is lit from within at night. A restaurant
and shop are located in a curving annex. Set on
a 110,250 m² site, the facility has a total floor
area of 21,914 m².

steht, wirkt beinahe außerirdisch – vor allem, wenn
er nachts von innen beleuchtet ist. Ein Restaurant
und ein Geschäft sind in einem sichelförmigen
Anbau untergebracht. Die Anlage steht auf einem
110 250 m² großen Grundstück.

apparence irréelle, presque extraterrestre, en
particulier la nuit lorsqu'il est éclairé de l'intérieur.
Un restaurant et une boutique sont aménagés
dans un bâtiment annexe incurvé. Sur un terrain
de 110 250 m², l'ensemble occupe une surface
de 21 914 m².

LIGHT AND TRANSLUCENT, THE DOME IS
MADE OF WOOD AND FIBERGLASS COMBINED
THROUGH THE USE OF ADVANCED TECH-
NOLOGY.

DIE LEICHTE UND LICHTDURCHLÄSSIGE
KUPPEL BESTEHT AUS HOLZ UND KUNSTFASER.

LÉGER ET TRANSLUCIDE, LE DOME EST EN BOIS
ET FIBRE DE VERRE ASSOCIÉS SELON DES
TECHNOLOGIES DE POINTE.

TOYO ITO

NAGAOKA LYRIC HALL

NAGAOKA, NIIGATA, JAPAN, 1993-96

CLIENT / BAUHERR: NAGAOKA CITY
FLOOR AREA / NUTZFLÄCHE / SURFACE
UTILE: 6 682 M²
COSTS / KOSTEN / COÛTS: 6 000 000 000 ¥

LIKE MANY OTHER RECENTLY BUILT JAPANESE
CULTURAL FACILITIES, THIS COMPLEX CONTAINS
A CONCERT HALL AND A THEATER.

TOYO ITO'S UNIQUE MASTERY OF LIGHTING
ARCHITECTURAL FORMS IS EVIDENT IN THE
NAGAOKA LYRIC HALL.

WIE VIELE NEUERE JAPANISCHE KULTUR-
BAUTEN ENTHÄLT AUCH DIESER KOMPLEX
EINE KONZERTHALLE UND EIN THEATER.

TOYO ITOS EINMALIGE BEHERRSCHUNG
LEICHTER ARCHITEKTURFORMEN WIRD IN
DER LYRIC HALL IN NAGAOKA DEUTLICH.

COMME BEAUCOUP DE NOUVEAUX ÉDIFICES
MODERNES JAPONAIS, CET COMPLEXE CON-
TIENT AUSSI UNE SALLE DE CONCERT ET UN
THÉÂTRE.

LA MAÎTRISE UNIQUE DES FORMES LÉGÈRES
EST TRÈS VISIBLE À THE LYRIC HALL DE
NAGAOKA.

Described by the architect as a "landscape," this $23 million structure is located in the Prefecture of Niigata in the west of Japan. Like Hasegawa's Niigata Performing Arts Center, it is set near the Shinano River. It contains a 450-seat proscenium theater and a 700-seat concert hall, as well as ten public rehearsal rooms of different sizes. An unusual aspect of the structure is that the three di-

Die 23 Millionen US$ teure Nagaoka Lyric Hall, die der Architekt als »Landschaft« bezeichnet, liegt in der Präfektur Niigata und wie Hasegawas Performing Arts Center am Fluß Shinano. Sie enthält ein Proszeniumtheater mit 450 und eine Konzerthalle mit 700 Sitzen sowie zehn Proberäume. Ungewöhnlich sind die gekrümmten Dächer, deren Form sich aus ihrer Funktion herleitet, dem reichli-

Présenté par l'architecte comme un «paysage», ce bâtiment de $23 millions se situe dans la préfecture de Niigata (ouest du Japon), au bord du fleuve Shinano, non loin du Centre des Arts du spectacle de Niigata. Il contient un théâtre à l'occidentale de 450 places, une salle de concerts de 700 places, et dix salles de répétition de différentes dimensions. Une de ses caractéristiques les plus étonnantes est

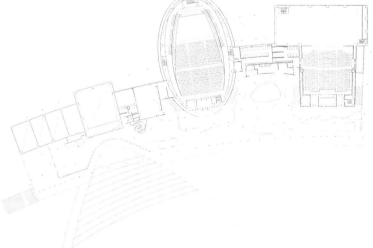

mensionally curved roofs are made to retain abundant winter snowfall, verifying Ito's own use of the word "landscape." The theater and concert hall stand above the curved roof in a rectangular and an oval corrugated glass volume. To the south of the building, a grass slope was created leading to the foyer. Set on a 39,700 m² site, the building has a total floor area of 6,682 m².

chen Schnee im Winter standzuhalten. So wird Itos Verwendung des Wortes »Landschaft« gerechtfertigt. Das Theater und die Konzerthalle erheben sich als rechteckiges bzw. ovales gläsernes Volumen über dem gekrümmten Dach. Im Süden wurde ein Grashang angelegt, der zum Foyer führt. Der Bau steht auf einem 39 700 m² großen Grundstück.

la conception de ses toits incurvés dans les trois dimensions pour retenir la neige abondante en hiver. Les salles de théâtre et de concert sont implantées au-dessus du toit incurvé dans deux volume de verres, l'un rectangulaire, l'autre ovale. Au sud du bâtiment, une pente herbeuse conduit au foyer. L'ensemble occupe une surface de 6 682 m² sur un terrain de 39 700 m².

TOYO ITO

OTA-KU RESORT COMPLEX

SHOUKEN DISTRICT, NAGANO, JAPAN, 1995-98

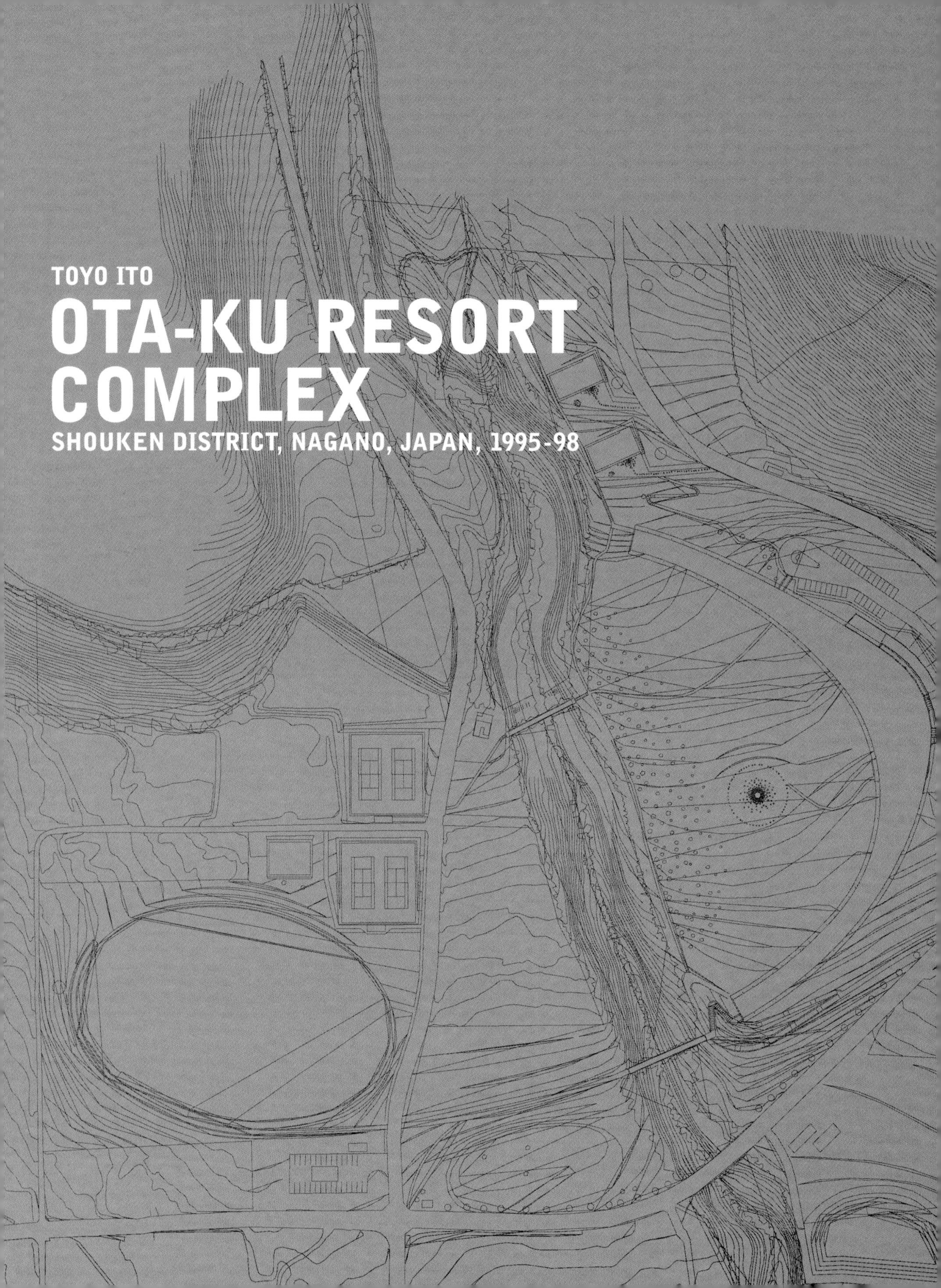

BUILT FOR THE STUDENTS OF A TOKYO SCHOOL
NEAR A WINTER RESORT AREA, THIS COMPLEX
CONTAINS CLASS, RESIDENCE AND SPORTS
FACILITIES.

DER FÜR SCHÜLER EINER TOKIOTER SCHULE
IN EINEM WINTERSPORTGEBIET ERBAUTE
KOMPLEX ENTHÄLT UNTERRICHTS- UND WOHN-
RÄUME SOWIE SPORTEINRICHTUNGEN.

CE COMPLEXE POUR LES ÉLÈVES D'UN COLLÈ-
GE DANS UNE RÉGION DE SPORTS D'HIVERS
CONTIENT DES SALLES DE COURS ET DE SPORT
AINSI QUE DES DORTOIRS.

P 270.271

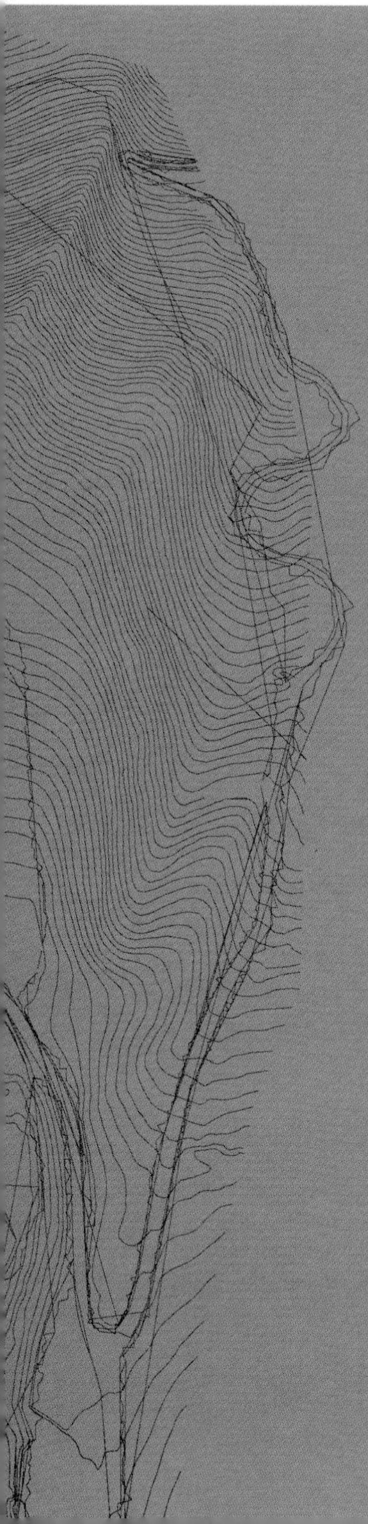

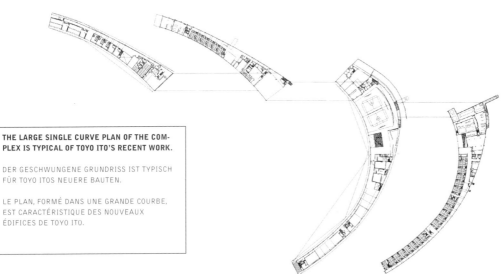

This complex was built for junior high school age students from the Tokyo area Ota-ku, who spend a period each year away from home. This is basically a school with integrated residence facilities, built in a particularly scenic part of the country near the so-called Japanese "Alps." It was important to the architect that all of the main facilities be associated in the same overall system. The lodgings are situated on the ground floor, with classrooms or sports

Dieser Freizeitkomplex wurde für Gymnasiasten aus dem Tokioter Stadtteil Ota-ku gebaut, die jährlich eine Zeit fern von zu Hause verbringen. Es handelt sich um eine Schule mit Internatsräumen, die in einem besonders schönen Teil des Landes liegt, den sogenannten »japanischen Alpen«. Ito legte Wert darauf, alle wichtigen Einrichtungen in ein System einzubinden. Die Schlafräume liegen im Erdgeschoß, darüber helle Klassen- und Sporträume.

Ce complexe a été édifié pour les élèves d'un collège d'Ota-ku, dans l'agglomération de Tokyo. Ils passent chaque année une certaine période loin de leur famille. Il s'agit essentiellement d'une école à internat à proximité des «Alpes japonaises». Il était important pour l'architecte que tous les équipements soient regroupés dans une même structure. Les dortoirs sont au rez-de-chaussée, surmontés par les salles de cours et de sport logées dans des volumes

COMPLETION / FERTIGSTELLUNG /
FIN DE LA CONSTRUCTION: 1998
CLIENT / BAUHERR: OTA-KU
FLOOR AREA / NUTZFLÄCHE /
SURFACE UTILE: 5 404 M²
COSTS / KOSTEN / COÛTS: WITHHELD /
UNGENANNT / NON COMMUNIQUÉS

rooms in bright, steel-framed spaces above. The structure, which is set on a slope, assumes the over-all shape of a crescent, the kind of elongated, ele-gant form that Ito excels in. An inclined, corrugated metal roof curves over the entire complex. The site also includes two pedestrian bridges and an annex made from "materials recycled from an old private dwelling of the region." This annex is intended to give students some idea of local traditions.

Der an einem Hang gelegene Bau hat die Form eines Halbmonds – jene elegante Form, die Ito so vortrefflich beherrscht. Ein geneigtes Wellblech-dach wölbt sich über den gesamten Komplex. Zwei Fußgängerbrücken und ein Nebengebäude bestehen aus »wiederverwendeten Materialien von einem alten Wohnhaus aus der Gegend«. Dies soll den Schülern örtliche Traditionen vermitteln.

encadrés d'acier. Le bâtiment construit sur un terrain en pente prend à peu près la forme d'un croissant, type de forme allongée dans lequel ex-celle Ito. Un toit incliné en métal ondulé se replie par dessus l'ensemble. Le site comprend également deux passerelles piétonnières et une annexe en «matériaux récupérés dans d'anciennes habitations de la région, pour donner aux étudiants un certain sens des traditions locales».

VINCENT JAMES

Vincent James received his M. Arch. degree from the University of Wisconsin in Milwaukee in 1978. He worked as an intern at Hardy Holzman Pfeiffer Associates (1978-80), and at Chrysalis Corporation (1980-84) before founding Vincent James Associates in 1994. He received a National AIA Honor Award for the Type/Variant House in 1998. He has

Vincent James erwarb 1978 seinen Master of Architecture an der University of Wisconsin in Milwaukee. Danach arbeitete er als Praktikant bei Hardy Holzman Pfeiffer Associates (1978-80) und der Chrysalis Corporation (1980-84). 1994 gründete er Vincent James Associates. 1998 erhielt James den National AIA Honor Award für sein

Vincent James est titulaire d'un Master of Architecture de l'Université du Wisconsin-Milwaukee (1978). Il travaille chez Hardy Holzman Pfeiffer Associates (1978-80) et à Chrysalis Corporation (1980-84), avant de fonder Vincent James Associates en 1994. Il reçoit un National AIA Honor Award pour sa Type/Variant House en 1998. Il a

THE TYPE/VARIANT HOUSE PUBLISHED HERE IS
ONE OF THE MOST NOTABLE WORKS BUILT TO
DATE BY VINCENT JAMES, A YOUNG ARCHITECT
FROM WISCONSIN.

DAS HIER VERÖFFENTLICHTE TYPE/VARIANT
HOUSE GEHÖRT ZU DEN BEMERKENSWERTE-
STEN BAUTEN, DIE VINCENT JAMES, EIN JUN-
GER ARCHITEKT AUS WISCONSIN, BISHER
AUSGEFÜHRT HAT.

LA TYPE/VARIANT HOUSE, REPRÉSENTÉE ICI,
EST À CE JOUR L'UNE DES ŒUVRES LES PLUS
REMARQUABLES DE VINCENT JAMES, JEUNE
ARCHITECTE DU WISCONSIN.

VINCENT JAMES ASSOCIATES INC
314 CLIFTON AVENUE SOUTH
MINNEAPOLIS, MINNESOTA 55403
UNITED STATES

TEL: + 1 612 872 6370
FAX: + 1 612 872 6380
E-MAIL: james016@maroon.tc.umn.edu

worked on the K. N. Dayton Residence (Minneapolis, Minnesota, 1996-97), Brooklyn Children's
Museum Master Plan (Brooklyn, New York, 1997-
98), the Minneapolis Rowing Club (Minneapolis,
1998), and on the CALA Addition and Remodeling,
University of Minnesota, Minneapolis, with Steven
Holl Architects (1998).

Type/Variant-Haus. Er baute das Wohnhaus K. N.
Dayton in Minneapolis, Minnesota (1996-97), das
Brooklyn Children's Museum in New York (1997-
98), das Gebäude des Minneapolis Rowing Club in
Minneapolis (1998) und, in Zusammenarbeit mit
Steven Holl, den CALA-Neu- und Umbau der Uni-
versity of Minnesota in Minneapolis (1998).

réalisé la K. N. Dayton Residence (Minneapolis,
Minnesota, 1996-97), le plan directeur du Brooklyn
Children's Museum (Brooklyn, New York, 1997-
98), le Minneapolis Rowing Club (Minneapolis,
1998) et l'extension et la restructuration de CALA,
University of Minnesota, Minneapolis, avec Steven
Holl Architects, 1998.

VINCENT JAMES
TYPE/VARIANT HOUSE
NORTHERN WISCONSIN, UNITED STATES, 1994-97

CLIENT / BAUHERR: WITHHELD AT OWNER'S
REQUEST / UNGENANNT / NON COMMUNIQUÉ
FLOOR AREA / NUTZFLÄCHE / SURFACE UTILE:
740 M²
COSTS / KOSTEN / COÛTS: WITHHELD AT
OWNER'S REQUEST / UNGENANNT / NON
COMMUNIQUÉS
FURNISHINGS AND STORAGE / AUSSTATTUNG /
MOBILIER: VINCENT JAMES

Set on a 2 hectare site near a lake in northern Wisconsin, this house is intended as a gathering place for a large family. Clad in copper, the house is characterized by a strict rectilinearity. The "type" referred to by the architect in the name of the house is related to the repeated use of rectangular volumes. Each volume is then differentiated, explaining the term "variant." Two tower-like structures facing in opposite directions, one 10.7 m tall and the other 7.3 m, contain facilities for guests.

Das auf einem 2 ha großen Grundstück an einem See im Norden Wisconsins errichtete Type/Variant-Haus ist für eine große Familie gedacht. Charakteristisch für den Bau ist seine strenge Geradlinigkeit. Der »Typ«, auf den sich der Name des Hauses bezieht, meint die Verwendung rechtwinkliger Volumina. Jedes Volumen wird differenziert, was den Begriff »Variante« erklärt. Zwei turmähnliche Bauteile – 10,7 m bzw. 7,3 m hoch – beherbergen Gästezimmer. Von diesen Türmen abgesehen, ist

Située sur un terrain de 2 hectares au bord d'un lac du nord du Wisconsin, cette maison est le lieu où se retrouve périodiquement une vaste famille. Recouverte de cuivre, elle se caractérise par sa stricte rectilinéarité. Le «type» auquel se réfère l'architecte dans le nom de son projet évoque la répétition de volumes rectangulaires mais différenciés, d'où le second terme de «variant». Deux tours, orientées dans des directions opposées, l'une de 10,7 m de haut, l'autre de 7,3 m, contiennent les chambres

DESPITE ITS RECTILINEAR VOLUMES, THE TYPE / VARIANT HOUSE IS CLOSELY INVOLVED WITH ITS NATURAL SETTING.

GROSSZÜGIGE AUSBLICKE VERBINDEN DAS STRENG WIRKENDE TYPE/VARIANT HOUSE MIT SEINER NATÜRLICHEN UMGEBUNG.

SES VOLUMES RECTILIGNES N'EMPÊCHENT PAS LA TYPE/VARIANT HOUSE DE S'INTÉGRER ÉTROITEMENT DANS SON CADRE NATUREL.

side from these towers, the 740 m² of space are divided into a living and dining room, kitchen and main bedroom on the ground floor, four bedrooms on the second floor, and a studio and roof deck on the third floor. The client chose the copper cladding, which is intended to turn green with time and blend into the forest. Douglas fir paneling is used extensively inside the house, on walls, ceilings and some floors, and windows frame views out onto the natural, wooded environment.

die Nutzfläche aufgeteilt in Wohn- und Eßraum, Küche und Schlafzimmer im Erdgeschoß, vier Schlafräume im ersten und Atelier mit Dachterrasse im zweiten Obergeschoß. Der Bauherr wählte eine Kupferverkleidung, die im Laufe der Zeit Patina ansetzt und so optisch mit dem Wald verschmilzt. Im Innern sind Wände, Decken und ein Teil der Fußböden großzügig mit Douglasfichte vertäfelt.

d'amis. Le reste de la surface utile de 740 m² est divisé en un séjour-salle à manger, une cuisine, et la chambre à coucher principale au rez-de-chaussée, quatre chambres au premier étage, un studio et une terrasse au troisième. Le client a choisi ce revêtement de cuivre qui devrait virer au vert avec le temps et se fondre dans la forêt. Les lambris en pin de Douglas recouvrent la quasi-totalité de l'intérieur, murs, plafonds et quelques sols. Les fenêtres cadrent l'environnement boisé et naturel.

WARO KISHI

APPROACHING FIFTY YEARS OF AGE, WARO KISHI IS A LEADING FIGURE IN JAPAN'S MOVEMENT TOWARD A HIGHLY REDUCTIVE VERSION OF MODERNISM, A KIND OF MINIMALISM IN ARCHITECTURE.

Born in Yokohama in 1950, Waro Kishi graduated from the Department of Electronics of Kyoto University in 1973, and from the Department of Architecture of the same institution two years later. He completed his postgraduate studies in Kyoto in 1978, and worked in the office of Masayuki Kurokawa in Tokyo from 1978 to 1981. He created Waro Kishi + K. Associates, Architects in Kyoto in

Waro Kishi, geboren 1950 in Yokohama, studierte an der Universität Tokio bis 1973 Elektrotechnik und bis 1975 Architektur. Sein Graduiertenstudium an der Universität Kioto schloß er 1978 ab und arbeitete danach bis 1981 im Büro von Masayuki Kurokawa. 1993 gründete Kishi in Kioto seine eigene Firma Waro Kishi + K. Associates, Architects. In Kioto hat er den Automobilsalon Autolab

Né à Yokohama en 1950, Waro Kishi est diplômé du département d'électronique de l'Université de Kyoto en 1973, et du département d'architecture en 1975. Il termine ses études de spécialisation à Kyoto en 1978, et travaille dans l'agence de Masayuki Kurokawa à Tokyo (1978-81), avant de créer Waro Kishi + K. Associates, Architects à Kyoto en 1993. Parmi ses réalisations au Japon: le

P 280.281

WARO KISHI IST EINER DER FÜHRENDEN
VERTRETER DES JAPANISCHEN TRENDS
ZU EINER STARK REDUZIERTEN VERSION
DER MODERNE, ZU EINEM AUSGEPRÄGTEN
MINIMALISMUS.

WARO KISHI EST L'UN DES LEADERS JAPONAIS
D'UNE VERSION HAUTEMENT RÉDUCTRICE DU
MODERNISME, SORTE DE MINIMALISME ARCHI-
TECTURAL.

WARO KISHI + K. ASSOCIATES, ARCHITECTS
3F YAMASHITA BLDG. 10 NISHIMOTOMACHI
KOYAMA, KITA-KU, KYOTO 603-8113
JAPAN

TEL: + 81 75 492 5175
FAX: + 81 75 492 5185
E-MAIL: warox@ja2.so-net.ne.jp

993. In Japan he completed the Autolab Automobile Showroom (Kyoto, 1989), Kyoto-Kagaku
research Institute (Kizu-cho, Kyoto, 1990), Yuno-
abashi Bridge (Ashikita-cho, Kumamoto, 1991),
onobe SD Office (Sonobe-cho, Funai-gun, Kyoto,
993), and numerous private houses. Recent work
ncludes his Memorial Hall (Ube, Yamaguchi,
997), and a house in Higashi-nada (Kobe, 1997).

(1989) und das Forschungsinstitut Kioto-Kagaku
in Kizucho, (1990), die Yunokabashi-Brücke in
Ashikita-cho, Kumamoto (1991), das Bürogebäude
Sonobe SD in Sonobe-cho, Funai-gun, Kioto (1993)
und zahlreiche Wohnhäuser gebaut. Zu seinen jüngsten Werken gehören die Memorial Hall in Ube,
Yamaguchi (1997) und ein Wohnhaus in Higashi-
nada, Kobe (1997).

showroom automobile Autolab (Kyoto, 1989), l'Institut de recherche Kyoto-Kagaju, Kizu-cho (Kyoto,
1990), le pont Yunokabashi (Ashikita-cho, Kumamoto, 1991), les bureaux Sonobe SD (Sonobe-cho,
Funai-gun, Kyoto, 1993), ainsi que de nombreuses
résidences privées. Il a récemment achevé le Hall
du souvenir (Ube, Yamaguchi, 1997) et une
résidence privée à Higashi-nada, Kobe (1997).

PLANNING / PLANUNG: 5/95-4/96
CONSTRUCTION / BAU: 7/96-4/97
CLIENT / BAUHERR: WITHHELD / UNGENANNT /
NON COMMUNIQUÉ
FLOOR AREA / NUTZFLÄCHE / SURFACE UTILE:
186 M²
COSTS / KOSTEN / COÛTS: WITHHELD /
UNGENANNT / NON COMMUNIQUÉS

THE STRICT LINES AND PURITY OF THIS
HOUSE CORRESPOND NOT ONLY TO A FASHION-
ABLE ARCHITECTURAL STYLE, BUT ALSO TO
THE JAPANESE WAY OF LIVING.

DIE KLAREN LINIEN UND DER PURISMUS DIE-
SES HAUSES ENTSPRECHEN NICHT NUR EINEM
MODERNEN STIL, SONDERN AUCH DER JAPANI-
SCHEN LEBENSWEISE.

LES LIGNES STRICTES ET LA PURETÉ FORMEL-
LE DE CETTE MAISON CORRESPONDENT NON
SEULEMENT À UN STYLE ARCHITECTURAL À LA
MODE, MAIS ÉGALEMENT AU STYLE DE VIE
JAPONAIS.

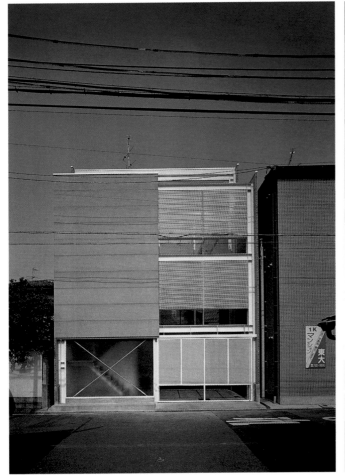

WARO KISHI

HOUSE

HIGASHI-OSAKA, OSAKA, JAPAN, 1995-97

As is typical for houses in the outskirts of Osaka,
this residence is set on a small (110 m²) site. The
total floor area of 186 m² is actually rather large
for a Japanese house, as is the 4.2 m frontage on
the street side. An inner courtyard open to the sky
is a frequent feature of Osaka houses as well. The
three-story steel frame structure is designed to provide an ample 4 m high living-dining space on the
third floor, together with a small terrace. Bedrooms

Wie alle typischen Einfamilienhäuser in den Außen-
bezirken Osakas steht auch dieses auf einem kleinen
Grundstück von 110 m². Die Gesamtnutzfläche von
186 m² ist für japanische Verhältnisse eigentlich
recht groß, ebenso wie die 4,2 m breite Fassade an
der Straßenseite. Der offene Innenhof ist ebenfalls
charakteristisch für Wohnhäuser in Osaka. Das
dreigeschossige Stahlskelett ermöglicht einen groß-
zügigen, 4 m hohen Wohn-/Eßbereich im zweiten

Comme il est de tradition dans les banlieues d'Osaka, cette maison est édifiée sur une petite parcelle
de 110 m². Sa surface totale de 186 m² est en fait
importante pour une résidence privée japonaise, de
même que sa façade sur la rue de 4,2 m de large.
L'ossature en acier est conçue pour permettre un
vaste espace de séjour-salle à manger de 4 m de
haut au deuxième étage, ainsi qu'une petite terrasse
Les chambres sont au premier étage. Comme beau-

are located on the second floor. Like much of the work of Waro Kishi this house can be described as strict or minimalist in its conception. Though the influence of Mies van der Rohe is often cited in reference to the work of Waro Kishi, this house is as much related to Japanese tradition as it is to European Modernism.

Obergeschoß. Wie viele Bauten von Waro Kishi kann auch die Anlage dieses Hauses als streng strukturiert oder minimalistisch bezeichnet werden. Obgleich in Verbindung mit Kishis Werk oft der Einfluß Mies van der Rohes erwähnt wird, ist dieses Haus der japanischen Tradition ebenso verbunden wie der europäischen Moderne.

coup de réalisations de l'architecte, cette maison est de conception stricte, voire minimaliste. Bien que l'influence de Mies van der Rohe soit souvent citée en référence, elle s'appuie autant sur la tradition japonaise que sur le modernisme européen.

KOHN PEDERSEN FOX

KPF was founded in 1976. With offices in New York, London and Tokyo, KPF currently has work in 30 countries. The 206-person firm is led by 12 principals: A. Eugene Kohn, William Pedersen, Robert L. Cioppa, William Louie, Lee Polisano, David Leventhal, Gregory Clement, Paul Katz, James von Klemperer, Kevin Kennon, Michael Greene, and Peter Schubert. KPF's projects of note include the DG Bank Headquarters (Frankfurt, Germany, 1993), the World Bank (Washington D.C., 1996), IBM Corporate Headquarters (Armonk, New York, 1997), and the Shanghai World Financial Center

Das 1976 gegründete Büro Kohn Pedersen Fox (KPF) hat Niederlassungen in New York, London und Tokio und arbeitet gegenwärtig in 30 Ländern. Es hat insgesamt 206 Mitarbeiter und wird von zwölf Architekten geleitet: A. Eugene Kohn, William Pedersen, Robert L. Cioppa, William Louie, Lee Polisano, David Leventhal, Gregory Clement, Paul Katz, James von Klemperer, Kevin Kennon, Michael Greene und Peter Schubert. Zu den bedeutenden Bauten von KPF zählen die Hauptverwaltung der DG-Bank in Frankfurt am Main (1993), die World Bank in Washington, D.C. (1996),

L'agence KPF, fondée en 1976, possède des bureau à New York, Londres et Tokyo, et travaille dans 30 pays. Elle compte 206 collaborateurs et est animée par douze associés dont A. Eugene Kohn, William Pedersen, Robert L. Cioppa, William Louie, Lee Polisano, David Leventhal, Gregory Clement, Paul Katz, James von Klemperer, Kevin Kennon, Michael Greene et Peter Schubert. Parmi ses projets les plus remarqués figurent le siège de la DG Bank (Francfort-sur-le-Main, Allemagne, 1993), la Banque Mondiale (Washington, D.C., 1996), le siège social d'IBM (Armonk, New York, 1997) et le Shanghai

BEST-KNOWN AS THE ARCHITECTS OF LARGE
CORPORATE PROJECTS, BUILT IN AMERICA AND
ALL OVER THE WORLD, KPF STILL TAKES ON
SOME PROJECTS ON A SMALLER SCALE LIKE
THE RODIN PAVILION BY KEVIN KENNON.

KPF, DIE VOR ALLEM MIT GROSSEN BÜRO-
BAUTEN IN AMERIKA UND IN DER GESAMTEN
ÜBRIGEN WELT BEKANNT SIND, ÜBERNEHMEN

NACH WIE VOR AUCH KLEINERE PROJEKTE WIE
DEN RODIN-PAVILLON VON KEVIN KENNON.

SURTOUT CONNU POUR SES GRANDS PROJETS
DE SIÈGES SOCIAUX ÉDIFIÉS EN AMÉRIQUE ET
DANS LE MONDE ENTIER, KPF NE SE DÉSINTÉ-
RESSE PAS POUR AUTANT DE CHANTIERS PLUS
MODESTES COMME CE PAVILLON RODIN DE
KEVIN KENNON.

KOHN PEDERSEN FOX ASSOCIATES
ARCHITECTS & PLANNING CONSULTANTS
111 WEST 57TH STREET
NEW YORK, NEW YORK 10019
UNITED STATES

TEL: + 1 212 977 6500
FAX: + 1 212 956 2526
E-MAIL: clee@kpf.com
WEB: www.kpf.com

Shanghai, 2001). Kevin Kennon, the design principal of the Rodin Pavilion, was born in 1958, and
was educated at Princeton University and Amherst
College. The attention to issues of transparency
seen in the Rodin project is also featured in his
other projects, such as the Sotheby's Headquarters
in New York, the Morgan Stanley Headquarters at
Rockefeller Center, New York, and the new prototype store for Bloomingdale's in San Francisco.

die IBM-Hauptverwaltung in Armonk, New York
(1997) und das Shanghai World Financial Center
(2001). Kevin Kennon, der Planungschef des Rodin-
Pavillons, wurde 1958 geboren und studierte an der
Princeton University und am Amherst College. Sein
besonderes Interesse an transparenten Strukturen
wird am Rodin-Pavillon wie an seinen anderen Entwürfen deutlich, so an den Sotheby's Headquarters,
den Morgan Stanley Headquarters im Rockefeller
Center in New York und dem neuen Ladenlokal-
Prototyp für Bloomingdale's in San Francisco.

World Financial Center (2001). Kevin Kennon,
responsable du Pavillon Rodin, né en 1958, a
étudié à Princeton University et Amherst College.
L'attention portée aux enjeux de la transparence
que l'on observe dans le projet Rodin se retrouve
dans d'autres réalisations, comme le siège de
Sotheby's à New York, celui de la Morgan Stanley
au Rockefeller Center, New York, et dans le nouveau prototype de magasin pour Bloomingdale's
à San-Francisco.

KOHN PEDERSEN FOX

RODIN PAVILION

SEOUL, SOUTH KOREA, 1995-97

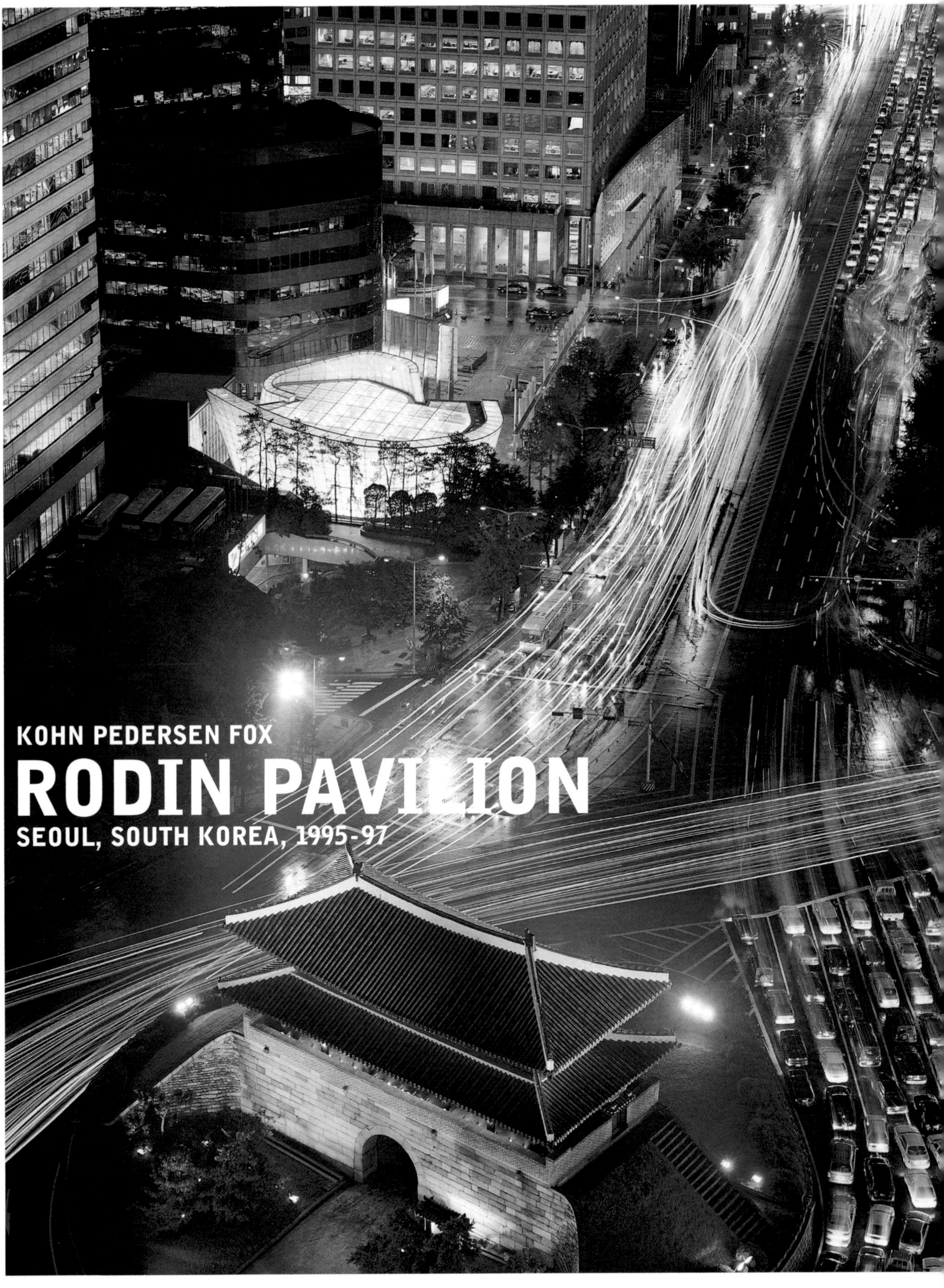

CLIENT / BAUHERR: SAMSUNG GROUP
FLOOR AREA / NUTZFLÄCHE / SURFACE
UTILE: 5000 SQ FT
COSTS / KOSTEN / COÛTS: US$ 10 000 000

SET DIRECTLY INTO THE URBAN COMPLEXITY
OF SEOUL, THE RODIN PAVILION STANDS OUT
FROM ITS ENVIRONMENT, FACING A MORE
TRADITIONAL BUILDING.

IN DER KOMPLEXEN BEBAUUNG VON SEOUL
HEBT SICH DER RODIN-PAVILLON VON SEINER
UMGEBUNG UND DEM GEGENÜBERLIEGENDEN
TRADITIONELLEN GEBÄUDE AB.

NOYÉ DANS LA COMPLEXITÉ URBAINE DE
SÉOUL, LE PAVILLON RODIN SE DÉTACHE DE
SON ENVIRONNEMENT MODERNISTE, FACE
À UN IMMEUBLE PLUS TRADITIONNEL.

Located at the Samsung Center, along the main
road leading from the South Gate to Seoul City
Hall, this glass pavilion was designed by Kevin
Kennon of KPF, and built for a cost of $10 million.
It is intended for the permanent exhibition of two
sculptures by Rodin, casts of the "Burghers of
Calais" and the "Gates of Hell." The installation
of the second work was delayed because of the recent financial problems of South Korea, but was
carried out in the spring of 1999. The pavilion is
set between three existing buildings, which are approximately 30 stories tall. The walls of the pavilion are made of exterior and interior glass skins
supported by structural tempered glass fins. An
airspace almost 1 m in width separates the two
layers of the glass walls. This thickness is apparent
near the curving walls at the entrance, which have
been compared to sculptures by Richard Serra, his
"Torqued Ellipses." Much of the glass is acid etched
and sandblasted, giving a translucent appearance.
Round structural steel columns support the glass
roof. Despite the irregular form of the pavilion, the
glass panels are rectangular, permitting easy
replacement.

Dieser Glaspavillon gehört zum Samsung Center
in Seoul, das an der Hauptstraße vom Südtor zum
Rathaus liegt. Er wurde von Kevin Kennon vom
Büro KPF geplant und für 10 Millionen US$
erbaut. In ihm sollen Abgüsse der »Bürger von
Calais« und des »Höllentors« von Auguste Rodin
ausgestellt werden. Die Aufstellung der zweiten
Skulptur wurde wegen der finanziellen Probleme
Südkoreas zunächst verschoben und erst im Frühjahr 1999 durchgeführt. Der Pavillon ist zwischen
drei bestehende Bauten gesetzt, die etwa 30 Ge-
schosse hoch sind. Seine Wände bestehen aus einer
äußeren und einer inneren Glashaut, die von Stre-
ben aus Hartglas gehalten werden. Die beiden Glaswände sind durch eine fast 1 m tiefe Luftschicht
voneinander getrennt. Diese Tiefe ist an den gekrümmten Wänden am Eingang erkennbar, die mit
Richard Serras Skulpturen »Torqued Ellipses« verglichen worden sind. Ein Großteil des Glases ist
mattgeätzt und sandgestrahlt. Runde Stahlstützen
tragen das Glasdach. Obwohl der Pavillon keine
regelmäßige Form hat, sind die Glasplatten recht-
eckig und damit leicht zu ersetzen.

Situé dans le Samsung Center, sur la route principale qui mène de la Porte du Sud à l'Hôtel de Ville
de Séoul, ce pavillon de verre a été conçu par Kevin
Kennon de KPF, et a coûté $10 millions. Sa fonc-
tion est l'exposition permanente de deux sculptures
de Rodin, des fontes des «Bourgeois de Calais»
et des «Portes de l'Enfer». L'installation de la seconde œuvre a été retardée par la crise financière
que connaît la Corée du Sud, mais finalement
effectuée au printemps 1999. Le pavillon s'insère
entre trois immeubles existants d'environ 30 étages
de haut. Ses murs sont constitués de deux peaux
de verre rigidifiées par des ailettes en verre trempé
et séparées par une lame d'air de presque 1 m
d'épaisseur. Cet écartement très apparent près des
murs incurvés à l'entrée, qui ont été comparés à une
sculpture de Richard Serra, les «Torqued Ellipses».
La plus grande partie du verre est sablé et décapé
à l'acide pour lui donner une apparence translucide.
Des colonnes cylindriques d'acier structurel soutien-
nent le toit de verre. Malgré la forme irrégulière du
Pavillon, les panneaux de verre sont rectangulaires
ce qui facilite leur remplacement éventuel.

P 288.289

SPENDING $10 MILLION TO EXHIBIT TWO WORKS OF ART DID NOT SEEM INAPPROPRIATE IN KOREA PRIOR TO ITS ECONOMIC DIFFICULTIES.

VOR DER WIRTSCHAFTSKRISE GALT ES IN KOREA NICHT ALS UNANGEMESSEN, 10 MILLIONEN $ FÜR DIE AUSSTELLUNG VON ZWEI KUNSTWERKEN AUSZUGEBEN.

DÉPENSER $10 MILLIONS POUR N'EXPOSER QUE DEUX ŒUVRES D'ART, NE SEMBLAIT PAS EXTRAORDINAIRE DANS LA CORÉE D'AVANT LA CRISE ÉCONOMIQUE.

THE COMPLEX GLASS FORMS OF THE PAVILION
OF COURSE UNDERLINE THE WORKS BY RODIN,
BUT THEY ALSO MAKE FOR A POWERFUL
URBAN PRESENCE.

DIE KOMPLEXEN GLÄSERNEN FORMEN DES
PAVILLONS GEBEN DEN KUNSTWERKEN VON
RODIN VIEL RAUM UND LICHT.

LES FORMES VITRÉES COMPLEXES DU PAVIL-
LON METTENT EN VALEUR LES ŒUVRES DE
RODIN, TOUT EN CONFÉRANT AU BÂTIMENT
UNE FORTE PRÉSENCE URBAINE.

REM KOOLHAAS

REM KOOLHAAS IS ONE OF THE MOST INFLUENTIAL ARCHITECTS CURRENTLY WORKING IN THE WORLD, BOTH BECAUSE OF HIS FEW BUILT WORKS AND BECAUSE OF HIS PUBLISHED BODY OF ARCHITECTURAL THEORY.

Rem Koolhaas was born in The Hague in 1944. Before studying at the Architectural Association in London, he worked as a journalist for the *Haagse Post* and as a screenwriter. He founded the Office for Metropolitan Architecture (OMA) in London in 1975, and became well known after the 1978 publication of his book *Delirious New York*. His built work includes apartments at Nexus World (Fukuoka, Japan, 1991), and the Villa dall'Ava (Saint-

Rem Koolhaas, geboren 1944 in Den Haag, arbeitete vor seinem Studium an der AA als Journalist bei der »Haagse Post« und als Drehbuchautor. 1975 gründete er in London das Office for Metropolitan Architecture (OMA); mit seinem Buch »Delirious New York« wurde er 1978 weithin bekannt. Zu seinen Bauten gehören Wohnungen in Nexus World, Fukuoka, Japan (1991) und die Villa dall'Ava in Saint-Cloud, Frankreich (1985-91). 1988 wurde

Né à La Haye en 1944, Rem Koolhaas est journaliste au «Haagse Post» et scénariste, avant d'étudier l'architecture à l'Architectural Association de Londres. Il crée l'Office for Metropolitan Architecture (OMA) à Londres en 1975, et se fait connaître à travers son ouvrage «Delirious New York» (1978). Il a construit un ensemble d'appartements pour Nexus World (Fukuoka, Japon, 1991) et la Villa dall'Ava (Saint-Cloud, 1985-91). Nommé architecte

REM KOOLHAAS IST GEGENWÄRTIG EINER DER
EINFLUSSREICHSTEN ARCHITEKTEN DER WELT.
SEIN ANSEHEN GRÜNDET SICH SOWOHL AUF
SEINE – WENN AUCH NUR WENIGEN – AUS-
GEFÜHRTEN BAUTEN ALS AUCH AUF SEINE
ARCHITEKTURTHEORETISCHEN SCHRIFTEN.

REM KOOLHAAS EST L'UN DES ARCHITECTES
LES PLUS INFLUENTS DU MOMENT PLUS POUR
SES OUVRAGES DE THÉORIE ARCHITECTURALE
QUE POUR SES RARES RÉALISATIONS.

P 292.293

OFFICE FOR METROPOLITAN ARCHITECTURE
STEDEBOUW B. V.
149 BOKELWEG HEER
ROTTERDAM 3032 AD
THE NETHERLANDS

TEL: + 31 10 243 8200
FAX: + 31 10 243 8202

Cloud, France, 1985-91). He was named head architect of the Euralille project in Lille, France, in
1988, and has worked on a design for the new
Jussieu University Library in Paris. With his 1,400-
page book *S,M,L,XL* (Benedikt Taschen Verlag,
1997, new ed.) he has become an influential writer.
Recent work includes a house (Bordeaux, France,
1998), movie studios in California, and the campus
center at the Illinois Institute of Technology.

ihm die Leitung des Euralille-Projekts in Lille über-
tragen, außerdem arbeitete er an einem Entwurf
für die neue Bibliothek der Universität Jussieu in
Paris. Mit seinem 1 400 Seiten – Buch »S,M,L,XL«
(Taschen Verlag, 1997, Neuaufl.) hat er sich erneut
als einflußreicher Autor erwiesen. Neuere Projekte
sind ein Wohnhaus in Bordeaux (1998), Filmstudios
in Kalifornien und das Campus-Zentrum des Illinois
Institute of Technology in Chicago.

en chef du projet Euralille à Lille en 1988, il a travaillé sur le projet de la nouvelle bibliothèque universitaire de Jussieu à Paris. Son livre de 1 400 pages «S,M,L,XL» (Benedikt Taschen Verlag, 1997,
nouvelle éd.) a fait de lui un auteur influent. Parmi ses réalisations récentes: une maison à Bordeaux
(1998), des studios de cinéma en Californie et le
Campus Center de l'Illinois Institute of Technology.

REM KOOLHAAS
EDUCATORIUM, UNIVERSITY OF UTRECHT
UTRECHT, THE NETHERLANDS, 1995-97

CLIENT / BAUHERR: UNIVERSITY OF UTRECHT
FLOOR AREA / NUTZFLÄCHE / SURFACE UTILE:
45 000 M²
COSTS / KOSTEN / COÛTS: US$ 12 600 000

P 294.295

THE ANGLED FLOOR DESIGN OF THE BUILDING
RESEMBLES THAT EMPLOYED BY KOOLHAAS IN
THE KUNSTHAL ROTTERDAM.

DER ENTWURF MIT SCHRÄGER GESCHOSS-
GESTALTUNG ÄHNELT DEM FÜR DIE KUNSTHAL
ROTTERDAM.

LES PLANS INCLINÉS FONT PENSER À
CEUX UTILISÉS PAR L'ARCHITECTE POUR
LE KUNSTHAL ROTTERDAM.

P 296.297

This 45,000 m² facility, built for a modest $12.6 million, was inaugurated in September 1997. The office of Koolhaas, OMA began work on the development plans of the University of Utrecht in 1985. The Educatorium contains a campus cafeteria with seating for 1,000, as well as two large lecture halls, seating respectively 400 and 500 persons. The skewed design of these lecture halls brings to mind a similar space designed by Koolhaas for the Kunsthal Rotterdam. Detailing is reminiscent of the Grand Palais in Lille, part of the Euralille complex. The cafeteria is placed below the lecture halls, whose rear forms the distinctive rounded "snout" of the building. Much of the circulation in the building is routed through inclined ramps, and views onto the external environment such as the neighboring botanical garden are both frequent and ample.

Das 45 000 m² umfassende Educatorium der Universiteit Utrecht wurde mit dem bescheidenen Budget von 12,6 Millionen US $ errichtet und im September 1997 eröffnet. OMA, das Büro von Koolhaas, nahm 1985 die Arbeit an den Bebauungsplänen für die Universität auf. Der Bau beherbergt ein Studentencafé mit 1 000 Plätzen und zwei große Hörsäle für 400 bzw. 500 Personen. Die schräge Form der Hörsäle geht auf Koolhaas' Entwurf für die Kunsthal Rotterdam zurück; die Detailgestaltung erinnert an das Grand Palais in Lille, das Teil des Euralille-Komplexes ist. Die Cafeteria liegt unterhalb der Hörsäle, deren Rückseite die charakteristische, abgerundete »Schnauze« des Bauwerks bildet. Ein Großteil des Besucherverkehrs wird über Rampen geführt; große Glasfronten ermöglichen Ausblicke in die Umgebung, etwa in den benachbarten botanischen Garten.

Cet équipement universitaire de 45 000 m², construit pour un modeste budget de $12,6 millions, a été inauguré en septembre 1997. L'agence de Koolhaas, OMA, a commencé à travailler sur les plans de développement de l'Université d'Utrecht dès 1985. L'Educatorium contient la cafétéria du campus d'une capacité de 1 000 places, deux grandes salles de conférences de 400 et 500 places. La conception en biais des ces salles rappelle des espaces similaires conçu par l'architecte pour la Kunsthal Rotterdam. L'aménagement des détails rappelle le complexe d'Euralille. La cafétéria est logée sous les salles de conférences dont la partie arrière forme le «mufle» caractéristique du bâtiment. Une grande partie des circulations se fait par des plans inclinés, et les multiples ouvertures sur l'environnement extérieur, comme le jardin botanique voisin, sont à la fois fréquentes et généreuses.

KOOLHAAS USES UNEXPECTED COMBINATIONS OF OFTEN INEXPENSIVE MATERIALS TO CREATE A LIVELY, EXCITING ENVIRONMENT.

KOOLHAAS VERWENDET HÄUFIG UNGEWÖHN-LICHE KOMBINATIONEN AUS PREISWERTEN MATERIALIEN UND SCHAFFT SO EIN KONTRAST-REICHES AMBIENTE.

KOOLHAAS COMBINE SOUVENT DES MATÉ-RIAUX ÉCONOMIQUES DE FAÇON INATTENDUE POUR CRÉER UN ENVIRONNEMENT ANIMÉ ET SÉDUISANT.

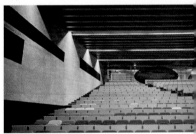

THE SWEEPING ROUNDED SHAPE OF THE BUILDING AND ITS ANGLED FLOOR GIVE IT A DECIDEDLY CONTEMPORARY FEELING FROM THE FIRST GLANCE.

DIE GESCHWUNGENE FORM DES GEBÄUDES UND SEINE SCHRÄGEN DECKEN VERLEIHEN IHM EINE ENTSCHIEDEN MODERNE WIRKUNG.

LES FORMES ARRONDIES ET ENVELOPPANTES DU BÂTIMENT ET SON SOL INCLINÉ EXPRIMENT AU PREMIER REGARD SA MODERNITÉ SENSIBLE.

KENGO KUMA

Born in 1954 in Kanagawa, Japan, Kengo Kuma graduated in 1979 from the University of Tokyo, with a Masters in architecture. In 1985-86 he received an Asian Cultural Council fellowship grant, and was a Visiting Scholar at Columbia University. In 1987 he established the Spatial Design Studio, and in 1991 he created Kengo Kuma & Associates. His work includes the Gunma Toyota Car Show Room (Maebashi, 1989), Maiton Resort Complex (Phuket, Thailand, 1991), Rustic and Doric, Office Buildings (Tokyo, 1991), M2, Headquarters for Mazda New Design Team (Tokyo, 1991), Kinjo Golf

Kengo Kuma, geboren 1954 in Kanagawa, Japan, schloß sein Studium an der Universität Tokio 1979 mit dem Master of Architecture ab. 1985-86 arbeitete er mit einem Stipendium des Asian Cultural Council als Gastwissenschaftler an der Columbia University in New York. 1987 gründete Kuma in Tokio das Spatial Design Studio und 1991 das Büro Kengo Kuma & Associates. Zu seinen ausgeführten Bauten gehören der Gunma Toyota Car Show Room in Maebashi, Japan (1989), die Ferienanlage Maiton in Phuket, Thailand (1991), die Bürogebäude Rustic und Doric sowie M2, die Hauptverwaltung

Né en 1954 à Kanagawa, Japon, Kengo Kuma obtient son Master of Architecture à l'Université de Tokyo en 1979. En 1985-86, il reçoit une bourse de l'Asian Cultural Council et devient chercheur invité à Columbia University. En 1987, il crée le Spatial Design Studio et, en 1991, Kengo Kuma & Associates. Parmi ses réalisations: le Showroom Gunma Toyota (Maebashi, 1989), le complexe balnéaire Maiton (Phuket, Thailande), les immeuble de bureaux Rustic et Doric (Tokyo), et le siège du département de design de Mazda M2 (Tokyo), tous en 1991; le Club House du Kinjo Golf Club (Okayama,

AT THE AGE OF 45, KENGO KUMA STANDS APART FROM MUCH OF CONTEMPORARY JAPANESE ARCHITECTURE, DARING TO CREATE BUILDINGS WHICH CAN BE ASSIMILATED TO WORKS OF ART IN AND OF THEIR OWN RIGHT.

KENGO KUMA DISTANZIERT SICH VOM GROSS-TEIL DER ZEITGENÖSSISCHEN JAPANISCHEN ARCHITEKTUR UND ERRICHTET BAUTEN, DIE

ZU RECHT ALS KUNSTWERKE BEZEICHNET WERDEN KÖNNEN.

À 45 ANS, KENGO KUMA SE DISTINGUE D'UNE BONNE PARTIE DE SES CONFRÈRES JAPONAIS ET N'HÉSITE PAS À METTRE EN ŒUVRE DES PROJETS QUI PEUVENT ÊTRE ASSIMILÉS À DES ŒUVRES D'ART EN SOI.

KENGO KUMA & ASSOCIATES
2-12-12-9F MINAMIAOYAMA
MINATO-KU, TOKYO 107-0062
JAPAN

TEL: + 81 3 3401 7721
FAX: + 81 3 3401 7778
E-MAIL: kuma@ba2.so-net.or.jp

lub, Club House (Okayama, 1992), Kiro-san Ob-ervatory (Ehime, 1994), Guest House for Bandai orp (Atami, 1992-95), Karuizawa Resort Hotel Karuizawa, 1993), Tomioka Lakewood Golf Club louse (Tomioka, 1993-96), a Noh stage (Toyama ity, 1996), and the Japanese Pavilion for the enice Biennale (Venice, Italy, 1995). Kengo uma is currently working on a Stone Museum nd a Museum of Ando Hiroshige, both in Tochigi, apan, and scheduled to be completed in 2000.

für das neue Designteam von Mazda, alle 1991 in Tokio entstanden; das Klubhaus des Kinjo Golf Club in Okayama (1992), das Observatorium Kiro-san in Ehime (1994), das Gästehaus für die Firma Bandai in Atami (1992-95), ein Hotel in Karuizawa (1993), das Klubhaus des Lakewood Golf Club in Tomioka (1993-96), das Noh-Theater in Toyama City (1996) und der Japanische Pavillon auf der Biennale in Venedig (1995). Gegenwärtig arbeitet Kuma an einem Steinmuseum und einem Museum für Ando Hiroshige, beide in Tochigi, Japan, die im Jahr 2000 fertiggestellt werden sollen.

1992), l'observatoire Kiro-san (Ehime, 1994), le pavillon d'invités Atami pour Bandai Corp. (Atami, 1992-95), l'hôtel de vacances Karuizawa (Karuiza-wa, 1993), le Club House du Tomiota Lakewood Golf Club (Tomioka, 1993-96), le Théâtre Nô de Toyama City (1996) et le pavillon japonais pour la Biennale de Venise (Venise, 1995). Il travaille actuellement à un Musée de la pierre et au Musée d'Ando Hiroshige, tous deux à Tochigi, qui devraient être achevés en l'an 2000.

KENGO KUMA
NOH STAGE IN THE FOREST
TOYAMA CITY, TOYAMA, JAPAN, 1996

The intention of this project was to return the Noh Theater to its original environment – an outdoor setting. Until the completion of this project, the local form of theater, called Toyama Noh, was performed in the gymnasium of the local high school. Set on the northern edge of the town of Toyama, which is in the west of the country near the Sea of Japan, the Noh Stage is used on a daily basis by local residents for the tea ceremony as well as for dancing. A light latticework of Douglas fir was employed to preserve the openness of the stage, and

Diesem Entwurf liegt der Gedanke zugrunde, das Noh-Theater in seine ursprüngliche Umgebung im Freien zurückzuführen. Bis zur Fertigstellung des Projekts wurde in Toyama die lokale Variante des Noh-Theaters, Toyama Noh genannt, in der Turnhalle des Gymnasiums aufgeführt. Die Noh-Bühne liegt am Nordrand der Stadt im Westen des Landes am Japanischen Meer. Sie wird von den Einwohnern täglich für die Teezeremonie und für Tanzveranstaltungen genutzt. Ein leichtes Gitterwerk aus Douglasfichte sollte die Offenheit der Bühne und

L'intention de ce projet est de rendre le théâtre Nô à son environnement original: l'extérieur. Jusqu'à son achèvement, les pièces de Nô local (Toyama Nô), étaient données dans le gymnase d'un collège. Dans le nord de la ville de Toyama (dans l'ouest du Japon, non loin de la mer du Japon), ce théâtre est utilisé quotidiennement par les habitants pour la cérémonie du thé ou la danse. Un léger treillis en pin de Douglas sert à préserver l'ouverture de la scène et les vues vers l'environnement naturel. La conception ouverte de ce projet, et en particulier la

P 306.307

KUMA'S SUCCESS IN THIS INSTANCE IS RELATED TO HIS INTERPRETATION OF THE TRADITIONAL FORMS OF THE NOH STAGE FROM A MODERN POINT OF VIEW.

KUMA INTERPRETIERT DIE TRADITIONELLEN FORMEN DER NOH-BÜHNE AUF MODERNE ART.

LA RÉUSSITE DE KUMA TIENT ICI À LA RÉINTERPRÉTATION MODERNE DES FORMES TRADITIONNELLES DE LA SCÈNE DE THÉÂTRE NÔ.

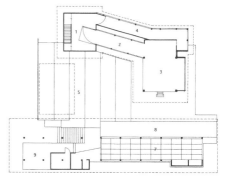

...ne views toward the surrounding environment. The ...pen nature of this design, and in particular the ...tage surface, which is "expressed as a thin plane," ...re unusual in a type of architecture that is normal- ...y highly codified in Japan. Set on a 1,700 m² site, ...ne building has a total floor area of 498 m², in- ...luding a small exhibition space. Since the stage is ...et just at the entrance to the forest at the town's ...dge, it is conceived as an "interface" or transition ...etween the two areas.

den Ausblick in die Umgebung erhalten. Der offene Charakter des Entwurfs und besonders die dünne Fläche des Bühnenbodens sind ungewöhnlich für diesen Bautyp, der in Japan streng kodifiziert ist. Das auf einem 1700 m² großen Grundstück stehende Gebäude hat eine Gesamtnutzfläche von 498 m², einen kleinen Ausstellungsraum eingeschlossen. Die Bühne liegt am Stadtrand direkt am Wald und bildet so als »Nahtstelle« den Übergang zwischen zwei Bereichen.

surface de la scène, sorte de «plan mince», sont inhabituelles dans un type d'architecture normalement très codifié. Aménagé sur un terrain de 1700 m², le bâtiment offre une surface totale de 498 m², y compris un petit espace d'exposition. La scène, en lisière de forêt, se veut une «interface» entre la nature et la ville.

THE USE OF SOME HISTORICIST DETAIL WAS
IMPOSED BY THE THEATRICAL FUNCTION OF
THE STAGE COMPLEX.

DIE FUNKTION DER BÜHNENANLAGE ALS
THEATER LEGTE DIE VERWENDUNG HISTO-
RISIERENDER DETAILS NAHE.

L'UTILISATION DE QUELQUES DÉTAILS HISTO-
RIQUES A ÉTÉ IMPOSÉE PAR LA FONCTION
THÉÂTRALE DE CETTE PETITE SCÈNE.

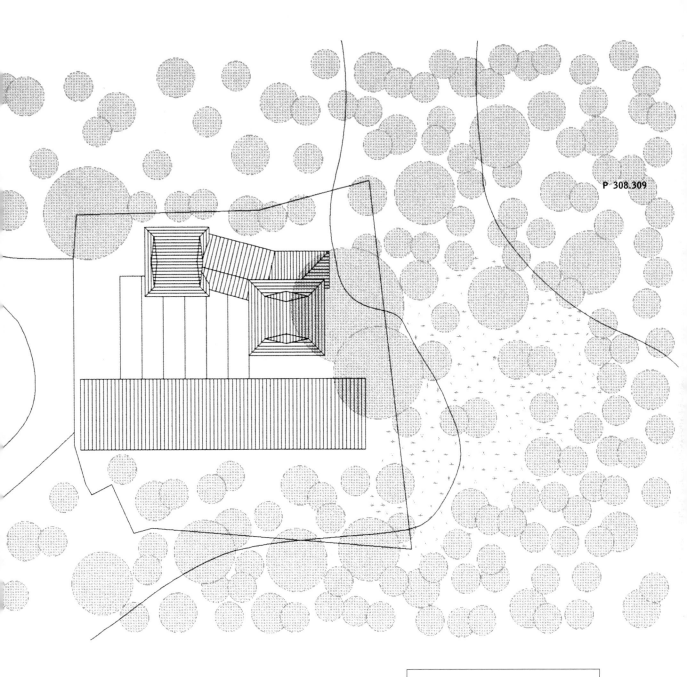

CLIENT / BAUHERR: TOWN OF TOYAMA
FLOOR AREA / NUTZFLÄCHE / SURFACE
UTILE: 498 M²
COSTS / KOSTEN / COÛTS: 195 000 000 ¥

DANIEL LIBESKIND

Born in Poland in 1946 and now a US citizen, Daniel Libeskind studied music in Poland, Israel and New York before taking up architecture at the Cooper Union in New York. He has taught at Harvard, Yale, Hanover, Graz, Hamburg, and UCLA. His work includes the Jewish Museum in Berlin (1989-99), and numerous projects such as his 1997 plan for an extension to the Victoria & Albert Museum in London, and his prize-winning scheme for the Bremen Philharmonic Hall (1995). Like Zaha

Daniel Libeskind, geboren 1946 in Polen, ist amerikanischer Staatsbürger. Zunächst studierte er Musik in Polen, Israel und New York, anschließend Architektur an der Cooper Union in New York. Er hat in Harvard, Yale, Hannover, Graz, Hamburg und an der UCLA gelehrt. Seine wichtigsten Projekte sind das kürzlich eröffnete Jüdische Museum in Berlin (1989-99), ein Entwurf zur Erweiterung des Victoria & Albert Museum in London (1997) und der preisgekrönte Wettbewerbsentwurf für die

Né en Pologne en 1946, et aujourd'hui citoyen américain, Daniel Libeskind étudie la musique en Pologne, en Israël et à New York avant de s'orienter vers l'architecture à Cooper Union, New York. Il a enseigné à Harvard, Yale, Hanovre, Graz et UCLA. Il est l'auteur, entre autres, du Musée juif de Berlin (1989-99) et de nombreux projets comme l'extension du Victoria & Albert Museum à Londres et la Salle philharmonique de Brême, primée en 1995. Comme Zaha Hadid, Libeskind a exercé une

LIKE ZAHA HADID AND COOP HIMMELB(L)AU, DANIEL LIBESKIND HAS BEEN ASSOCIATED WITH THE EMERGENCE OF DECONSTRUCTIVISM IN THE 1980S. LIKE THEM, HE IS NOW STARTING TO BUILD MUCH MORE.

WIE ZAHA HADID UND COOP HIMMELB(L)AU WIRD DANIEL LIBESKIND MIT DEM DEKON-STRUKTIVISMUS DER 80ER JAHRE VERBUNDEN,

UND WIE SIE BEGINNT ER JETZT, MEHR PROJEKTE ZU VERWIRKLICHEN.

COMME ZAHA HADID ET COOP HIMMELB(L)AU, DANIEL LIBESKIND A PARTICIPÉ À L'ÉMERGEN-CE DU DÉCONSTRUCTIVISME DES ANNÉES 1980. COMME EUX, IL EST AUJOURD'HUI ENTRÉ DANS UNE PHASE DE CONSTRUCTION ACTIVE.

ARCHITEKTUR STUDIO LIBESKIND
WINDSCHEIDSTRASSE 18
10627 BERLIN
GERMANY

TEL: + 49 30 324 9963
FAX: + 49 30 324 9591

adid, he has had a considerable influence through is theory and his projects, rather than through his mited built work. The Felix Nussbaum Museum Osnabrück, Germany, is in fact one of his first ompleted works. His current work includes pro-cts for the Imperial War Museum, London, and r the Shoah Centre in Manchester, the Jewish useum, San Francisco, California, and the JVG niversity-Colleges of Public Administration, uadalajara, Mexico.

Philharmonie in Bremen (1995). Wie Zaha Hadid hat er mehr Einfluß ausgeübt durch seine Theorien und Entwürfe als durch seine wenigen ausgeführten Bauten, deren erstes das Felix-Nußbaum-Haus in Osnabrück war. Zur Zeit arbeitet er an Projekten für das Imperial War Museum in London und das Shoah Centre in Manchester, England, das Jewish Museum in San Francisco und die JVG University-Colleges of Public Administration in Guadalajara, Mexiko.

influence considérable à travers ses théories et ses écrits plus qu'à travers ses réalisations en nombre limité. Le Felix Nussbaum Museum d'Osnabrück, Allemagne, est en fait l'une de ses premières œuvres achevées. Il travaille actuellement à un projet pour l'Imperial War Museum à Londres et pour le Shoah Centre de Manchester, Grande-Bretagne, le Musée juif de San-Francisco, Californie, et le collège d'administration publique de l'Université JVG de Guadalajara, Mexique.

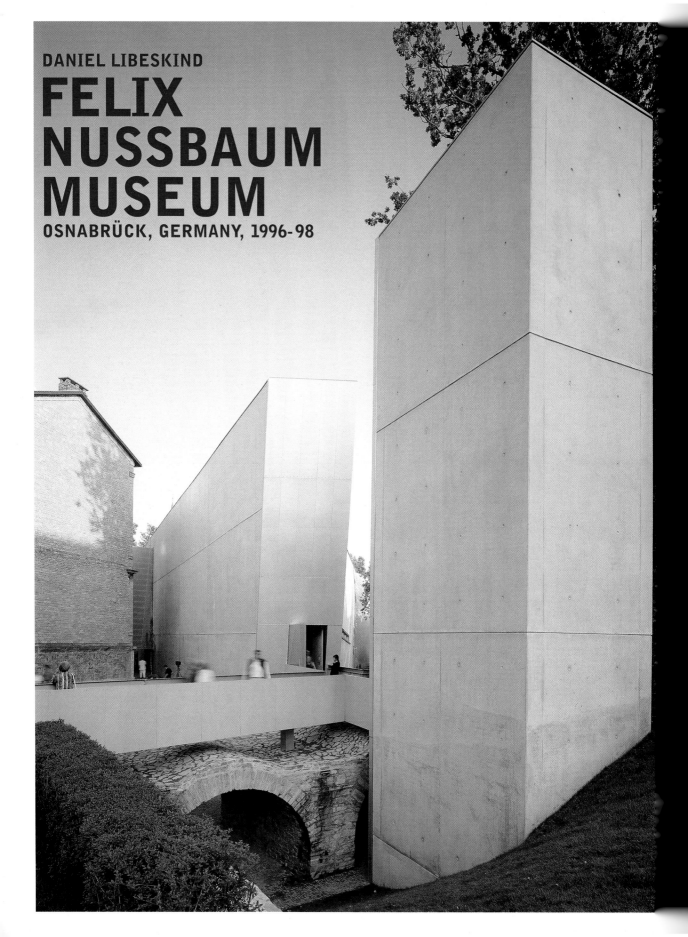

DANIEL LIBESKIND

FELIX NUSSBAUM MUSEUM

OSNABRÜCK, GERMANY, 1996-98

OPENED / ERÖFFNET / OUVERTURE: 7/98
CLIENT / BAUHERR: CITY OF OSNABRÜCK
USER / NUTZER / UTILISATEUR: KULTUR-
GESCHICHTLICHES MUSEUM OSNABRÜCK
FLOOR AREA / NUTZFLÄCHE / SURFACE
UTILE: 1 890 M²
COSTS / KOSTEN / COÛTS: 14 600 000 DM

HERE, AS IN HIS MUSEUM IN BERLIN,
LIBESKIND FOCUSES AS MUCH ON THE IDEA OF
ABSENCE AS ON THAT OF ARCHITECTURAL
PRESENCE.

WIE BEI SEINEM BERLINER MUSEUM VER-
SUCHT LIBESKIND AUCH HIER, DIE GEDANKEN
VON TOD UND ERINNERUNG FORMAL UMZU-
SETZEN.

COMME DANS SON MUSÉE DE BERLIN, LIBES-
KIND SE CONCENTRE ICI AUSSI BIEN SUR
L'IDÉE DE L'ABSENCE QUE SUR L'IDÉE DE
PRÉSENCE DANS L'ARCHITECTURE.

A CENTRAL FEATURE OF THE MUSEUM IS A
46 M LONG GALLERY THAT IS ONLY 3 M WIDE.

ZENTRALES ELEMENT DES MUSEUMS IST
DER 46 M LANGE, ABER NUR 3 M BREITE
»NUSSBAUM-GANG«.

UNE DES CARACTÉRISTIQUES PRINCIPALES
DU MUSÉE EST SA GALERIE DE 46 M DE LONG
SUR 3 M DE LARGE.

P 314.315

This is the first completed building by one of the best-known architects of the moment. It is related in form to Libeskind's Jewish Museum in Berlin, which had been scheduled to open earlier. Its three intersecting volumes are clad in oak, zinc, and concrete. Built to commemorate the work of the Jewish painter, Felix Nussbaum, who was killed in Auschwitz in 1944 aged 40, the structure is intended to evoke a "Museum without Exit." In practical terms this means that the architect has made the movement of visitors through the space intentionally difficult. One of its central features is an unusual 46 m long, 3 m wide gallery called the "Nussbaum Passage." The lines formed by the building are intended to lead to important sites in the life of the artist and of the town, such as the former synagogue, burned by the Nazis in 1938. According to the architect, "every element of the spatial organization, geometry and programmatic content of this scheme refers to the paradigmatic destiny of Nussbaum ..." As Libeskind himself points out, the very presence of the Felix Nussbaum Museum, like its architecture in this conservative town, is unexpected.

Dies ist der erste ausgeführte Bau eines der bekanntesten zeitgenössischen Architekten. In der Form ist es seinem Jüdischem Museum in Berlin verwandt. Die drei einander durchdringenden Baukörper sind mit Eichenholz und Zink verkleidet. Der Bau wurde zum Gedenken an den jüdischen Maler Felix Nußbaum errichtet, der 1944 im Alter von 40 Jahren in Auschwitz ermordet wurde. Es soll ein »Museum ohne Ausgang« sein, was konkret bedeutet, daß der Architekt den Gang durch die Räume bewußt schwierig gestaltet hat. Zentrales Element des Baus ist die ungewöhnliche, 46 m lange und 3 m breite Galerie, der sogenannte »Nußbaum-Gang«. Die Linien des Gebäudes sollen zu wichtigen Orten im Leben des Künstlers und in der Stadt führen, so zur Synagoge, die 1938 von den Nationalsozialisten in Brand gesteckt wurde. Nach Libeskind »bezieht sich jedes Element dieses Entwurfs, die räumliche Organisation, die Geometrie und der programmatische Inhalt, auf das paradigmatische Schicksal Nußbaums ...« Wie er selbst betont, ist das Museum und seine Architektur ungewöhnlich für diese konservative Stadt.

Premier bâtiment achevé par l'un des architectes les plus connus du moment, il n'est pas sans liens formels avec le Musée juif de Berlin qui aurait dû ouvrir ses portes le premier. Ses trois volumes qui s'entrecoupent sont plaqués de chêne, de zinc et de béton. Edifié pour commémorer l'œuvre du peintre juif Felix Nussbaum, mort à Auschwitz en 1944 à l'âge de 40 ans, ce bâtiment veut évoquer un «Musée sans issue». En termes concrets, l'architecte a volontairement compliqué le parcours des visiteurs. L'une de ses caractéristiques principales est une galerie de 46 m de long sur 3 de large appelée le «Nussbaum Passage». Les axes du bâtiment sont orientés vers des sites qui ont compté dans la vie de l'artiste et de la ville, comme l'ancienne synagogue incendiée par les nazis en 1938. Pour l'architecte: «Chaque élément de l'organisation spatiale, de sa géométrie et de son contenu en termes de programme se réfère au destin paradigmatique de Nussbaum ...» Il fait également remarquer que la présence d'un tel musée et d'une telle architecture dans une ville conservatrice est surprenante.

MODULATING MATERIAL AND STRUCTURAL ANGULARITY, DANIEL LIBESKIND CREATES A BUILDING THAT RESEMBLES A SCULPTURE.

DURCH AUFEINANDER ABGESTIMMTE MATE-RIALIEN UND SCHRÄGE WINKEL HAT LIBES-KIND EIN BAUWERK GESCHAFFEN, DAS EINER SKULPTUR ÄHNELT.

MODULATION DES MATÉRIAUX ET STRUCTURE ANGULEUSE: DANIEL LIBESKIND A CRÉÉ UN BÂTIMENT QUI RESSEMBLE À UNE SCULPTURE.

DANIEL LIBESKIND
JEWISH MUSEUM
BERLIN, GERMANY, 1989-99

COMPETITION / WETTBEWERB / CONCOURS:
1989
START OF PLANNING / PLANUNGSBEGINN /
DÉBUT DES ÉTUDES: 1989
CONSTRUCTION / BAU: 1991-99
FLOOR AREA / NUTZFLÄCHE / SURFACE
UTILE: 12 500 M²
EXHIBITION SPACE / AUSSTELLUNGSFLÄCHE /
SURFACE D'EXPOSITION: 9 500 M²
COSTS / KOSTEN / COÛTS: 72 100 000 DM

DANIEL LIBESKIND'S LONG AWAITED JEWISH
MUSEUM IN BERLIN OPENED ITS DOORS DEVOID
OF ANY COLLECTION.

DANIEL LIBESKINDS LANG ERWARTETES
JÜDISCHES MUSEUM ÖFFNETE SEINE PFORTEN,
OHNE EINE SAMMLUNG ZU BEHERBERGEN.

LONGTEMPS ATTENDU, LE MUSÉE JUIF CONÇU
PAR LIBESKIND POUR BERLIN A OUVERT SES
PORTES SANS LA MOINDRE COLLECTION À
PRÉSENTER.

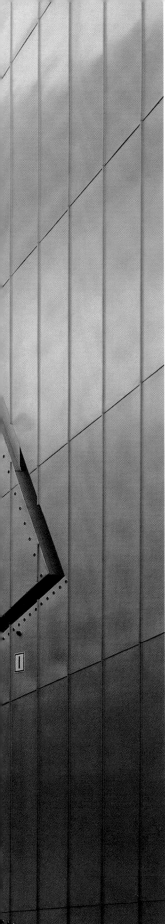

A ZIGZAGGING PATTERN OF OPENINGS EVOKES THE IDEA OF RUPTURE, DESTRUCTION AND ABSENCE.

DIE IM ZICKZACK-SYSTEM ANGELEGTEN ÖFFNUNGEN RUFEN DIE VORSTELLUNG VON BRÜCHEN, ZERSTÖRUNG UND ABWESENHEIT HERVOR.

UN MOTIF DE DÉCOUPES EN ZIGZAG ÉVOQUE L'IDÉE DE RUPTURE, DE DESTRUCTION ET D'ABSENCE.

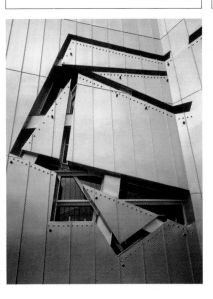

 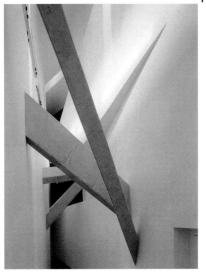

JUST AS SOME CONTEMPORARY ART SEEKS
OUT THE UNCOMFORTABLE, SO THE JEWISH
MUSEUM PROPOSES NO EASY SOLUTIONS.

WHERE MUCH CONTEMPORARY ARCHITECTURE
SEEKS SIMPLICITY AND EASE, THIS DESIGN IS
INTENTIONALLY DIFFICULT.

DAS JÜDISCHE MUSEUM ERSCHLIESST SICH
DEM BESUCHER NICHT OHNE WEITERES.

IM GEGENSATZ ZU VIELEN ANDEREN BAUTEN
IST DAS MUSEUM BEWUSST KOMPLIZIERT
GESTALTET.

DE MÊME QUE CERTAINES ŒUVRES D'ART CON-
TEMPORAIN CHERCHENT À METTRE LE SPEC-
TATEUR MAL À L'AISE, LE MUSÉE JUIF NE
PROPOSE PAS D'INTERPRÉTATION ÉVIDENTE.

ALORS QUE LA PLUPART DES ŒUVRES ARCHI-
TECTURALES CONTEMPORAINES RECHER-
CHENT LA SIMPLICITÉ, LA CONCEPTION DU
MUSÉE JOUE LA DIFFICULTÉ.

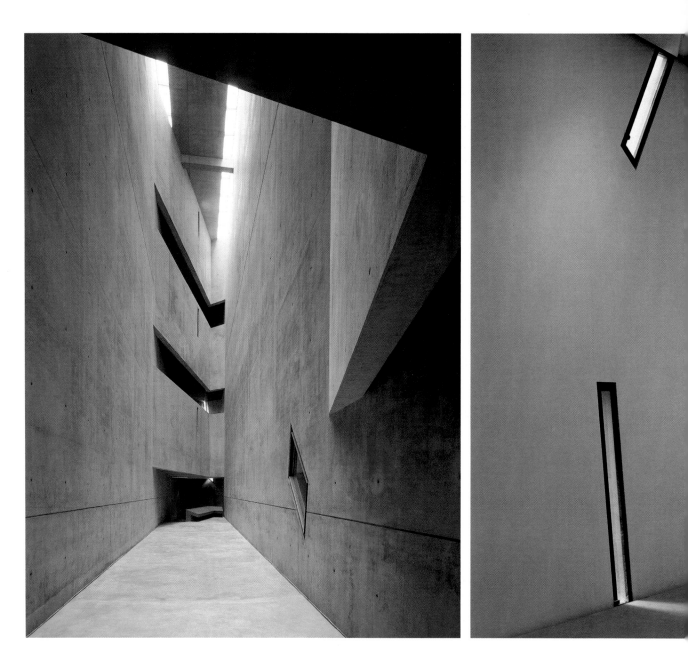

The Jewish Museum has had a long and compli-
cated history. The project was launched in 1988
as an addition to the Berlin Museum, originally intended to contain a "Jewish Department," as well
as theater, fashion and toy displays. Daniel Libeskind's project won first prize in a competition held
in 1989. The fall of the Berlin Wall and the decision to return the capital to the now unified city
affected plans. A decision to include "the entire history of the relationship between German Jews and
non-Jews from Roman times to the present," in the
words of the museum's director W. Michael Blu-

Das Jüdische Museum hat eine lange Vorgeschichte.
Das Projekt wurde 1988 als Erweiterung des Berlin-
Museums ins Leben gerufen und war ursprünglich
für die Aufnahme einer »Jüdischen Abteilung« sowie von Theater-, Mode- und Spielzeugexponaten
gedacht. Libeskinds Entwurf erhielt im Wettbewerb
von 1989 den ersten Preis. Der Fall der Mauer und
der Beschluß, das wiedervereinigte Berlin zur Bun-
deshauptstadt zu erklären, hatten eine Änderung
der Pläne zur Folge. Die Entscheidung, »die gesamte Geschichte der Beziehungen zwischen deutschen
Juden und Nichtjuden von der Zeit der Römer bis

L'histoire du musée juif est complexe. Le projet a
été lancé en 1988 en extension du Berlin Museum,
qui prévoyait de s'équiper d'un «département juif»,
d'un théâtre, et d'expositions de mode et de jouets.
Le projet de Libeskind a remporté le premier prix
lors d'un concours organisé en 1989. La chute du
mur de Berlin et la décision de réinstaller la capitale de l'Allemagne dans la ville réunifiée affecta
le projet. La décision d'inclure «la totalité de l'histoire de la relation entre les Juifs allemands et
les non-Juifs de l'époque romaine à aujourd'hui»,
selon les mots du directeur du musée, W. Michael

menthal, has left the structure at least temporarily without any exhibition or other contents. A fractured Star of David, or a fragment of the SS symbol? Such are the suggested sources of the plans of this structure, which is unlike any other contemporary museum. Many sections of the building will in any case remain intentionally empty, symbolizing the void left by the absence of Jews who died as a result of the Holocaust.

zur Gegenwart« darzustellen, wie der Museumsdirektor W. Michael Blumenthal es formulierte, hat dazu geführt, daß das Museum zumindest vorerst ohne Exponate geblieben ist. Die Form eines gebrochenen Davidsterns (oder der SS-Runen) sind als Quellen für den Grundriß des Baus vorstellbar, der sich von allen anderen zeitgenössischen Museen deutlich abhebt. Viele Teile des Hauses werden bewußt leer bleiben, um die Leere zu symbolisieren, die durch den Verlust der im Holocaust ermordeten Juden entstand.

Blumenthal, a eu pour conséquence que le bâtiment se trouve pour l'instant sans expositions ni collections. Une étoile de David fracturée – ou un fragment du symbole SS – a pu inspirer les plans de ce bâtiment très différent de tous les musées récemment construits. Plusieurs de ses parties resteront volontairement vides pour symboliser le sentiment d'absence laissé par la disparition des Juifs victimes de l'Holocauste.

GIVEN LIBESKIND'S IDEAS ABOUT THE CONCEPT OF ABSENCE IN THIS ARCHITECTURE, MEANING THAT OF THE ABSENCE OF THE JEWS WHO WERE MURDERED, THE FACT THAT IT OPENED EMPTY SEEMS APPROPRIATE.

DIE TATSACHE, DASS DAS MUSEUM OHNE EXPONATE ERÖFFNET WURDE, UNTERSTREICHT LIBESKINDS IDEE VON DER »ABWESENHEIT«,

WOMIT ER DIE ABWESENHEIT DER ERMORDETEN JUDEN MEINT.

QUE LE MUSÉE SOIT VIDE ILLUSTRE AUSSI LE CONCEPT D'ABSENCE DE SON ARCHITECTURE EXPRIMANT LA DISPARITION DES JUIFS ASSASSINÉS.

FUMIHIKO MAKI

Born in Tokyo in 1928, Fumihiko Maki received his B. Arch. degree from the University of Tokyo in 1952, and M. Arch. degrees from the Cranbrook Academy of Art (1953) and the Harvard Graduate School of Design (1954). He worked for Skidmore, Owings and Merrill in New York (1954-55) and Sert Jackson and Associates in Cambridge, Massachusetts (1955-58) before creating his own firm, Maki and Associates, in Tokyo in 1965. Notable buildings include Fujisawa Municipal Gymnasium (Fujisawa, Kanagawa, 1984), Spiral (Minato-ku,

Fumihiko Maki, geboren 1928 in Tokio, erwarb 1952 den Bachelor of Architecture an der Universität Tokio, den Master of Architecture 1953 an der Cranbrook Academy of Art und 1954 an der Harvard Graduate School of Design. Er arbeitete in den Büros Skidmore, Owings and Merrill in New York (1954-55) und Sert Jackson and Associates in Cambridge, Massachusetts (1955-58), bevor er 1965 seine eigene Firma Maki and Associates in Tokio gründete. Zu seinen herausragenden Bauten gehören die Städtische Sporthalle in Fujisawa,

Né à Tokyo en 1928, Fumihiko Maki est B. Arch. de l'Université de Tokyo et a obtenu deux Masters of Architecture à la Cranbrook Academy of Art (1953) et à l'Harvard Graduate School of Design (1954). Il travaille pour Skidmore, Owings and Merrill à New York (1954-55), puis Sert Jackson and Associates à Cambridge, Massachusetts (1955-58) avant de créer sa propre agence, Maki and Associates, à Tokyo en 1965. Parmi ses réalisations les plus connues figurent le Gymnase municipal (Fujisawa, Kanagawa, 1984), Spiral (Minato-ku, Tokyo,

WINNER OF THE 1999 PRAEMIUM IMPERIALE, FUMIHIKO MAKI IS ONE OF THE MOST URBANE AND REFINED OF JAPAN'S CONTEMPORARY ARCHITECTS, ALWAYS RETAINING HIS INNATE ABILITY TO BE RESOLUTELY MODERN.

FUMIHIKO MAKI, DER GEWINNER DES PRAE-MIUM IMPERIALE VON 1999, ZÄHLT ZU DEN AM STÄRKSTEN INTERNATIONAL AUSGERICHTETEN ZEITGENÖSSISCHEN ARCHITEKTEN JAPANS. ER

HAT SICH STETS DIE FÄHIGKEIT BEWAHRT, EIN-DEUTIG MODERN ZU BAUEN.

TITULAIRE DU PRAEMIUM IMPERIALE 1999, FUMIHIKO MAKI EST L'UN DES PLUS URBAINS ET DES PLUS RAFFINÉS ARCHITECTES CONTEM-PORAINS JAPONAIS, DOUÉ D'UN DON MODER-NISTE INNÉ.

MAKI AND ASSOCIATES
HILLSIDE WEST BUILDING C
13-4 HACHIYAMA-CHO
SHIBUYA-KU, TOKYO 150-0035
JAPAN

TEL: + 81 3 3780 3880
FAX: + 81 3 3780 3881
E-MAIL: brendon@maki-and-associates.co.jp

Tokyo, 1985), National Museum of Modern Art (Sakyo-ku, Kyoto, 1986), Tepia (Minato-ku, Tokyo, 1989), Nippon Convention Center Makuhari Messe (Chiba, 1989), Tokyo Metropolitan Gymnasium (Shibuya, Tokyo, 1990), and Yerba Buena Center for the Arts (San Francisco, California, 1993). Recent projects include Nippon Convention Center Makuhari Messe Phase II, Chiba, completed in 1997, and the Hillside West buildings, completed in 1998, part of his ongoing Hillside Terrace project.

Kanagawa (1984), das Medienzentrum Spiral, Minato-ku, Tokio (1985), das Staatliche Museum für moderne Kunst in Sakyo-ku, Kioto (1986), das Tepia-Gebäude in Minato-ku, Tokio (1989), das Nippon Convention Center Makuhari Messe in Chiba (1989), die Städtische Sporthalle in Shibuya, Tokio (1990) und das Yerba Buena Center for the Arts in San Francisco (1993). 1998 wurden die Hillside West-Gebäude als Teil seines laufenden Projekts Hillside Terrace fertiggestellt.

1985), le Musée national d'art moderne (Sakyo-ku, Kyoto, 1986), Tepia (Minato-ku, Tokyo, 1989), le Nippon Convention Center Makuhari Messe (Chiba, 1989), le Gymnase métropolitain (Shibuya, Tokyo, 1990) et le Yerba Buena Center for the Arts (San Francisco, Californie, 1993). Ses projets récents comprennent le Nippon Convention Center Maku-hari Messe, phase II (Chiba, 1997) et les Hillside West buildings (1998) qui font partie d'un projet en cours de développement, Hillside Terrace.

FUMIHIKO MAKI
KAZE-NO-OKA
CREMATORIUM
NAKATSU, OITA, JAPAN, 1995-97

P 330.331

COMPLETION / FERTIGSTELLUNG /
FIN DE LA CONSTRUCTION: 2/97
CLIENT / BAUHERR: NAKATSU CITY
FLOOR AREA / NUTZFLÄCHE / SURFACE
UTILE: 2 260 M²
COSTS / KOSTEN / COÛTS: 1 350 240 000 ¥

VOLUNTARILY SCULPTURAL IN ITS DESIGN, THIS CREMATORIUM TAKES INTO ACCOUNT INFLUENCES AS DIVERSE AS JAPANESE TRADITION AND MINIMALIST ART.

DAS KREMATORIUM WURDE BEWUSST PLASTISCH GESTALTET, NIMMT ABER AUCH SO UNTERSCHIEDLICHE EINFLÜSSE WIE DIE DER JAPANISCHEN TRADITION UND DER MINIMALISTISCHEN KUNST AUF.

VOLONTAIREMENT SCULPTURAL DANS SON CONCEPT, CE CRÉMATORIUM PREND EN COMPTE DES INFLUENCES AUSSI DIVERSES QUE LA TRADITION JAPONAISE ET L'ART MINIMALISTE.

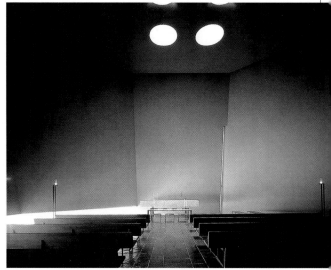

Located on the southern island of Kyushu in a town of 65,000 inhabitants, this 2,260 m² building is designed to represent the Japanese idea of a return to nature after death. It is made up of three main elements: a brick funeral hall, a concrete crematorium, and a waiting area. Its name is derived from the hill where it is set: the Kaze-no-Oka or "hill of the winds." The building is set in a park designed by Maki with Toru Mitani. The architect wanted to create a place that would be in opposition to the

Das Krematorium liegt auf der Insel Kyushu, in der 65 000 Einwohner zählenden Stadt Nakatsu. Maki wollte die japanische Vorstellung von der Rückkehr der Toten zur Natur verdeutlichen. Es hat drei Hauptelemente: eine Trauerhalle aus Backstein, eine Kremationskammer aus Beton und einen Vorraum für die Trauergäste. Der Name des Krematoriums ist dem Berg entlehnt, auf dem es steht: dem »Hügel der Winde«. Der Bau liegt in einem von Maki und Toru Mitani gestalteten Park. Der Archi-

Situé sur l'île méridionale de Kyushu dans une ville de 65 000 habitants, ce bâtiment de 2 260 m² est conçu dans le respect du concept japonais de retour à la nature après la mort. Il se compose de trois éléments principaux: un hall funéraire en brique, un crématorium en béton et une zone d'attente. Son nom vient de celui de la colline sur laquelle il s'élève, «la colline des vents». Le parc qui l'entoure a été dessiné par Maki, en collaboration avec Toru Mitani. L'architecte souhaitait créer un lieu très

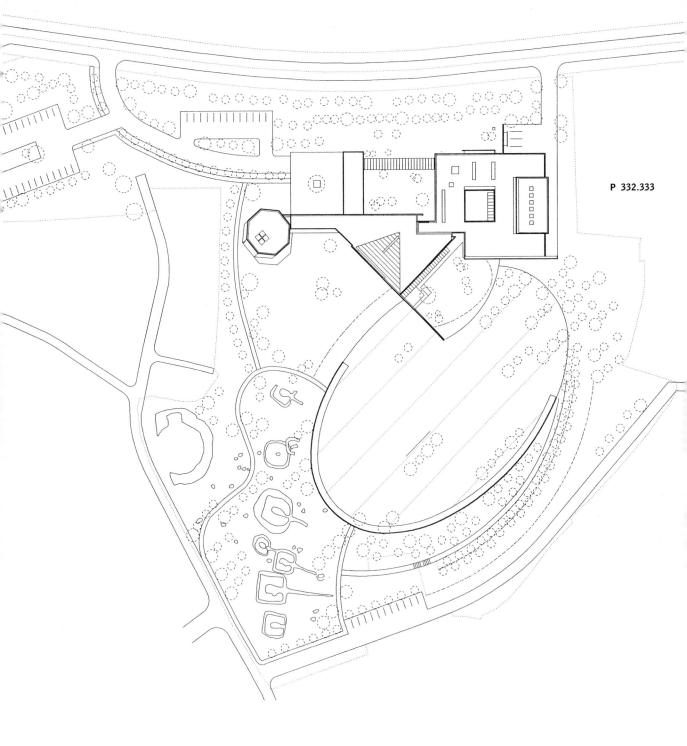

generally ornate crematoriums in Japan. The result is an austerity befitting the function of the structure, which also approaches a kind of sculptural minimalism, an impression heightened by the use of a large, angled Corten steel wall that shields the waiting area. Highlighting the idea of a connection to nature expressed by the park, Maki says that for the building and its interiors, "we decided to use colors ranging from gray to black, to express dignity, and brown, to create a feeling of gentleness."

tekt wollte einen Ort schaffen, der sich von den in Japan üblichen überladenen Krematorien unterscheidet. Das Ergebnis ist streng und funktional – ein Eindruck, der durch die große, abgewinkelte Stahlwand verstärkt wird, die den Vorraum abtrennt. Maki sagt über den Bau und seine Innenräume: »Wir haben uns entschieden, Farben von Grau bis Schwarz zu verwenden, um Würde auszudrücken, und Braun, um ein Gefühl der Sanftheit zu vermitteln.«

différent des crématoriums typiques du Japon. Son austérité est adaptée à sa fonction et atteint à une sorte de minimalisme sculptural, dont l'impression est renforcée par un vaste mur incliné en acier Corten. En soulignant le concept de connexion avec la nature exprimée par le parc, Maki explique que pour le bâtiment et son intérieur, «nous avons décidé de nous servir de couleurs qui vont du gris au noir, pour exprimer la dignité, et le brun, pour créer un sentiment d'humanité».

THE IDEA OF SOLEMNITY AND PEACE IS EVERYWHERE PRESENT IN THE SPACES WITHIN THE CREMATORIUM.

FEIERLICHKEIT UND FRIEDEN SIND IN ALLEN RÄUMEN DES KREMATORIUMS SPÜRBAR.

L'IDÉE DE SOLENNITÉ ET DE PAIX EST OMNI-PRÉSENTE DANS LES VOLUMES INTÉRIEURS.

COMPLETION / FERTIGSTELLUNG /
FIN DE LA CONSTRUCTION: 9/97
CLIENT / BAUHERR: CHIBA PREFECTURE
FLOOR AREA / NUTZFLÄCHE / SURFACE
UTILE: 33 413 M²
COSTS / KOSTEN / COÛTS: 22 000 000 000 ¥

FUMIHIKO MAKI

MAKUHARI MESSE PHASE II

NAKASE, CHIBA, JAPAN, 1996-97

Located on the outskirts of Tokyo, near the road leading to Narita Airport, this 33,413 m² facility is an extension to a 131,043 m² structure built by Maki in 1989. Maki rejected the possibility of merely extending the first building, and decided to set the rectangular volume of Phase II at a perpendicular to Phase I. The roof, which sweeps up like a wave, spanning 96 m, and rising to a maximum height of 32 m, is made from a series of curved steel girders suspended at 12 m intervals and held

Dieser 33 413 m² große Bau liegt in einem Außenbezirk Tokios an der Straße zum Flughafen Narita und ist die Erweiterung der 1989 von Maki errichteten Makuhari-Messe mit 131 043 m² Gesamtnutzfläche. Der Architekt beschloß, den Baukörper im rechten Winkel zum bestehenden Teil anzulegen. Das aufsteigende Dach überspannt 96 m und erreicht eine Firsthöhe von 32 m. Es besteht aus einer Folge gekrümmter Stahlbinder, die in Abständen von je 12 m aufgehängt sind, und wird von Sei-

Dans la banlieue de Tokyo, près de l'axe qui mène à l'aéroport de Narita, ces bâtiments de foire de 33 413 m² sont une extension des 131 043 m² déjà édifiés par Maki en 1989. L'architecte a écarté l'idée d'un simple agrandissement du premier bâtiment et a implanté le volume rectangulaire de sa Phase II perpendiculairement à celui de la Phase I. Le toit, soulevé comme une vague, présente une portée de 96 m pour une hauteur maximum de 32 m. Il se compose d'une succession de poutres d'acier

up by cables connected to an overhead walkway. Like many of Maki's buildings, the Makuhari Messe Phase II has a bright silver gleam that sets it apart from most neighboring structures. Ramps lead up to first-floor entrances, providing visitors with a view of the complex before they enter. The main exhibition area covers nearly 9,000 m², with a good deal of natural light that is admitted near the "crest" of the wave-like roof.

len gehalten, die an einem darüberliegenden Laufgang befestigt wurden. Wie viele Bauwerke Makis hat auch dieses eine silbrig glänzende Außenhaut, die es von den benachbarten Bauten unterscheidet. Rampen führen zu den Eingängen im Obergeschoß und bieten einen Blick auf die Gesamtanlage. Der Hauptausstellungsbereich erstreckt sich über fast 9 000 m² und ist (durch ein Oberlicht unterhalb der Dachkante) vorwiegend natürlich belichtet.

incurvées suspendues à intervalles de 12 m et maintenues par des câbles reliés à une coursive en partie supérieure. Comme beaucoup des réalisations de Maki, celle-ci est d'un gris argent étincelant. Des rampes mènent aux entrées et offrent aux visiteurs une vision préalable de l'ensemble. Le principal espace d'exposition couvre près de 9 000 m². Il est pour une bonne part éclairé par la lumière naturelle qui pénètre par des ouvertures disposées à proximité de la crête de la vague du toit.

MECANOO

Henk Döll (center), Chris de Weijer (left), Francine Houben (right) and Erick van Egeraat (who left the group in 1995) created Mecanoo in 1984 in Delft. Döll and de Weijer were born in 1956, and Francine Houben a year earlier. All three attended the Technical University of Delft, graduating in 1983 and 1984. Their work included large housing projects such as the Herdenkingsplein in Maastricht, Netherlands (1990-92), and smaller-scale projects such as their 1990 Boompjes Pavilion (a cantilevered structure overlooking the harbor of Rotter-

Mecanoo wurde 1984 von Henk Döll, Chris de Weijer, Francine Houben und Erik van Egeraat (der die Gruppe 1995 verließ) gegründet. Döll (Mitte, geboren 1956), de Weijer (links, geboren 1956) und Houben (rechts, geboren 1955) besuchten die Technische Universität Delft und schlossen ihr Studium 1983 bzw. 1984 ab. Zu ihren Bauten zählen große Wohnbauprojekte wie Herdenkingsplein in Maastricht (1990-92) und kleinere Objekte wie der Boompjes-Pavillon (1990), ein Gebäude am Rotterdamer Hafen nahe der neuen Erasmus-Brücke und

Henk Döll (au milieu), Chris de Weijer (à gauche), Francine Houben (à droite) et Erik van Egeraat (qui a quitté le bureau en 1995) ont créé Mecanoo à Delft en 1984. H. Döll et C. de Weijer sont nés en 1956, et Francine Houben un an plus tôt. Tous les trois ont étudié à l'Université Technique de Delft dont ils sont sortis diplômés en 1983 et 1984. Leurs recherches comprennent de grands projets de logements comme le Herdenkingsplein à Maastricht (1990-92) et d'autres plus petites comme le Boompjes Pavillon (1990), une structure

BACK AS A CREATIVE FORCE AFTER THE DEPARTURE OF ONE OF THEIR FOUNDING MEMBERS, MECANOO IS ONCE AGAIN BREAKING NEW GROUND WITH THEIR LIBRARY FOR THE DELFT TECHNICAL UNIVERSITY, WHERE THE FIRM'S PRINCIPALS STUDIED.

MECANOO BETRITT NACH AUSSCHEIDEN EINES SEINER GRÜNDUNGSMITGLIEDER NEULAND MIT SEINER BIBLIOTHEK DER TECHNISCHEN

UNIVERSITÄT DELFT – AN DER DIE LEITER DES BÜROS STUDIERT HABEN.

REGAIN DE CRÉATIVITÉ APRÈS LE DÉPART DE L'UN DE SES MEMBRES FONDATEURS: MECANOO FAIT À NOUVEAU PARLER DE LUI AVEC SA BIBLIOTHÈQUE DE L'UNIVERSITÉ DE TECHNOLOGIE DE DELFT, OÙ SES ASSOCIÉS ONT ÉTUDIÉ.

MECANOO ARCHITECTEN B.V.
OUDE DELFT 203
2611 HD DELFT
THE NETHERLANDS

TEL: + 31 15 214 7445
FAX: + 31 15 214 0987
E-MAIL: mecanoo@.pi.net
WEB: www.xs4all.nl/~mecanoo

P 340.341

dam, close to the new Erasmus Bridge), and a private house in Rotterdam (1989-91). Signature features of these projects include unexpected use of materials, as in the Rotterdam house, where bamboo and steel are placed in juxtaposition with concrete, for example, or an apparent disequilibrium, as in the Boompjes Pavilion. Current projects of Mecanoo include a new 9,300 m² library, music school and museum, Canadaplein, Alkmaar (1997-2000), and an office for a Housing Association, Site Woondiensten, Doetinchem (1998-2000).

ein Wohnhaus in Rotterdam (1989-91). Charakteristisch für ihre Bauten sind die Verwendung ungewöhnlicher Materialien oder ein beabsichtigtes Ungleichgewicht, wie im Boompjes-Pavillon. Gegenwärtige Projekte von Mecanoo sind eine Bibliothek, eine Musikschule und ein Museum am Canadaplein in Alkmaar (1997-2000) sowie ein Bürogebäude für die Wohnungsbaugesellschaft Site Woondiensten in Doetinchem (1998-2000), alle in den Niederlanden.

en porte-à-faux qui donne sur le port de Rotterdam, ou une résidence privée à Rotterdam (1989-91). On retrouve dans leurs projets un recours à des matériaux inattendus ou à certains déséquilibres apparents. Parmi les projets actuels de l'agence: une bibliothèque de 9 300 m², une école de musique et un musée à Canadaplein, Alkmaar (1997-2000), et un bureau pour une association se consacrant au logement (Site Woondiensten, Doetinchem, 1998-2000), tous aux Pays-Bas.

MECANOO

CENTRAL LIBRARY, DELFT TECHNICAL UNIVERSITY

DELFT, THE NETHERLANDS, 1993-98

PLANNING / PLANUNG: 1993-95
CONSTRUCTION / BAU: 4/96-5/98
CLIENT / BAUHERR: ING VASTGOED
ONTWIKKELING B.V., DEN HAAG / TECHNICAL
UNIVERSITY, DELFT
FLOOR AREA / NUTZFLÄCHE / SURFACE
UTILE: 15 000 M²
COSTS / KOSTEN / COÛTS: 60 000 000 NLG

P 342.343

WEITHIN SICHTBAR IST DER ZENTRALE KEGEL
DER BIBLIOTHEK, DEREN SCHRÄGES DACH MIT
GRAS GEDECKT IST.

DER KEGEL DIENT ZUR BELICHTUNG DER
UNTEREN EBENE. SCHRÄGE FASSADEN UND
STÜTZEN SIND WEITERE UNGEWÖHNLICHE
MERKMALE.

LE CÔNE CENTRAL SIGNALE LA PRÉSENCE DE
LA BIBLIOTHÈQUE DONT LE TOIT INCLINÉ EST
RECOUVERT DE GAZON.

LE CÔNE A ÉGALEMENT POUR FONCTION
D'ORIENTER LA LUMIÈRE NATURELLE
JUSQU'AU REZ-DE-CHAUSSÉE. LES FAÇADES
INCLINÉES ET LES COLONNES SONT ORIGI-
NALES.

THE CENTRAL CONE SIGNALS THE PRESENCE
OF THE LIBRARY WHOSE SLOPING ROOF IS
COVERED WITH GRASS.

THE CONE ALSO SERVES TO BRING LIGHT INTO
THE LOWER LEVEL. ANGLED FACADES AND
COLUMNS ARE OTHER UNUSUAL FEATURES.

With a total floor area of approximately 15,000 m², this library costs 60 million florins to build. As the architects say about the unusual structure of the new building: "It has a grass roof that rises at an angle from ground level, like a sheet of paper lifted at one corner." The grass roof provides excellent insulation for a large, 1,000-seat reading room, equipped with 300 computers. Seasonal or "ground cooling" is used to avoid the necessity of cooling installations, through the circulation of water stored

Bei einer Nutzfläche von fast 15 000 m² betrugen die Baukosten für dieses Gebäude 60 Millionen Gulden. Die Architekten erläutern die ungewöhnliche Form der neuen Bibliothek so: »Sie hat ein Grasdach, das sich vom Bodenniveau erhebt wie ein an einer Ecke angehobenes Blatt Papier.« Das begehbare Grasdach ist eine ausgezeichnete Isolierung für den großen, 1 000 Personen fassenden Lesesaal, der mit 300 Computern ausgestattet ist. Je nach Jahreszeit wird, um Klimaanlagen zu ver-

Pour une surface totale d'environ 15 000 m², ce bâtiment a coûté 60 millions de florins. Les architectes expliquent ainsi la forme exceptionnelle de la nouvelle bibliotheque: «Son toit gazonné s'élève en biais à partir du sol, comme une feuille de papier que l'on soulèverait par un coin.» Le toit semé d'herbe offre une excellente isolation thermique à la vaste salle de lecture de 1 000 places, équipée de 300 postes informatiques. Un système de pompe à chaleur alimenté par de l'eau emmagasinée dans

deep underground and channeled through tubes to a heat exchanger. A high stucco-clad concrete cone with a metal point projects above the reading room, signaling the presence of the library, and bringing some light into the space below. The stacks of the library are located below ground, obviating the need for extensive climate control. The so-called "noise-producing areas" are grouped in order to provide the most tranquil working environment possible.

meiden, »Bodenkühlung« durch den Umlauf von Wasser erzeugt, das tief im Untergrund gelagert und durch Rohre zu einem Wärmetauscher geleitet wird. Ein hoher, verputzter Betonkegel mit Metallspitze über dem Lesesaal läßt Tageslicht in den darunterliegenden Raum fallen. Die Magazine liegen unterirdisch, wodurch sich aufwendige Klimatisierung erübrigt. Die sogenannten »lärmerzeugenden Bereiche« sind zusammengefaßt, um größtmögliche Ruhe in den Arbeitsräumen zu gewährleisten.

des citernes profondément enfouies évite un conditionnement d'air classique. Un cône de béton recouvert de stuc et terminé par une pointe de métal se projette au-dessus de la salle de lecture pour signaler la présence du bâtiment et apporter un peu de lumière à l'espace qu'il recouvre. Les rayonnages sont implantés en sous-sol pour éviter, là encore, le recours à la climatisation. Les «zones à bruit» sont regroupées pour offrir un environnement de travail aussi paisible que possible.

THE GRASS-COVERED ROOF (SEE P 342.343) DISGUISES THE SIZE (15,000 M²) OF THE LIBRARY'S SPACES.

DAS GRASGEDECKTE DACH (SIEHE P 342.343) KASCHIERT DIE GRÖSSE (15 000 M²) DER BIBLIOTHEK.

LE TOIT RECOUVERT DE GAZON (VOIR P 342.343) MASQUE LA TAILLE RÉELLE (15 000 M²) DE LA BIBLIOTHÈQUE.

RICHARD MEIER

BORN IN 1934, DESIGNER OF THE GETTY CEN-
TER IN LOS ANGELES, RICHARD MEIER IS ONE
OF THE MOST CONSISTENT AND RIGOROUS OF
CONTEMPORARY ARCHITECTS, RELYING ON
STRICT GRID SYSTEMS AND ALMOST ALWAYS
ON WHITE CLADDING.

RICHARD MEIER, ERBAUER DES GETTY CENTER
IN LOS ANGELES, IST EINER DER KONSEQUEN-
TESTEN UND NÜCHTERNSTEN ZEITGENÖSSI-

Born in Newark, New Jersey, in 1934, Richard Meier received his architectural training at Cornell University, and worked in the office of Marcel Breuer (1960-63) before establishing his own practice in 1963. He won the Pritzker Prize, 1984, and the Royal Gold Medal, 1988. Notable buildings include The Atheneum (New Harmony, Indiana, 1975-79), Museum for the Decorative Arts (Frankfurt,

Richard Meier, geboren 1934 in Newark, New Jersey, studierte Architektur an der Cornell University und arbeitete bei Marcel Breuer (1960-63), bevor er 1963 sein eigenes Büro eröffnete. Er wurde 1984 mit dem Pritzker Prize und 1988 mit der Royal Gold Medal ausgezeichnet. Zu seinen bedeutendsten Bauten gehören das Atheneum in New Harmony, Indiana (1975-79), das Museum für Kunsthand-

Né à Newark, New Jersey en 1934, Richard Meier étudie l'architecture à Cornell University, et travaille dans l'agence de Marcel Breuer (1960-63) avant de s'établir à son compte en 1963. Pritzker Prize 1984; Royal Gold Medal 1988. Parmi ses réalisations les plus connues: Atheneum (New Harmony, Indiana, 1975-79), Musée des Arts Décoratifs (Francfort-sur-le-Main, Allemagne, 1979-85), High

SCHEN ARCHITEKTEN, DER MIT STRENGEN
RASTERSYSTEMEN ARBEITET UND WÄNDE
MEIST WEISS VERKLEIDET.

RICHARD MEIER, AUTEUR DU GETTY CENTER
À LOS ANGELES, EST L'UN DES ARCHITECTES
LES PLUS RIGOUREUX ET LES PLUS CONSTANTS
DANS SA DÉMARCHE. IL TRAVAILLE À PARTIR
D'UN SYSTÈME DE TRAME ET A RECOURS À UN
REVÊTEMENT EXTÉRIEUR BLANC.

RICHARD MEIER & PARTNERS
475 TENTH AVENUE
NEW YORK, NEW YORK 10018
UNITED STATES

TEL: + 1 212 967 6060
FAX: + 1 212 967 3207
E-MAIL: rmp@richardmeier.com
WEB: www.richardmeier.com

Germany, 1979-85), High Museum of Art (Atlanta, Georgia, 1980-83), Canal+ Headquarters (Paris, 1988-92), City Hall and Library (The Hague, 1990-95), Barcelona Museum of Contemporary Art (1988-95), and Getty Center (Los Angeles, California, 1984-97). Current work includes a US Courthouse and Federal Building (Phoenix, Arizona, 1995-2000).

werk in Frankfurt a. M. (1979-85), das High Museum of Art, Atlanta (1980-83), die Hauptverwaltung von Canal+, Paris (1988-92), Rathaus und Bibliothek, Den Haag (1990-95), das Museum für Zeitgenössische Kunst, Barcelona (1988-95) und das Getty Center, Los Angeles (1984-97). Gegenwärtig arbeitet er am U. S. Courthouse and Federal Building, Phoenix, Arizona (1995-2000).

Museum of Art (Atlanta, Géorgie, 1980-83), siège de Canal+ (Paris, 1988-92), Hôtel de Ville et bibliothèque (La Haye, 1990-95), Musée d'Art Contemporain (Barcelone, 1988-95) et Getty Center (Los Angeles, Californie, 1984-97). Il travaille actuellement sur le projet de U. S. Courthouse and Federal Building, à Phoenix, Arizona (1995-2000).

RICHARD MEIER

CHURCH
OF THE YEAR 2000

ROME, ITALY, 1996-2000

P 352.353

CLIENT / BAUHERR: VICARIATO DI ROMA
FLOOR AREA / NUTZFLÄCHE /
SURFACE UTILE: 882 M²
COSTS / KOSTEN / COÛTS: WITHHELD /
UNGENANNT / NON COMMUNIQUÉS

Beginning in the early 1990s, the Vicariato di Roma began plans for the construction of 50 new parish churches to celebrate the Jubilee Year in 2000. Few of these churches will in fact be completed on time, but special significance was given to one of them. An international competition was organized for that church, which would symbolize the importance of the Jubilee, and renew the commitment of the Catholic Church to the arts. The invited architects were Günter Behnisch, Santiago Calatrava, Peter Eisenman, Frank O. Gehry, and Richard Meier. Meier won, and his design is being built in the Tor Tre Teste area of Rome. Designed in Meier's trademark white like a series of sails, the three curved walls of the church, symbolizing the Holy Trinity, admit ample light. Light is also a constant factor in the architecture of Richard Meier, and as applied to a religious context it naturally assumes a symbolic power and significance. The pews are set perpendicular to the last and largest of the sail-like walls, making for a plan that does not specifically bring to mind the traditional configuration of Christian churches.

Anfang der 90er Jahre begann der Vicariato di Roma mit der Planung von 50 neuen Pfarrkirchen, um das Heilige Jahr 2000 zu feiern. Wenige dieser Kirchen werden tatsächlich termingerecht ausgeführt sein; besondere Bedeutung wird jedoch einer von ihnen zugeschrieben: Ein internationaler Wettbewerb wurde für diesen Bau ausgelobt, der die Bedeutung des Jubiläums symbolisieren und die Verpflichtung der katholischen Kirche gegenüber den Künsten erneut bekräftigen soll. Eingeladen wurden die Architekten Günter Behnisch, Santiago Calatrava, Peter Eisenman, Frank O. Gehry und Richard Meier, der den Wettbewerb gewann. Die drei in Form aufgespannter Segel gestalteten, gekrümmten Wände der Kirche in dem für Meiers Architektur typischen Weiß symbolisieren die Heilige Dreifaltigkeit und sorgen für eine ausreichende Belichtung des Kirchenraums. Das Licht ist ein allgegenwärtiges Element in der Architektur Richard Meiers; in religiösem Kontext angewandt, gewinnt es an Bedeutung und Symbolkraft. Die Bestuhlung steht rechtwinklig zur letzten und größten dieser segelförmigen Wände.

C'est au début des années 90 que le vicariat de Rome a lancé les plans de construction de 50 nouvelles églises paroissiales pour célébrer le Jubilé de l'an 2000. Peu de ses projets seront en fait terminés à temps, mais une importance particulière à été donnée à l'un d'entre eux. Un concours international a en effet été organisé pour édifier un lieu de culte chargé de symboliser l'événement du Jubilé, et de manifester le renouveau d'intérêt de l'Église pour les arts. Les architectes invités furent Günter Behnisch, Santiago Calatrava, Peter Eisenman, Frank O. Gehry et Richard Meier, dont le projet pour le quartier de Tor Tre Teste fut retenu. Conçus dans le style blanc, caractéristique de l'architecte, les trois murs en forme voile de l'église et symbolisant la Sainte Trinité laissent pénétrer une abondante lumière. Celle-ci est une des grandes constantes de l'œuvre de Meier. Dans un contexte religieux, elle prend un sens et une puissance renouvelés. Les bancs sont perpendiculaires au dernier et plus grand des trois murs-voiles, selon un plan différent de la configuration intérieure traditionnelle des églises chrétiennes.

TOSHIKO MORI
AND GWENAEL NICOLAS

Toshiko Mori attended the Cooper Union School of Art and School of Architecture (1970-76), and received an Honory Master of Architecture degree from the Harvard School of Design in 1996. She is currently a Professor at Harvard. She has worked on numerous retail stores, such as Comme des Garçons (New York, 1998), and Kyoto Arts & Fashions (New York, 1989) as well as corporate offices such as Sony Research Laboratories, New

Toshiko Mori studierte an der Cooper Union in New York (1970-76) und erwarb 1996 den Honory Master of Architecture an der Harvard School of Design, wo sie zur Zeit eine Professur innehat. Sie hat viele Ladenlokale geplant, so etwa Comme des Garçons (1998) und Kyoto Arts & Fashions (1989), beide in New York, außerdem Bürobauten wie die Sony Research Laboratories (1996) und Nigel French International (1991), ebenfalls in

Toshiko Mori a étudié aux Cooper Union School of Design et School of Architecture (1970-76). Elle est Honory Master of Architecture de la Harvard School of Design en 1996, et enseigne actuellement à Harvard. Elle a créé de nombreux magasins dont Comme des Garçons, New York (1998), Kyoto Arts & Fashions, New York (1989) ainsi que des sièges d'entreprise dont Sony Research Laboratories, New York, 1996, ou celui de Nigel French International,

IN A SMALL SPACE IN THE SOHO AREA OF NEW YORK, MORI AND NICOLAS HAVE CREATED A FUNCTIONAL BOUTIQUE. THEIR SENSE OF COLOR AND HIGH-TECH MATERIALS TRANSFORMS AND BRINGS THE VOLUME ALIVE.

IN EINEM KLEINEN RAUM IM NEW YORKER BEZIRK SOHO HABEN MORI UND NICOLAS EINE FUNKTIONALE BOUTIQUE GESCHAFFEN. DAS SICHERE GEFÜHL DER ARCHITEKTEN FÜR

FARBEN UND HIGH-TECH-MATERIALIEN VERÄNDERT DEN RAUM UND ERWECKT IHN ZUM LEBEN.

C'EST DANS UN PETIT LOCAL DU QUARTIER DE SOHO À NEW YORK QUE MORI ET NICOLAS ONT CRÉÉ CETTE BOUTIQUE TRÈS FONCTIONNELLE. LEUR SENS DES COULEURS ET DES MATÉRIAUX HIGH-TECH ONT RÉUSSI À TRANSFORMER ET ANIMER CE VOLUME.

TOSHIKO MORI ARCHITECT
145 HUDSON STREET, 4TH FLOOR
NEW YORK, NEW YORK 10013
UNITED STATES

TEL: + 1 212 274 8687
FAX: + 1 212 274 9043
E-MAIL: TMoriArch@AOL.com

GWENAEL NICOLAS
CURIOSITY INC.
1-52-4 #403 YOYOGI
SHIBUYA-KU, TOKYO 151-0053
JAPAN

TEL: + 81 3 5333 8525
FAX: + 81 3 5333 8526
E-MAIL: nicolas@curiosity.co.jp

York (1996), and Nigel French International, New York (1991). Born in 1966 in France, Gwenael Nicolas studied at the École Supérieure d'Arts Graphiques et d'Architecture d'Intérieure (ESAG) in Paris, 1984-88. He has worked on Pleats Please boutiques for Issey Miyake in Paris and Japan as well as New York, and worked on the bottle and package design for the Miyake perfume "Le Feu d'Issey."

New York. Gwenael Nicolas, geboren 1966 in Frankreich, studierte an der École Supérieure d'Arts Graphiques et d'Architecture d'Interieur (ESAG) in Paris (1984-88). Er arbeitete an den Pleats Please-Boutiquen von Issey Miyake in Paris, Japan und New York und an der Gestaltung von Flacon und Verpackung des Miyake-Parfums »Le Feu d'Issey«.

New York (1991). Né en France en 1966, Gwenael Nicolas a étudié à l'École Supérieure d'Arts Graphiques et d'Architecture d'Intérieur (ESAG) à Paris (1984-88). Il a travaillé sur les boutiques Pleats Please d'Issey Miyake à Paris, au Japon et à New York, ainsi que sur la bouteille et le packaging du parfum de Miyake « Le Feu d'Issey ».

TOSHIKO MORI AND GWENAEL NICOLAS

ISSEY MIYAKE PLEATS PLEASE BOUTIQUE

NEW YORK, NEW YORK, UNITED STATES, 1998

This very small boutique for the Japanese clothing designer Issey Miyake is sited at the corner of Wooster and Prince Streets in the Soho area of New York. It is located on the ground floor of an 1853 brick and brownstone building, and is the result of collaboration between the New York architect Toshiko Mori and the Tokyo-based French designer Gwenael Nicolas. They applied a surprising polymer resin film developed by Sumitomo Chemical to the glass surfaces, which makes the inside of the boutique look blurry from a distance

Diese sehr kleine Boutique des japanischen Mode-machers Issey Miyake liegt an der Ecke Wooster und Prince Street im New Yorker Stadtteil Soho. Sie befindet sich im Erdgeschoß eines 1853 in Backstein und Brownstone (braunem Sandstein) erbauten Hauses und ist Ergebnis einer Zusammen-arbeit der New Yorker Architektin Toshiko Mori mit dem in Tokio ansässigen Designer Gwenael Nicolas. Die Schaufenster sind mit einem speziellen, von Sumitomo Chemical entwickelten Kunstharzfilm beschichtet, der das Innere der Boutique aus der

Cette petite boutique conçue pour le couturier japo-nais Issey Miyake se trouve au pied d'un immeuble de briques et de brownstones de 1853, à l'angle des rues Wooster et Prince, dans le quartier de Soho à New York. L'architecte new-yorkaise et le designer français basée à Tokyo ont appliqué sur les surfaces vitrées une étonnante résine polymère de Sumitomo Chemical qui rend l'intérieur du magasin flou lorsqu'on le regarde de loin et net vu de près. Cet effet de flou souligne le mystère de cet espace tout en donnant une impression de plus grande profon-

CLIENT / BAUHERR: ISSEY MIYAKE USA
CORPORATION
FLOOR AREA / NUTZFLÄCHE / SURFACE
UTILE: 612 SQ FT
COSTS / KOSTEN / COÛTS: WITHHELD /
UNGENANNT / NON COMMUNIQUÉS

**THE POLYMER RESIN FILM APPLIED TO THE
GLASS SURFACES, MAKES THEM TRANSLU-
CENT OR TRANSPARENT ACCORDING TO THE
VIEWING ANGLE.**

DER AUF DIE GLASFLÄCHEN AUFGEBRACHTE
KUNSTHARZFILM MACHT SIE JE NACH BLICK-
WINKEL ENTWEDER VERSCHWOMMEN ODER
DURCHSICHTIG.

LE FILM DE RÉSINE POLYMÈRE APPLIQUÉ SUR
LES VITRINES LES RENDENT TRANSPARENTES
OU TRANSLUCIDES, EN FONCTION DE L'ANGLE
DE VUE.

and clear when viewed from close. The blurring
effect serves to heighten the mystery of the space,
but also to give an impression of greater depth.
Inside, colors such as the bright green of the cash-
ier's enclosure, which appears to float above the
floor, highlight the shapes and colors of Miyake's
Pleats Please line. Although the building is not an
official New York City Landmark, the Landmarks
Preservation Commission was very favorable to the
architect's strict respect for the existing stonework
facade.

Entfernung verschwommen und aus der Nähe
klar erkennen läßt. Der nebelhafte Eindruck soll
das Geheimnisvolle des Raums verstärken, aber
auch größere Tiefenwirkung erzeugen. Im Innern
heben Farben – so das leuchtende Grün des Kassen-
bereichs, der über dem Boden zu schweben scheint
– die Formen und Farbtöne von Miyakes Pleats
Please-Kollektion hervor. Obgleich das Gebäude
nicht als Baudenkmal registriert ist, begrüßte die
Denkmalbehörde den respektvollen Umgang mit
der alten Fassade.

deur. À l'intérieur la coloration – dont le vert
éclatant de la caisse qui semble flotter au-dessus
du sol – met en valeur les formes et les tons de la
ligne Pleats Please. Bien que l'immeuble ne soit pas
protégé, la Commission new-yorkaise de classement
s'est montrée très favorable au strict respect de
la façade existante par l'architecte.

GLENN MURCUTT

Glenn Murcutt, born in London in 1936 of Australian parents. He studied at the Sydney Technical College, University of New South Wales, and worked in the offices of Levido & Baker (1956), Neville Gruzman (1958-59), and Allen & Jack (1962), before creating his own office in 1969. He has taught at the University of New South Wales, and traveled extensively in Europe and the United States. His

Glenn Murcutt, als Sohn australischer Eltern 1936 in London geboren, studierte am Sydney Technical College der University of New South Wales und arbeitete in den Büros Levido & Baker (1956), Neville Gruzman (1958-59) und Allen & Jack (1962), bevor er 1969 sein eigenes Büro gründete. Er lehrte an der University of New South Wales und unternahm ausgedehnte Reisen nach Europa und in die

Glenn Murcutt naît à Londres en 1936 de parents australiens. Il étudie l'architecture au Sydney Technical College, University of New South Wales, et fait ses débuts dans les agences de Levido & Baker (1956), Neville Gruzman (1958-59) et Allen & Jack (1962), avant de s'établir à son compte en 1969. Il a enseigné à son université, et a beaucoup voyagé en Europe et aux États-Unis. Parmi ses

GLENN MURCUTT IS A LEGENDARY FIGURE IN AUSTRALIAN ARCHITECTURE, MAINLY KNOWN FOR HIS PRIVATE HOUSES, AND YET HE IS SO LITTLE CONCERNED WITH HIS PERSONAL PUBLICITY THAT HE DOES NOT HAVE A PICTURE OF HIMSELF.

GLENN MURCUTT, VOR ALLEM DURCH SEINE WOHNHÄUSER BEKANNT, IST EINE LEGENDÄRE GESTALT DER AUSTRALISCHEN ARCHITEKTUR-SZENE. DENNOCH IST ER SO WENIG UM SEINE PUBLICITY BEDACHT, DASS ER NICHT EINMAL EIN FOTO VON SICH BESITZT.

ESSENTIELLEMENT CONNU POUR SES MAISONS INDIVIDUELLES, GLENN MURCUTT EST UNE FIGURE LÉGENDAIRE DE L'ARCHITECTURE AUSTRALIENNE. IL EST SI PEU SENSIBLE À LA PUBLICITÉ, QU'IL NE DISPOSE MÊME PAS D'UN PORTRAIT DE LUI.

GLENN MURCUTT & ASSOCIATES P/L
176A RAGLAN STREET
MOSMAN NSW 2088
AUSTRALIA

TEL/FAX: + 61 2 99 69 77 97

built work includes numerous private houses, such as the Magney House (Bingi Point, NSW, 1982-84), the Meagher House (Bowral, NSW, 1988-92), and the Marika-Alderton House (Yirrkala, Northern Territory, 1991-94), as well as the Museum of Local History and Tourism Office (Kempsey, NSW, 1979-82, 1986-88), and a Restaurant (Berowra Waters, Sydney, 1977-78, 1982-83).

Vereinigten Staaten. Sein Werk umfaßt zahlreiche Privathäuser: Haus Magney in Bingi Point, NSW (1982-84), Meagher in Bowral, NSW (1988-92) und Marika-Alderton in Yirrkala, Northern Territory, (1991-94), außerdem das Heimatmuseum und Fremdenverkehrsamt in Kempsey, NSW (1979-82, 1986-88) und das Restaurant Berowra Waters in Sydney (1977-78, 1982-83).

réalisations: Magney House (Bingi Point, Nouvelles-Galles du Sud, 1982-84), Meagher House (Bowral, Nouvelles-Galles du Sud, 1988-92), ou Marika-Alderton House (Yirrkala, Northern Territory, 1991-94), le Museum of Local History and Tourism Office (Kempsey, Nouvelles-Galles du Sud, 1979-82 et 1986-88) et un restaurant à Berowra Waters (Sydney, 1977-78 et 1982-83).

GLENN MURCUTT
PRIVATE RESIDENCE
MOUNT WILSON, NEW SOUTH WALES, AUSTRALIA, 1989-94

CLIENT / BAUHERR: WITHHELD / UNGENANNT / NON COMMUNIQUÉ
COSTS / KOSTEN / COÛTS: $ 2 300 PER M²

Situated in the Blue Mountains, 150 km northwest of Sydney, this residence is set on a 3 hectares site at an altitude of 1,000 m. The spartan design for a retired couple includes a house and an atelier, which is separated by an elevated wooden walkway and a basin. This presence of wood is exceptional in a house that is made of aluminum, painted steel, glass, and polished concrete for the floors. Characterized by an evident horizontality, the house is strictly aligned except for the atelier, which is set

Das in den Blue Mountains 150 km nordwestlich von Sydney gelegene Haus steht auf einem 3 ha großen Grundstück in 1 000 m Höhe. Der spartanische Entwurf umfaßt ein Wohnhaus und ein Atelier, die durch einen erhöhten hölzernen Steg verbunden sind, sowie ein Wasserbecken. Die Verwendung von Holz bei einem Haus aus Aluminium, gestrichenem Stahl, Glas und geschliffenen Betonböden wirkt außergewöhnlich. Das langgestreckte Gebäude ist streng rechtwinklig ausgerichtet, mit Ausnahme des

Située dans les Blue Montains, à 150 km au nord-ouest de Sydney, cette résidence se dresse sur un terrain de 3 hectares à 1 000 m d'altitude. Ce projet spartiate conçu pour un couple de retraités comprend une maison et un atelier séparés par une allée de bois surélevée et un bassin. La présence du bois est étonnante dans cette maison toute d'aluminium, acier laqué, verre et sols de béton poli. Résolument horizontal, le plan de la maison est entièrement aligné, à l'exception de l'atelier im-

REFUGE MODERNE, IMAGINÉ PAR MURCUTT À PARTIR DE PRINCIPES DE SIMPLICITÉ ET DE LUMINOSITÉ.

AU MILIEU DES BOIS ET EN HARMONIE AVEC EUX, LA MAISON N'EN A PAS MOINS SU SE CRÉER SON TERRITOIRE.

at a slight angle to the rest of the composition because of a rock outcropping. The house faces toward the east and northeast, and the bedrooms are lodged toward the rear under the lower point of the sloping roof. The inclined roof and rectilinear layout bring to mind Murcutt's Meagher House (Bowral, New South Wales, 1988-92). Despite its apparently extreme austerity and simplicity, the house took more than five years to design and build.

Ateliers, das einem Felsen ausweicht und im leichten Winkel zum Rest der Anlage steht. Das Gebäude ist nach Osten und Nordosten orientiert; die Schlafräume liegen im rückwärtigen Bereich unter der tiefer gezogenen Seite des Schrägdachs. Dies und der rechtwinklige Grundriß erinnern an Murcutts Haus Meagher (Bowral, NSW, 1988-92). Trotz seiner extremen Strenge und Schlichtheit betrugen Planungs- und Bauzeit mehr als fünf Jahre.

planté légèrement en biais pour éviter un affleurement de rocher. La façade regarde vers l'est et le nord-est et les chambres sont installées à l'arrière, sous la partie la plus basse du toit. L'inclinaison de celui-ci et le plan rectiligne font penser à la Meagher House, également de Murcutt (Bowral, Nouvelle-Galles du Sud, 1988-92). Malgré cette apparente austère simplicité, il a fallu plus de cinq ans pour concevoir et construire la maison.

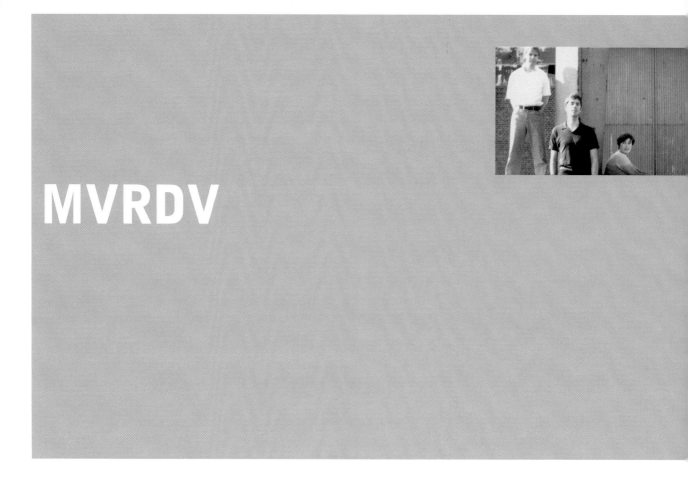

MVRDV

Winy Maas (left), Jacob van Rijs (center) and Nathalie de Vries (right) created MVRDV in 1992. The name of the firm is made up of the initials of the surnames of the partners. Born in 1959, Maas, like his two partners (both born in 1964), studied at the Technical University in Delft. Both Maas and van Rijs worked for OMA. Maas and de Vries worked in the office of Ben van Berkel before founding MVRDV. Aside from the Villa VPRO, their work includes the RVU Building, Hilversum,

Winy Maas (links), Jacob van Rijs (Mitte) und Nathalie de Vries (rechts) gründeten MVRDV im Jahre 1992; der Name des Büros ist aus den Initialen ihrer Nachnamen gebildet. Maas (geboren 1959), van Rijs (geboren 1964) und de Vries (geboren 1964) studierten an der Technischen Universität Delft. Maas und van Rijs arbeiteten zuvor für OMA; Maas und de Vries bei Ben van Berkel. Zu ihren Werken gehören das RVU-Gebäude in Hilversum (1994-97), ein Doppelhaus in Utrecht (1995-97)

Winy Maas (né en 1959, à gauche), Jacob van Rijs (né en 1964, au milieu) et Nathalie de Vries (née en, 1964, à droite) ont créé MVRDV en 1992, dont le nom reprend leurs initiales. W. Maas, comme ses deux associés, a étudié l'architecture à l'Université Technique de Delft. Avec J. van Rijs il a travaillé pour l'agence OMA, et avec N. de Vries pour Ben van Berkel. En dehors de leur Villa VPRO ils ont construit le RVU Building à Hilversum (1994-97), une maison jumelée à Utrecht (1995-

USING THEIR OWN INITIALS FOR THEIR FIRM'S
NAME, MAAS, VAN RIJS AND DE VRIES HAVE
SET THE PACE IN THE YOUNGER GENERATION
OF DUTCH ARCHITECTURE THAT IS INFLUENCED
BY REM KOOLHAAS.

MAAS, VAN RIJS UND DE VRIES, DIE IHRE
INITIALEN ZUM FIRMENNAMEN MACHTEN,
GEBEN DAS TEMPO DER JUNGEN GENERATION

IN DER HOLLÄNDISCHEN ARCHITEKTURSZENE
AN, DIE VON REM KOOLHAAS BEEINFLUSST IST.

SOUS CETTE DÉNOMINATION COMPOSÉE DE
LEURS INITIALES, MAAS, VAN RIJS ET DE VRIES
DONNENT LE TON À UNE NOUVELLE GÉNÉRA-
TION D'ARCHITECTES NÉERLANDAIS INSPIRÉS
PAR REM KOOLHAAS.

MVRDV
POSTBUS 63136
3002 JC ROTTERDAM
THE NETHERLANDS

TEL: + 31 10 477 2860
FAX: + 31 10 477 3627
E-MAIL: mvrdv@archined.nl
WEB: www.archined.nl/mvrdv/mvrdv.html

etherlands (1994-97), a Double House in Utrecht, etherlands (1995-97), and WoZoCo, 100 apartments for elderly people, Amsterdam-Osdorp (1997). hey have also worked on urban development chemes such as their "Shadow City Bergen Op oom" project (1993), or the masterplan for Parkane Airport, Eindhoven, Netherlands. The Villa 'PRO bears some similarity to a 1993 project for church in Barendrecht that evolved from a cheme involving "folded" shapes.

sowie WoZoCo, ein Komplex mit 100 Senioren-wohnungen in Amsterdam-Osdorp (1997). Darüber hinaus haben sie städtebauliche Planungen wie das Projekt »Shadow City Bergen Op Zoom« (1993) oder den Bebauungsplan für den Flughafen Parklane in Eindhoven erarbeitet. Die Villa VPRO weist gewisse Ähnlichkeiten mit dem Entwurf für eine Kirche in Barendrecht von 1993 auf, der ebenfalls aus einem System »gefalteter« Formen entwickelt ist.

97), ainsi que WoZoCo, 100 appartements pour personnes âgées à Amsterdam-Osdorp (1997). Ils ont également travaillé à des programmes d'urbanisme comme leur projet de «Shadow City Bergen Op Zoom» (1993), ou le plan directeur de l'aéroport Parklane à Eindhoven. La Villa VPRO présente certaines similarités avec leur projet d'église pour Barendrecht (1993), issu d'une étude sur les espaces «pliés».

MVRDV
VILLA VPRO
HILVERSUM, THE NETHERLANDS, 1993-97

CLIENT / BAUHERR: VPRO, HILVERSUM
ENGINEERING AND BUILDING CONSULTANCY /
KONSTRUKTION UND BAUBERATUNG / ÉLABO-
RATION DU PLAN ET CONSEIL TECHNIQUE:
BUREAU BOUWKUNDE ROTTERDAM
FLOOR AREA / NUTZFLÄCHE / SURFACE UTILE:
10 500 M²
COSTS / KOSTEN / COÛTS: 22 000 000 NLG

P 366.367

HIGHLY UNEXPECTED FEATURES INCLUDE
INCLINED FLOORS WITH ORIENTAL RUGS AND
A CRYSTAL CHANDELIER.

THE BUILDING CLEVERLY ALTERNATES OPACITY
AND WEIGHT WITH TRANSPARENCY AND LIGHT-
NESS.

ORIENTTEPPICHE UND EIN KRONLEUCHTER
AUS KRISTALL SIND ÄUSSERST UNGEWÖHN-
LICHE ELEMENTE IN DIESEM MODERNEN
GEBÄUDE.

DAS GEBÄUDE IST EINE GELUNGENE KOMBI-
NATION VON DICHTE UND SCHWERE MIT
TRANSPARENZ UND LEICHTIGKEIT.

CARACTÉRISTIQUES SORTANT DE L'ORDINAIRE
POUR CETTE PETITE VILLA: SOLS INCLINÉS,
TAPIS ORIENTAUX ET LUSTRE DE CRISTAL.

LA MAISON ALTERNE AVEC INTELLIGENCE
OPACITÉ ET MASSE, TRANSPARENCE ET
LÉGÈRETÉ.

This headquarters and studio building for the VPRO public broadcasting company, formerly housed in a group of 13 villas, offers 10,000 m² of floor space. The intention of the architects was to reproduce some of the positive aspects of the former villas. The raised, grass-covered roof covers what the architects call a "geological formation made up of the different floors," connected to each other

Dieser Verwaltungs- und Studiobau für den Radio-sender VPRO ersetzt eine Gruppe von 13 Villen. Die Architekten versuchten, einige Vorzüge der Villen zu übernehmen. Das angehobene Grasdach erstreckt sich über die von den Architekten so be-zeichnete »geologische Formation aus verschiede-nen Ebenen«, die durch Rampen, abgestufte Böden und kleine Steigungen zu einem Raumkontinuum

Le nouveau siège et les studios de la station de radio publique VPRO, qui occupaient naguère 13 villas, offrent une surface de 10 000 m². Les archi-tectes ont voulu reprendre à leur compte certains avantages de l'installation éclatée précédente. Le toit soulevé et semé d'herbe recouvre ce que l'archi-tecte appelle une «formation géologique composée des différents niveaux», réunis entre eux par des

by ramps, stepped floors and small rises in what amounts to a continuous space. The architects' intention is also to connect interior and exterior through views and openings. Rather than being placed in the ceilings, the air, data and electricity conduits are in the floors. 35 different types of glass of varying color and reflectivity are used in the building, intended for a workforce of 300.

vereint sind. Absicht der Architekten war zudem, Inneres und Äußeres miteinander zu verbinden. Die Leitungen für Klima, Datentransfer und Elektrizität sind in den Fußböden und nicht wie üblich in den Decken verlegt. In dem Bau, der für 300 Arbeitsplätze ausgelegt ist, wurden insgesamt 35 Glasarten in verschiedenen Farben verwendet. Obgleich Betonböden die Regel sind, präsentiert sich der Eingangs-

rampes, des sols inclinés et de légers soulèvements tout au long d'un espace traité en continu. L'intérieur et l'extérieur sont mis en connexion par des vues calculées et des ouvertures. Les réseaux de fluides – air, données, électricité – passent par les sols et non par les plafonds. 35 variétés de verre de différentes couleurs et réflexivités sont utilisés dans ce bâtiment conçu pour 300 personnes. Bien que les

Although concrete floors are the rule, the entrance boasts an incongruous chandelier and Persian carpets. Nets of black nylon hung from steel cables replace more traditional guardrails, while steel chains have taken over for the more common exterior drainpipes. By calling on young, relatively little known architects, the VPRO Company, known for its own anti-establishment attitude, seems to have gotten exactly what it bargained for.

bereich mit Kronleuchter und Perserteppichen. Schwarze, an Stahlseilen aufgehängte Nylonnetze ersetzen die traditionellen Handläufe, während Stahlketten die Aufgabe der üblichen Fallrohre übernehmen. Durch die Auftragsvergabe an relativ unbekannte Architekten hat der unkonventionelle Sender VPRO ein Gebäude erhalten, das zu ihm paßt.

sols en béton soient de règle, l'entrée n'en est pas moins décorée d'un lustre incongru et des tapis persans. Des filets de nylon noir suspendus à des câbles d'acier remplacent les rampes traditionnelles, et des chaînes d'acier les descentes de pluie extérieures. En faisant appel à de jeunes architectes relativement peu connus, VPRO, célèbre pour son attitude anti-establishment, semble avoir exactement obtenu ce qu'elle recherchait.

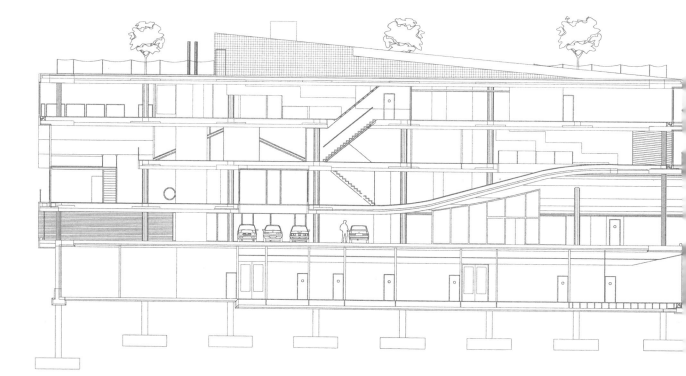

SECTIONS AND PHOTOS SHOW HOW THE IN-
CLINED FLOOR PLAN IS INSERTED INTO THE
DESIGN.

SCHNITTE UND FOTOS ZEIGEN, WIE DIE SCHRÄ-
GEN BÖDEN IN DEN ENTWURF INTEGRIERT
SIND.

LES COUPES ET LES PHOTOS MONTRENT DE
QUELLE FAÇON LE SOL INCLINÉ S'INSÈRE DANS
LE PLAN.

P 372.373

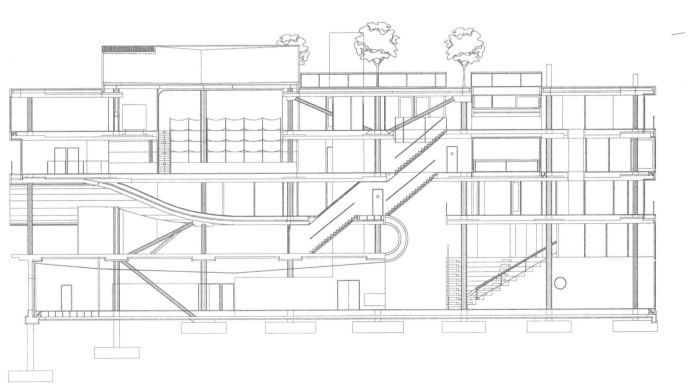

MZRC

This unusual group of architects was put together specifically to build the Stade de France. The architects were in fact strongly encouraged to work together by the builders' consortium. Michel Macary (right) and Aymeric Zublena (left) have been working together in the firm they created jointly (SCAU) since 1971. Macary has been the chief architect for Marne-la-Vallée, Lanau, Carcans-Maubuisson, and the Nouveau Bercy project. His best-known job before the Stade was his collaboration with I. M. Pei on the Grand Louvre project.

Diese ungewöhnliche Architektengruppe hat sich eigens zum Bau des Stade de France zusammengefunden; die Mitglieder wurden vom Baukonsortium nachdrücklich darum gebeten. Michel Macary (rechts) und Aymeric Zublena (links) arbeiteten schon seit 1971 in der von ihnen gegründeten Firma SCAU zusammen; Macary trug die Verantwortung für die Projekte Marne-la-Vallée, Lanau, Carcans-Maubuisson und Nouveau Bercy. Vor dem Bau des Stadions war er vor allem durch seine Mitarbeit an Ieoh Ming Peis Grand Louvre bekannt

Ce groupe d'architectes s'est constitué pour construire le Stade de France, avec les encouragements d'un consortium de constructeurs. Michel Macary (à droite) et Aymeric Zublena (à gauche) ont travaillé ensemble dans leur propre agence, SCAU, créée en 1971. Macary a été architecte-en-chef des villes de Marne-la-Vallée, Lanau, Carcans-Maubuisson et du projet du Nouveau Bercy. Il a par ailleurs collaboré avec I. M. Pei sur le Grand Louvre. Zublena a travaillé sur les plans d'urbanisme de Buenos Aires et de Marne-la-Vallée. L'hô-

AGENCE MACARY ZUBLENA
5, RUE LEMAIGNAN
75014 PARIS, FRANCE

TEL: + 33 1 40 78 84 00
FAX: + 33 1 40 78 85 98
E-MAIL:
scau@architectes.net
WEB: www.scau.newz.net

COSTANTINI REGEMBAL
19, RUE DE LA FORGE
ROYALE
75011 PARIS
FRANCE

TEL: + 33 1 43 72 50 44
FAX: + 33 1 43 72 36 08
WEB: www.costantini-
regembal.com

P 374.375

A GROUPING OF ARCHITECTS CREATED SPECIF-
ICALLY FOR THE CONSTRUCTION OF THE STADE
DE FRANCE IN PARIS, MZRC IS SIMPLY THE
SUM OF TWO PRACTICES ENCOURAGED TO
WORK TOGETHER.

DIESE VEREINIGUNG VON ARCHITEKTEN, DIE
SICH SPEZIELL FÜR DEN BAU DES STADIONS
ZUSAMMENGEFUNDEN HAT, BESTEHT AUS ZWEI

BÜROS, DIE ZUR KOOPERATION VERPFLICHTET
WURDEN.

REGROUPEMENT D'ARCHITECTES CONSTITUÉ
À L'OCCASION DU PROJET DU STADE DE
FRANCE À PARIS, MZRC EST LA SOMME DE
DEUX AGENCES INCITÉES À COLLABORER
PAR LES PROMOTEURS DU PROJET.

Zublena worked on the urban plans of Buenos Aires and on Marne-la-Vallée as well. His recently completed Georges-Pompidou Hospital in Paris confirms his mastery of hospital construction. Michel Regembal and Claude Costantini have worked together for 20 years. They built the Légion d'Honneur School in Saint-Denis, and numerous administrative buildings such as the Departmental Offices of the Loiret region, and the Tax Authority building in Aix-en-Provence.

geworden. Zublena arbeitete an den städtebaulichen Entwürfen für Buenos Aires und Marne-la-Vallée. Mit dem kürzlich fertiggestellten Georges Pompidou-Krankenhaus in Paris hat er seine Fähigkeiten erneut unter Beweis gestellt. Michel Regembal und Claude Costantini arbeiten seit 20 Jahren zusammen. Sie bauten die Schule der Légion d'Honneur in Saint-Denis und zahlreiche Bürohäuser, darunter das Verwaltungsgebäude des Départements Loiret und das Finanzamt in Aix-en-Provence, alle in Frankreich.

pital Georges-Pompidou qu'il a récemment achevé à Paris témoigne de sa compétence dans le domaine hospitalier. Michel Regembal et Claude Costantini collaborent depuis 20 ans. Ils ont construit l'École de la Légion d'Honneur à Saint-Denis et de nombreux bâtiments administratifs, comme les bureaux du département du Loiret ou l'immeuble du Centre des Impôts d'Aix-en-Provence.

STADE DE FRANCE
SAINT-DENIS, FRANCE, 1994-97

PLANNING / PLANUNG: 1994-95
CONSTRUCTION / BAU: 1995-97
CLIENT / BAUHERR: CONSORTIUM STADE DE FRANCE
FLOOR AREA / NUTZFLÄCHE / SURFACE UTILE: 140 000 M²
COSTS / KOSTEN / COÛTS: 2 600 000 000 FF
PLACES / PLÄTZE: FOOTBALL: 80 000; ATHLETHICS: 75 000; CONCERTS: 105 000

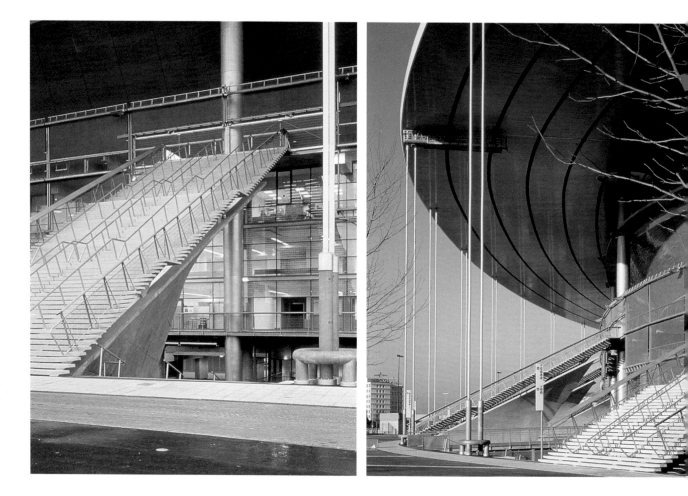

In 1992, France was chosen as the organizer of the 1998 World Cup. The site for the main stadium in Saint-Denis was chosen in 1993, and work actually began on the massive structure in May 1995. Although the competition was marred by some controversy, the project designed by Michel Macary and his associates has since been widely praised. Several matches and most notably the final of the 1998 World Cup were held in the Stade de France for capacity audiences. The 80,000-seat stadium was built for about 2.6 billion French francs. The longer axis of the oval measures 274 m and the

1992 wurde Frankreich zum Organisator der Fußball-Weltmeisterschaft 1998 gewählt. Die Entscheidung, das Hauptstadion in Saint-Denis zu bauen, wurde 1993 getroffen, und die Bauarbeiten an der gewaltigen Konstruktion begannen im Mai 1995. Obgleich der Wettbewerb von Kontroversen geprägt war, ist der von Michel Macary und seinen Partnern geplante Entwurf überwiegend gelobt worden. Mehrere Spiele und vor allem das Endspiel der WM 1998 wurden im ausverkauften Stade de France abgehalten. Bei 80 000 Sitzplätzen betrugen die Baukosten etwa 2,6 Milliarden Francs. Die Längs-

En 1992, la France a été désignée pour organiser la Coupe du monde de football 1998. En 1993, la ville de Saint-Denis fut retenue pour le site du grand stade prévu, dont les travaux ont débuté en mai 1995. Bien que le concours ait été l'objet d'une controverse, le projet de Michel Macary et de ses associés a été largement applaudi. Plusieurs matches et surtout la finale de la Coupe se sont joués dans cet immense stade de 80 000 places qui aura coûté 2,6 milliards de francs. L'axe le plus long de l'ovale mesure 274 m et l'ensemble couvre 17 hectares. Le toit, élément majeur du projet, est suspen-

P 378.379

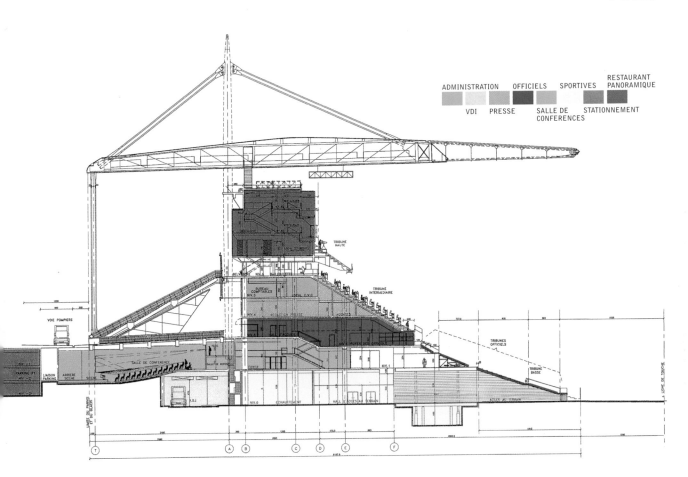

ADMINISTRATION   OFFICIELS   SPORTIVES   RESTAURANT PANORAMIQUE

VDI   PRESSE   SALLE DE CONFERENCES   STATIONNEMENT

whole covers 17 hectares. The roof, a major element of the design, is suspended from 18 steel poles and measures a total of 6 hectares in area. There are approximately 5,000 parking spaces near the stadium, and two rapid transit public transport stations (RER) were built near the site to encourage visitors not to come by car. The design permits visitors to actually see the playing field before they enter through one of the 120 entrances, a factor that reduces the usual feeling of claustrophobia in these circumstances.

achse des ovalen Stadions mißt 274 m, das Gelände der gesamten Anlage 17 ha. Das Dach als Hauptelement des Entwurfs ist an 18 Stahlmasten aufgehängt, seine Fläche beträgt insgesamt 6 ha. In unmittelbarer Nähe des Stadions befinden sich etwa 5 000 Parkplätze und zwei Stationen der Schnellbahn (RER). Die Form des Stadions erlaubt den Zuschauern einen Blick auf das Spielfeld, noch ehe sie durch einen der 120 Eingänge die Tribünen betreten. Dieser Kunstgriff vermindert das klaustrophobische Gefühl, das solche Bauten oft vermitteln.

du à 18 poteaux d'acier et mesure 6 hectares. Environ 5 000 places de parking ont été prévues, et deux stations de RER ont été construites pour encourager les spectateurs à venir par les transports publics. La conception des accès permet aux spectateurs de voir le terrain de jeu avant d'arriver à leur place par une des 120 entrées, facteur qui réduit le sentiment de claustrophobie fréquemment lié à ce type de construction.

P 380.381

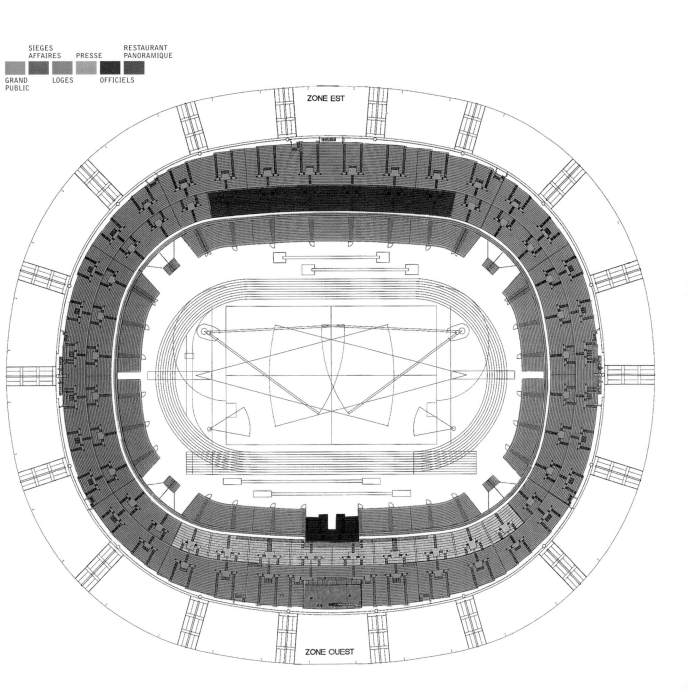

JEAN NOUVEL

AT 55 YEARS OF AGE, JEAN NOUVEL HAS FRE-QUENTLY BEEN CALLED THE MOST INVENTIVE AND ONE OF THE MOST INFLUENTIAL ARCHI-TECTS OF HIS GENERATION. HIS BOLD FORMS AND UNEXPECTED USE OF MATERIALS SET HIM APART FROM MANY OTHER FRENCH ARCHI-TECTS.

DER 55JÄHRIGE JEAN NOUVEL IST HÄUFIG ALS DER PHANTASIEVOLLSTE UND EINER DER EINFLUSSREICHSTEN ARCHITEKTEN SEINER GENERATION BEZEICHNET WORDEN. SEINE KÜHNEN FORMEN UND DIE UNGEWÖHNLICHE VERWENDUNG VON MATERIALIEN UNTER-SCHEIDEN IHN VON VIELEN ANDEREN FRAN-ZÖSISCHEN ARCHITEKTEN.

Born in 1945 in Fumel, France, Jean Nouvel was admitted to the École des Beaux-Arts in Bordeaux in 1964. In 1970 he created his first office with François Seigneur. His first widely noticed project was the Institut du Monde Arabe in Paris (1981-87, with Architecture Studio). Other works include his Nemausus housing (Nîmes, France, 1985-87), offices for the CLM/BBDO advertising firm (Issy-les-Moulineaux, 1988-92), Lyons Opera House (1986-93), Vinci Conference Center (Tours, 1989-

Jean Nouvel, geboren 1945 in Fumel, Frankreich, studierte ab 1964 an der École des Beaux-Arts in Bordeaux. 1970 gründete er zusammen mit Fran-çois Seigneur sein erstes Büro. Weithin bekannt wurde Nouvel mit seinem Institut du Monde Arabe in Paris (1981-87, bei dem er mit Architecture Studio zusammenarbeitete. Weitere herausragende Werke sind die Wohnanlage Nemausus in Nîmes (1985-87), die Büros der Werbeagentur CLM/BBDO in Issy-les-Moulineaux (1988-92), das Opernhaus in

Né en 1945 à Fumel, Jean Nouvel est admis à l'École des Beaux-Arts de Bordeaux en 1964. En 1970, il crée sa première agence avec François Seigneur. Son premier projet très remarqué est l'Institut du Monde Arabe à Paris (1981-87, avec Architecture Studio). Il réalise également l'im-meuble de logements Nemausus à Nîmes (1985-87), les bureaux de l'agence de publicité CLM/BBDO à Issy-les-Moulineaux (1988-92), l'Opéra de Lyon (1986-93), le Vinci Centre International de

À 55 ANS, JEAN NOUVEL EST SOUVENT CONSIDÉRÉ COMME L'UN DES ARCHITECTES LES PLUS INVENTIFS ET LES PLUS INFLUENTS DE SA GÉNÉRATION. SES FORMES AUDACIEUSES ET SON UTILISATION PERSONNELLE DES MATÉRIAUX LUI CONFÈRENT UNE PLACE À PART DANS L'ARCHITECTURE FRANÇAISE.

ARCHITECTURES JEAN NOUVEL
10, CITÉ D'ANGOULÈME
75011 PARIS
FRANCE

TEL: + 33 1 49 23 83 83
FAX: + 33 1 43 14 81 10
E-MAIL: ajn01@FranceNet.fr

93), Euralille Shopping Center (Lille, 1991-94), Fondation Cartier (Paris, 1991-95), and the Galeries Lafayette, Berlin (1992-96). Among his unbuilt projects are the "Tour sans fins" (La Défense, Paris, 1989), Grand Stade for the 1998 World Cup (Paris, 1994), and Tenaga National Tower (Kuala Lumpur, Malaysia, 1995). His largest current commission is the Music and Conference Center in Lucerne, Switzerland, whose concert hall was inaugurated in 1998.

Lyon (1986-93), das Kongreßzentrum Vinci in Tours (1989-93), das Einkaufszentrum Euralille in Lille (1991-94) und die Fondation Cartier in Paris (1991-95). Außerdem baute Nouvel die Galeries Lafayette in Berlin (1992-96) und plante die 400 m hohe »Tour sans fins« in La Défense, Paris (1989), das Grand Stade für die Fußball-Weltmeisterschaft von 1998 (1994) und den Tenaga National Tower in Kuala Lumpur, Malaysia (1995), die aber alle nicht realisiert wurden.

Congrès de Tours (1989-93), le centre commercial Euralille à Lille (1991-94), la Fondation Cartier à Paris (1991-95) et les Galeries Lafayette à Berlin (1992-96). Ses projets non réalisés sont: une tour de 400 m de haut («Tour sans fins», La Défense, Paris, 1989), le Grand Stade pour la Coupe du Monde de football (Paris, 1994) et la Tenaga National Tower (Kuala Lumpur, Malaisie, 1995). Sa plus importante commande actuelle est le Centre de Musique et de Conférences de Lucerne (Suisse).

JEAN NOUVEL

LUCERNE CULTURE
AND CONGRESS CENTER

LUCERNE, SWITZERLAND, 1992-99

THE OVERHANGING ROOF OF COURSE PROTECTS VISITORS FROM THE WEATHER, BUT ITS RAZOR-SHARP FORM ALSO DEFINES THE VISUAL IDENTITY OF THE COMPLEX.

DAS AUSKRAGENDE DACH DIENT ALS WETTER-SCHUTZ, SEINE RASIERMESSERSCHARFE FORM VERLEIHT DEM KOMPLEX ABER AUCH VISUELLE IDENTITÄT.

LE TOIT EN SURPLOMB PROTÈGE LES VISI-TEURS DE LA PLUIE, MAIS SA FORME DE RASOIR EFFILÉ DÉFINIT ÉGALEMENT L'IDEN-TITÉ VISUELLE DU CENTRE.

START OF PLANNING / PLANUNGSBEGINN /
DÉBUT DES ÉTUDES: 1992
CONSTRUCTION / BAU: 1995-98 (1. PHASE),
1995-99 (2. PHASE)
CLIENT / BAUHERR: TRÄGERSTIFTUNG KULTUR-
UND KONGRESSZENTRUM LUZERN
FLOOR AREA / NUTZFLÄCHE / SURFACE UTILE:
35 000 M²
COSTS / KOSTEN / COÛTS: 209 400 000 SFR

Set in a highly visible location in Lucerne, next to the railroad station and at the edge of the lake, this is the most important building by Jean Nouvel since his Fondation Cartier in Paris (1995). Intended to provide a 1,900-seat symphony hall, a 900-seat multi-purpose hall, a 300-seat congress hall, a 2,400 m² *kunsthalle* and three restaurants, the complex will have a total usable floor area of 35,000 m². The approximate budget for the building, whose symphony hall opened in 1998, is 200 million Swiss francs. A first proposal by Nouvel made in 1989 that would have modified the existing shores of the

Weithin sichtbar, neben dem Bahnhof und am Ufer des Vierwaldstätter Sees gelegen, ist das Luzerner Kultur- und Kongreßzentrum der bedeutendste Bau Jean Nouvels seit seiner Fondation Cartier in Paris (1995). Der Komplex wird aus einem Konzertsaal mit 1 900, einer Mehrzweckhalle mit 900 und einer Kongreßhalle mit 300 Sitzen bestehen. Hinzu kommen eine 2 400 m² großer Kunstsaal und drei Restaurants. Das voraussichtliche Budget des Gebäudes, dessen großer Konzertsaal 1998 eröffnet wurde, beträgt 200 Millionen Schweizer Franken. Ein erster Vorschlag Nouvels von 1989, der eine in den

Occupant une position particulièrement en vue au centre de Lucerne, près de la gare et en bordure du lac, ce Centre est la plus importante réalisation de Jean Nouvel depuis la Fondation Cartier à Paris (1995). Une fois achevé, il abritera sur une surface totale de 35 000 m² une salle de concerts symphoniques de 1 900 places (inaugurée en 1998), une salle polyvalente de 900 places, une salle de congrès de 300 places, une galerie d'art de 2 400 m² et trois restaurants. Le budget de construction devrait s'élever approximativement à 200 millions de francs suisses. En 1989, une première proposition

P 390.391

P 390.391

INSIDE, JEAN NOUVEL RETAINS HIS TASTE FOR UNEXPECTED MATERIALS, AND CREATES SPACES THAT ARE LESS CLAUSTROPHOBIC THAN THOSE OF THE LYON OPERA HOUSE FOR EXAMPLE.

IM INNERN BEWEIST NOUVEL SEIN GESCHICK IM UMGANG MIT UNGEWÖHNLICHEN MATERIALIEN UND ERZEUGT RÄUME, DIE WENIGER ENG WIRKEN ALS ZUM BEISPIEL IN SEINEM OPERNHAUS VON LYON.

À L'INTÉRIEUR, NOUVEL MANIFESTE SON GOÛT POUR LES MATÉRIAUX INATTENDUS ET CRÉE DES ESPACES MOINS CLAUSTROPHOBIQUES QUE CEUX DE L'OPÉRA DE LYON.

lake by building out into the water was rejected by a referendum, and the city asked him to propose a new scheme in 1992. The most stunning feature of the Center is its razor-thin roof, which projects out toward the lake and the tour boat dock. A truly mature work, it is full of surprises, ranging from the use of light to the surprising materials. Another unexpected feature of the building is that Nouvel actually brings water inside, with long, narrow basins separating each unit of the complex.

See hineinragende Bebauung vorsah, wurde in einem Referendum verworfen. 1992 forderte die Stadt ihn zu einem neuen Entwurf auf. Das auffälligste Merkmal des Zentrums ist sein papierdünnes Dach, das über den See und die Anlegestelle der Ausflugsboote auskragt. Dieses wahrhaft meisterliche Werk steckt voller Überraschungen – von der Nutzung des Lichts bis zu den ungewöhnlichen Materialien. Eine weitere Eigenheit des Baus besteht darin, daß Nouvel das Wasser – mittels langer, schmaler Becken, welche die einzelnen Trakte voneinander trennen – in den Innenraum führt.

de l'architecte qui modifiait le profil de la rive du lac en édifiant le bâtiment au-dessus de l'eau, avait été rejetée par référendum. La ville lui demanda un nouveau projet en 1992. L'élément le plus étonnant est le toit en lame de rasoir qui se projette vers le lac et un appontement. Œuvre de grande maturité, ce bâtiment réserve de nombreuses surprises, de la maîtrise de la lumière à celle de matériaux inhabituels, en passant par de longs bassins étroits qui séparent intérieurement chaque partie du bâtiment.

THE MAIN CONCERT HALL SEATS 1,900 PER-
SONS. ITS FORM AND MATERIALS ARE NATUR-
ALLY RELATED TO ACOUSTICAL CONSIDER-
ATIONS.

P 392.393

DIE GROSSE KONZERTHALLE FASST 1900 PER-
SONEN. IHRE FORM UND DIE WAHL DER MATE-
RIALIEN SIND DURCH AKUSTISCHE ANFORDE-
RUNGEN BEDINGT.

LA SALLE DE CONCERT PRINCIPALE COMPTE
1900 PLACES. SA FORME ET SES MATÉRIAUX
SONT DÉTERMINÉS PAR DES CONSIDÉRATIONS
ACOUSTIQUES.

NOX

Lars Spuybroek, who founded NOX in 1991, was born in 1959 in Rotterdam. He studied at the Technical University in Delft. His work has won several prizes (Archiprix 1989, Mart Stam Incentive Prize 1992, Iakov Chernikov Award 1997, Zeeland Architecture Award 1998). Recent work includes Foam Home, a housing project for the KAN area near Nijmegen (1997), OffTheRoad/103.8 MHz, housing and noise barrier, Eindhoven, (1998/99), and the V2_Engine, proposed facade for the V2_Organisation (Rotterdam, 1997-99). Right from the start, his architectural design has been influenced by other media: simultaneously with the formation

Lars Spuybroek, geboren 1959 in Rotterdam, studierte an der Technischen Universität Delft und gründete 1991 das Büro NOX. Seine Bauten wurden mit verschiedenen Preisen ausgezeichnet (Archiprix 1989, Mart Stam Incentive Prize 1992, Iakov Chernikov 1997, Zeeland Architecture Award 1998). Zu seinen neueren Arbeiten gehören das Foam Home, ein Wohnbauprojekt für das Gebiet KAN bei Nijmegen (1997), OffTheRoad/103.8 Mhz, Wohnungsbau und Schallschutzmauer in Eindhoven (1998-99) sowie V2_Engine, ein Fassadenentwurf für die V2_Organisation in Rotterdam (1997-99). Von Anfang an wurden seine Entwürfe durch an-

Né à Rotterdam en 1959, Lars Spuybroek a fait ses études à l'Université Technique de Delft et a fondé NOX en 1991. Il a remporté différents prix (Archiprix 1989, Mart Stam Incentive Prize 1992, Iakov Chernikov Award 1997, Zeeland Architecture Award 1998). Parmi ses travaux récents figurent le Foam Home, projet d'habitation pour la zone d'aménagement KAN près de Nimègue (1997), les OffThe-Road/103.8 Mhz, logements et barrière anti-bruit, (Eindhoven, 1998) et le V2_Engine, projet de façade pour la V2_Organisation (Rotterdam, 1997-99). Dès le début, ses projets ont été influencés par d'autres médias : parallèlement à la fondation de NOX-

LARS SPUYBROEK AND NOX ARE CONVINCED THAT COMPUTER-GENERATED FORMS ARE THE WAVE OF THE FUTURE, PERMITTING THE DESIGN AND CONSTRUCTION OF HITHERTO UNIMAGINABLE FORMS.

LARS SPUYBROEK UND NOX SIND DAVON ÜBERZEUGT, DASS DIE ZUKUNFT COMPUTER-GENERIERTEN ENTWÜRFEN GEHÖRT, DA DIESE

DIE PLANUNG UND AUSFÜHRUNG BISHER UNVORSTELLBARER FORMEN ERMÖGLICHEN.

LARS SPUYBROEK ET NOX SONT CONVAINCUS QUE LES FORMES CONÇUES PAR ORDINATEUR REPRÉSENTENT LE FUTUR ET PERMETTRONT LA CONCEPTION ET LA MISE EN ŒUVRE DE SOLUTIONS JUSQUE LÀ INIMAGINABLES.

NOX
MATHENESSERLAAN 443
3023 GJ ROTTERDAM
THE NETHERLANDS

TEL/FAX: + 31 10 477 2853
E-MAIL: nox@luna.nl

of NOX architects, Spuybroek created *NOX* magazine in collaboration with Maurice Nio. He has also been editor of the journal *Forum* (1995-98) and he regularly lectures and publishes in Holland and abroad. Inspired by the ideas of "the liquid" and "metamorphosis," Lars Spuybroek moves freely between the media of architecture, computer design, video productions ("NOX' Soft City"), and installations ("Armed Response", Den Bosch; "Heavenly Bodies", Eindhoven).

dere Medien beeinflußt: Gleichzeitig mit der Eröffnung des Büros gründete er zusammen mit Maurice Nio die Zeitschrift »NOX«, von 1995-98 war er zudem Herausgeber der Zeitschrift »Forum«. Außerdem lehrt und publiziert er regelmäßig in Holland und im Ausland. Inspiriert durch die Idee des »Liquiden« und der »Metamorphose«, schafft Lars Spuybroek fließende Übergänge zwischen den Medien Architektur, Computerdesign, Video (»NOX' Soft City«) und Installation (»Armed Response«, Den Bosch; »Heavenly Bodies«, Eindhoven).

Architects, il a crée la revue « NOX » avec Maurice Nio. Éditeur de la revue « Forum » de 1995 à 1998, il donne régulièrement des conférences et publie des ouvrages en Hollande et à l'étranger. Inspiré par l'idée du « liquide » et de la « métamorphose », Lars Spuybroek passe librement des médias de l'architecture au design informatique, aux productions vidéo (« NOX' Soft City ») et aux installations (« Armed Response », Den Bosch ; « Heavenly Bodies », Eindhoven).

NOX
WATER PAVILION
H₂O EXPO
NEELTJE JANS, THE NETHERLANDS, 1994-97

START OF PLANNING / PLANUNGSBEGINN / DÉBUT DES ÉTUDES: 1994
CONSTRUCTION / BAU: 3/96-5/97
CLIENT / BAUHERR: DELTA EXPO / MINISTRY OF TRANSPORT, PUBLIC WORKS AND WATER MANAGEMENT
FLOOR AREA / NUTZFLÄCHE / SURFACE UTILE: 800 M²
COSTS / KOSTEN / COÛTS: 2 150 000 NLG (ART INSTALLATION: 2 000 000 NLG)

THE AQUATIC PAVILION IS LOCATED NEXT TO THE "DELTA PROJECT" SEAWALLS. THE DARKER SECTION ATTACHED TO THE SILVER FORM IS A "SALT WATER PAVILION" DESIGNED BY OOSTERHUISASSOCIATES.

DER WASSERPAVILLON LIEGT AN DEN DEICHEN DES »DELTA-PROJEKTS«. DER DUNKLERE, AN DIE SILBERFARBENE FORM ANGEFÜGTE TRAKT

IST DER VON OOSTERHUISASSOCIATES ENTWORFENE »SALZWASSERPAVILLON«.

LE WATER PAVILION SE DRESSE NON LOIN DES DIGUES DU «DELTA PROJECT». LE BÂTIMENT SOMBRE CONTRE LA FORME ARGENTÉE EST LE «PAVILLON DE L'EAU DE MER», CONÇU PAR OOSTERHUISASSOCIATES.

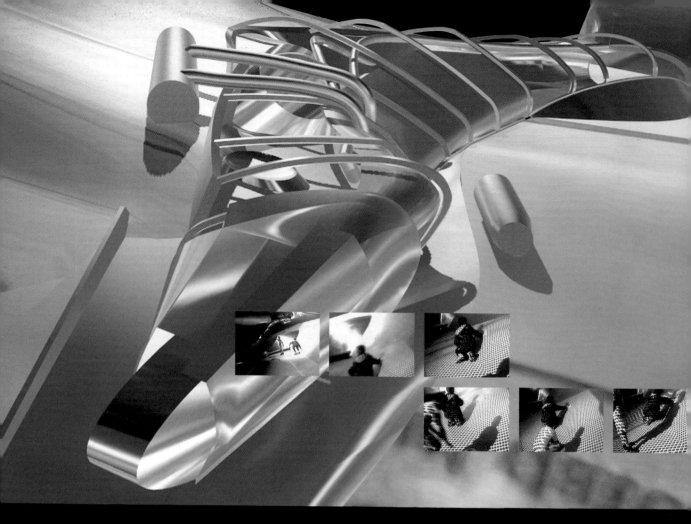

This highly unusual structure is the result of the melding of two projects, designed respectively by the Rotterdam architects Lars Spuybroek of NOX, and Kas Oosterhuis of oosterhuisassociates. It is set on the artificial island of Neeltje Jans, located to the southwest of Rotterdam. It is part of the popular Neeltje Jans Waterland. As Lars Spuybroek says, his H_2O expo, the Fresh Water Pavilion, "is conceived as a dynamic system within which there is a constant, computer-mediated interaction between users, environment and building." He uses the term "liquid architecture" to describe the structure, in which there are no right angles or straight surfaces. Rather the visitor wanders through an often interactively lit interior filled with surprising effects related to water. Spuybroek designed the H_2O expo.

Dieses sehr ungewöhnliche Bauwerk ist das Ergebnis der Verbindung zweier Projekte, entworfen von den Rotterdamer Architekten Lars Spuybroek, dem Leiter von NOX, und Kas Oosterhuis von oosterhuisassociates. Es steht auf einer künstlichen Insel südwestlich von Rotterdam und ist Teil des beliebten Neeltje Jans Waterland. Spuybroek über die H_2O expo, den von ihm entworfenen Süßwasserpavillon: »Das Gebäude wurde als dynamisches System geplant, innerhalb dessen eine ständige computergenerierte Interaktion zwischen User, Umwelt und Bauwerk stattfindet.« Er benutzt den Ausdruck »fließende Architektur«, um den Bau zu beschreiben, in dem es keine rechten Winkel oder geraden Flächen gibt. Vielmehr wandert der Besucher durch das meist spärlich beleuchtete Innere, das überra-

Ce très curieux bâtiment est le résultat de la fusion de deux projets, conçus respectivement par les architectes de NOX à Rotterdam, sous la direction de Lars Spuybroek, et par Kas Oosterhuis de oosterhuisassociates. Il se trouve sur une île artificielle au sud-ouest de Rotterdam et fait partie de Neeltje Jans Waterland, très apprécié des touristes. Comme l'indique Spuybroek à propos de H_2O, son Pavillon de l'eau douce: « Le pavillon est un système dynamique à l'intérieur duquel se déroulent en permanence des interactions entre utilisateurs, environnement et bâtiment via l'informatique. » Il utilise le terme d'« architecture liquide » pour décrire ce projet sans angles droits ni surfaces planes. Le visiteur se promène dans ce pavillon souvent faiblement éclairé qui propose des effets aquatiques

P 398.399

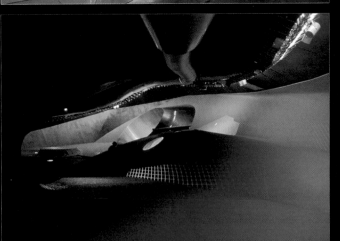

PHOTOS AND COMPUTER IMAGES GIVE AN IDEA OF THE UNEXPECTED NON-GEOMETRIC WALLS AND FLOORS OF THE PAVILION.

FOTOS UND COMPUTERBILDER VERMITTELN EINE VORSTELLUNG VON DEN UNGEWÖHNLI-CHEN, NICHT GEOMETRISCHEN WÄNDEN UND EBENEN DES PAVILLONS.

PHOTOS ET IMAGES DE SYNTHÈSE DONNENT UNE IDÉE DES MURS ET DES SOLS SUR-PRENANTS DE CE PAVILLON.

measuring about 61 m in length. It has an elong-ated, wave-like form, and is clad in stainless steel. The Salt Water Pavilion by Kas Oosterhuis is dark gray, tapered and angular, and about 42 m long. Inside, as Lars Spuybroek says of the H₂O expo, "there is no distinction between horizontal and ver-ical, between floors, walls and ceilings. Building and exhibition have fused: mist blows around your ears, a geyser erupts, water gleams and splatters all around you, projections fall directly onto the building and its visitors, the air is filled with inter-actively created waves of electronic sound and light. In that sense it is not an exhibition about water but visitors become part of the water, they have to 'level' their behavior with the continuously changing atmosphere."

schende Effekte bereithält. Der etwa 61 m lange Süßwasserpavillon hat eine langgezogene Wellen-form und ist mit Edelstahl verkleidet. Der eckige Meerwasserpavillon von Oosterhuis ist dunkelgrau, verjüngt sich nach oben und ist etwa 42 m lang. Im Innern der H₂O expo »gibt es keinen Unterschied ... zwischen Böden, Wänden und Decken. Gebäude und Ausstellung sind zu einer Einheit geworden: Gischt weht einem um die Ohren, ein Geysir springt hoch, Wasser glänzt und spritzt umher, Bilder werden direkt auf das Gebäude und die Besucher projiziert, die Luft ist von interaktiv erzeugten Klängen und Licht erfüllt. ... Es ist keine Ausstellung über das Wasser, die Besucher werden vielmehr zu einem Teil des Wassers, sie müssen ihr Verhalten der stän-dig sich verändernden Umgebung angleichen.«

surprenants. Long de 61 m, le Pavillon de l'eau douce a la forme d'une vague allongée et est recou-vert d'acier inoxydable. Le Pavillon de l'eau de mer d'Oosterhuis est gris foncé, angulaire, se rétrécit vers le haut et mesure environ 42 m de long. A l'intérieur de H₂O expo, « il n'y a pas de distinction ... entre les sols, les murs et les plafonds. Le bâti-ment et l'exposition ont fusionné : le vent du large souffle dans vos oreilles, un geyser se soulève, l'eau scintille et éclabousse tout autour de vous, des pro-jections d'images se font directement sur le bâti-ment et les visiteurs, l'air est envahi d'un jeu inter-actif de sons et lumières. ... Ce n'est pas une expo-sition ayant l'eau pour thème. Les visiteurs font partie de l'eau, ils doivent s'adapter à un environne-ment en perpétuelle mutation. »

NOX
V2_MEDIA LAB
ROTTERDAM, THE NETHERLANDS, 1998

Architect Lars Spuybroek conceived the V2_Media-Lab as part of the renovation of the V2 building located on the Eendrachtsstraat near the well-known Witte de Withstraat in Rotterdam. It was developed entirely by "computer with animation software that allows for a non-linear and time-dependent architecture." As Spuybroek writes, in his very personal style, "Instead of regarding the renovation as something that tranquilizes the existing structure and refurbishes it to death, architecture here assumes the attitude of the furniture and the textile as something that introduces movement into the existing situation, accelerates it, vectorizes, seduces and flexes. In this way we progress seam-

Lars Spuybroek entwarf das V2_MediaLab im Zuge des Umbaus des V2-Gebäudes, das in der Rotterdamer Eendrachtsstraat, nahe der bekannten Witte de Withstraat liegt. Geplant wurde es ausschließlich mit Hilfe von »Computern mit Animationssoftware, die eine nichtlineare und zeitgemäße Architektur ermöglicht«. Spuybroek schreibt weiter: »Statt den Umbau als Maßnahme aufzufassen, die das bestehende Bauwerk ruhigstellt und ›zu Tode saniert‹, erfüllt die Architektur hier eine Aufgabe, die auch Möbel und Textilien haben: Sie bringt Bewegung in die Situation, macht sie reizvoll und wandlungsfähig. So gehen wir nahtlos über von einem computergenerierten Prozeß der Kräfte,

L'architecte Lars Spuybroek a conçu le V2_Media-Lab dans le cadre de la rénovation de l'immeuble V2 situé sur la Eendrachtsstraat près de la fameuse Witt de Withstraat, à Rotterdam. Il a été entièrement mis au point par «ordinateur à l'aide d'un logiciel d'animation qui permet d'imaginer une architecture non linéaire et déterminée par le temps» Comme l'écrit Spuybroek dans son style très personnel: «Au lieu de considérer la rénovation comme quelque chose qui apaise la structure existante et la nettoie à mort, l'architecture reprend la fonction du mobilier et du textile, comme quelque chose qui introduit le mouvement dans une situation existante, l'accélère, le transmet, l'infléchit et séduit. De cette

THE V2_MEDIA LAB, SET IN A TRADITIONAL ROTTERDAM STREET, IS DESIGNED TO RESEMBLE THE SPACES IN COMPUTER GAMES.

DAS V2_MEDIA LAB, IN EINER TRADITIONELLEN ROTTERDAMER STRASSE GELEGEN, SOLL DIE WIRKUNG VON RÄUMEN AUS COMPUTER-SPIELEN VERMITTELN.

LE V2_MEDIA LAB, IMPLANTÉ DANS UNE RUE TRADITIONNELLE DE ROTTERDAM EST INSPIRÉ DE L'ESTHÉTIQUE DES JEUX D'ORDINATEUR.

CLIENT / BAUHERR: V2_ORGANISATION, ROTTERDAM
FLOOR AREA/NUTZFLÄCHE/SURFACE UTILE: 140 M²
COSTS / KOSTEN / COÛTS: 150 000 NLG

lessly from a computer-generated process of forces, vectors and springs, to inflections in plywood sheets and PVC pipes, to ... the undulations of the floor, to the chairs with adjustable spring legs, to tensions in the 4 mm thick plastic wall (stretched with steel cables and springs), to the flowing transition between floor and tables and then to the tensions within the human body: the arm and leg muscles that provide a constant neuro-electrical background to all human behavior taking place here ... In this, the design attempts to produce a shift from the optical domain where architecture is always judged towards the haptic where everything is proximity."

Vektoren und Federn zu Sperrholztafeln und PVC-Rohren, zu ... wellenförmigen Fußböden, zu Stühlen mit Beinen aus verstellbaren Sprungfedern, zu der durch Stahlseile und -federn gespannten, 4 mm dikken Kunststoffwand, zum fließenden Übergang vom Boden zu den Tischen und auch hin zu den Spannungen im menschlichen Körper: den Arm- und Beinmuskeln, die einen konstanten neuro-elektrischen Hintergrund für jegliches menschliche Verhalten bilden ... Dies alles in Betracht ziehend, versucht der Entwurf, eine Verlagerung vom Optischen – nach dem Architektur immer beurteilt wird – zum Haptischen zu bewirken, bei dem alles Nähe und Berührung ist.«

façon, nous progressons imperceptiblement d'un processus de forces généré par ordinateur, de vecteurs et de sauts, à des inflexions en feuilles de contreplaqué et des tuyaux de PVC, jusqu'aux ... ondulations du sol, aux sièges à pieds à ressorts réglables, aux tensions dans le mur de plastique de 4 mm d'épaisseur et à la transition en flux entre le sol et les tables, puis aux tensions internes au corps humain: les muscles des bras et des jambes qui fournissent un contexte neuro-électrique constant à tout comportement humain qui se déroule ici ... En cela, le projet essaye de produire un glissement du contexte optique dans lequel l'architecture est toujours jugée, vers l'haptique où tout est proximité. »

THE INTENTIONALLY UNEVEN FLOORS OF THIS
SPACE USED FOR COMPUTER DESIGN PROVIDE
A CHALLENGE TO CHAIR MANUFACTURERS.

P 402.403

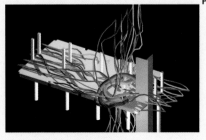

DIE UNEBEN GESTALTETEN BÖDEN DES RAUMS,
DER FÜR COMPUTERGESTÜTZTES ENTWERFEN
(CAD) GENUTZT WIRD, SIND EINE HERAUSFOR-
DERUNG FÜR STUHLFABRIKANTEN.

LES SOLS VOLONTAIREMENT INÉGAUX DE CET
ESPACE RÉSERVÉ À LA CONCEPTION PAR ORDI-
NATEUR REPRÉSENTENT UN DÉFI POUR LES
FABRICANTS DE SIÈGES.

RENZO PIANO

RENZO PIANO BUILDING WORKSHOP
VIA P. P. RUBENS, 29
16158 GENOVA
ITALY

TEL: + 39 010 6171 1
FAX: + 39 010 6171 350
E-MAIL: renzopianobwit@bwge.it
WEB: www.rpwf.org

Born in 1937 in Genoa, Italy, Renzo Piano studied at the University of Florence and at the Milan Polytechnic (1964). He formed his own practice (Studio Piano) in 1965, and then joined Richard Rogers (Piano & Rogers, 1971-78). They completed the Centre Pompidou in Paris in 1977. From 1978 to 1980, Piano worked with Peter Rice (Piano & Rice Associates). He created the Renzo Piano Building Workshop in 1981 in Genoa and Paris. He received the RIBA Gold Medal in 1989, and the Pritzker Prize in 1998. His built work includes Menil

Renzo Piano, geboren 1937 in Genua, studierte an der Florentiner Universität und am Mailänder Polytechnikum (1964). 1965 gründete er sein eigenes Büro Studio Piano und ging später eine Partnerschaft mit Richard Rogers ein (Piano & Rogers, 1971-78). Sie errichteten 1977 das Centre Pompidou in Paris. Von 1978 bis 1980 arbeitete Piano mit Peter Rice zusammen (Piano & Rice Associates). 1989 wurde ihm die Gold Medal des Royal Institute of British Architects verliehen, 1998 erhielt er den Pritzker Prize. 1981 gründete den

Né en 1937 à Gênes, Italie, il fait ses études à l'Université de Florence et à l'Institut Polytechnique de Milan (1964). Il crée son agence (Studio Piano) en 1965, puis s'associe à Richard Rogers (Piano & Rogers, 1971-78). Ils réalisent le Centre Pompidou (1977). De 1978 à 1980, Piano travaille avec Peter Rice (Piano & Rice Associates). Gold Medal du RIBA en 1989, Pritzker Prize 1998. Le Renzo Piano Building Workshop est fondé en 1981 à Gênes et Paris. Parmi ses réalisations: Menil Collection Museum (Houston, Texas, 1981-86), le

BASED IN GENOA AND PARIS, RENZO PIANO
COMBINES A SENSE FOR POWERFUL MODERN
FORMS AND DESIGN WITH A DISTINCTIVE
ABILITY TO ADAPT HIS WORK TO LOCAL CONDI-
TIONS AND TRADITIONS.

DER IN GENUA UND PARIS ANSÄSSIGE RENZO
PIANO HAT SOWOHL DIE BEGABUNG FÜR KRAFT-
VOLLE MODERNE FORMEN UND GESTALTUNGEN
ALS AUCH DIE AUSGEPRÄGTE FÄHIGKEIT, SEINE

BAUTEN ÖRTLICHEN BEDINGUNGEN UND
TRADITIONEN ANZUPASSEN.

BASÉ À GÊNES ET PARIS, RENZO PIANO RÉUNIT
UN SENS DES FORMES PUISSANTES ET MODER-
NES ET UNE RÉFLEXION REMARQUABLEMENT
RESPECTUEUSE DES CONDITIONS ET DES
TRADITIONS LOCALES.

Collection Museum (Houston, Texas, 1981-86), San Nicola Stadium (Bari, Italy, 1987-90), extension for the IRCAM, Paris, and renovation of Lingotto complex (Turin, Italy, 1989), Mercedes-Benz Design Center (Stuttgart, Germany, 1992-96), and Kansai International Airport Terminal (Osaka, Japan, 1988-94). Recent works are Cité Internationale de Lyon (France, 1985-96), the New Metropolis Science Center, Amsterdam, and Beyeler Foundation, Basel.

Renzo Piano Building Workshop in Genua und Paris. Zu seinen Bauten gehören das Museum der Menil Collection in Houston, Texas (1981-86), das San Nicola-Stadion in Bari (1987-90), die Erwei-terung des IRCAM in Paris (1989), die Umgestal-tung des Lingotto-Komplexes in Turin (1993), das Design-Zentrum Mercedes-Benz in Sindelfingen bei Stuttgart (1992-96), der Kansai International Airport Terminal bei Osaka, Japan (1988-94), das Wissenschaftszentrum New Metropolis in Amster-dam und die Fondation Beyeler bei Basel.

stade San Nicola (Bari, Italie, 1987-90), l'exten-sion de l'IRCAM (Paris, 1989), la rénovation de l'ensemble du Lingotto (Turin, 1989), le Mercedes-Benz Design Center (Stuttgart, Allmagne, 1992-96) et le terminal de l'aéroport international de Kansai (Osaka, Japon, 1988-94). Plus récemment, il a conçu la Cité Internationale de Lyon (1985-96), ainsi que des projets près de la Potsdamer Platz à Berlin, le New Metropolis Science Center à Amsterdam, et la Fondation Beyeler à Bâle.

RENZO PIANO

JEAN-MARIE TJIBAOU CULTURAL CENTER

NOUMÉA, NEW CALEDONIA, 1992-98

INSPIRED BY LOCAL ARCHITECTURE, THE COMPLEX IS MEANT TO RESEMBLE A VILLAGE OF WOODEN HUTS.

DIE VON DER LOKALEN ARCHITEKTUR INSPI-RIERTE ANLAGE IST EINEM DORF MIT HOLZ-HÜTTEN NACHEMPFUNDEN.

INSPIRÉ DE L'ARCHITECTURE LOCALE, CE COM-PLEXE CULTUREL RESSEMBLE À UN VILLAGE DE HUTTES MODERNES.

COMPETITION / WETTBEWERB / CONCOURS: 1991
CONCEPTUAL DESIGN / ENTWURF / PLANS: 1992
CONSTRUCTION / BAU: 1994-98
CLIENT / BAUHERR: AGENCY FOR THE
DEVELOPMENT OF KANAK CULTURE, MARIE
CLAUDE TJIBAOU (PRESIDENT)
FLOOR AREA / NUTZFLÄCHE / SURFACE
UTILE: 7 650 M²
COSTS / KOSTEN / COÛTS: 200 000 000 FF

From the outset, Renzo Piano included the question of the identity of the Kanak people in his concept for a cultural center named after a local proponent of independence from France. Specifically non-European in its concept, this alignment of ten conical wooden "houses" connected by a glass and wood corridor drawn out over some 250 m is surrounded by a garden of carefully chosen local plants. The ten structures are aligned in three groups according to their function: entrance, exhibition space and cafeteria; multimedia and temporary exhibitions;

Von Anfang an bezog Renzo Piano die Frage nach der Identität der Südseeinsulaner in seinen Entwurf für ein Kulturzentrum ein, das nach einem Kämpfer für die Unabhängigkeit Neukaledoniens von Frankreich benannt ist. Die Folge von zehn kegelförmigen hölzernen »Häusern«, die durch einen etwa 250 m langen Korridor aus Glas und Holz miteinander verbunden sind, ist von einem Garten mit sorgfältig ausgewählten einheimischen Pflanzen umgeben. Die zehn Bauten sind entsprechend ihrer Funktion in drei Gruppen aufgeteilt: Eingang, Ausstellungs-

Dès le départ, Renzo Piano a intégré dans son projet qui porte le nom d'un leader indépendantiste assassiné, le problème de l'identité du peuple kanak. De concept non-européen, cet alignement de dix «maisons» coniques en bois réunies par un corridor en bois et en verre, se développe sur environ 250 m de long, entouré d'un jardin de plantes locales choisies avec soin. Les deux structures sont disposées en trois groupes selon leur fonction: entrée, espace d'exposition et cafétéria; expositions temporaires et multi-média; salles vidéo et salles de cours sur la

P 410.411

video rooms, and classrooms for courses in local
culture. The naturally ventilated "houses" turn their
curved backs to the ocean, which is to say against
the prevailing winds that can attain a hurricane
force of over 240 km/h. There was no question
of the architect copying any local architecture –
rather he has given a sensitive and unexpected
contemporary interpretation to the design of this
center, which is located on a small peninsula
10 km northwest of the capital, Nouméa.

bereich und Cafeteria; Multimedia und Wechselaus-
stellungen; Video- und Unterrichtsräume für das
Studium der einheimischen Kultur. Die natürlich
belüfteten »Häuser« wenden ihre gekrümmten Rück-
seiten dem Meer zu und trotzen dem Wind, der hier
eine Geschwindigkeit von mehr als 240 km/h erreichen kann. Piano hat die regionale Architektur mit
dieser Anlage auf einer kleinen Halbinsel 10 km
nordwestlich der Hauptstadt Nouméa ebenso ein-
fühlsam wie überraschend interpretiert.

culture locale. Les «maisons» qui bénéficient d'une
ventilation naturelle tournent leurs dos arrondi à
l'océan, et donc aux vents dominants qui peuvent
atteindre jusqu'à 240 km/h. Plutôt que de copier
l'architecture locale, Piano a préféré en donner une
interprétation sensible et inattendue. Le Centre se
dresse sur une péninsule à 10 km au nord-ouest de
la capitale, Nouméa.

RENZO PIANO
DEBIS TOWER
BERLIN, GERMANY, 1993-99

AT THE LEADING EDGE OF A LARGE SITE SHARED WITH RAFAEL MONEO, ARATA ISOZAKI AND HANS KOLLHOFF, THE DEBIS TOWER STANDS OUT AGAINST THE BERLIN SKYLINE.

AUF DER HAUPTSEITE EINES GROSSEN GRUND-STÜCKS, DAS RAFAEL MONEO, ARATA ISOZAKI UND HANS KOLLHOFF BEBAUEN, STEHT DER DEBIS-TURM VOR DER BERLINER SKYLINE.

DANS UN EMPLACEMENT EXCEPTIONNEL EN BORDURE D'UN VASTE TERRAIN PARTAGÉ ENTRE PIANO, RAFAEL MONEO, ARATA ISOZAKI ET HANS KOLLHOFF, LA TOUR DEBIS ANIME DÉJÀ LE PANORAMA URBAIN BERLINOIS.

COMPETITION / WETTBEWERB / CONCOURS: 1992
PLANNING / PLANUNG: 1993-95
CONSTRUCTION / BAU: 1995-99
CLIENT / BAUHERR: DAIMLER-BENZ AG
FLOOR AREA / NUTZFLÄCHE / SURFACE
UTILE: 45 000 M²
HEIGHT / HÖHE / HAUTEUR: 106 M
CAPACITY / KAPAZITÄT / CAPACITÉ:
1 000 EMPLOYEES / MITARBEITER / EMPLOYÉS

Piano was given a large responsibility for a group of buildings totaling 600,000 m² on the Potsdamer Platz in Berlin, near Mies van der Rohe's National Gallery, and Hans Scharoun's National Library. The other structures are being built by Hans Kollhoff, Rafael Moneo, Richard Rogers, Lauber + Wöhr, and Arata Isozaki; Piano's own Debis Tower, named after one of the companies in the Daimler Benz group, was completed in 1998 in association with Christoph Kohlbecker. The highest structure in the complex, this tower contains an ample, skylit atrium, and is marked by surprising, glass emergency stairways that jut out from the building, giving the impression that it is far thinner than it actually is. In fact, the architect alternates slabs covered in terracotta panels with these glass elements. On the east, south and west sides of the tower, there is an innovative double glazing, with one layer of panels about 69 cm in front of another. This double layering insulates the structure in winter and provides ventilation during the summer.

Im Rahmen der städtebaulichen Neuordnung des Potsdamer Platzes übernahm Renzo Piano die Verantwortung für das Debis-Grundstück, benannt nach einer Firma der Daimler-Benz-Gruppe. Die Bauten liegen in der Nähe von Mies van der Rohes Nationalgalerie und Hans Scharouns Staatsbibliothek. Pianos Debis-Hochhaus wurde 1998 in Zusammenarbeit mit Christoph Kohlbecker fertiggestellt. Die übrigen Bauten wurden von Hans Kollhoff, Rafael Moneo, Richard Rogers, Lauber + Wöhr und Arata Isozaki geplant. Dieser Bau, der höchste des Komplexes, enthält ein weiträumiges, von oben belichtetes Atrium und wird durch die ungewöhnlichen, verglasten Feuertreppen charakterisiert, die aus der Flucht des Gebäudes vorspringen. An der Fassade wechseln Terrakottaplatten und verglaste Elemente einander ab. Drei Fassaden des Hochhauses sind mit einer innovativen Doppelverglasung versehen, die aus zwei Schichten im Abstand von etwa 69 cm besteht. Die doppelte Glasschicht isoliert das Gebäude im Winter und kann im Sommer geöffnet werden.

Piano est l'urbaniste responsable d'un ensemble d'immeubles, totalisant 600 000 m², sur la Potsdamer Platz à Berlin, près de la Galerie Nationale de Mies van der Rohe et de la Bibliothèque nationale de Hans Scharoun. La Tour Debis (du nom d'une des sociétés du groupe Daimler-Benz), achevée en 1998 en association avec Christoph Kohlbecker, est ainsi entourée de réalisations de Hans Kollhoff, Rafael Moneo, Richard Rogers, Lauber + Wöhr et Arata Isozaki. La tour se distingue par un vaste atrium à éclairage zénithal, et de surprenants escaliers de secours en verre, qui se projettent de la façade, en donnant l'impression que l'immeuble est beaucoup plus mince qu'en réalité. En fait l'architecte a alterné des dalles recouvertes de panneaux de terre cuite et ces éléments de verre. À l'est, au sud et à l'ouest de la tour, une double peau de verre d'un type nouveau se compose de panneaux séparés par une lame d'air de 69 cm d'épaisseur. Ce système protège l'immeuble du froid en hiver et, en position ouverte, permet une ventilation naturelle en été.

RICHARD ROGERS

RICHARD ROGERS PARTNERSHIP
THAMES WHARF, RAINVILLE ROAD
LONDON W6 9HA
ENGLAND

TEL: + 44 20 7 385 1235
FAX: + 44 20 7 385 8409
E-MAIL: enquiries@richardrogers.co.uk
WEB: www.richardrogers.co.uk

Born 1933 in Florence, Italy, of British parents, Richard Rogers studied at the Architectural Association in London (1954-59). He received his M. Arch. degree from the Yale University School of Architecture in 1962, and created partnerships with his wife Su Rogers, Norman and Wendy Foster (Team 4, London, 1964-66), and with Renzo Piano in London, Paris and Genoa (1971-77). In 1977 he founded Richard Rogers Partnership in London. He has taught at Yale, and been Chairman of the

Richard Rogers, geboren 1933 als Sohn britischer Eltern in Florenz, studierte von 1954 bis 1959 an der Architectural Association in London. Seinen Master of Architecture erwarb er 1962 an der Yale University School of Architecture. Mit seiner Frau Su sowie Norman und Wendy Foster gründete er 1964 in London Team 4, das bis 1966 bestand. Von 1971 bis 1977 arbeitete er in Partnerschaft mit Renzo Piano in London, Paris und Genua. 1977 gründete er Richard Rogers Partnership in London.

Né à Florence en 1933 de parents britanniques, Richard Rogers étudie à l'Architectural Association de Londres (1954-59). Diplômé d'architecture de la Yale University School of Architecture en 1962, il fonde une agence avec son épouse Su Rogers, Norman et Wendy Foster (Team 4, Londres, 1964-66), puis avec Renzo Piano à Londres, Paris et Gênes (1971-77). Il crée Richard Rogers Partnership à Londres en 1977. Il a enseigné à Yale et a été président du Conseil d'administration de la Tate

A PARTNER OF RENZO PIANO FOR THE CON-STRUCTION OF THE CENTRE POMPIDOU IN PARIS (1971-77), LORD ROGERS IS, WITH LORD NORMAN FOSTER, THE BEST-KNOWN BRITISH ARCHITECT, A MASTER OF TECHNOLOGICALLY ORIENTED DESIGN.

LORD ROGERS, SEINERZEIT PARTNER VON RENZO PIANO BEIM BAU DES CENTRE POMPI-DOU IN PARIS (1971-77), IST NEBEN LORD NORMAN FOSTER DER BEKANNTESTE BRITI-SCHE ARCHITEKT, EIN MEISTER DES TECHNO-LOGISCH ORIENTIERTEN DESIGN.

PARTENAIRE DE RENZO PIANO DANS LA CONS-TRUCTION DU CENTRE POMPIDOU À PARIS (1971-77), RICHARD ROGERS EST AVEC NORMAN FOSTER L'UN DES ARCHITECTES BRITANNIQUES LES PLUS CONNUS, UN DES MAÎTRES DE L'AR-CHITECTURE TECHNOLOGIQUE.

Trustees of the Tate Gallery, London (1981-89). His main buildings include the Centre Pompidou (Paris, with Renzo Piano, 1971-77), Lloyd's of London headquarters (1978-86), Channel 4 television headquarters (London, 1990-94), European Court of Human Rights (Strasbourg, France, 1989-95), Bordeaux Palais de Justice (1993-98), Daimler Benz Offices and Housing (Potsdamer Platz, Berlin, 1994-98).

Er hat in Yale gelehrt und war Vorstand des Kura-toriums der Tate Gallery in London (1981-89). Zu seinen wichtigsten Bauten gehören das Centre Pom-pidou in Paris (mit Renzo Piano, 1971-77), die Hauptverwaltung Lloyd's of London (1978-86), die Hauptverwaltung von Channel 4 in London (1990-94), der Europäische Gerichtshof für Menschen-rechte in Straßburg (1989-95) sowie die Büros und Wohnungen für Daimler-Benz am Potsdamer Platz (1994-98).

Gallery, (Londres, 1981-89). Parmi ses principales réalisations: le Centre Pompidou (Paris, avec Renzo Piano, 1971-77), le siège de Lloyd's of London (Londres, 1978-86), le siège de Channel 4 (Londres, 1990-94), la Cour européenne des droits de l'hom-me (Strasbourg, 1989-95), le Palais de justice de Bordeaux (1993-98), ainsi que des bureaux et des logements pour Daimler Benz (Potsdamer Platz, Berlin, 1994-98).

RICHARD ROGERS
LAW COURTS
BORDEAUX, FRANCE, 1993-98

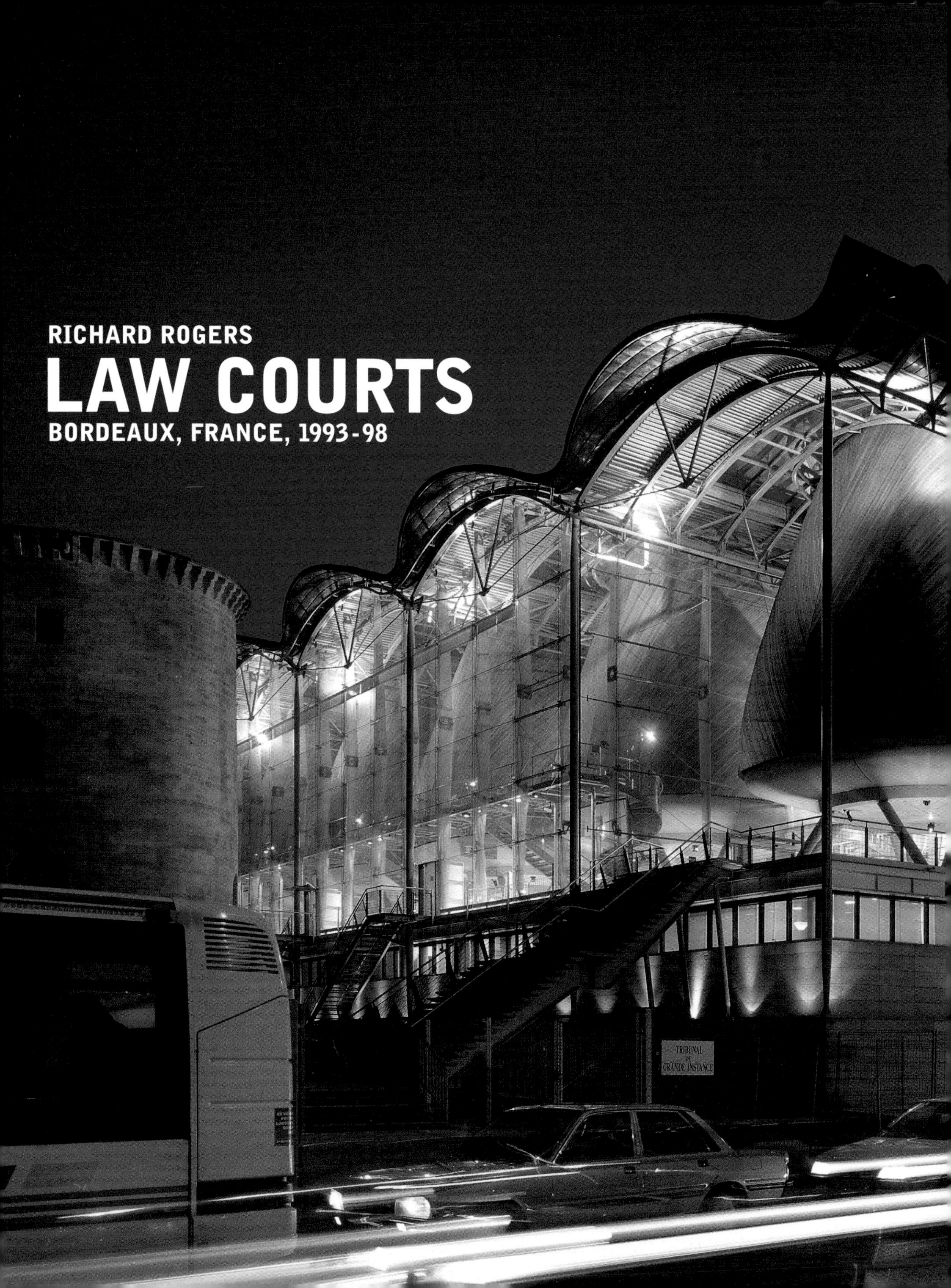

TRIBUNAL
DE
GRANDE INSTANCE

The Bordeaux Palais de Justice is located near the Neo-Classical heart of this south-western French city. Intended to be light and open, symbolizing the transparency of the justice system, the building contains seven pod-like wood-clad courtroom structures, aligned behind a 20 x 76 m glass wall. Made with a concrete base and a wood-frame superstructure, the courtroom pods are lined with plywood with an overlay of cedar strips. They are approached by an open and exposed walkway that

Das Palais de Justice liegt nahe dem klassizistischen Zentrum von Bordeaux und ist als helles und offenes Gebäude geplant, um die Transparenz des Justizsystems zu symbolisieren. Der Bau enthält sieben holzverkleidete Gerichtssäle, aufgereiht hinter einer 20 x 76 m großen Glaswand. Die aus einer Betonbasis und einer Holzkonstruktion als Überbau bestehenden Gerichtssäle sind mit Sperrholz und darüberliegenden Zedernholzstreifen verkleidet. Sie sind über einen offenen Steg erschlos-

Le Palais de Justice de Bordeaux (13 000 m²) est situé non loin du centre néoclassique de la ville. Voulu ouvert et aérien pour symboliser la transparence du système judiciaire, il contient sept structures de chambres de justice en forme de coques recouvertes de bois, alignées derrière une paroi de verre de 20 x 76 m. Structures en bois montées sur une base de béton, ces coques sont doublées de contreplaqué recouvert de bardeaux de cèdre. On y accède par une passerelle ouverte assez exposée qui

THE WOOD-CLAD PODS CONTAIN THE COURT-ROOM SPACES. A CENTRAL GLASS PASSAGE-WAY LINKS THEM.

DIE HOLZVERKLEIDETEN GEHÄUSE ENTHALTEN DIE GERICHTSSÄLE, DIE DURCH EINEN ZEN-TRALEN, VERGLASTEN GANG MITEINANDER VERBUNDEN SIND.

LES ENCEINTES RECOUVERTES DE BOIS CONTIENNENT LES SALLES DES TRIBUNAUX. ELLES SONT RELIÉES PAR UNE PASSERELLE DE VERRE.

COMPETITION / WETTBEWERB / CONCOURS: 11/1992
PLANNING / PLANUNG: 1993-94
CONSTRUCTION / BAU: 1995-98
COMPLETION / FERTIGSTELLUNG / FIN DE LA CONSTRUCTION: 2000 (EXTERNAL WORKS)
FLOOR AREA / NUTZFLÄCHE / SURFACE UTILE: 25 000 M²
COSTS / KOSTEN / COÛTS: £ 27 000 000

reveals the full height of the building. Known for his mechanically oriented design, Rogers here appears to make a successful foray into the domain of more organic forms. Directly abutting an ancient wall and surrounded largely by the classical stone buildings of Bordeaux, the Palais de Justice is at once surprising and coherent in this context.

sen, der die große Höhe des Gebäudes spürbar macht. Rogers, der für seine High-Tech-Entwürfe bekannt ist, macht hier offenbar einen erfolgreichen Abstecher in den Bereich eher organischer Formen. Das direkt an eine alte Mauer angrenzende und überwiegend von klassizistischen Gebäuden umgebene Palais de Justice wirkt in diesem Kontext zugleich überraschend wie auch dazugehörig.

permet de prendre conscience de la hauteur du bâtiment. Connu pour son approche technologique, Rogers semble avoir fait ici une incursion réussie dans des formes plus organiques. Appuyé directement contre un ancien rempart et entouré en grande partie d'immeubles classiques de pierre blanche typiques de Bordeaux, ce Palais de Justice est à la fois surprenant et cohérent dans son contexte.

THE INTERNAL OPENNESS OF THE BUILDING
CONTRASTS WITH THE WOODEN DISCRETION
OF THE ACTUAL COURTROOMS.

DIE TRANSPARENZ DER ÖFFENTLICH ZUGÄNG-
LICHEN INNENRÄUME STEHT IM KONTRAST
ZUR GESCHLOSSENHEIT DER HOLZVERKLEIDE-
TEN GERICHTSSÄLE.

L'IMPRESSION D'OUVERTURE TRÈS SENSIBLE
À L'INTÉRIEUR DU BÂTIMENT CONTRASTE AVEC
LA NEUTRALITÉ DU DÉCOR DES SALLES DE
TRIBUNAL.

AXEL SCHULTES AND CHARLOTTE FRANK
HAVE GAINED INTERNATIONAL RECOGNITION
AS WINNERS OF THE 1993 SPREEBOGEN COM-
PETITION. TODAY, THEY HAVE COMPLETED A
REMARKABLY POWERFUL AND SIMPLE CREMA-
TORIUM, ALSO IN BERLIN.

AXEL SCHULTES AND CHARLOTTE FRANK

Born in 1943 in Dresden, Axel Schultes graduated from the Technical University of Berlin in 1969. He worked in partnership with Dietrich Bangert, Bernd Jansen and Stefan Scholz from 1974 to 1991 (BJSS), with whom he built the Kunstmuseum, Bonn. He created his own firm in 1992, and participated in both the Reichstag and Spreebogen competitions in Berlin in 1993, as well as many other competitions such as that for the Alexandria Library in 1989, or the Potsdamer Platz in Berlin

Axel Schultes wurde 1943 in Dresden geboren und schloß 1969 sein Studium an der TU Berlin ab. Von 1974 bis 1991 arbeitete er bei BJSS zusammen mit Dietrich Bangert, Bernd Jansen und Stefan Scholz, mit denen er das Bonner Kunstmuseum baute. 1992 gründete er sein eigenes Büro. Schultes beteiligte sich an den Wettbewerben zur Bibliothek von Alexandria (1989), zum Potsdamer Platz (1991) und zum Reichstag (1993). Sein Wettbewerbsbeitrag zur Bebauung des Spreebogens in

Né à Dresde en 1943, Axel Schultes sort diplômé de l'Université Technique de Berlin en 1969. Il travaille ensuite en association avec Dietrich Bangert, Bernd Jansen et Stefan Scholz de 1974 à 1991 (BJSS), avec lesquels il construit le Kunstmuseum de Bonn. Il fonde sa propre agence en 1992, et participe aux concours du Reichstag et de la boucle de la Spree (Spreebogen) en 1993, ainsi qu'à de nombreux autres dont celui pour la Bibliothèque d'Alexandrie en 1989, ou de la Potsdamer Platz à Berlin

AXEL SCHULTES UND CHARLOTTE FRANK
HABEN ALS PREISTRÄGER DES SPREEBOGEN-
WETTBEWERBS INTERNATIONALES RENOMMEE
ERWORBEN. NUN HABEN SIE, EBENFALLS IN
BERLIN, EIN KRAFTVOLLES UND SCHLICHTES
KREMATORIUM GEBAUT.

AXEL SCHULTES ET CHARLOTTE FRANK ONT
ACCÉDÉS À LA NOTORIÉTÉ INTERNATIONALE
EN REMPORTANT EN 1993 LE CONCOURS
DE LA BOUCLE DE LA SPREE. ILS VIENNENT
D'ACHEVER UN CRÉMATORIUM D'UNE SIMPLI-
CITÉ ET D'UNE FORCE REMARQUABLES,
TOUJOURS À BERLIN.

AXEL SCHULTES ARCHITEKTEN
LÜTZOWPLATZ 7
10785 BERLIN
GERMANY

TEL: + 49 30 230 888 0
FAX: + 49 30 230 888 88
E-MAIL: schultes.architekten@snafu.de

in 1991. The Spreebogen competition, which he won, was executed in collaboration with Charlotte Frank, born in Kiel in 1959, who has been his partner since 1992. Built work includes the Büropark am Welfenplatz, Hanover (1993). Recent projects are offices in Berlin, Leipziger Platz, and the Baumschulenweg Crematorium, Berlin, published here.

Berlin (Bundeskanzleramt, 1993) gewann den ersten Preis. An diesem Projekt ist Charlotte Frank (1959 in Kiel geboren) beteiligt, die seit 1992 mit Schultes zusammenarbeitet. Weitere Projekte sind der Büropark am Welfenplatz (Hannover, 1993), Bürohäuser am Leipziger Platz (1998) und das hier vorgestellte Krematorium Baumschulenweg in Berlin.

en 1991. Le projet pour la boucle de la Spree, qui lui vaut de remporter le concours, a été mis au point en collaboration avec Charlotte Frank, née à Kiel en 1959, son associée depuis 1992. Parmi ses réalisations: le Büropark am Welfenplatz, Hanovre (1993). Il travaille actuellement sur des immeubles de bureaux, Leipziger Platz, Berlin et sur le crématorium, Baumschulenweg, Berlin.

COMPETITION / WETTBEWERB / CONCOURS: 1992
COMPLETION / FERTIGSTELLUNG / FIN DE LA CONSTRUCTION: 1998
CLIENT / BAUHERR: BEZIRKSAMT TREPTOW, BERLIN
FLOOR AREA / NUTZFLÄCHE / SURFACE UTILE: 9.339 M²
COSTS / KOSTEN / COÛTS: 60 000 000 DM

AXEL SCHULTES AND CHARLOTTE FRANK

BAUMSCHULENWEG CREMATORIUM

BERLIN, GERMANY, 1992-98

A RECTANGULAR PLAN AND SIMPLE CONCRETE FORMS CREATE A CONTRAST BETWEEN THE HEAVY AND THE LIGHT BOTH IN FIGURATIVE AND IN METAPHORICAL TERMS, JUST AS AXEL SCHULTES AND CHARLOTTE FRANK WANTED.

EIN RECHTWINKLIGER GRUNDRISS UND SCHLICHTE BETONFORMEN ERZEUGEN DEN VON AXEL SCHULTES UND CHARLOTTE FRANK ANGESTREBTEN KONTRAST VON SCHWERE UND

LEICHTIGKEIT – IM WÖRTLICHEN WIE IM ÜBER-TRAGENEN SINN.

LE PLAN RECTANGULAIRE ET LA SIMPLICITÉ DES FORMES EN BÉTON CRÉENT UN CONTRAS-TE ENTRE LE LOURD ET LE LÉGER EN TERMES AUSSI BIEN FIGURATIFS QUE MÉTAPHORIQUES, CE QUE SOUHAITAIENT SCHULTES ET FRANK.

This Crematorium is both powerful and extremely simple in its conception. The architects' stated intention was to create "a place of calm, a silent space which balances the transient and final nature of the experience, which makes what is heavy clear and what is light possible." Set at the entrance to a cemetery, this concrete rectangular form can hold 1,000 mourners. Looking to an inspiration in pagan rituals, Schultes has chosen Orpheus as the programmatic "spirit" behind his design. 29 columns give a rhythm to the interior, while circular openings in the roof around these columns bring daylight into the heart of the space. Although it calls upon a minimalistic modern vocabulary, the Crematorium has a monumentality that has not been typical of recent funerary architecture. In this, the architect does indeed look back to history, and evokes as he says, the distant pagan spirit that predates the Christian era.

Das Krematorium wirkt kraftvoll und zugleich in seiner Anlage äußerst schlicht. Erklärtes Ziel der Architekten war, einen »Ort der Ruhe« zu schaffen, »einen Raum der Stille, der das Vergängliche und das Endgültige des Ereignisses ausbalanciert, das Schwere deutlich und das Leichte möglich macht.« Der rechtwinklige Betonbau am Eingang des Friedhofs bietet bis zu 1 000 Trauergästen Raum. Der griechische Orpheus-Mythos war das Vorbild für den programmatischen »Geist« des Entwurfs. 29 kräftige Rundstützen rhythmisieren den Raum und münden in runde Deckenöffnungen, die Tageslicht einlassen. Trotz seines modernen, minimalistischen Vokabulars besitzt das Krematorium eine Monumentalität, die für jüngere Friedhofsarchitektur ungewöhnlich ist. Hierin bezieht Schultes sich auf die Geschichte und evoziert, wie er sagt, den Geist einer Zeit, die der christlichen voranging.

Ce crématorium est de conception à la fois massive et extrêmement simple. Pour les architectes, il s'agissait de créer un lieu de sérénité, espace qui par son silence vienne en contrepoint de la nature définitive et implacable de sa fonction. Implanté à l'entrée du cimetière, ce massif parallélogramme de béton peut recevoir jusqu'à 1 000 personnes à la fois. S'inspirant de rituels païens, Axel Schultes s'est placé sous l'invocation d'Orphée. 29 puissantes colonnes rythment l'intérieur, tandis que des ouvertures circulaires dans le toit pratiquées autour des colonnes laissent pénétrer la lumière du jour au cœur du bâtiment. À travers son vocabulaire minimaliste contemporain, ce crématorium possède une monumentalité assez rare dans l'architecture funéraire récente. Schultes s'est ainsi tourné vers des sources historiques, dont certaines sont plus anciennes que le christianisme.

SHAFTS OF LIGHT PENETRATE THE SOLID CON-
CRETE FORMS OF THE CREMATORIUM. THOUGH
MINIMALISTIC IN ITS DESIGN IT IS ALSO MONU-
MENTAL.

THE EXTREME AUSTERITY OF THE INTERIOR OF
THE CREMATORIUM AND ITS LARGE COLUMNS
BRING TO MIND THE ARCHITECT'S INTEREST IN
THE "PAGAN SPIRIT."

LICHTSCHÄCHTE DURCHBRECHEN DIE GE-
SCHLOSSENEN FORMEN DES KREMATORIUMS.
DER RAUM SELBST WIRKT SCHLICHT UND
ZUGLEICH MONUMENTAL.

DIE EXTREME STRENGE DES INNENRAUMS
UND DIE HOHEN STÜTZEN ZEUGEN VON
SCHULTES' INTERESSE FÜR ANTIKE FORMEN.

DES PUITS DE LUMIÈRE PERCENT LES ÉPAIS-
SES PAROIS DE BÉTON DU CRÉMATORIUM, À
LA FOIS MINIMALISTE ET MONUMENTAL.

L'EXTRÊME AUSTÉRITÉ DE L'INTÉRIEUR DU
CRÉMATORIUM ET DE SES IMPRESSIONNANTES
COLONNES RENVOIE À CERTAINE EXPRESSIONS
PAÏENNES.

SCHWEGER + PARTNER

Born in 1935 in Medias, Rumania, Peter Schweger attended the Technical University, Budapest, and the University of Zurich, Eidgenössische Technische Hochschule (ETH) Zurich, where he received his diploma in 1959. From 1959 to 1962 he had an office in Vienna, Austria. In 1960 he had a research assignment for the Körber-Stiftung, Hamburg, and from 1968-69 a visiting professorship at the Hochschule für Bildende Künste, Hamburg and one at the University of Hanover's Institute for

Peter Schweger, geboren 1935 in Medias in Siebenbürgen (im heutigen Rumänien), studierte an der Technischen Universität Budapest, der Universität Zürich und der Eidgenössischen Technischen Hochschule (ETH) Zürich, wo er 1959 sein Diplom erwarb. Von 1959 bis 1962 leitete er ein Büro in Wien. 1960 erhielt er einen Forschungsauftrag der Körber-Stiftung in Hamburg. 1968-69 war er Gastprofessor an der Hochschule für Bildende Künste in Hamburg und an der Universität Hannover. 1968

Né en 1935 à Medias, Roumanie, Peter Schweger suit les cours de l'Université Technique de Budapest, de l'Université de Zurich et de la Eidgenössische Technische Hochschule de Zurich (ETH), dont il est diplômé en 1959. De 1959 à 1962, il anime une agence à Vienne. Il a été chercheur pour la Körber-Stiftung, Hambourg (1960), puis professeur invité à la Hochschule für Bildende Künste, Hambourg et à l'Institut d'Architecture de l'Université de Hanovre (1968-69). Il crée l'agence Graaf +

NAHM DIE SCHWIERIGE AUFGABE, EINE
MUNITIONSFABRIK IN EIN ZENTRUM FÜR
MODERNE MEDIENKUNST UMZUBAUEN.

DE PLUS EN PLUS DE MUSÉES ET D'INSTITU-
TIONS CULTURELLES S'EMPARENT D'ESPACES
INDUSTRIELS. PETER SCHWEGER A ÉTÉ CHAR-
GÉ DE LA TÂCHE DÉLICATE DE TRANSFORMER
UNE FABRIQUE DE MUNITIONS EN CENTRE
POUR LES ARTS MULTIMÉDIAS.

ARCHITEKTEN SCHWEGER + PARTNER
VALENTINSKAMP 30
20355 HAMBURG
GERMANY

TEL: + 49 40 350 959 0
FAX: + 49 40 350 959 95

**MORE AND MORE MUSEUMS AND CULTURAL
INSTITUTIONS ARE OCCUPYING OLD INDUSTRIAL
SPACES. PETER SCHWEGER WAS GIVEN THE
DAUNTING TASK OF TURNING A MUNITIONS FAC-
TORY INTO A CENTER FOR ADVANCED MEDIA
ARTS.**

IMMER MEHR ALTE INDUSTRIEBAUTEN WER-
DEN ZU MUSEEN UND KULTUREINRICHTUNGEN
UMFUNKTIONIERT. PETER SCHWEGER ÜBER-

Architecture. In 1968 he founded the office of
Graaf + Schweger (from 1987 Architekten
Schweger + Partner) and was Professor at the
University of Hanover, Institute for Architecture in
1972. Current work includes Poseidon-Haus (office
building, Hamburg, 1990-95), Deutscher Industrie-
und Handelstag headquarters (Berlin, 1994-97),
and the ZKM Center for Art and Media Technology
(Karlsruhe, Germany, 1993-97).

gründete Schweger das Büro Graaf + Schweger
(ab 1987 Architekten Schweger + Partner). Seit
1972 ist Peter Schweger Professor an der Universität Hannover. Zu den neueren Arbeiten des
Büros gehören das Bürogebäude Poseidon-Haus
in Hamburg (1990-95), die Hauptverwaltung des
Deutscher Industrie- und Handelstags in Berlin
(1994-97) und das Zentrum für Kunst und Medientechnologie (ZKM) in Karlsruhe (1993-97).

Schweger en 1968 (depuis 1987 Architekten
Schweger + Partner). Professeur à l'Université de
Hanovre, à l'Institut d'Architecture (1972). Parmi
ses réalisations récentes: Poseidon-Haus, immeuble
de bureaux (Hambourg, 1990-95), siège de la
Deutscher Industrie- und Handelstag (Berlin,
1994-97) et ZKM Centre d'art et de technologie
des médias (Karlsruhe, Allemagne, 1993-97).

SCHWEGER + PARTNER

ZKM CENTER FOR ART AND MEDIA TECHNOLOGY

KARLSRUHE, GERMANY, 1993-97

COMPETITION / WETTBEWERB / CONCOURS: 1993
CONSTRUCTION / BAU: 1993-97
CLIENT / BAUHERR: CITY OF KARLSRUHE / KOMMUNALBAU KARLSRUHE GMBH
EXHIBITION AREA / AUSSTELLUNGSFLÄCHE / SURFACE D'EXPOSITION: 15 940 M²
COSTS / KOSTEN / COÛTS: 153 400 000 DM

P 436.437

In 1992 the German city of Karlsruhe chose to reconvert a 1918 landmark munitions plant, after abandoning a proposed new building to be designed by Rem Koolhaas for the ZKM Center for Art and Media Technology. Surprisingly undamaged during the war, the 312 m long structure was one of the first concrete skeleton designs built in Germany. It was left largely intact by Schweger, who placed a priority on maintaining its industrial character. They did place a blue cube at the entrance, which contains the Institute for Music and Acoustics, but

Nachdem der Plan eines Neubaus von Rem Koolhaas für das ZKM aufgegeben werden mußte, beschloß die Stadt Karlsruhe 1992 die Umnutzung einer unter Denkmalschutz stehenden Munitionsfabrik von 1918. Das im Krieg erstaunlicherweise unbeschädigt gebliebene, 312 m lange Bauwerk ist einer der frühesten Stahlbetonskelettbauten Deutschlands. Schweger hat ihn weitgehend unverändert belassen und räumte der Erhaltung seines industriellen Charakters Priorität ein. An den Eingang setzte er einen blauen Kubus, der das

En 1992, la ville de Karlsruhe en Allemagne a choisi de reconvertir une usine de munitions historique datant de 1918, après avoir abandonné un projet de bâtiment neuf de Rem Koolhaas. Laissée intact par la guerre, cette structure de 312 m de long fut l'une des premières ossatures de béton construite en Allemagne. Schweger qui souhaitait lui conserver son caractère industriel, l'a respecté pour l'essentiel. Un cube bleu à l'entrée contient l'Institut de musique et d'acoustique, mais par ailleurs il s'est contenté d'adapter l'espace à ses nou-

P 438.439

THE BLUE CUBE CONTAINS THE ZKM INSTITUTE FOR MUSIC AND ACOUSTICS. THE REST OF THE ZKM IS LOCATED IN THE PRE-EXISTING FACTORY BUILDING.

DER NEU ERRICHTETE BLAUE KUBUS BE-
HERBERGT DAS INSTITUT FÜR MUSIK UND
AKUSTIK. ALLE ÜBRIGEN EINRICHTUNGEN
DES MUSEUMS SIND IN DER ALTEN FABRIK
UNTERGEBRACHT.

LE CUBE BLEU CONTIENT L'INSTITUT ZKM POUR
LA MUSIQUE ET L'ACOUSTIQUE. LES AUTRES
ACTIVITÉS DE ZKM SONT INSTALLÉES DANS UN
ANCIEN BÂTIMENT INDUSTRIEL.

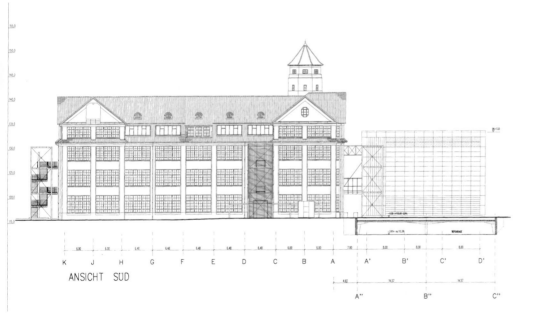

ANSICHT SÜD

otherwise concentrated on intervening only where it was necessary for the required functions. Those functions include space for the Institute for Visual Media, which sees itself as "a forum for the creative and critical analysis of a constantly changing media culture," the Media Museum, and the Museum of Contemporary Art, as well as a media library. The former factory also houses the State Academy of Design and the Municipal Gallery of the City of Karlsruhe.

Institut für Musik und Akustik beherbergt. Die üb-rigen Veränderungen ergaben sich aus den vorgese-henen Funktionen. Der Bau umfaßt die Räume des Instituts für Bildmedien, das sich selbst als »Forum für die kreative und kritische Analyse einer sich ständig wandelnden Medienkultur« sieht, das Me-dienmuseum und das Museum für Neue Kunst sowie eine Mediathek und ein Medientheater. Weiterhin sind in der früheren Fabrik die Staatliche Hoch-schule für Gestaltung und die Städtische Galerie untergebracht.

velles fonctions: l'Institut pour les médias visuels «forum de création et d'analyse critique d'une cul-ture des médias en changement continu», Musée des médias, et Musée d'art contemporain, ainsi qu'une bibliothèque des médias. L'ancienne cons-truction abrite également l'Académie d'État de Dessin et la Galerie municipale de la ville de Karlsruhe.

VAST OPEN SPACES MARK THE INTERIOR OF THIS 1918 LANDMARK FACTORY STRUCTURE.

WEITE, OFFENE RÄUME KENNZEICHNEN DAS INNERE DES FABRIKGEBÄUDES AUS DEM JAHRE 1918.

CETTE ANCIENNE USINE QUI DATE DE 1918 SE CARACTÉRISE PAR LES IMPRESSIONNANTES DIMENSIONS DE SES ESPACES INTÉRIEURS.

SITE

TRAINED AS A SCULPTOR, JAMES WINES, THE PRESIDENT OF SITE, HAS EXPANDED THE HORIZONS OF CONTEMPORARY ARCHITECTURE TO INCLUDE FORMS MORE OFTEN RELATED TO THE VISUAL ARTS.

JAMES WINES, DER ALS BILDHAUER UND INNENARCHITEKT AUSGEBILDETE LEITER VON SITE, HAT DIE GEGENWARTSARCHITEKTUR BELEBT, INDEM ER FORMEN VERWENDET, DIE DER BILDENDEN KUNST ENTSTAMMEN.

SCULPTEUR DE FORMATION, JAMES WINES, PRÉSIDENT DE SITE, A ÉLARGI LES HORIZONS DE L'ARCHITECTURE CONTEMPORAINE À DES FORMES SOUVENT PROCHES DES ARTS PLASTIQUES.

James Wines, founding principal of SITE (Sculpture in the Environment) was born in Chicago, Illinois, in 1932 and studied art and art history at Syracuse University, (B.A., 1956). Between 1965 and 1967 he worked as a sculptor. He created SITE with Alison Sky and Michelle Stone in 1970. Notable buildings include Indeterminate Facade Showroom (Houston, Texas, 1975), Ghost Parking Lot (Hamden, Connecticut, 1978), Highway 86, World Exposition (Vancouver, 1986), Four

Der Gründer von SITE (Sculpture in the Environment), James Wines, wurde 1932 in Chicago geboren. Er studierte Kunst und Kunstgeschichte an der Syracuse University und erwarb 1956 den B.A. Von 1965 bis 1967 arbeitete er als Bildhauer. 1970 schloß er sich mit Alison Sky und Michelle Stone zu SITE zusammen. SITE entwarf den Indeterminate Facade Showroom in Houston, Texas (1975), das Ghost Parking Lot in Hamden, Connecticut (1978), Highway 86 auf der Weltausstellung

James Wines, associé-fondateur de SITE (Sculpture in the Environment), est né à Chicago, Illinois, en 1932, et a étudié l'art et l'histoire de l'art à Syracuse University dont il sort B.A. en 1956. Il se consacre à la sculpture de 1965 à 1967. Il crée SITE avec Alison Sky et Michelle Stone en 1970. Parmi leurs réalisations les plus notables: Indeterminate Facade Showroom (Houston, Texas, 1975), Ghost Parking Lot (Hamden, Connecticut, 1978), Highway 86, World Exposition (Vancouver, 1986),

SITE
25 MAIDEN LANE
NEW YORK, NEW YORK 10038
UNITED STATES

TEL: + 1 212 285 0120
FAX: + 1 212 285 0125
E-MAIL: sitejw@interport.net
WEB: www.siteenvirodesign.com

Continents Bridge (Hiroshima, 1989), Avenue Number Five, Expo '92 (Seville, Spain, 1992), and Ross's Landing Plaza and Park (Chattanooga, Tennessee, 1992). Recent work includes landscape design and promenades for MCA Garden – Universal Studios (Orlando, Florida, 1996), Brinker International Chili's Restaurant, prototype restaurant design (Denver, Colorado, 1998), and the Rossini Estate Memorial Pavilion (Briosco, Italy), a 1998 project in its conceptual design phase.

in Vancouver, (1986), die Brücke der Vier Kontinente in Hiroshima (1989), Avenue Number Five auf der Expo '92 in Sevilla (1992) sowie Ross's Landing Plaza und Park in Chattanooga, Tennessee (1992), Landschaftsplanungen und Promenaden für MCA Garden – Universal Studios in Orlando, Florida (1996), einen Restaurant-Prototyp für Brinker International Chili's Restaurant in Denver, Colorado (1998) und den Rossini-Gedächtnispavillon in Briosco, Italien (Projekt).

Four Continents Bridge (Hiroshima, 1989), Avenue Number Five, Expo '92 (Séville, Espagne, 1992) et Ross's Landing Plaza and Park (Chattanooga, Tennessee, 1992). Plus récemment, il a réalisé des aménagements paysagers et des promenades pour MCA Garden – Universal Studios (Orlando, Floride, 1996), le prototype de restaurant de Brinker International Chili's Restaurant (Denver, Colorado, 1998) et le Pavillon mémorial Rossini (Briosco, Italie, 1998), projet encore en phase de conception.

SITE
MUSEUM
OF ISLAMIC ARTS
DOHA, QATAR, 1997 (PROJECT)

This unbuilt project was submitted as part of an international competition organized with the assistance of the Aga Khan Trust. According to SITE President James Wines, "this project for a new Museum of Islamic Arts was designed as a total fusion of architecture, exhibition spaces, communications technology, and the surrounding context." His idea was to express "the spiritual unity of Islam" through a tripartite plan including a 12 m grid intended to "dematerialize" on the exterior to define a public

Dieses nicht realisierte Projekt entstand als Beitrag zu einem internationalen Wettbewerb, der mit Unterstützung des Aga Khan Trust durchgeführt wurde. Nach den Worten von James Wines, dem Vorsitzenden von SITE, »wurde dieser Entwurf eines neuen Museums für islamische Kunst als vollständige Verschmelzung von Architektur, Ausstellungsräumen, Kommunikationstechnologie und Umgebung geplant.« Mauern, die sich von außen nach innen fortsetzen, und eine Folge »gewellter Dachflächen«

Ce projet non réalisé est la participation de SITE au concours international organisé avec le soutien de l'Aga Khan Trust. Selon James Wines, président de l'agence: « Ce projet d'un nouveau musée d'arts islamiques représente une fusion totale de l'architecture, des espaces d'exposition, des technologies de communication et du contexte environnant. » Pour exprimer « l'unité spirituelle de l'Islam », il fait appel à un plan tripartite et à une trame de 12 m afin de « dématérialiser » l'extérieur et délimiter un

SITE'S PROPOSAL FOR THE MUSEUM INCLUDED
WALLS THAT CONTINUE FROM THE INTERIOR
INTO THE GARDEN SPACES, THUS "DEMATERI-
ALIZING" THE EXTERIOR.

P 444.445

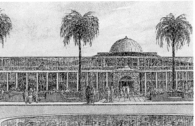

SITES ENTWURF FÜR DAS MUSEUM ENTHIELT
MAUERN, DIE VOM INNENRAUM BIS IN DEN
GARTEN FÜHREN UND SO DIE KONTUR »ENT-
MATERIALISIEREN«.

LA PROPOSITION DE SITE POUR LE MUSÉE
COMPRENAIT DES MURS QUI SE CONTINUAIENT
DANS LE JARDIN, POUR «DÉMATÉRIALISER»
LA RUPTURE INTÉRIEUR/EXTÉRIEUR.

CLIENT / BAUHERR: THE SPECIAL PROJECTS
OFFICE
FLOOR AREA / NUTZFLÄCHE / SURFACE
UTILE: 25 590 M²
COSTS / KOSTEN / COÛTS: US$ 32 000 000

garden, a series of walls that continue from outside to inside, and a series of "undulating roof planes" contributing to the impression of a continuity between exterior and interior. The use of radiant cooling, deflected daylight, shade walls, light-reflecting colors, green air-handling and "dehumidification technology" ensures that this structure would have been as environmentally conscious as possible in an extremely warm, humid climate.

sollten die Verbindung von Außen- und Innenraum verstärken. Trotz des extrem heißen und feuchten Klimas in Qatar, das besondere Anforderungen an Architektur und Technik stellt, versuchte man den Bau durch den Einsatz von Strahlungskühlung, gestreutem Tageslicht, schattenspendenden Wänden, reflektierenden Farben, ökologisch verträglicher Belüftung und »Entfeuchtungstechnologie« so umweltbewußt wie möglich zu planen.

jardin public, à une série de murs partant de l'extérieur vers l'intérieur, et à une succession de plans de toiture ondulés qui contribuent à l'impression de continuité entre l'intérieur et l'extérieur. L'utilisation d'une climatisation radiante, de la lumière du jour indirecte, de murs pare-soleil, de couleurs réfléchissantes, d'une ventilation naturelle et d'une «technologie de déhumidification» permet à cette structure d'être aussi écologique que possible sous un climat extrêmement chaud et humide.

THE BEST-KNOWN LIVING PORTUGUESE ARCHI-
TECT, ÁLVARO SIZA IS THE MASTER OF A VERY
PERSONAL AND RATHER LYRICAL FORM OF
MODERNISM. WINNER OF THE 1992 PRITZKER
PRIZE, HE IS NOW INTERNATIONALLY RECOG-
NIZED.

ÁLVARO SIZA

Born in Matosinhos, Portugal, in 1933, Álvaro Siza studied at the University of Porto School of Architecture (1949-55). He created his own practice in 1954, and worked with Fernando Tavora from 1955 to 1958. Since 1976 he has been Professor of Construction at the University of Porto, receiving the European Community's Mies van der Rohe Prize in 1988, and the Pritzker Prize in 1992. He built a large number of small-scale projects in Portugal, and more recently has worked on the restructuring

Álvaro Siza, geboren 1933 in Matosinhos, Portugal, studierte Architektur an der Universität Porto (1949-55). 1954 gründete er sein eigenes Büro, in dem er von 1955 bis 1958 mit Fernando Tavora zusammenarbeitete. Seit 1976 lehrt Siza als Professor an der Universität Porto. 1988 wurde ihm der Mies van der Rohe-Preis der Europäischen Gemeinschaft verliehen, 1992 erhielt er den Pritzker Prize. In Portugal hat er viele kleinere Bauten ausgeführt, seit 1989 arbeitet er am Wiederaufbau des

Né à Matosinhos, Portugal, en 1933, Álvaro Siza étudie à l'École d'architecture de l'Université de Porto (1949-55). Il crée sa propre agence en 1954 et travaille avec Fernando Tavora de 1955 à 1958. Il est professeur de construction à l'Université de Porto depuis 1976 et reçoit le Prix Mies van der Rohe de la Communauté Européenne en 1988, et le Pritzker Prize en 1992. Il réalise de multiples petits chantiers au Portugal et, plus récemment, a participé à la restructuration du quartier du

ÁLVARO SIZA, DER BEKANNTESTE PORTUGIESI-
SCHE ARCHITEKT, VERTRITT EINE PERSÖN-
LICHE, EHER LYRISCH GEPRÄGTE FORM DER
MODERNE. ER WURDE 1992 MIT DEM PRITZKER-
PREIS AUSGEZEICHNET UND IST HEUTE INTER-
NATIONAL ANERKANNT.

LE PLUS CÉLÈBRE DES ARCHITECTES PORTU-
GAIS VIVANTS, ÁLVARO SIZA EST À L'ORIGINE
D'UNE FORME LYRIQUE ET TRÈS PERSONNELLE
DE MODERNISME. PRITZKER PRIZE 1992, IL EST
AUJOURD'HUI CONNU DANS LE MONDE ENTIER.

ÁLVARO SIZA - ARQUITECTO, LDA
RUA DO ALEXIO, 53-2°
4150-043 PORTO
PORTUGAL

TEL: + 351 2 61 67 27 0
FAX: + 351 2 61 67 27 9

of the Chiado, Lisbon, Portugal since 1989, the
Meteorology Center (Barcelona, Spain, 1989-92),
the Vitra Furniture Factory (Weil am Rhein, Germany, 1991-94), the Porto School of Architecture,
Porto University (1986-95), and the University
of Aveiro Library (Aveiro, Portugal, 1988-95). His
latest projects are the Portuguese Pavilion for the
Expo '98 (Lisbon, 1998), and the Serralves Foundation (Porto, Portugal, 1998).

Lissabonner Chiado-Viertels. Neuere Bauten sind
das Meteorologische Zentrum in Barcelona (1989-
92), die Möbelfabrik Vitra in Weil am Rhein (1991-
94), die Architekturschule der Universität Porto
(1986-95) und die Bibliothek der Universität
Aveiro (1988-95) in Portugal sowie der Portugiesische Pavillon auf der Expo '98 in Lissabon (1998)
und die Stiftung Serralves in Porto (1998).

Chiado (Lisbonne, depuis 1989). Il est l'auteur du
Centre de météorologie de Barcelone (1989-92), de
l'usine de meubles Vitra (Weil am Rhein, Allemagne,
1991-94), de l'École d'Architecture de Porto, Université de Porto (Portugal, 1986-95) et de la Bibliothèque de l'Université d'Aveiro (Portugal, 1988-
95). Parmi ses projets les plus récents figurent le
Pavillon du Portugal Expo '98 (Lisbonne, 1998) et
la Fondation Serralves (Porto, 1998).

ÁLVARO SIZA

CHURCH AND PARISH CENTER

MARCO DE CANAVEZES, PORTUGAL, 1990-96

PLANNING / PLANUNG: 1990-93
CONSTRUCTION / BAU: 1994-96
CLIENT / BAUHERR: COMISSÃO FABRIQUEIRA DO MARCO DE CANAVEZES
FLOOR AREA / NUTZFLÄCHE / SURFACE UTILE: 3 477 M²
COSTS / KOSTEN / COÛTS: US$ 1 263 PER M²

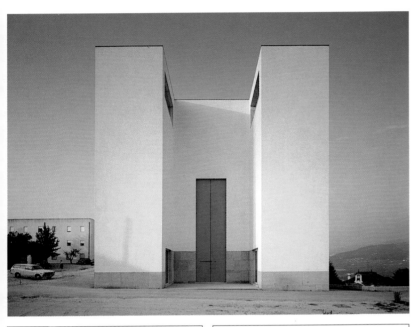

THE POWERFUL SIMPLICITY OF THE CHURCH
IS EVIDENT IN ITS UNADORNED FACADE AND
INTERIOR.

THE ENTRANCE DOORS, WHICH WILL EVENTU-
ALLY BE REPLACED BY BRONZE ONES, ARE
10 M HIGH.

DIE AUSDRUCKSVOLLE SCHLICHTHEIT DER
KIRCHE ZEIGT SICH IM INNENRAUM WIE
AUCH IN DER UNDEKORIERTEN FASSADE.

DIE 10 M HOHEN EINGANGSTÜREN AUS HOLZ
SOLLEN SPÄTER EVENTUELL DURCH BRONZE-
TÜREN ERSETZT WERDEN.

LA SIMPLICITÉ ET LA FORCE DE CETTE ÉGLISE
SE TRADUISENT DANS SA FAÇADE ET SON
INTÉRIEUR PRESQUE SANS AUCUN DÉCOR.

LA PORTE D'ENTRÉE QUI SERA ÉVENTUEL-
LEMENT REMPLACÉE PAR UN MODÈLE EN
BRONZE, MESURE 10 M DE HAUT.

Designed in close collaboration with the parish priest, Father Nuno Higino, the spare, white church of Santa Maria at Marco de Canavezes is one of Álvaro Siza's purest and most powerful works. The simple, 30 m long nave has 10 m high twin doors that open out onto the future square where the Parish Center is to be built when the church raises sufficient funds. Within the church, Siza has taken great care in the design of numerous details, ran-

Die bescheidene, in enger Zusammenarbeit mit dem Gemeindepriester Nuno Higino geplante Kirche Santa Maria in Marco de Canavezes gehört zu Álvaro Sizas klarsten und kraftvollsten Bauten. Das schlichte, 30 m lange Mittelschiff hat 10 m hohe Doppeltüren, die sich zu einem Vorplatz öffnen, auf dem das Gemeindezentrum erbaut werden soll, sobald Mittel vorhanden sind. Im Innern der Kirche hat Siza zahlreiche Details, von der Bestuhlung

Conçue en collaboration étroite avec le prêtre de la paroisse, le Père Nuno Higino, l'austère église immaculée de Sainte-Marie à Marco de Canavezes est l'une des plus pures et plus puissantes œuvres de Siza. Sa simple nef de 30 m de long se termine sur deux étroites portes de 10 m de haut, qui donnent sur la place où s'élèvera un centre paroissial lorsque l'église aura trouvé les fonds nécessaires. À l'intérieur, Siza a apporté le plus grand soin au des-

ging from the chairs to the altar and even to the gilt wood cross, which stands to the right of the altar as the priest faces the congregation. Local construction techniques were used to reduce costs, but Siza's touch is visible at every point, particularly in the very successful "light chimneys" that bring two bands of light down behind the altar, suggesting the presence of a cross without actually drawing it out. These light-wells also serve the funerary chapel

über den Altar bis hin zum vergoldeten Holzkreuz rechts vom Altar, selbst gestaltet. Regionale Bauweisen kamen zum Tragen, um die Kosten zu reduzieren; Sizas Handschrift ist aber überall erkennbar, besonders in den gelungenen »Lichtkaminen«, durch die Tageslicht in zwei Streifen hinter den Altar fällt und ein Kreuz andeutet. Diese Lichtschächte beleuchten auch die direkt unter dem Altar gelegene Kapelle. Ungewöhnliche Details, wie

sin de nombreux détails, allant des sièges à l'autel et même à la croix de bois doré qui se dresse à droite de l'autel. Des techniques de construction locales ont permis de réduire les coûts, mais la signature de l'architecte reste omniprésente, en particulier dans les très réussies «cheminées de lumière» qui orientent deux bandeaux lumineux à l'arrière de l'autel pour suggérer la présence d'une croix. Ces puits de lumière éclairent également la

USING LOCAL PLASTER TECHNIQUES, SIZA
HAS CREATED SUBTLE UNDULATING WALL SUR-
FACES.

THE BAPTISMAL FONT, ALSO DESIGNED BY
SIZA, IS PLACED IN A TILED AREA TO THE LEFT
OF THE CHURCH ENTRANCE.

UNTER VERWENDUNG LOKALER PUTZTECH-
NIKEN HAT SIZA LEICHT GESCHWUNGENE
WANDFLÄCHEN GESCHAFFEN.

DAS EBENFALLS VON SIZA ENTWORFENE
TAUFBECKEN STEHT IN EINER GEKACHELTEN
TAUFKAPELLE LINKS VOM EINGANG.

GRÂCE À DES TECHNIQUES LOCALES D'APPLI-
CATION DU PLÂTRE, SIZA A CRÉÉ DES SUR-
FACES MURALES SUBTILEMENT ONDULÉES.

LES FONTS BAPTISMAUX, ÉGALEMENT DESSI-
NÉS PAR SIZA, SONT SITUÉS DANS UNE PIÈCE
CARRELÉE À GAUCHE DE L'ENTRÉE DE
L'ÉGLISE.

located directly below the altar. Unusual features such as the tile-clad baptistery area sited immediately to the left of the main entrance, and the low strip window that offers the 400 seated parishioners a view of neighboring mountains, ensure that this church is full of surprises, despite its apparent austerity.

die mit Kacheln verkleidete Taufkapelle links vom Haupteingang und das niedrige Fensterband, das von den 400 Sitzplätzen einen Blick auf die nahegelegenen Berge bietet, beweisen, daß diese Kirche trotz ihrer Nüchternheit voller Überraschungen steckt.

chapelle funéraire située juste sous l'autel. Par ses détails inhabituels comme le baptistère en carrelage directement à gauche de l'entrée et la longue baie en bandeau qui offre aux 400 fidèles une vue sur les montagnes avoisinantes, cette église apparemment austère ne manque pas de surprendre.

ÁLVARO SIZA
VIEIRA DE CASTRO HOUSE
FAMALICÃO, PORTUGAL, 1984-98

SET INTO A ROCKY OUTCROP OVERLOOKING
THE TOWN OF FAMALICÃO, THE HOUSE IS
DECEPTIVELY SIMPLE WHEN SEEN FROM
THE EXTERIOR.

DAS AUF EINEN FELSVORSPRUNG ÜBER DER
STADT FAMALICÃO GESTELLTE WOHNHAUS IST
EIN SEHR SCHLICHTER BAUKÖRPER.

IMPLANTÉE SUR UNE EXCROISSANCE ROCHEU-
SE QUI DOMINE LA VILLE DE FAMALICÃO, LA
MAISON REVÊT UNE APPARENCE SIMPLE MAIS
TROMPEUSE VUE DE L'EXTÉRIEUR.

P 454.455

CLIENT / BAUHERR: DAVID VIEIRA DE CASTRO
FLOOR AREA / NUTZFLÄCHE / SURFACE
UTILE: 550 M²
COSTS / KOSTEN / COÛTS: WITHHELD /
UNGENANNT / NON COMMUNIQUÉS

More than 14 years in the making, this house built for a local businessman is on a hilltop site above the modern town of Famalicão, north of Porto. A forest path approaches it, and the visitor first encounters sculptural Corten steel entry gates. Like the rusticated stone walls that define the terraces of the residence, these gates are Siza's work. The visitor is led along a path between the rectangular outdoor swimming pool and an existing rocky outcrop to the discreet main door. Indoors, a gently

Die Entstehung des Hauses Vieira de Castro, das für einen ortsansässigen Geschäftsmann entworfen wurde, hat sich über 14 Jahre hingezogen. Es liegt auf einer Anhöhe oberhalb der Stadt Famalicão nördlich von Porto. Das Haus ist über einen Waldweg erreichbar, und der Blick des Besuchers fällt zuerst auf die Tore aus Corten-Stahl, die wie Skulpturen wirken. Sie wurden, ebenso wie das Rustikamauerwerk aus Natursteinen, das die Terrasse des Hauses einfaßt, von Siza gestaltet. Innen führt ein

Il a fallu 14 ans pour mener à bien la construction de cette maison réalisée pour un chef d'entreprise local, au sommet d'une colline qui surplombe la ville moderne de Famalicão, au nord de Porto. Le visiteur se trouve d'abord face à deux portes sculpturales en acier Corten, œuvres de Siza, de même que les murs de pierre rustiquée qui délimitent les terrasses. Une allée conduit à la porte d'entrée en se glissant entre la piscine rectangulaire et un affleurement de rocher. A l'intérieur, un couloir par-

THE ROCK WALLS AND UNEXPECTED METAL ENTRANCE GATES WERE DESIGNED BY SIZA AS WAS THE ENTIRE INTERIOR.

DIE NATURSTEINMAUERN UND DIE EINGANGS-TORE AUS CORTEN-STAHL WURDEN EBENSO WIE DIE GESAMTE INNENAUSSTATTUNG VON SIZA GESTALTET.

LES MURETS DE PIERRE ET LE PORTAIL D'ENTRÉE EN MÉTAL ONT ÉTÉ DESSINÉS PAR SIZA, COMME TOUS LES AMÉNAGEMENTS INTÉRIEURS.

P 456.457

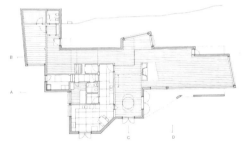

sloping, slightly curved wooden passage leads down to the living room, with its many views onto the neighboring mountainous countryside. The chimney, the living and dining room furniture, the kitchen fixtures, all are designed by Siza. Committed to a lengthy and complex process, the owners waited patiently for the last pieces of furniture to arrive. Although clearly a house for wealthy clients, a modern discretion bordering on austerity is the rule in this light-filled residence.

sanft abfallender, leicht gekrümmter Holzkorridor hinunter zum Wohnraum mit seinen zahlreichen Ausblicken in die bergige Landschaft. Der Kamin, die Möblierung des Wohn- und Eßzimmers und die Kücheneinrichtung wurden ebenfalls von Siza entworfen. Obgleich es sich hier eindeutig um ein Werk für wohlhabende Bauherren handelt, ist das lichterfüllte Haus durch eine moderne, fast an Nüchternheit grenzende Zurückhaltung geprägt.

queté en pente douce et légèrement incurvé mène à la salle de séjour. La cheminée, le mobilier du séjour et de la salle à manger, les meubles de cuisine, tous ont été dessinés par Siza. Les propriétaires ont patiemment attendu que les derniers meubles soient livrés pour s'installer. Maison à l'évidence construite pour de riches clients, sa discrétion moderniste et lumineuse frise l'austérité.

ÁLVARO SIZA
PORTUGUESE PAVILION EXPO '98
LISBON, PORTUGAL, 1996-98

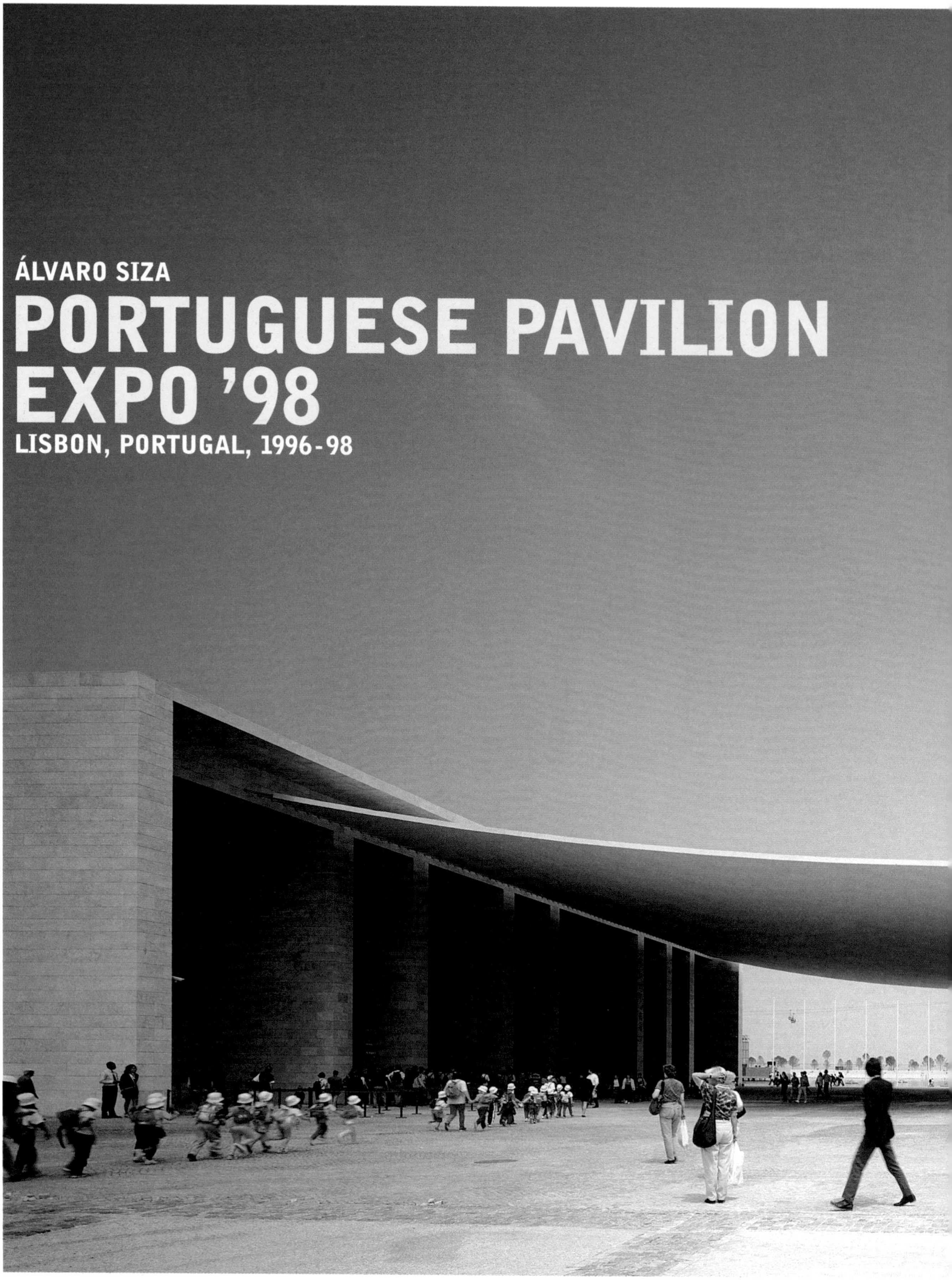

THE MOST SPECTACULAR ARCHITECTURAL
ELEMENT OF THE PAVILION IS THE ENORMOUS
SUSPENDED CONCRETE "VEIL" THAT COVERS
AN OUTDOOR SQUARE.

DAS SPEKTAKULÄRSTE ELEMENT DES
PAVILLONS IST DAS RIESIGE BETON-»SEGEL«,
DAS EINEN WEITLÄUFIGEN FREIBEREICH
ÜBERDECKT.

LE PLUS SPECTACULAIRE ÉLÉMENT ARCHITEC-
TURAL DU PAVILLON EST UN ÉNORME «VOILE»
DE BÉTON SUSPENDU QUI ABRITE UNE PLACE
INTÉRIEURE.

P 458.459

Built on the shores of the Tagus, the Portuguese
Pavilion occupies an axial site not far from the
main entrance to Expo '98. As opposed to many of
the surrounding buildings, Siza chose a discreet,
horizontal design. His brief included a large outside
space for ceremonial functions. He met this require-
ment with an unusual curved concrete "veil", which
is suspended at either end from steel cables. Red
and green ceramic cladding is used at the ends
of this outdoor space, marking one of Siza's first
exterior uses of a traditional Portuguese building

Der am Ufer des Tejo errichtete Portugiesische
Pavillon steht auf einem symmetrischen Grundstück
nahe dem Haupteingang zur Expo '98. Siza gab
dem Gebäude eine langgestreckte einfache Form,
die im Kontrast zu vielen Bauten der Umgebung
steht. Den in der Ausschreibung geforderten Platz
für Feste schuf Siza durch einen Beton-»Segel«,
eine Art Hängedach aus Beton, das auf beiden Seiten an Stahlseilen aufgehängt ist. Die Wände des
Freibereichs sind mit roter und grüner Keramik
verkleidet. Siza verwendet dieses traditionelle por-

Edifié au bord du Tage, ce Pavillon officiel occupe
un site majeur, non loin de l'entrée principale de
l'Expo '98. À la différence des nombreux bâtiments
environnants, Siza a choisi un parti de discrétion et
d'horizontalité. Le programme prévoyait un vaste
espace extérieur pour les cérémonies officielles,
obligation à laquelle il a répondu par un surprenant
«voile» de béton suspendu par des câbles à ses
deux extrémités. Des placages de carreaux de céra-
mique rouges et verts – première utilisation extérieure par Siza d'un matériau typiquement portu-

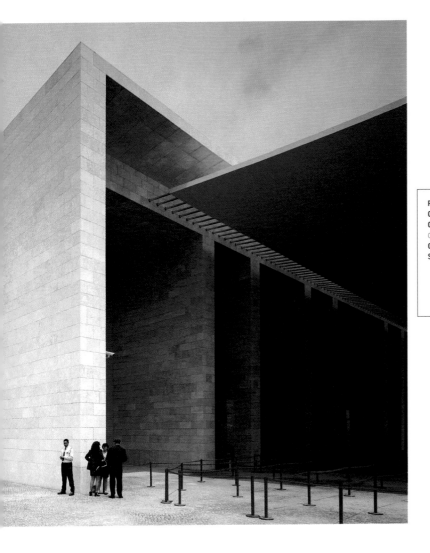

P 460.461

PLANNING / PLANUNG: 1995-96
CONSTRUCTION / BAU: 1996-97
COMPLETION / FERTIGSTELLUNG / FIN DE LA
CONSTRUCTION: 1998
CLIENT / BAUHERR: EXPO '98
SITE AREA / FLÄCHE / SURFACE: 14 000 M²

material. The main structure, now serving as the seat of the Portuguese Council of Ministers, is designed for maximum flexibility. The large, high-ceilinged rooms on the ground floor were used for the Expo '98 multimedia presentation, in spaces designed by Eduardo Souto de Moura. On the upper level, around a central courtyard, the so-called "VIP" rooms, including the large table for the Council of Ministers, are entirely designed and decorated by Siza.

tugiesische Baumaterial hier erstmals an einem Außenbau. Der Haupttrakt, der jetzt als Sitz des Portugiesischen Ministerrats dient, sollte äußerst flexibel sein. Die großen, hohen Räume im Erd-geschoß beherbergten während der Expo '98 eine Multimedia-Präsentation und wurden von Eduardo Souto de Moura gestaltet. Die um einen zentralen Innenhof angeordneten sogenannten »VIP«-Räume im Obergeschoß wurden, einschließlich des großen Tischs für den Ministerrat, ebenfalls von Siza entworfen.

gais – marquent les deux limites de cet espace extérieur. Le bâtiment principal, qui abrite au-jourd'hui le siège du Conseil des ministres, a été conçu pour permettre le maximum de souplesse. Au rez-de-chaussée, les vastes salles à haut plafond ont accueilli des expositions multimédias lors de l'Expo '98 dans une mise en espace d'Eduardo Souto de Moura. Au niveau supérieur, autour d'une cour centrale, les salons VIP, dont la grande table du Conseil, ont été entièrement conçus et décorés par Siza.

AUCH DIE INNENBEREICHE, EINSCHLIESSLICH
DER MÖBEL UND WANDZEICHNUNGEN, WUR-
DEN ÜBERWIEGEND VON SIZA GESTALTET.
EINE AUSNAHME BILDET DER GROSSE AUS-
STELLUNGSBEREICH, DEN SEIN MITARBEITER
EDUARDO SOUTO DE MOURA AUSGESTATTET
HAT.

LA PLUPART DES INTÉRIEURS ONT ÉTÉ DESSI-
NÉS PAR SIZA, Y COMPRIS LE MOBILIER ET LES
DESSINS DES MURS.
LA SEULE EXCEPTION À L'INTERVENTION DE
SIZA EST LE VASTE ESPACE D'EXPOSITION
CONÇU PAR SON CONFRÈRE EDUARDO SOUTO
DE MOURA.

MOST INTERIOR AREAS OF THE BUILDING
WERE ENTIRELY DESIGNED BY SIZA, INCLUDING
FURNITURE AND WALL DRAWINGS.
ONE EXCEPTION TO SIZA'S CONTROL IS THE
LARGE EXHIBITION SPACE DESIGNED BY HIS
COLLEAGUE EDUARDO SOUTO DE MOURA.

THOMAS SPIEGELHALTER

ATELIER PROF. SPIEGELHALTER + ASSOZIIERTE
POSTFACH-5107
79018 FREIBURG
GERMANY

TEL: + 49 761 47 46 11
FAX: + 49 761 47 46 12
E-MAIL: tspiegelh@t-online.de

Thomas Spiegelhalter was born in Freiburg, Germany, in 1959. He works in Freiburg as a sculptor, architect and communications designer. He obtained degrees in sculpture, 3-D visual communication and architecture in Bremen, Flensburg and in Berlin. He has taught architecture and visual arts in Kaiserslautern, at the Technische Hochschule in

Thomas Spiegelhalter, geboren 1959 in Freiburg, arbeitet dort als Bildhauer, Architekt und Kommunikationsdesigner. Er erwarb Diplome in Bildhauerei, dreidimensionaler visueller Kommunikation und Architektur in Bremen, Flensburg und Berlin; heute lehrt er an der Universität Kaiserslautern und der Technischen Hochschule Leipzig, seit August 1999

Thomas Spiegelhalter est né à Freiburg en 1959. Il travaille d'abord comme sculpteur, architecte et concepteur en communication. Il obtient des diplômes de sculpture, de communication visuelle en 3-D et d'architecture à Brême, Flensburg et à Berlin et a enseigné l'architecture et les arts visuels à Kaiserslautern et à la Technische Hochschule de

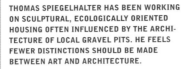

THOMAS SPIEGELHALTER HAS BEEN WORKING ON SCULPTURAL, ECOLOGICALLY ORIENTED HOUSING OFTEN INFLUENCED BY THE ARCHITECTURE OF LOCAL GRAVEL PITS. HE FEELS FEWER DISTINCTIONS SHOULD BE MADE BETWEEN ART AND ARCHITECTURE.

THOMAS SPIEGELHALTER PLANT PLASTISCHE, ÖKOLOGISCH ORIENTIERTE WOHNBAUTEN. ER IST DER ANSICHT, DASS ZWISCHEN KUNST UND

ARCHITEKTUR WENIGER UNTERSCHIEDE GEMACHT WERDEN SOLLTEN.

SOUVENT INFLUENCÉ PAR L'ARCHITECTURE DES GRAVIÈRES LOCALES, THOMAS SPIEGELHALTER TRAVAILLE SUR DES LOGEMENTS ÉCOLOGIQUES. POUR LUI, LES DISTINCTIONS ENTRE L'ART ET L'ARCHITECTURE NE SONT PAS VRAIMENT PERTINENTES.

P 466.467

Leipzig. Since August 1999 he has been teaching at the University of Houston. Starting January 2000 he will be teaching at the Carnegie Mellon University. His projects include sculptural works, sometimes related to his interest in the Freiburg gravel pits. Since 1989 he has worked on the design of energy-efficient homes.

an der University of Houston und ab Jaunuar 2000 an der Carnegie Mellon University. Seine Projekte umfassen eine Reihe plastischer Werke, die sein Interesse an den südbadischen Kieswerken widerspiegeln. Seit 1989 arbeitet er an der Planung von Energiesparhäusern.

Leipzig. Depuis août 1999 il enseigne à l'University of Houston, et en janvier 2000 il enseignera à la Carnegie Mellon University. Ses réalisations comprennent un certain nombre de travaux de sculpture, parfois liés à son intérêt pour les gravières de la région de Freiburg. Depuis 1989, il travaille sur l'habitat écologique.

THOMAS SPIEGELHALTER

EXPERIMENTAL HOUSING

FREIBURG, GERMANY, 1996-97

THE SOMEWHAT "BRISTLY" APPEARANCE OF
THIS HOUSING IS DUE IN PART TO ITS ECO-
LOGICALLY EFFICIENT DESIGN.

DAS ETWAS »RUPPIGE« ERSCHEINUNGSBILD
DIESER WOHNANLAGE IST ZUM TEIL AUF DIE
ÖKOLOGISCHE BAUWEISE ZURÜCKZUFÜHREN.

L'APPARENCE UN PEU CHAOTIQUE DE CET
IMMEUBLE EST JUSTIFIÉE EN PARTIE PAR
DES RAISONS ÉCOLOGIQUES.

Thomas Spiegelhalter is an unusual figure, although his attitude fits in well with the particular interest of Germany in ecologically conscious architecture. "I think the traditional division into 'art on this side and architecture on the other' is quite obsolete and stifles communication between the various media," he says. He is also opposed to the priority of computer-generated digital reality, in such projects as his recent very sculptural house in Breisach am Rhein, inspired by the forms of the machinery of a local gravel pit. His efforts in Freiburg in this four-story structure are related to the city's plans to drastically reduce the heating requirements of new buildings. Passive solar energy, efficient insulation and thermal storage are used to reduce energy consumption, while the curving roof on the south-facing side houses photovoltaic panels and protects the housing from the sun. Rainwater is accumulated for use in the bathrooms. Less eccentric in its form than the house in Breisach, this new building is evidence of the maturity of Spiegelhalter and the viability of ecologically sound architecture.

Thomas Spiegelhalter läßt sich einer Bewegung zum ökologischen Bauen zuordnen, durch seine experimentellen Formen setzt er sich aber deutlich von anderen Architekten ab. »Ich glaube, daß die traditionelle Aufteilung zwischen ›Kunst einerseits und Architektur andererseits‹ völlig überholt ist und die Kommunikation zwischen den verschiedenen Medien behindert«, sagt er. Spiegelhalter stellt sich gegen die Vorherrschaft der computergenerierten digitalen Realität. Sein Entwurf viergeschossiger Experimentalwohnbauten für Freiburg bezieht sich auf Pläne der Stadtverwaltung, den Aufwand für die Heizung von Neubauten drastisch zu reduzieren. Passive Solarenergie, wirksame Isolierung und Wärmespeicherung werden genutzt, um den Energieverbrauch zu senken, während das gekrümmte Dach auf der Sonnenseite Photovoltaik-Elemente enthält und das Haus zugleich vor der Sonne schützt. Regenwasser wird aufgefangen und für Bad und Toilette verwendet. Der Bau zeigt Spiegelhalters durchdachte Arbeit und das Kraftpotential ökologischer Architektur.

Thomas Spiegelhalter est un personnage original, même si ses positions correspondent bien à l'intérêt que portent les Allemands à l'architecture écologique. «Je pense que la division traditionnelle entre ‹l'art d'un côté et l'architecture de l'autre› est assez obsolète et paralyse la communication entre les divers médias», explique-t-il. Il est par ailleurs opposé à la priorité donnée à la réalité numérique des ordinateurs, comme le montre la maison qu'il vient d'achever à Breisach am Rhein inspirée par les formes des installations d'une gravière voisine. Son projet de bâtiment pour Freiburg illustre la politique de la ville qui veut réduire la consommation de chauffage des nouvelles constructions. L'énergie solaire passive, une isolation thermique efficace et l'accumulation de chaleur servent à réduire la consommation d'énergie, tandis qu'au sud le toit est équipé de panneaux photovoltaïques. L'eau de pluie est utilisée dans les salles de bains. Ce nouveau bâtiment est la preuve de la maturité de cet architecte et de la viabilité d'une architecture authentiquement préoccupée d'écologie.

FLOOR AREA / NUTZFLÄCHE / SURFACE
UTILE: 200-300 M² PER STUDIO-HOUSE
COSTS / KOSTEN / COÛTS: 1 800 DM PER M²

THE CURVED ROOF, FACING SOUTH, HOLDS AN
ARRAY OF PHOTOVOLTAIC CELLS TO GENERATE
SOLAR ENERGY.

DAS NACH SÜDEN ORIENTIERTE, GEKRÜMMTE
DACH ENTHÄLT PHOTOVOLTAIK-ELEMENTE ZUR
GEWINNUNG VON SOLARENERGIE.

LE TOIT INCURVÉ, FACE AU SUD, EST ÉQUIPÉ
D'UN RÉSEAU DE CELLULES PHOTOVOLTAÏQUES
GÉNÉRATRICES D'ÉNERGIE.

PHILIPPE STARCK
AND LUC ARSÈNE-HENRY

Philippe Starck (left) was born in Paris in 1949, and attended the École Nissim de Camondo in the same town. His projects include the Café Costes (Paris, 1984), Royalton Hotel (New York, 1988), Laguiole Knife Factory (France, 1988), the Paramount Hotel (New York, 1990), Asahi Beer Building (Tokyo, 1989), the Teatriz Restaurant (Madrid, 1990), and his Baron Vert building in Osaka, Japan

Philippe Starck (links), geboren 1949 in Paris, studierte an der École Nissim de Camondo in Paris. Zu seinen Projekten zählen das Café Costes in Paris (1984), das Royalton Hotel (1988) und das Paramount Hotel (1990), beide in New York, die Messerfabrik in Laguiole (Frankreich, 1988) sowie das Gebäude der Asahi-Brauerei (Tokio, 1989), das Baron Vert Building in Osaka (1990) und das

Philippe Starck (à gauche), né en 1949, est élève de l'École Nissim de Camondo, Paris. Parmi ses réalisations: le Café Costes (Paris, 1984), le Royalton Hotel (New York, 1988), une usine de coutellerie (Laguiole, 1988), le Paramount Hotel (New York, 1990), un immeuble pour la bière Asahi (Tokyo, 1989), le restaurant Teatriz (Madrid, 1990) et l'immeuble Baron Vert (Osaka, Japon, 1990). Luc

PHILIPPE STARCK HAS CULTIVATED THE IMAGE OF THE "BAD BOY" OF DESIGN. BEST-KNOWN FOR OBJECTS AND INTERIORS, HERE HE VENTURES INTO ARCHITECTURE IN THE COMPANY OF LUC ARSÈNE-HENRY FROM BORDEAUX.

PHILIPPE STARCK HAT SEINEN RUF ALS »ENFANT TERRIBLE« DES DESIGNS KULTIVIERT. DURCH SEINE OBJEKTE UND INTERIORS BEKANNT GEWORDEN, WIDMET ER SICH HIER, GEMEINSAM MIT LUC ARSÈNE-HENRY AUS BORDEAUX, DER ARCHITEKTUR.

PHILIPPE STARCK CULTIVE UNE IMAGE «D'ENFANT TERRIBLE» DU DESIGN. SURTOUT CONNU POUR SES OBJETS ET SES AMÉNAGEMENTS INTÉRIEURS, IL S'AVENTURE ICI DANS LE DOMAINE DE L'ARCHITECTURE EN COMPAGNIE DE LUC ARSÈNE-HENRY, ARCHITECTE BORDELAIS.

PHILIPPE STARCK
27, RUE PIERRE POLI
92130 ISSY-LES-MOULINEAUX
FRANCE

TEL: + 33 1 41 08 82 82
FAX: + 33 1 41 08 96 65

LUC ARSÈNE-HENRY JR & ALAIN TRIAUD
ARCHITECTES ASSOCIÉS
EXPOBURO
COURS CHARLES BRICAUD
33300 BORDEAUX
FRANCE

TEL: + 33 5 56 69 35 10
FAX: + 33 5 56 50 98 56
E-MAIL: lah.at@wanadoo.fr

(1990). Luc Arsène-Henry (right) was born in 1949 in Neuilly. He studied at the École des Beaux-Arts in Paris from 1967, and went to work for an architectural agency in Bordeaux in 1973. He created his present firm in 1992, and has worked with Philippe Starck on the control tower for the Bordeaux Merignac Airport and for a waste treatment plant in Vitry-sur-Seine, France.

Restaurant Teatriz in Madrid (1990). Luc Arsène-Henry (rechts), geboren 1949 in Neuilly-sur-Seine, studierte an der École des Beaux-Arts in Paris und arbeitete seit 1973 in einem Architekturbüro in Bordeaux; 1992 gründete er eine eigene Firma. Mit Philippe Starck arbeitete er am Kontrollturm des Flughafens Merignac in Bordeaux und an einer Müllverwertungsanlage in Vitry-sur-Seine.

Arsène-Henry (à droite) est né en 1949 à Neuilly-sur-Seine. Après des études à l'École des Beaux-Arts de Paris, débutées en 1967, il travaille pour une agence d'architecture bordelaise en 1973, puis crée sa propre structure en 1992. Il a déjà collaboré avec Philippe Starck au projet de la Tour de contrôle de l'aéroport de Bordeaux-Mérignac et à une usine de traitement d'ordures ménagères à Vitry-sur-Seine.

PHILIPPE STARCK AND LUC ARSÈNE-HENRY

NATIONAL SCHOOL OF DECORATIVE ARTS

PARIS, FRANCE, 1995-98

CLIENT / BAUHERR: MINISTÈRE DE LA CULTURE
ET DE LA COMMUNICATION
FLOOR AREA / NUTZFLÄCHE / SURFACE
UTILE: 8 500 M²
COSTS / KOSTEN / COÛTS: 100 000 000 FF

P 474.475

This apparently unusual building was strongly op-posed by associations of local residents. Since completion, its entirely blank marble street-side face has not been unanimously praised. In fact, behind a facade that some liken to a tomb, this extension to the National School of Decorative Arts is actually a relatively straightforward modern building, used for classroom areas and for offices. The rear, north facade of the building, which faces a tree-filled inner courtyard, is entirely glazed, admitting light to almost all of the interior spaces. Unexpectedly, this facade is inclined toward the garden. Colors like a dark red make the interiors relatively warm. Although some might expect this collaborative venture between Philippe Starck and the architect Luc Arsène-Henry to have yielded unusual interior spaces, like those in Starck's buildings in Japan, this is not really the case. Aside from the "event" of the facade, and the side entrance, the rest of the building is functional and modern in a relatively traditional sense.

Gegen dieses Gebäude haben Bürgerinitiativen Einspruch erhoben – vor allem die vollkommen glatte, marmorne Fassade zur Straßenseite wurde kritisiert. Der Neubau der Pariser École Nationale Supérieure des Arts Décoratifs, von vielen mit einem Grabstein verglichen, ist ein modernes Gebäude mit Unterrichtsräumen und Büros. Die rückwärtige, zum baumbestandenen Innenhof geneigte Nordfassade ist verglast und läßt Tageslicht in fast alle Innenräume fallen. Warme Farben wie Dunkelrot prägen die Innenräume. Manch einer hatte erwartet, daß diese Zusammenarbeit von Philippe Starck mit dem Architekten Luc Arsène-Henry zu so ungewöhnlichen Innenräumen wie denen von Starcks japanischen Bauten führen würde, was jedoch nicht der Fall ist. Abgesehen von der marmorverkleideten Fassade und dem seitlich gelegenen Eingang entspricht der Bau durchaus traditionellen Vorstellungen von Funktionalität und Moderne.

Ce bâtiment étonnant a fait face à une forte opposition de son voisinage. Depuis son achèvement, sa façade aveugle sur la rue, entièrement plaquée de marbre blanc, n'a pas fait l'unanimité. En fait, derrière cette façade, que certains ont comparée à celle d'un mausolée, se cache un bâtiment de bureaux et de salles de cours modernes et relativement classiques. À l'arrière, la façade nord, qui donne sur une cour intérieur arborée, est entièrement vitrée, afin d'éclairer la quasi-totalité des espaces intérieurs. Cette façade est curieusement inclinée vers le jardin. La coloration interne qui fait appel à un rouge sombre produit un effet assez chaleureux. Si l'on avait pu espérer de la collaboration Arsène-Henry-Starck des espaces intérieurs aussi originaux que ceux créés par le second au Japon, on ne peut qu'être déçu. En dehors de sa spectaculaire façade et de l'entrée latérale, le reste de l'immeuble est presque traditionnellement moderne et fonctionnel.

SHIN TAKAMATSU

Born in Shimane Prefecture in 1948, Shin Takamatsu graduated from Kyoto University in 1971, and from the Graduate School of the same institution in 1979. He created his own office in Kyoto in 1975 and has taught at Kyoto Technical University and at the Osaka University of Arts. Profiting amply from the building boom of the 1980s in Japan, Takamatsu completed a large number of structures including Origin I, II and III (Kamigyo,

Shin Takamatsu, geboren 1948 in der japanischen Präfektur Shimane, studierte an der Universität Kioto, wo er 1971 seinen ersten akademischen Grad erwarb und 1979 die Graduate School absolvierte. 1975 gründete er ein eigenes Büro in Kioto. Er lehrte an der Technischen Universität Kioto und an der Osaka University of Arts. Vom Bauboom der 80er Jahre profitierte er nachhaltig und realisierte eine große Anzahl von Gebäuden, darunter Origin I,

Né dans la préfecture de Shimane en 1948, Shin Takamatsu est diplômé de l'Université de Kyoto en 1971 et de la Graduate School de la même institution en 1979. Il crée sa propre agence à Kyoto en 1975 et a enseigné à l'Université Technique de Kyoto et à l'Université des Arts d'Osaka. Profitant largement de l'essor immobilier des années 80 au Japon, il réalise un grand nombre de projets dont Origin I, II et III (Kamigyo, Kyoto, 1980-86), le

KNOWN FIRST FOR HIS MECHANICALLY ORI-
ENTED ARCHITECTURE IN THE REGION OF
KYOTO, SHIN TAKAMATSU HAS MORE RECENTLY
ADAPTED AN INCREASINGLY MINIMALIST
VOCABULARY.

DER FÜR SEINE TECHNISCH ORIENTIERTE
ARCHITEKTUR IN DER REGION VON KIOTO
BEKANNTE SHIN TAKAMATSU HAT SICH NEUER-
DINGS EIN ZUNEHMEND MINIMALISTISCHES
VOKABULAR ANGEEIGNET.

CONNU INITIALEMENT POUR SES RÉALISA-
TIONS MÉCANISTES DANS LA RÉGION DE KYOTO,
SHIN TAKAMATSU S'EST PLUS RÉCEMMENT
TOURNÉ VERS UN LANGAGE DE PLUS EN PLUS
MINIMALISTE.

SHIN TAKAMATSU ARCHITECT & ASSOCIATES
195 JYOBODAIIN-CHO
TAKEDA, FUSHIMI-KU
KYOTO 612-8445
JAPAN

TEL: + 81 75 621 6002
FAX: + 81 75 621 6079
E-MAIL: syntax@magical.egg.or.jp

Kyoto, 1980-86), the Kirin Plaza Osaka (Chuo, Osaka, 1985-87), and Syntax (Sakyo-ku, Kyoto, 1988-90). In his more recent, less mechanical style, Takamatsu has completed the Kirin Head-quarters (Chuo-ku, Tokyo, 1993-95), the Shoji Ueda Museum of Photography (Kishimoto-cho, Tottori, 1993-95), and the Nagasaki Port Terminal Building (1994-95).

II und III (Kamigyo, Kioto, 1980-86), Kirin Plaza Osaka (Chuo, Osaka, 1985-87) und Syntax (Sakyo-ku, Osaka, 1988-90). Das Kirin-Verwaltungs-gebäude in Chuo-ku, Tokio (1993-95), das Shoji Ueda Museum für Fotografie in Kishimoto-cho, Tottori (1993-95) und der Terminal des Hafens Nagasaki (1994-95), alle in Japan, lassen Taka-matsus neuen, weniger technisch orientierten Stil erkennen.

Kirin Plaza Osaka (Chuo, Osaka, 1985-87) et Syntax (Sakyo-ku, Kyoto, 1988-90). Dans son style actuel, moins mécaniste que par le passé, il a réali-sé le siège de Kirin (Chuo-ku, Tokyo, 1993-95), le Musée de photographie Shoji Ueda (Kishimoto-cho, Tottori, 1993-95) et le terminal du port de Nagasaki (1994-95).

SHIN TAKAMATSU
SHOJI UEDA MUSEUM OF PHOTOGRAPHY
KISHIMOTO, TOTTORI, JAPAN, 1993-95

QUITE DIFFERENT FROM TAKAMATSU'S EARL-
IER WORK, THE SHOJI UEDA MUSEUM HAS A
MINIMALISTIC CONCRETE DESIGN.

IM GEGENSATZ ZU TAKAMATSUS FRÜHEREN
BAUTEN HAT DAS SHOJI UEDA MUSEUM EINE
KLARE, REDUZIERTE FORM.

ASSEZ DIFFÉRENT DES RÉALISATIONS ANTÉ-
RIEURES DE TAKAMATSU, CE MUSÉE TOUT
EN BÉTON EST D'ESPRIT MINIMALISTE.

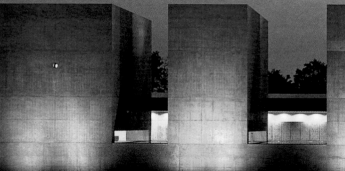

CLIENT / BAUHERR: TOWN OF KISHIMOTO
FLOOR AREA / NUTZFLÄCHE /
SURFACE UTILE: 2825 M²
COSTS / KOSTEN / COÛTS: WITHHELD /
UNGENANNT / NON COMMUNIQUÉS

THE JAPANESE PLACE GREAT IMPORTANCE ON GEOGRAPHIC FEATURES SUCH AS THE DAISEN MOUNTAIN.

DIE JAPANER MESSEN LANDSCHAFTLICHEN ELEMENTEN, WIE HIER DEM BERG DAISEN, GROSSE BEDEUTUNG BEI.

LES JAPONAIS ATTACHENT BEAUCOUP D'IMPORTANCE À CERTAINS SITES GÉOGRAPHIQUES COMME LE MONT DAISEN.

Better known in the past for the mechanical metaphors employed in his designs, Shin Takamatsu has matured to the point where his style has become much purer and more in tune with the current affinity for minimalist designs. This is certainly the case in his Shoji Ueda Museum of Photography, a reinforced concrete building with a total floor area of 2,825 m². The three-story museum is made up

Shin Takamatsu, der durch die mechanistischen Metaphern seiner Entwürfe bekannt wurde, hat heute eine Reife erreicht, in der sein Stil klarer ist und im Einklang mit der gegenwärtigen Vorliebe für minimalistische Gestaltung steht. Dies trifft zweifellos auf sein Shoji Ueda Museum für Fotografie zu, einen Stahlbetonbau mit drei Geschossen. Das Museum besteht aus vier Baukörpern, in denen die

Connu dans le passé pour le vocabulaire mécaniste de ses projets Shin Takamatsu a mûri et son style va jusqu'à rejoindre aujourd'hui les courants minimalistes. C'est le cas de ce musée de photographie Shoji Ueda, bâtiment de trois niveaux en béton armé de 2825 m² de surface. Il se compose de quatre blocs de béton pour les salles d'exposition, qui donnent une «atmosphère de village», et de

of four concrete block exhibition areas meant to
give a "village-like atmosphere," and three pools
designed to reflect the nearby Daisen Mountain.
A curved wall is also intended as a metaphorical
reference to the same mountain. Takamatsu likens
these reflections to the act of "pulling scenery into
architecture."

Ausstellungsbereiche untergebracht sind. Sie sollen
an einzelne Häuser erinnern und so eine »dorfähn-
liche Atmosphäre« erzeugen. In den drei Wasserbecken spiegelt sich der nahegelegene Berg Daisen;
die geschwungene Wand scheint seine Konturen
nachzuziehen. Takamatsu bezeichnet diese Bezüge
als Akt der »Einbeziehung von Landschaft in
Architektur«.

trois bassins qui reflètent la montagne de Daisen
à proximité. Un mur en courbe se veut également
une métaphore de la même montagne. Takamatsu
compare ces reflets à une tentative «d'attirer le
paysage dans l'architecture».

WHETHER IN HIS EARLIER, MORE MECHANIC-
ALLY ORIENTED WORK, OR IN THIS GEOMETRIC
COMPOSITION, TAKAMATSU STRIVES FOR
POWERFUL FORMS.

SOWOHL IN SEINEN FRÜHEREN, STÄRKER
TECHNISCH ORIENTIERTEN BAUTEN ALS
AUCH IN DIESER KLAREN GEOMETRISCHEN
KOMPOSITION BEVORZUGT TAKAMATSU EINE
KRAFTVOLLE FORMENSPRACHE.

QUE CE SOIT DANS SES RÉALISATIONS
D'ESPRIT PLUS MÉCANIQUE OU DANS SES
COMPOSITIONS GÉOMÉTRIQUES, TAKAMATSU
PRIVILÉGIE LES FORMES PUISSANTES.

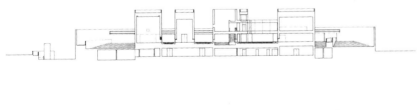

SHIN TAKAMATSU
METEOR PLAZA
MIHONOSEKI, SHIMANE, JAPAN, 1994-95

CLIENT / BAUHERR: TOWN OF MIHONOSEKI / SHIMANE PREFECTURAL GOVERNMENT
FLOOR AREA / NUTZFLÄCHE / SURFACE UTILE: 5 588 M²
COSTS / KOSTEN / COÛTS: WITHHELD / UNGENANNT / NON COMMUNIQUÉS

THE DISTINCTIVE SHAPE OF THE METEOR PLAZA IS INTENDED TO REUNITE ITS DISPARATE FUNCTIONS UNDER A SINGLE ROOF.

DIE AUFFÄLLIGE GESTALT DES METEOR PLAZA VEREINT UNTERSCHIEDLICHSTE FUNKTIONEN UNTER EINEM DACH.

LA FORME TRÈS ORIGINALE DU METEOR PLAZA A POUR FONCTION DE RÉUNIR PLUSIEURS FONCTIONS DISPARATES SOUS UN MÊME TOIT.

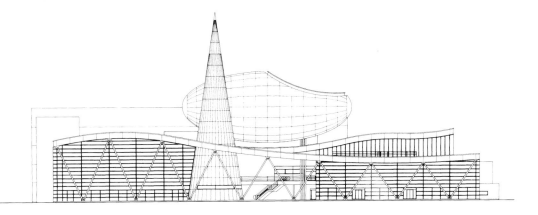

This project was the result of the combination of a unique series of functions: a ferry terminal for navigation to and from the island of Oki, a "Thalasso-Therapy" center making use of sea water, a city meeting hall for 500 persons, and an exhibition hall to show a meteor that fell on the city three years prior to the construction (thus the name Meteor Plaza). It is a four-story steel and reinforced con-

Takamatsu hatte die Aufgabe, eine Reihe ganz verschiedener Funktionen in einem Bau zu vereinen: einen Fährschiff-Terminal für den Schiffsverkehr zur Insel Oki, ein »Thalasso-Therapie«-Zentrum zur medizinischen Nutzung des Meerwassers, eine Stadthalle für 500 Personen und die Ausstellungshalle für einen Meteoriten, der drei Jahre zuvor auf die Stadt fiel (daher der Name Meteor Plaza). Die

Ce projet est né de la combinaison d'une série de fonctions plutôt rare: un terminal de ferries vers l'île d'Oki, un centre de thalassothérapie, une salle municipale de réunions de 500 places, et une salle d'exposition qui présente un météore tombé sur la ville trois ans avant le début des travaux, d'où le nom de ce complexe. Le bâtiment en acier et béton armé de quatre niveaux offre une surface de

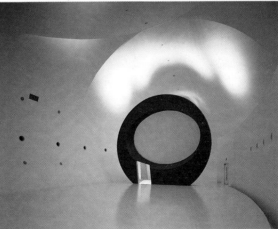

crete building with a total floor area of 5,588 m². Each of the disparate functions of the center is combined under a wave-like roof intended to evoke the neighboring sea. Specific volumes were then assigned to the components giving the whole the appearance of a "temporary composition," to paraphrase the architect.

Halle, ein viergeschossiges Gebäude aus Stahl und Stahlbeton mit einer Gesamtnutzfläche von 5 588 m², vereint die verschiedenen Nutzungen des Zentrums unter einem wellenförmigen Dach, das auf das nahe Meer verweist. Den einzelnen Funktionen wurden spezifische Formen zugewiesen, so daß der Gesamtbau – in den Worten des Architekten – wie »vorläufig zusammengestellt« wirkt.

5 588 m². Toutes les fonctions sont donc regroupées sous un toit en forme de vague qui évoque la mer toute proche. Les volumes spécifiques assignés à chacune d'entre elles donnent à l'ensemble un aspect de «composition temporaire», selon l'architecte.

SHIN TAKAMATSU
WORSHIP HALL SEIREI
KAWANISHI, HYOGO, JAPAN, 1996-98

CLIENT / BAUHERR: KANSAI SINNYO-JI, NOSE
MYOKEN-ZAN (BUDDHIST NICHIREN SECT.)
FLOOR AREA / NUTZFLÄCHE / SURFACE
UTILE: 901 M²
COSTS / KOSTEN / COÛTS: WITHHELD /
UNGENANNT / NON COMMUNIQUÉS

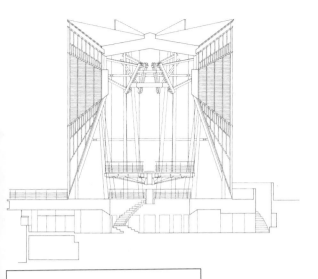

P 490.491

LOCAL CEDAR AND PINE WERE USED TO RE-CALL JAPANESE TRADITION NOT IN A LITERAL BUT IN A "MENTAL" WAY, ACCORDING TO THE ARCHITECT.

NACH AUSSAGE DES ARCHITEKTEN WURDE DAS HEIMISCHE ZEDERN- UND KIEFERNHOLZ NICHT IN FORMALER, SONDERN IN »GEISTIGER« ANLEHNUNG AN DIE JAPANISCHE TRADITION VERWENDET.

LE CÈDRE ET LE PIN LOCAUX ABONDAMMENT UTILISÉS RAPPELLENT LA TRADITION JAPO-NAISE DE MANIÈRE NON LITTÉRALE MAIS «MENTALE», EXPLIQUE L'ARCHITECTE.

THE VISUAL COMPLEXITY OF THE HALL RELATES IT TO SOME OF TAKAMATSU'S SMALL EARLY BUILDINGS IN KYOTO.

DIE KOMPLEXITÄT DER HALLE ERINNERT AN EINIGE VON TAKAMATSUS FRÜHEN, KLEINEREN BAUTEN IN KIOTO.

LA COMPLEXITÉ VISUELLE DE CE LIEU DE CULTE RAPPELLE CERTAINES DES RÉALISA-TIONS ANTÉRIEURES MOINS IMPORTANTES DE TAKAMATSU À KYOTO.

This reinforced concrete and steel frame building is set on a 2,645 m² site, and has a total floor area of 901 m². It is intended as a place of worship near the top of Mount Myoken-zan, replacing an older facility that was in poor condition. Since this location is related to the local cedar and pine trees by the Buddhist saint Myoken Bosatsu, it was decided to make use of locally cut wood. Wood of course has particular significance in Japanese architecture, although the protection of natural areas has made it increasingly difficult to build with locally felled timber. Takamatsu links the use of wood, which is unexpected in this technologically oriented architect, to Japanese tradition, not in a figurative way, but in terms of its "mental" value.

Die Gebetshalle am Gipfel des Bergs Myoken-zan wurde als Ersatz für ein altes, baufälliges Gebäude errichtet. Der Stahlbetonbau erhebt sich auf einem 2 645 m² großen Grundstück und hat eine Gesamt-nutzfläche von 901 m². Für den Bau wurde vor Ort geschlagenes Holz verwendet, um die Verbindung zu den dort stehenden Zedern und Kiefern des bud-dhistischen Heiligen Myoken Bosatsu aufzuzeigen. Holz spielt in der japanischen Architektur eine große Rolle, obgleich der Naturschutz die Nutzung einheimischen Holzes zunehmend erschwert. Taka-matsu will durch die Verwendung von Holz, die bei einem technisch orientierten Architekten wie ihm erstaunt, dem Ort entsprechend vor allem »geistige« und nicht formale Bezüge zur japanischen Tradition herstellen.

Ce bâtiment en béton armé et structure d'acier se dresse sur un terrain de 2 645 m² et offre une sur-face utile totale de 901 m². Au sommet du Mont Myoken-zan, il remplace un ancien lieu de culte en mauvais état. Dans cet endroit célèbre pour ses cèdres et ses pins chantés par le saint bouddhiste Myoken Bosatsu, il a été décidé d'utiliser des bois coupés sur place. Ce matériau présente une signifi-cation particulière dans l'architecture japonaise, mais la protection dont bénéficient aujourd'hui les espaces naturels fait qu'il est de plus en plus diffi-cile de construire avec les bois locaux. Takamatsu se sert du bois, inattendu chez cet architecte d'habi-tude plus intéressé par la haute technologie, dans l'esprit et le «mental» de la tradition japonaise et non au sens strictement utilitaire.

THE OCTAGONAL INTERIOR SPACE, WHERE
CONCRETE REPLACES THE WOOD, IS OPEN AND
FILLED WITH LIGHT.

DER ACHTECKIGE INNENRAUM, IN DEM BETON
ANSTELLE VON HOLZ VERWENDET WURDE, IST
OFFEN UND LICHTDURCHFLUTET.

DANS LES ESPACES INTÉRIEURS DE FORME
OCTOGONALE, OUVERTS ET LUMINEUX, LE
BÉTON REMPLACE LE BOIS.

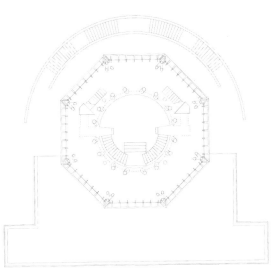

TEN ARQUITECTOS

TEN ARQUITECTOS HAVE RAISED THE STAND-
ARDS OF LATIN AMERICAN ARCHITECTURE TO
NEW LEVELS, WINNING THE 1998 MIES VAN
DER ROHE AWARD FOR THEIR TELEVISA SER-
VICES BUILDING.

Enrique Norten was born in Mexico City in 1954, and graduated as an architect from the Universidad Iberoamericana there in 1978. He received a Masters degree in architecture from Cornell University in 1980. He was partner in Albin y Norten Arquitectos (1981-84) before founding TEN Arquitectos in 1986. Bernardo Gómez-Pimienta was born in Brussels in 1961 and studied at the Universidad

Enrique Norten, geboren 1954 in Mexico City, beendete dort 1978 sein Studium an der Universidad Iberoamericana. An der Cornell University erwarb er 1980 den Master of Architecture. Bevor er 1986 TEN Arquitectos gründete, war Norten Partner im Büro Albin y Norten (1981-1984). Bernardo Gómez-Pimienta, geboren 1961 in Brüssel, studierte an der Universidad Anahuac in Mexico City und

Né à Mexico en 1954, Enrique Norten est architecte diplômé de la Universidad Iberoamericana en 1978. Il obtient un Master of Architecture de la Cornell University en 1980. Après avoir été associé à Albin y Norten Arquitectos (1981-84), il crée TEN Arquitectos en 1986. Bernardo Gómez-Pimienta naît à Bruxelles en 1961, et étudie à l'Universidad Anahuac de Mexico et à Columbia University. Il est

TEN ARQUITECTOS
CUERNAVACA 114-PB
COL. CONDESA
MEXICO CITY 06 140
MEXICO

TEL: + 52 5 211 8004
FAX: + 52 5 286 1735
E-MAIL: tenarq@mail.internet.com.mx

TEN ARQUITECTOS HABEN DEN STANDARD DER LATEINAMERIKANISCHEN ARCHITEKTUR AUF EIN NEUES NIVEAU GEHOBEN. 1998 ERHIELT IHR TELEVISA SERVICES BUILDING DEN MIES VAN DER ROHE AWARD.

L'AGENCE TEN ARQUITECTOS A RELEVÉ LES STANDARDS DE L'ARCHITECTURE LATINO-AMÉRICAINE. ELLE A REMPORTÉ LE PRIX MIES VAN DER ROHE 1998 POUR L'IMMEUBLE TELEVISA SERVICES.

Anahuac in Mexico City and at Columbia University, New York. He has been partner in TEN Arquitectos since 1987. Their work in Mexico includes a Cultural Center (Lindavista, 1987-92), the National Theater School (Churubusco, 1993), a workers' Restaurant (San Angel, 1993), House LE (Mexico City, 1995), and the Museum of Sciences (Mexico City, 1997, project).

an der Columbia University. Seit 1987 ist er Partner von TEN Arquitectos. Zu ihrem Werk gehören ein Kulturzentrum in Lindavista (1987-92), die Staatliche Schauspielschule in Churubusco, Mexico City (1993), ein Arbeiterrestaurant in San Angel (1993), das Haus LE (1995) und das Museo de Historia Natural in Mexico City (1997, Projekt).

un des associés de TEN Arquitectos depuis 1987. Leurs réalisations au Mexique comprennent entre autres: un Centre culturel (Lindavista, 1987-92), l'École Nationale du Théâtre (Churubusco, 1993), un restaurant pour travailleurs (San Angel, 1993) et la Maison LE (Mexico, 1995). Le Musée des Sciences (Mexico, 1997) est un de ses projets non réalisés.

TEN ARQUITECTOS
TELEVISA
SERVICES BUILDING
MEXICO CITY, MEXICO, 1993-95

THE SWEEPING CURVE OF THE BUILDING GIVES
IT A DYNAMIC, MODERN APPEARANCE WHILE
MEETING STRICT BUDGETARY RESTRICTIONS.

DIE GESCHWUNGENE FORM DES GEBÄUDES
VERLEIHT IHM EIN DYNAMISCHES, MODERNES
ERSCHEINUNGSBILD.

LA COURBE ÉLÉGANTE DE L'IMMEUBLE
GÉNÈRE UNE DYNAMIQUE ET UNE MODERNITÉ,
TOUT EN RESTANT DANS LE RESPECT DES
CONTRAINTES BUDGÉTAIRES.

PLANNING / PLANUNG: 1993-94
CONSTRUCTION / BAU: 1994-95
CLIENT / BAUHERR: TELEVISA S.A. DE C.V.
FLOOR AREA / NUTZFLÄCHE / SURFACE
UTILE: 7500 M²
COSTS / KOSTEN / COÛTS: US$ 24 000 000

A LARGE OPEN SPACE UNDER THE CURVING ALUMINUM ROOF IS DEVOTED TO A DINING AREA.

EIN GROSSER, OFFENER RAUM UNTER DEM GEWÖLBTEN ALUMINIUMDACH WIRD ALS KANTINE GENUTZT.

LE VASTE ESPACE OUVERT SOUS LE TOIT D'ALUMINIUM INCURVÉ EST CONSACRÉ AU RESTAURANT D'ENTREPRISE.

This structure was the recipient of the 1998 Mies van der Rohe Award for Latin American Architecture, given at the Museum of Modern Art in New York. The 7,500 m² facility, including parking, offices, an employee dining room, conference rooms, and meeting space, was built using concrete seismic walls and concrete slab supported by steel framing at a cost of $24 million. The roof is clad in Alucobond panels. Intended to replace a group of several

1998 erhielten TEN Arquitectos für diesen Bau den Mies van der Rohe Award for Latin American Architecture des Museum of Modern Art in New York. Der Komplex aus Parkhaus, Büros, einer Kantine sowie Konferenz- und Sitzungsräumen wurde mit erdbebensicheren Wänden und Betondecken, die von einem Stahlskelett getragen werden, errichtet. Das Dach ist mit Alucobond-Platten gedeckt. Der Bau ersetzt eine Gruppe von Häusern, in denen die

Ce bâtiment, édifié pour remplacer une groupe de petits immeubles qui abritaient les mêmes fonctions jusqu'en 1995, a reçu le Prix Mies van der Rohe 1998 pour l'Amérique Latine, remis au Museum of Modern Art de New York. Mesurant 7 500 m², et ayant coûté $24 millions, il comprend des bureaux, des salles de conférence, des espaces de réunion, un restaurant pour le personnel et des parkings. Construit sur un terrain trapézoïdal, sa structure se

buildings, in which the same services were housed until 1995, the Televisa Services structure is set on an unusual trapezoidal site. As the architects say, the "soaring aluminum-paneled shell alludes to an industrial vernacular and it also represents a technically expedient method of construction." This "silvery blimp," which houses the employees' dining room, is set on a more weighty black concrete volume where the garage and offices are located.

Firma bis 1995 untergebracht war, und steht auf einem trapezförmigen Grundstück. Die Architekten erklärten, daß »die aluminiumverkleidete Schale auf regionale Industriebauten verweist und zugleich eine technisch ausgereifte Baumethode darstellt«. Der »silbrige Ballon«, in dem die Kantine untergebracht ist, wurde auf einen wuchtigen schwarzen »Betonsockel« gesetzt, in dem sich das Parkhaus und die Büros befinden.

compose de murs en béton anti-sismiques et d'une dalle de béton soutenue par une ossature d'acier. L'architecte explique que «la coque recouverte de panneaux d'aluminium est une allusion à l'architecture vernaculaire industrielle et représente également une méthode pratique de construction». La «bosse argentée» qui abrite le restaurant repose sur un volume de béton noir plus massif dans lequel ont été implantés les bureaux et les parkings.

MAKOTO SEI WATANABE

Born in 1952 in Yokohama, Makoto Sei Watanabe attended Yokohama National University, from which he graduated with a M. Arch. in 1976. In 1979 he went to work for Arata Isozaki & Associates, and in 1984 he established Makoto Sei Watanabe/Architects' Office. His first work, the Aoyama Technical College built in the Shibuya-ku area of Tokyo in 1989, brought him international attention because of its spectacular forms influenced by cartoon graphics. His other work includes

Makoto Sei Watanabe, geboren 1952 in Yokohama, studierte an der Staatlichen Universität Yokohama, wo er 1976 seinen Master of Architecture erwarb. 1979 begann er seine Tätigkeit bei Arata Isozaki & Associates und gründete 1984 Makoto Sei Watanabe/Architects' Office. Sein erster Bau, das Aoyama Technical College in Shibuya-ku, Tokio (1989), erfuhr mit seinen von der Cartoon-Graphik beeinflußten, spektakulären Formen internationale Beachtung. Zu Watanabes weiteren Arbeiten zählen

Né en 1952 à Yokohama, Makoto Sei Watanabe fait ses études à l'Université Nationale de Yokohama dont il obtient un M. Arch. en 1976. En 1979, il est engagé par Arata Isaozaki & Associates et, en 1984, crée Makoto Sei Watanabe/Architects' Office. Son premier chantier, le Collège technique d'Aoyama construit dans le quartier Shibuya-ku à Tokyo attire l'attention internationale pour ses formes spectaculaires influencées par la bande dessinée. Parmi ses autres réalisations: Chronospace

MAKOTO SEI WATANABE IS A PROVOCATIVE
INNOVATOR. HIS AOYAMA TECHNICAL COLLEGE
IN TOKYO (1989), MODELED AFTER A CARTOON
ROBOT, GAINED HIM INTERNATIONAL PRESS
COVERAGE.

MAKOTO SEI WATANABE IST EIN PROVOKATIVER
NEUERER. SEIN AOYAMA TECHNICAL COLLEGE
IN TOKIO (1989), DAS EINEM CARTOON-ROBOTER

NACHGEBILDET WURDE, HAT IHM INTERNATIO-
NALE BEACHTUNG EINGEBRACHT.

MAKOTO SE WATANABE EST UN NOVATEUR ET
UN PROVOCATEUR. SON COLLÉGE TECHNIQUE
AOYAMA, À TOKYO (1989), A PRIS L'ALLURE D'UN
ROBOT DE BANDE DESSINÉE. IL A ÉTÉ PUBLIÉ
DANS TOUTE LA PRESSE INTERNATIONALE.

MAKOTO SEI WATANABE / ARCHITECTS' OFFICE
#2806 AZUMABASHI 1-23-30
SUMIDA-KU, TOKYO 130-0001
JAPAN

TEL: + 81 3 3829 3221
FAX: + 81 3 3829 3837
E-MAIL: msw@makoto-architekt.com
WEB: www.makoto-architect.com

Chronospace (Minato-ku, Tokyo, 1991), Mura-no
Terrace gallery, information office and café,
Sakauchi Village (Ibi-gun, Gifu, 1995), "Fiber
Wave," environmental art (Gifu and Tokyo, 1995-
96), Atlas, housing (Suginami-ku, Tokyo, 1996),
K-Museum (Koto-ku, Tokyo, 1996), "Fiber Wave,"
environmental art, The Chicago Athenaeum (1998),
and Iidabashi Subway Stations (Bunkyo-ku and
Shinjuku-ku, Tokyo, under construction).

Chronospace in Minato-ku, Tokio (1991), Mura-no
Terrace in Sakauchi Village, Ibi-gun, Gifu (1995),
»Fiber Wave«-Environments in Gifu und Tokio
(1995-96), die Wohnanlage Atlas in Suginami-ku,
Tokio, und das K-Museum in Koto-ku, Tokio (beide
1996), das »Fiber Wave«-Environment für das
Chicago Athenaeum (1998) sowie die Iidabashi-
U-Bahn-Stationen Bunkyo-ku und Shinjuku-ku,
Tokio (im Bau).

(Minato-ku, Tokyo, 1991), Mura-no Terrace, galerie, bureau d'information et café, Sakauchi Village (Ibi-gun, Gifu, 1991), «Fiber Wave», art environnemental (Gifu et Tokyo, 1995-96), immeuble
de logements Atlas (Suginami-ku, Tokyo, 1996),
K-Museum (Koto-ku, Tokyo, 1996), «Fiber Wave»,
art environnemental au Chicago Athenaeum (1998)
et les stations de métro Iidabashi (Bunkyo-ku et
Shinjuku-ku, Tokyo, en construction).

MAKOTO SEI WATANABE
MURA-NO TERRACE
IBI-GUN, GIFU, JAPAN, 1994-95

Unexpectedly, the small town of Sakauchi, with a population of 750 persons, located in the mountains of central Honshu, found enough interest in contemporary design to ask the rather radical Tokyo architect Makoto Sei Watanabe to create a 389 m² information center and café. Located at the entrance to the town, it also serves as a gathering point for local residents, and sells food. The one-story steel

Die im bergigen Zentrum der Insel Honshu gelegene, nur 750 Einwohner zählende Stadt Sakauchi zeigte ein starkes Interesse an moderner Architektur, als sie den Tokioter Architekten Makoto Sei Watanabe mit der Planung eines Informationszentrums mit Café beauftragte. Der Bau dient unter anderem als Treffpunkt für die Bürger und enthält auch ein Lebensmittelgeschäft. Die eingeschossige

Il est assez surprenant que le village de Sakauchi, situé dans les montagnes centrale de Honshu, et ses 750 habitants se soient suffisamment intéressés à l'architecture contemporaine pour demander à l'architecte radical de Tokyo, Makoto Sei Watanabe, de créer ce centre d'information et café de 389 m². À l'entrée du village, il sert aussi de lieu de rencontre aux habitants et vend même de la nourritu-

P 502.503

PLANNING / PLANUNG: 1994
CONSTRUCTION / BAU: 1995
CLIENT / BAUHERR: SAKAUCHI-MURA VILLAGE, GIFU
FLOOR AREA / NUTZFLÄCHE / SURFACE UTILE: 389 M²

THE MURA-NO TERRACE SITS LIGHTLY ON ITS SITE, AS IF IT ARRIVED FROM ANOTHER PLANET.

WATANABES MURA-NO TERRACE SCHEINT ÜBER DEM FLUSS ZU SCHWEBEN.

LA MURO-NO TERRACE EST DÉLICATEMENT POSÉE SUR SON TERRAIN, COMME ARRIVÉE D'UNE AUTRE PLANÈTE.

frame structure juts out over the neighboring river. The architect also created a kind of technological garden near the structure that he calls "Edge of Water." Intended to be a "topographical model of the surroundings," it features a series of 150 carbon fiber rods with LEDs, powered by solar batteries, that light up at night and wave in the wind.

Stahlkonstruktion schwebt auf einer Seite frei über dem nahegelegenen Fluß. Watanabe gestaltete darüber hinaus einen »technischen Garten«, den er »Rand des Wassers« nennt und als »topographisches Modell der Umgebung« bezeichnet. Er besteht aus 150 Kohlenstoffaserstäben mit solarbetriebenen Dioden, die nachts leuchten und im Wind schwanken.

re. La structure à ossature d'acier de un niveau seulement s'avance au-dessus d'une rivière. L'architecte a également dessiné juste à côté une sorte de jardin technologique qu'il appelle «le bord de l'eau», «maquette topographique de son environnement», planté de 150 tiges de fibre de carbone équipées de LED alimentées par des piles solaires qui s'éclairent la nuit et ondulent dans le vent.

THE MAIN TERRACE, CANTILEVERED INTO
EMPTY SPACE, HEIGHTENS THE IMPRESSION OF
AN ALIEN OBJECT IN THIS RURAL SETTING.

DIE GROSSE, AUSKRAGENDE TERRASSE VER-
STÄRKT DEN EINDRUCK EINES AUSSERIRDI-
SCHEN OBJEKTS IN DIESER LÄNDLICHEN
UMGEBUNG.

LA TERRASSE PRINCIPALE, EN PORTE-À-FAUX
AU-DESSUS D'UN ESPACE VIDE, RENFORCE
L'IMPRESSION D'OBJET ÉTRANGER QUI AURAIT
ATTERRI DANS CE CADRE RURAL.

P 504.505

PLANNING / PLANUNG: 1995
CONSTRUCTION / BAU: 1996
CLIENT / BAUHERR: THE BUREAU OF PORT AND
HARBOUR / TOKYO METROPOLITAN GOVERN-
MENT / TOKYO WATER FRONT DEVELOPMENT,
INC
FLOOR AREA / NUTZFLÄCHE / SURFACE
UTILE: 245 M²

MAKOTO SEI WATANABE
K-MUSEUM
TOKYO, JAPAN, 1995-96

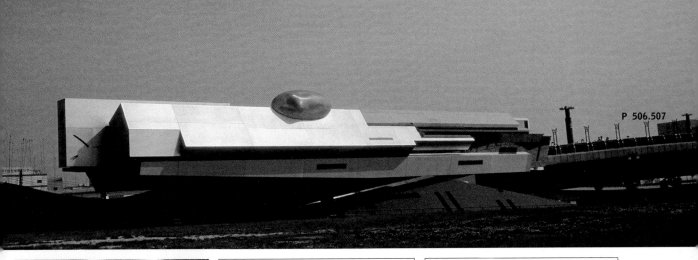

Located in an area of new construction bordering the Bay of Tokyo that the architect calls "the Tokyo frontier," the K-Museum was designed to heighten public awareness of a major utility tunnel that runs beneath it. It has been pointed out that this is a museum dedicated to a city that does not really exist as yet, and which may not exist for some time given the economic slowdown in Japan. Set on a base of black granite, the structure is shaped like an inclined bar coated with aluminum and stainless steel panels. Carbon fiber rods lining the approach to the museum contain light-emitting diodes and solar batteries, as is the case in the Mura-no Terrace building. With no source of energy other than the sun, they give off a bluish light at night. The museum has a small total floor area of 245 m², and is set on a 13,536 m² site. The interior display, using models and technologically advanced video presentations, leads visitors toward the tunnel, but as Watanabe says, "my idea from the outset is that the museum building itself is an item on display."

Das K-Museum liegt in einem Neubaugebiet an der Bucht von Tokio, das der Architekt als »Tokios Grenze« bezeichnet, und soll das Publikum auf einen großen Versorgungstunnel aufmerksam machen, der darunter verläuft. Dieses Museum ist für eine Stadt bestimmt, die in den 80er Jahren als Megaprojekt geplant wurde, jedoch angesichts der wirtschaftlichen Rezession in Japan auch in nächster Zeit nicht realisiert werden wird. Das auf einer Basis aus schwarzem Granit errichtete Bauwerk hat die Form eines geneigten Riegels, der mit Aluminium- und Edelstahlplatten verkleidet ist. Stäbe aus Kohlenstoffaser säumen den Zugang zum Museum. Sie enthalten, wie bei der Mura-no Terrace, Dioden mit Solarbatterien und leuchten nachts bläulich. Das Museum hat eine Gesamtnutzfläche von nur 245 m² und steht auf einem 13 536 m² großen Grundstück. Die Ausstellung, die Modelle und modernste Video-Präsentationen zeigt, führt die Besucher zum Tunnel. Watanabe sagt: »Nach meiner Vorstellung sollte das Museumsgebäude selbst ein Ausstellungstück sein.«

Dans une zone de constructions nouvelles en bordure de la baie de Tokyo que l'architecte appelle «la frontière de Tokyo», le K-Museum a été conçu pour éveiller l'intérêt du public pour un important tunnel qui passe juste en dessous. On a pu faire remarquer qu'il s'agissait d'un musée consacré à une ville qui n'existe pas encore et n'existera peut-être pas d'ici longtemps vu le ralentissement de la croissance économique du pays. Posé sur un socle de granit noir, le bâtiment est en forme de barre inclinée recouverte de panneaux d'aluminium et d'acier inoxydable. Des tiges en fibre de carbone qui bordent le chemin d'accès contiennent des diodes luminescentes et des batteries solaires, comme pour la Mura-no Terrace. Sans autre source d'énergie que le soleil, elles émettent la nuit une lumière bleuâtre. Edifié sur un terrain de 13 536 m², le musée en compte 245 m². La présentation intérieure informe les visiteurs sur le tunnel à l'aide de maquettes et de vidéo de haute technologie. «Mon idée depuis le départ est que ce musée soit lui-même un objet d'exposition», a expliqué Watanabe.

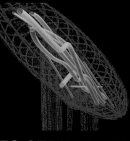

MAKOTO SEI WATANABE
NATIONAL DIET BUILDING
NEW CAPITAL, JAPAN, 1996 (PROJECT)

Like many Japanese tired of the bureaucratic tangles of his country, and particularly disappointed by the national Diet (parliament), symbolized by its neo-classical building, Makoto Sei Watanabe has proposed a new solution. Taking the idea of "transparency" in politics beyond its logical conclusion, he suggests that a new building for the Diet be totally transparent, with walls, ceilings and floors made of glass. He calls his structure "an extremely thin highscraper". Visitors and constituents would be able to enter the building by a system of transpar-

Makoto Sei Watanabe, der wie viele Japaner der bürokratischen Verstrickungen seines Landes überdrüssig ist, hat einen Neubau für das Parlament vorgeschlagen, das bisher durch ein klassizistisches Gebäude repräsentiert wird. Watanabe überträgt den Begriff der »Transparenz« in der Politik auf seine Architektur und gestaltet das neue Parlamentsgebäude vollkommen durchsichtig – mit Wänden, Decken und Böden aus Glas. Besucher und Wähler könnten das Gebäude durch ein System aus transparenten Röhren betreten und die Abgeordneten bei

Fatigué, comme de nombreux Japonais, de la complexité bureaucratique de son pays et particulièrement déçu par le Parlement que symbolise son siège néo-classique, Makoto Sei Watanabe a proposé une solution nouvelle. Poussant l'idée de «transparence» en politique au-delà de ses conséquences logiques, il a suggéré un bâtiment totalement transparent, dont les murs, les sols et les plafonds seraient en verre. Il parle d'un «highscraper» (gratte-hauteur) extrêmement mince. Les visiteurs pourraient le visiter grâce à un système de tubes transparents

P 508.509

WATANABE FÜHRT IN DIESEM PHANTASTISCH
ANMUTENDEN PARLAMENTSGEBÄUDE DIE IDEE
DER TRANSPARENZ IN DER POLITIK ZU NEUEN
HÖHEN.

WATANABE A POUSSÉ L'IDÉE DE TRANSPA-
RENCE DÉMOCRATIQUE DANS SES ULTIMES
RETRANCHEMENTS DANS CE PROJET POUR LE
PARLEMENT JAPONAIS.

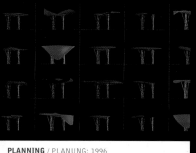

PLANNING / PLANUNG: 1996
BEGINNING OF CONSTRUCTION / BAUBEGINN /
DÉBUT DES TRAVAUX: 2001
CLIENT / BAUHERR: GIFU PREFECTURE
FLOOR AREA / NUTZFLÄCHE / SURFACE
UTILE: 200 000 M²

ent tubes that would allow the legislators to be seen at work, without actually disturbing them. Going even further, Watanabe suggests that the "exterior of the building is made of elastic covering, and minute actuators densely arranged on its inside maintain and adjust the form of the building. Consisting of small linked cells, the covering resembles the skin of a living organism. Photosynthesizing organs and chromatophores are built into the cells, and the cells are activated by sunlight."

ihrer Arbeit beobachten, ohne sie zu stören. Darüber hinaus schlägt Watanabe vor, »das Äußere des Gebäudes aus einer elastischen Abdeckung zu bilden und an der Innenseite in geringen Abständen winzige Spannvorrichtungen anzubringen, um das Gebäude in Form zu halten und diese Form zu regulieren. Die aus kleinen, miteinander verbundenen Zellen bestehende Hülle ähnelt der Haut eines lebenden Organismus. In die Zellen sind photosynthetische Organe und Farbstoffträger eingebaut, die bei Sonnenlicht aktiviert werden.«

à travers lesquels on pourrait voir les députés au travail sans les déranger. Allant plus loin encore, l'architecte suggère que «l'extérieur du bâtiment soit recouvert d'un parement élastique, dans lequel des activateurs instantanés maintiendraient et ajusteraient la forme de l'immeuble. Composé de petites cellules reliées entre elles, ce parement fait penser à la peau d'un organisme vivant. Des dispositifs de photosynthèse et des chromatophores insérés dans les cellules feraient activer celles-ci par la lumière solaire.»

WILLIAMS AND TSIEN

Tod Williams was born in Detroit in 1943, he gained his B.A. (1965) and Master of Fine Arts (1967) from Princeton University. After six years as associate architect with Richard Meier in New York, he began his own practice there in 1974. He taught at Cooper Union for more than 15 years, as well as at Harvard, Yale, the University of Virginia, and Southern California Institute of Architecture. He won the Prix de Rome in 1983. Billie Tsien, born in Ithaca, New York, in 1949, gained her B.A.

Tod Williams, geboren 1943 in Detroit, erwarb 1965 den Bachelor of Arts und 1967 den Master of Fine Arts an der Princeton University. Nach sechs Jahren Mitarbeit im Büro von Richard Meier machte er sich 1974 in New York selbständig. Er lehrte an der Cooper Union, in Harvard und Yale, an der University of Virginia und am Southern California Institute of Architecture. 1983 wurde ihm der Prix de Rome verliehen. Billie Tsien, geboren 1949 in Ithaca, schloß 1977 ihr Studium

Tod Williams, né à Detroit en 1943, Bachelor of Arts en 1965, Master of Fine Arts, 1967, Princeton University. Après avoir passé six ans dans l'agence new-yorkaise de Richard Meier, il se met à son compte en 1974, à New York. Il a enseigné à Cooper Union pendant plus de 15 ans ainsi qu'à Harvard, à Yale, à l'Université de Virginie et au Southern California Institute of Architecture. Prix de Rome en 1983. Billie Tsien, née à Ithaca, New York, 1949, Bachelor of Arts, Yale, M. Arch.,

ONE OF A NUMBER OF COUPLES WHO HAVE EMERGED ON THE CONTEMPORARY ARCHITECTURE SCENE IN AMERICA, WILLIAMS AND TSIEN HAVE AFFIRMED THEIR TASTE FOR A COMPLEX MODERNITY THAT PLAYS ON VARIED MATERIALS.

ALS EINES VON MEHREREN PAAREN DER AMERIKANISCHEN ARCHITEKTURSZENE HABEN WILLIAMS UND TSIEN IHRE VORLIEBE FÜR EINE KOMPLEXE MODERNITÄT IM SPIEL MIT VIELFÄLTIGEN MATERIALIEN BEWIESEN.

L'UN DE CES COUPLES D'ARCHITECTES AMÉRICAINS QUI SE SONT FAIT CONNAÎTRE AU COURS DES DERNIÈRES ANNÉES, WILLIAMS ET TSIEN AFFIRMENT LEUR GOÛT POUR UNE MODERNITÉ COMPLEXE QUI JOUE SUR LA VARIÉTÉ DES MATÉRIAUX.

TOD WILLIAMS, BILLIE TSIEN AND ASSOCIATES
222 CENTRAL PARK SOUTH
NEW YORK, NEW YORK 10019
UNITED STATES

TEL: + 1 212 582 2385
FAX: + 1 212 245 1984
E-MAIL: twbta@newyorknet.net

from Yale, and her M. Arch. from UCLA (1977). A painter and graphic designer (1971-75), she taught at Parsons School of Design, Southern California Institute of Architecture, Harvard and Yale. Their built work includes Feinberg Hall (Princeton, New Jersey, 1986), New College, University of Virginia (Charlottesville, Virginia, 1992), and the renovation and extension of the Museum of Fine Arts in Phoenix, Arizona.

an der UCLA mit dem M. Arch. ab, nachdem sie den B. A. an der Yale University erworben hatte. Von 1971 bis 1975 arbeitete sie als Malerin und Graphikerin. Sie lehrte an der Parsons School of Design, am SCI-Arc, in Harvard und Yale. Wichtige Bauten des Büros sind die Feinberg Hall in Princeton, New Jersey (1986), das New College der University of Virginia in Charlottesville, sowie der Umbau des Museum of Fine Arts in Phoenix.

UCLA. Peintre et graphiste de 1971 à 1975, elle a enseigné à la Parsons School of Design, au Southern California Institute of Architecture, à Harvard et à Yale. Parmi leurs projets réalisés: le Feinberg Hall (Princeton, New Jersey, 1986), le New College, University of Virginia (Charlottesville, Virginia, 1992) et l'extension et rénovation du Museum of Fine Arts de Phoenix, Arizona.

WILLIAMS AND TSIEN
NEW YORK CITY HOUSE
NEW YORK, NEW YORK, UNITED STATES, 1995-97

THIS HOUSE, LOCATED ON EAST 72ND STREET IN MANHATTAN, STANDS OUT IN A BLOCK WHERE OLDER BUILDINGS ARE THE RULE.

DIESES WOHNHAUS IN DER EAST 72ND STREET IN MANHATTAN FÄLLT AUS SEINER UMGEBUNG HERAUS, DIE ÜBERWIEGEND AUS ÄLTEREN GEBÄUDEN BESTEHT.

CETTE RÉSIDENCE SITUÉE SUR EAST 72ND STREET À MANHATTAN SE DÉTACHE EN FAÇADE D'UN BLOC DANS LEQUEL LES IMMEUBLES ANCIENS SONT DE RÉGLE.

P 512.513

CLIENT / BAUHERR: WITHHELD / UNGENANNT / NON COMMUNIQUÉ
FLOOR AREA / NUTZFLÄCHE / SURFACE UTILE: 1300 M²
COSTS / KOSTEN / COÛTS: WITHHELD / UNGENANNT / NON COMMUNIQUÉS
INTERIOR / INNENAUSSTATTUNG / DÉCORATION INTÉRIEURE: WILLIAMS AND TSIEN

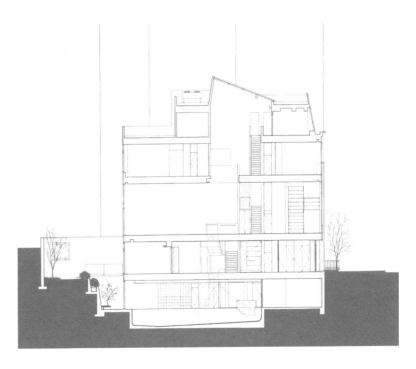

This new residence was built on the former lots of two demolished brownstones measuring a total of 9.2 x 30.5 m. A central element of the new facade is a rectangular 10 cm thick limestone wall, surrounded by glass, giving a degree of privacy to the residents and isolating them from the street. Interior design, including furniture and carpets, was also the responsibility of the architects. They used cherry wood for the cabinetwork and some floors. A skylit stairway serves to bring natural light into the six levels of the house. An underground pool and a

Dieses neue, 9,2 x 30,5 m große Wohnhaus wurde auf den Grundstücken zweier abgebrochener »Brownstone«-Häuser errichtet. Zentrales Element der neuen Glasfassade ist eine rechteckige, 10 cm dicke Platte aus Kalksandstein, die den Bewohnern die notwendige Privatsphäre bietet, indem sie sie von der Straße abschirmt. Die Innenausstattung samt Möblierung und Teppichen wurde ebenfalls von den Architekten gestaltet. Ein von oben belichtetes Treppenhaus erhellt alle sechs Etagen des Gebäudes. Weitere Besonderheiten sind ein Swimming-

Cet hôtel particulier a été édifié sur les terrains de deux «brownstones» démolies, formant au total une parcelle de 9,2 x 30,5 m. L'élément central de la façade est un rectangle d'épais calcaire de 10 cm d'épaisseur, entouré de verre, qui protège en partie l'intimité des occupants et les isole de la rue. Les architectes ont été également chargés des aménagements intérieurs, y compris le mobilier et les tapis. Une cage d'escalier fait fonction de puits de lumière et distribue celle-ci sur les six niveaux de la maison. Une piscine souterraine et un jardin sur deux

THE UNEXPECTED CONFRONTATION OF GLASS AND STONE NEAR A STAIRWAY IS TYPICAL OF THE WORK OF WILLIAMS AND TSIEN.

DER ÜBERRASCHENDE KONTRAST VON GLAS UND NATURSTEIN IM TREPPENHAUS IST TYPISCH FÜR DIE ARBEITEN VON WILLIAMS UND TSIEN.

LA CONFRONTATION INATTENDUE DU VERRE ET DE LA PIERRE PRÈS DE LA CAGE D'ESCA-LIER EST TYPIQUE DES INTERVENTIONS DE WILLIAMS ET TSIEN.

two-level garden are other features of the project. Although there have not been many such private houses built in Manhattan in recent years, Philip Johnson's 1950 Rockefeller Guest House is cited as a precedent. In fact, Johnson was interviewed by the clients before they chose Williams and Tsien. The floor area of the house is about 1,300 m², whereas New York zoning would have permitted more than twice as much, an unheard of luxury in this real-estate-conscious city.

pool im Souterrain und ein Garten über zwei Ebenen. In den vergangenen Jahren wurden nur wenige derartige Privathäuser in Manhattan errichtet; Philip Johnsons Rockefeller-Gästehaus von 1950 wird als Vorbild genannt. Die Nutzfläche des Hauses ist mit etwa 1 300 m² niedrig gehalten, obwohl die New Yorker Bauvorschriften mehr als das Doppelte zugelassen hätten – ein unerhörter Luxus in dieser Stadt mit ihrer ausgeprägten Grundbesitzermentalität.

niveaux ont été créés. Bien que l'on n'ait guère construit de résidences aussi luxueuses à Manhattan au cours de ces dernières années, la Rockefeller Guest House de Philip Johnson (1950) est citée comme précédent. En fait, Johnson a été consulté par les clients avant qu'ils se décident pour Williams et Tsien. La surface totale de la maison est d'environ 1 300 m² alors que les règlements d'urbanisme auraient permis de construire le double, luxe inouï dans cette ville si consciente du marché de l'immobilier.

JEAN-MICHEL WILMOTTE

Born in 1948, a graduate of the École Nissim de Camondo in Paris, Jean-Michel Wilmotte created his own firm, Governor, in 1975. Although he is best known for his work in interior design, including part of private apartments for the Élysée Palace, Wilmotte joined the Order of Architects in France in 1993. His recent work includes the fitting out of the Decorative Arts Department of the Louvre,

Jean-Michel Wilmotte, geboren 1948, studierte an der École Nissim de Camondo in Paris und gründete 1975 seine Firma Governor. Obwohl er vor allem als Innenarchitekt bekannt geworden ist – er gestaltete einen Teil der Privatwohnungen im Élysée-Palast –, trat er 1993 dem französischen Ordre des Architectes bei. Zu Wilmottes neueren Arbeiten zählen die Ausstattung der Abteilung für Ange-

Né en 1948, diplômé de l'École Nissim de Camondo à Paris, Jean-Michel Wilmotte a créé sa propre agence – Governor – en 1975. Bien qu'il soit surtout connu pour ses projets d'architecture intérieure, dont une partie des appartements privé au Palais de l'Élysée, il rejoint l'Ordre des Architectes en 1993. Parmi ses réalisations récentes: l'architecture intérieure du département des Arts décora-

SUBTIL, SEINE ARBEIT PROFESSIONELL UND
VIELFÄLTIG.

JEAN-MICHEL WILMOTTE, ARCHITECTE D'INTÉ-
RIEUR TRÈS CONNU EN FRANCE, S'EST LANCÉ
AVEC SUCCÈS DANS L'ARCHITECTURE. SON
GOÛT EST MODERNE ET SUBTIL, SES RÉALI-
SATIONS PROFESSIONNELLES ET VARIÉES.

**JEAN-MICHEL WILMOTTE, WELL KNOWN IN
FRANCE AS AN INTERIOR DESIGNER, HAS
SUCCESSFULLY BRANCHED OUT INTO ARCHITEC-
TURE. HIS TASTE IS MODERN AND SUBTLE, HIS
WORK PROFESSIONAL AND VARIED.**

DER IN FRANKREICH ALS INNENARCHITEKT
SEHR BEKANNTE JEAN-MICHEL WILMOTTE
BETÄTIGT SICH MIT ERFOLG AUCH ALS
ARCHITEKT. SEIN STIL IST MODERN UND

JEAN-MICHEL WILMOTTE
68 RUE DU FAUBOURG ST. ANTOINE
75012 PARIS
FRANCE

TEL: + 33 1 53 02 22 22
FAX: + 33 1 43 44 17 11

Richelieu Wing, with Ieoh Ming Pei (1989-93), and the Museum of Fashion, Marseilles. As an architect, Jean-Michel Wilmotte recently completed the International Executive Office building, Tokyo, and the New N° 3 Arai building, again in Tokyo, while he also carried out the furniture design for the Banque de Luxembourg building, completed by Arquitectonica in 1994.

wandte Kunst im Richelieu-Flügel des Louvre (1989-93), gemeinsam mit Ieoh Ming Pei, sowie die des Modemuseums in Marseille. Als Architekt vollendete Wilmotte kürzlich das International Executing Offices Building und das New N° 3 Arai-Gebäude, beide in Tokio; gleichzeitig entwarf er die Möbel für das von Arquitectonica entworfene Gebäude der Bank von Luxemburg (1994).

tifs du Musée du Louvre, aile Richelieu (1989-93), avec Ieoh Ming Pei, et le Musée de la Mode de Marseille. En tant qu'architecte il a récemment achevé le chantier de l'immeuble de l'International Executive Office, et l'immeuble New N°3 Arai, à Tokyo, tout en dessinant le mobilier de la Banque de Luxembourg signée Arquitectonica (1994).

JEAN-MICHEL WILMOTTE
GANA ART CENTER
SEOUL, SOUTH KOREA, 1996-98

Located in the Pyungchang-Dong area of Seoul, this 3,000 m² facility includes exhibition space, a cafeteria, bookshop, conference room, outdoor theater, and a sculpture garden. Pyungchang-Dong is a hilly residential district at the periphery of the Korean capital. Wilmotte has chosen to use abundant glazing in the greeting and restaurant areas, and to make the exhibition spaces more "solid" and "permanent" in their appearance by using a white stone that he finds particularly well adapted to the local lighting conditions. One room of this large

Das 3 000 m² große, in Seouls Stadtteil Pyungchang-Dong gelegene Gana Art Center beherbergt Ausstellungsbereiche, eine Cafeteria, eine Buchhandlung, einen Konferenzsaal, ein Freilichttheater und einen Skulpturengarten. Wilmotte entschied sich für die großzügige Verwendung von Glas in den Empfangs- und Restaurantbereichen und für eine »solider« und »dauerhafter« wirkende Gestaltung der Ausstellungsbereiche in weißem Naturstein, den er bei den gegebenen Lichtverhältnissen für besonders geeignet hielt. Ein Raum dieses großen

Ce bâtiment public de 3 000 m² comprend un espace d'exposition, une cafétéria, une librairie, une salle de conférences, un théâtre en plein air et un jardin de sculptures. Le quartier résidentiel vallonné de Pyungchang-Dong à Séoul, dans lequel il se trouve, est à la périphérie de la capitale. Wilmotte a choisi de privilégier le verre dans les zones d'accueil et de restauration et de donner dans le même temps aux espaces d'exposition un aspect plus «solide» et «permanent» au moyen d'une pierre de couleur blanche qu'il juge particulièrement adaptée à la

GENEROUS WOODEN TERRACES AND LARGE OPENINGS MAKE THIS GALLERY LOOK LIKE A MUSEUM.

GROSSZÜGIGE HOLZTERRASSEN UND WEITE ÖFFNUNGEN VERLEIHEN DEM MULTIFUNK-TIONALEN ART CENTER DEN EINDRUCK EINES MUSEUMS.

DES TERRASSES AU SOL DE BOIS ET DE VASTES BAIES DONNENT À CETTE GALERIE UN AIR DE MUSÉE.

international gallery was designed specifically for works by Pablo Picasso, with specially created display cases. Reversing the usual order for such interventions, the gallery sometimes asks artists to design works that take into account the architecture of the gallery spaces. Fully at ease with a cultural program of this type, Jean-Michel Wilmotte, who successfully carried out the renovation of the Decorative Arts Department of the Louvre in collaboration with Ieoh Ming Pei, here proves that he is also at ease working outside France.

Museums ist ausschließlich dem Werk Pablo Picassos gewidmet und mit eigens hierfür entworfenen Vitrinen ausgestattet. Jean-Michel Wilmotte, der mit derartigen Aufträgen vertraut ist – in Zusammenarbeit mit Ieoh Ming Pei hat er die Sanierung der Abteilung für Angewandte Kunst des Louvre durchgeführt –, beweist hier einmal mehr sein Können und seine Vielseitigkeit.

qualité de la lumière locale. Une salle de ce musée international a été spécialement conçue, ainsi que ses vitrines, pour accueillir des œuvres de Picasso. Inversant l'ordre habituel de ce type d'intervention, le musée demande parfois aux artistes de concevoir des œuvres qui prennent en compte l'architecture de ses espaces. Parfaitement à l'aise dans un programme de ce type, Wilmotte qui a mené avec succès la rénovation du Département des arts décoratifs du Louvre montre ici qu'il est tout aussi capable d'intervenir à l'étranger.

gana art center

CLIENT / BAUHERR: GANA RESEARCH &
CONSULTING DEPARTMENT
FLOOR AREA / NUTZFLÄCHE / SURFACE
UTILE: 3 000 M²
COSTS / KOSTEN / COÛTS: WITHHELD /
UNGENANNT / NON COMMUNIQUÉS

KEN YEANG

Born in 1948 in Penang, Malaysia, Ken Yeang attended the Architectural Association in London (1966-71), and Wolfson College, Cambridge University (1971-75). Much of his subsequent work was based on his PhD dissertation in Cambridge on ecological design. His work (with Tengku Robert Hamzah as TR Hamzah & Yeang, created in 1976 in Kuala Lumpur) includes the MBF Tower (Penang, 1990-93), the Menara Mesiniaga Tower

Ken Yeang, geboren 1948 in Penang, Malaysia, studierte von 1966 bis 1971 an der Architectural Association in London und von 1971 bis 1975 am Wolfson College der Cambridge University. Ein Großteil seiner späteren Projekte basiert auf seiner Dissertation über ökologische Architektur. Dazu gehören die Hochhäuser MBF in Penang (1990-93) und Menara Mesiniaga (1989-92) – letzteres 1995 mit dem Aga Khan Award ausgezeichnet –, ein

Né en 1948 à Penang, Malaisie, Ken Yeang a étudié à l'Architectural Association de Londres (1966-71) et à la Cambridge University (Wolfson College, 1971-75). Ses travaux reposent sur sa thèse de doctorat traitant de l'architecture écologique. Parmi ses réalisations (avec Tengku Robert Hamzah, agence TR Hamzah & Yeang, créée à Kuala Lumpur en 1976), la tour MBF à Penang (1990-93), la tour Menara Mesiniaga, Prix Aga Khan 1995 (1989-

**KEN YEANG IS ONE OF THE BEST-KNOWN
MALAYSIAN ARCHITECTS, PLEADING ACTIVELY
FOR A "BIOCLIMATIC" ARCHITECTURE WELL
SUITED TO THE DEMANDS OF HIS REGION.**

KEN YEANG IST EINER DER BEKANNTESTEN
ARCHITEKTEN MALAYSIAS, DER SICH AKTIV
FÜR EINE DIESER REGION ANGEMESSENE
»BIOKLIMATISCHE« ARCHITEKTUR EINSETZT.

KEN YEANG EST L'UN DES ARCHITECTES MA-
LAIS LES PLUS CONNUS. IL DÉFEND ACTIVE-
MENT UNE ARCHITECTURE «BIOCLIMATIQUE»
ADAPTÉE AUX CONDITIONS LOCALES DE CETTE
RÉGION DU MONDE.

P 522.523

T.R. HAMZAH & YEANG SDN. BHD.
8 JALAN 1, TAMAN SRI UKAY
68000 AMPANG, SELANGOR
MALAYSIA

TEL: + 60 3 4571 966 / + 60 3 4571 948
FAX: + 60 3 4561 005 / + 60 3 4569 330
E-MAIL: trhy@tm.net.my
WEB: www.trhamzah-yeang.com

(1989-92), a recipient of the 1995 Aga Khan Award, a tower in Ho Chi Minh City, Vietnam (1992-94), the Tokyo-Nara Tower, Japan (1997), and the Menara UMNO, Penang (1998). His published books include *The Architecture of Malaysia* (Kuala Lumpur, 1992), and *The Skyscraper, Bioclimatically Considered: A Design Primer* (London, 1997). Yeang was President of the Malaysian Institute of Architects from 1983 to 1986.

Hochhaus in Ho-Chi-Minh-Stadt, Vietnam (1992-94), das Projekt für den Tokio-Nara-Tower (1997) und das Gebäude Menara UMNO in Penang (1998). Er veröffentlichte unter anderem »The Architecture of Malaysia« (Kuala Lumpur, 1992) und »The Skyscraper, Bioclimatically Considered: A Design Primer« (London, 1997). Von 1983 bis 1986 war Ken Yeang Präsident des malaysischen Architektenverbands.

92), une tour à Ho Chi Minh Ville, Vietnam (1992-94), la tour Tokyo-Nara, Japon (1997) et l'immeuble Menara UMNO à Penang (1998). Il est l'auteur de plusieurs livres dont «The Architecture of Malaysia», 1992, Kuala Lumpur et «The Skyscraper, Bioclimatically Considered: A Design Primer», Londres, 1997. Ken Yeang a été président de l'Institut malais des architectes de 1983 à 1986.

KEN YEANG

GUTHRIE PAVILION

SHAH ALAM, SELANGOR, MALAYSIA, 1995-98

Built in a new area about 30 km to the west of Kuala Lumpur, this pavilion is intended to attract attention to a real-estate development project. Half its space (nearly 5,000 m²) is a golf clubhouse, and the other clearly delineated half is used by Guthrie Property Development to sell houses. The most striking feature of the building is its 2,500 m² wing-shaped air-inflated fabric canopy. Made from glass fabric on steel frames suspended from three

Der in einem 30 km westlich von Kuala Lumpur gelegenen Neubaugebiet errichtete Guthrie-Pavillon soll auf ein Erschließungsprojekt aufmerksam machen. Die Hälfte des Gebäudes (fast 5 000 m²) nimmt ein Golfklubhaus ein, die andere, deutlich abgegrenzte Hälfte wird vom Bauträger Guthrie als Immobilienbüro genutzt. Auffälligstes Merkmal des Komplexes ist ein 2 500 m² großes, flügelförmiges und luftgefülltes Dach aus Glasfasergewebe. Es ist

Construit dans une nouvelle zone d'urbanisation à l'ouest de Kuala Lumpur, ce pavillon a pour fonction la promotion d'un projet immobilier. La moitié de sa surface (près de 5 000 m²) est consacrée à un clubhouse de golf, et le reste à la vente des maisons de Guthrie Property Development. La caractéristique principale du projet est son auvent (2 500 m²) en forme d'aile irrégulière en tissu de verre gonflé, étudié pour résister à des vents de 125 km/h. Il est

BENEATH THE AIR-INFLATED GLASS FABRIC ARE BUILDINGS THAT ARE FAR MORE DOWN TO EARTH.

DIE GEBÄUDE UNTER DEM LUFTGEFÜLLTEN GLASFASERDACH WIRKEN DENNOCH BODEN-STÄNDIG.

SOUS LE TISSU DE VERRE GONFLÉ, LES ÉLÉMENTS CONSTRUITS SONT BEAUCOUP PLUS CLASSIQUES.

P 526.527

40 m masts by zinc-dipped spiral strand steel cables, the irregular canopy is designed to resist 125 km/h winds. The actual office buildings below the two wings are less innovative, but they do contribute to reinforcing the image of a landing bird that characterizes this complex. They are some-what irregular in their forms, but have a trad-itional concrete frame design.

mit verzinkten, stählernen Spanndrahtseilen an drei 40 m hohen Masten aufgehängt und kann auf-grund seiner ungleichmäßigen Form Böen von bis zu 125 km/h standhalten. Die unter den beiden Flügeln gelegenen Bürotrakte verstärken den für diesen Komplex charakteristischen Eindruck eines landenden Vogels. Sie sind ungewöhnlich geformt, haben aber ein traditionelles Betonskelett.

tendu sur une armature d'acier et suspendu à trois mâts de 40 m par des câbles toronnés en spirale et zingués. Les bureaux qu'il abrite sont moins novateurs mais renforcent l'image d'un oiseau qui se pose. De forme légèrement irrégulière ils font appel à une classique ossature en béton.

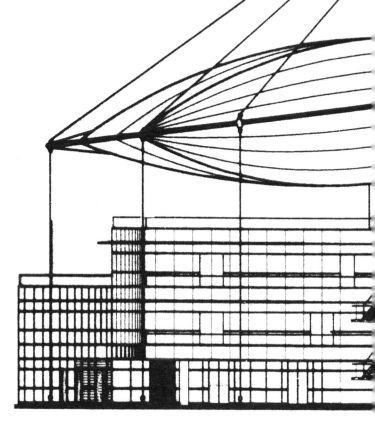

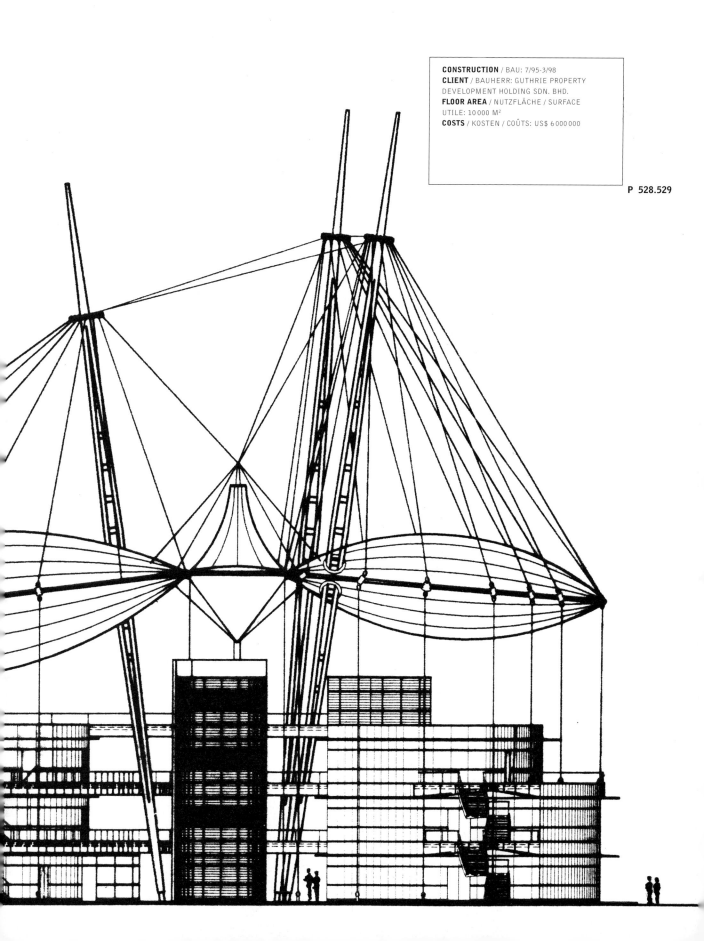

CONSTRUCTION / BAU: 7/95-3/98
CLIENT / BAUHERR: GUTHRIE PROPERTY
DEVELOPMENT HOLDING SDN. BHD.
FLOOR AREA / NUTZFLÄCHE / SURFACE
UTILE: 10 000 M²
COSTS / KOSTEN / COÛTS: US$ 6 000 000

P 528.529

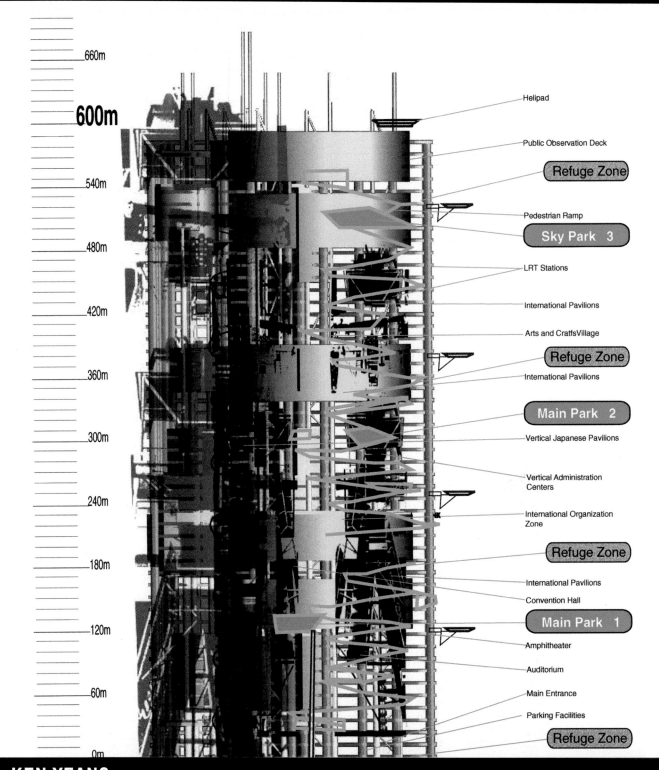

660m

600m

540m

480m

420m

360m

300m

240m

180m

120m

60m

0m

Helipad

Public Observation Deck

Refuge Zone

Pedestrian Ramp

Sky Park 3

LRT Stations

International Pavilions

Arts and CratfsVillage

Refuge Zone

International Pavilions

Main Park 2

Vertical Japanese Pavilions

Vertical Administration Centers

International Organization Zone

Refuge Zone

International Pavilions

Convention Hall

Main Park 1

Amphitheater

Auditorium

Main Entrance

Parking Facilities

Refuge Zone

KEN YEANG

NAGOYA EXPO 2005 TOWER

SETO, NAGOYA, JAPAN, 1997 (PROJECT)

AGAINST THE USUAL LOGIC, YEANG POINTS OUT THAT A TALL BUILDING SAVES PRECIOUS FOREST LAND.

KEN YEANG STELLT SICH GEGEN VERBREITETE AUFFASSUNGEN UND WEIST DARAUF HIN, DASS DURCH EIN HOHES GEBÄUDE WERTVOLLE WALDFLÄCHEN ERHALTEN BLEIBEN.

A L'INVERSE DE LA LOGIQUE HABITUELLE, YEANG FAIT ICI PRENDRE CONSCIENCE QU'UN IMMEUBLE DE GRANDE HAUTEUR PERMET D'ÉPARGNER UN PRÉCIEUX TERRAIN BOISÉ.

P 530.531

PLANNING / PLANUNG: 1997
CONSTRUCTION / BAU: 2000-2005 (PROJECTED)
BUILDING FOOTPRINT / GRUNDFLÄCHE /
SURFACE: 3 HA
FLOOR AREA / NUTZFLÄCHE / SURFACE
UTILE: 150 HA
BUDGET: US$ 1 500 000 000
HEIGHT / HÖHE / HAUTEUR: 600 M
EXPECTED VISITORS / ERWARTETE BESUCHER /
VISITEURS ATTENDUS: 25 000 000

Since the area near Seto City slated for the 2005 World's Fair is forested, Ken Yeang has proposed to put the entire exhibition into a 150-story, 600 m high skyscraper. This would permit avoiding the deforestation of some 160 hectares of land. Estimated costs for the project, which would be the world's tallest skyscraper, approach $1.5 billion. Yeang proposes to create a spiral monorail train on the exterior of the structure to replace more traditional elevators. He has specialized in environmentally conscious tall buildings, and naturally this project would take his expertise into account, calling on natural ventilation or solar heating for example. Planning would take into account the hypothesis that the tower would be converted to office, shop or factory space after the exhibition. Yeang also proposed an even higher 210-story, 800 m tower for a location somewhere between Tokyo and Nara.

Nachdem das Gebiet nahe der Stadt Seto für die Expo 2005 nominiert wurde, schlug Ken Yeang vor, die gesamte Ausstellung in einem Wolkenkratzer von 600 m Höhe mit 150 Geschossen unterzubringen, um so die Abholzung von etwa 160 ha Wald zu vermeiden. Die geschätzten Projektkosten – das Gebäude wäre das höchste der Welt – betragen etwa 1,5 Milliarden US$. Der Architekt plant anstelle der üblichen Aufzüge eine spiralförmig von außen um das Gebäude führende Einschienenbahn. Yeang hat sich auf umweltfreundliche Hochhäuser spezialisiert und seine bisherigen Erfahrungen, etwa im Hinblick auf natürliche Belüftung oder Solarheizung, in dieses Projekt eingebracht. Der Entwurf berücksichtigt ferner, daß das Hochhaus nach der Weltausstellung in Büro-, Laden- oder Produktionsräume umfunktioniert werden kann. Yeang hat einen noch höheren Wolkenkratzer für einen Standort zwischen Tokio und Nara entworfen.

Comme le terrain prévu par la ville de Seto pour accueillir la Foire mondiale de 2005 est boisé, Ken Yeang a proposé d'installer la totalité de l'exposition dans un gratte-ciel de 150 niveaux et 600 m de haut. Cette solution permettrait d'éviter la déforestation de quelque 160 hectares de terrain. Le budget estimé pour le projet de ce qui serait le plus haut gratte-ciel du monde approche $1,5 milliard. L'architecte envisage de créer un monorail extérieur en spirale pour remplacer les ascenseurs traditionnels. Yeang s'est spécialisé dans les immeubles écologiques de grande hauteur et ce projet s'appuie sur son expérience en particulier de la ventilation naturelle et du chauffage solaire. À l'issue de l'exposition, l'immeuble serai reconverti en bureaux, commerces et espaces d'activité. L'architecte a proposé une tour encore plus haute – 210 niveaux, 800 m – entre Tokyo et Nara.

SHOEI YOH

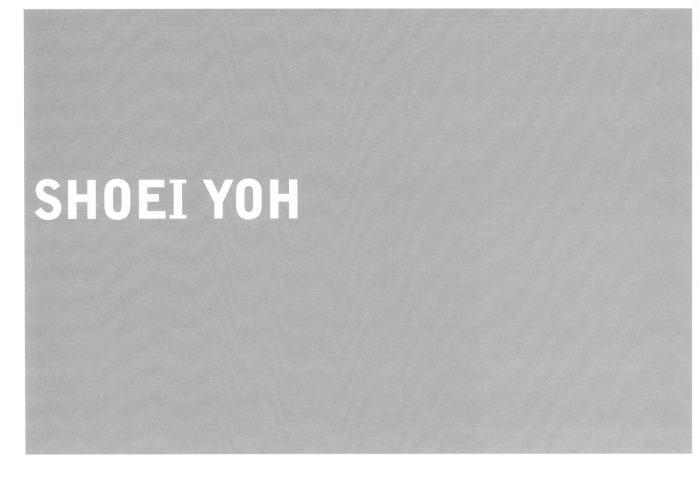

Born in 1940 in Kumamoto City, Japan, Shoei Yoh received a degree in economics from Keio Gijuku University, Tokyo (1962), and studied fine and applied arts at Wittenberg University in Springfield, Ohio (1964). Self-trained as an architect, he founded Shoei Yoh + Architects in Fukuoka in 1970, and gained a local reputation in industrial and interior design. His Stainless-Steel House with Light Lattice (Nagasaki, 1980) was widely published. More recent

Shoei Yoh, geboren 1940 in Kumamoto, beendete 1962 das Studium der Wirtschaftswissenschaften an der Universität Keio Gijuku in Tokio. 1964 begann er ein Kunststudium an der Wittenberg University in Springfield, Ohio. Obwohl er kein ausgebildeter Architekt ist, gründete Yoh 1970 das Büro Yoh + Architects in Fukuoka und errang lokales Ansehen in Industriebau und Innenarchitektur. Sein Stainless-Steel House with Light Lattice in Naga-

Né en 1940 à Kumamoto, Shoei Yoh est diplômé en économie de l'Université Keio Gijuku de Tokyo (1962), et étudie les beaux-arts et les arts appliqués à la Wittenberg University de Springfield, Ohio (1964). Architecte autodidacte, il ouvre l'agence Shoei Yoh + Architects à Fukuoka en 1970, appréciée localement pour ses créations de design industriel et d'architecture intérieure. Sa Stainless-Steel House with Light Lattice (Nagasaki, 1980) a

SHOEI YOH DOES NOT FIT READILY INTO ANY
SCHOOL OF ARCHITECTURE. HIS IS AN EXHIL-
ARATING MODERNITY WHOSE SHAPE CHANGES
ACCORDING TO THE CIRCUMSTANCES.

SHOEI YOH LÄSST SICH NICHT OHNE WEITERES
EINER ARCHITEKTURRICHTUNG ZUORDNEN.
ER VERTRITT EINE LEBENDIGE MODERNE,
DEREN FORMEN SICH DEN JEWEILS GESTELL-
TEN BAUAUFGABEN ENTSPRECHEND WANDELN.

P 532.533

SHOEI YOH NE S'INTÈGRE PAS AISÉMENT
AU CADRE D'UNE ÉCOLE D'ARCHITECTURE.
SA MODERNITÉ PLEINE DE VIE CHANGE DE
FORME SELON LES CIRCONSTANCES.

SHOEI YOH + ARCHITECTS
1-12-30 HEIWA
MINAMI-KU, FUKUOKA-SHI 815-0071
JAPAN

TEL: + 81 92 521 4782
FAX: + 81 92 521 6718
E-MAIL: yohshoei@jade.dti.ne.jp

work, such as his Kanada Children Training House
(Fukuoka, 1994) and his Uchino Community Center
for Seniors & Children (Kaho, Fukuoka, 1995),
shows his flair for spectacular forms, which draw,
in their sense of space or in certain techniques, on
Japanese tradition. Shoei Yoh is a professor of
architecture and urban design at the Graduate
School of Keio University.

saki (1980) wurde mehrfach veröffentlicht. Das
Kanada Children Training House in Fukuoka (1994),
und das Gemeindezentrum Uchino in Kaho, Fukuoka (1995), verraten Yohs Neigung zu spektakulären Formen, die in ihrer Raumwirkung und in
gewissen Techniken von der traditionellen japanischen Architektur beeinflußt sind. Shoei Yoh ist
Professor für Architektur und Städtebau an der
Keio-Universität.

été largement publiée. Des réalisations plus récentes comme sa maison Kanada pour l'éducation des
enfants (Fukuoka, 1994) et son Centre communautaire Uchino pour personnes âgées et enfants (Kaho,
Fukuoka, 1995) témoignent son penchant pour les
formes spectaculaires qui s'appuient dans leur sens
de l'espace sur certaines techniques traditionnelles.
Il est professeur d'architecture et d'urbanisme à
l'Université Keio.

SHOEI YOH

PROSPECTA '92 TOYAMA OBSERVATORY TOWER

KOSUGI, TOYAMA, JAPAN, 1990-92

CONCEIVED AS AN OBSERVATION PLATFORM
OR A "MID-AIR" MUSEUM, THE TOWER STANDS
OUT AGAINST THE NIGHT ENVIRONMENT.

DER ALS OBSERVATORIUM ODER »FREISCHWE-
BENDES« MUSEUM GEPLANTE TURM ZEICHNET
SICH GEGEN DEN NACHTHIMMEL AB.

CONÇUE COMME UNE PLATE-FORME D'OBSER-
VATION OU UN MUSÉE «FLOTTANT», LA TOUR
MARQUE SON ENVIRONNEMENT NOCTURNE.

PLANNING / PLANUNG: 6/90-1/91
CONSTRUCTION / BAU: 4/91-4/92
CLIENT / BAUHERR: TOYAMA PREFECTURE
FLOOR AREA / NUTZFLÄCHE / SURFACE
UTILE: 1150 M²
COSTS / KOSTEN / COÛTS: 910 000 000 ¥

ESSENTIALLY CUBIC IN FORM, PROSPECTA '92 IS ENTIRELY HOLLOW IN THE MIDDLE.

DER WÜRFELFÖRMIGE TURM IST AN DEN SEITEN VOLLKOMMEN OFFEN.

DE FORME ESSENTIELLEMENT CARRÉE, PROSPECTA '92 EST ENTIÈREMENT CREUSE DANS SA PARTIE CENTRALE.

P 536.537

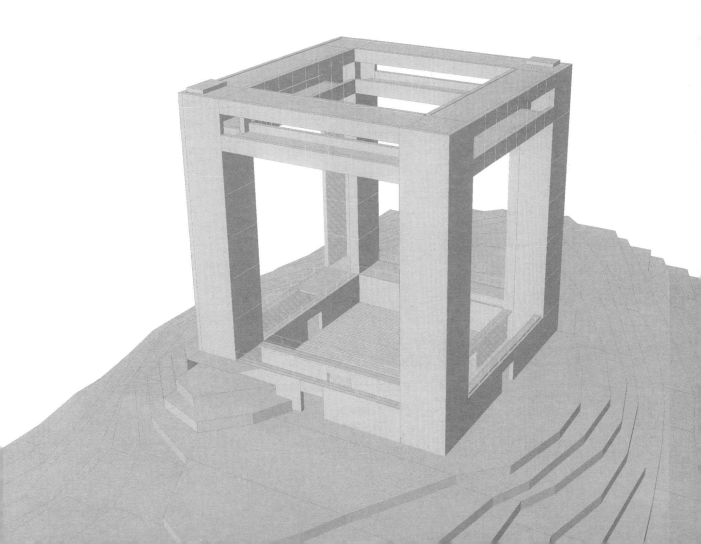

This 30 x 32 x 32 m observation tower was "conceived as a mid-air museum dedicated to the beauty of the earth and the universe." One of the architect's goals was to permit visitors to contemplate the beauty of nearby mountains, a popular pastime in Japan. He likens the 32 m high observation deck to an open-air theater, where the spectacle of nature is reinforced by such devices as a fog-generating

Das Observatorium mit den Ausmaßen von 30 x 32 x 32 m wurde »als freischwebendes, den Schönheiten der Erde und des Universums gewidmetes Museum« geplant. Ziel des Architekten war, den Besuchern die kontemplative Betrachtung der Schönheit der nahen Berge zu ermöglichen. Yoh gestaltete die Dachterrasse wie ein Freilichttheater und unterstreicht das Naturschauspiel auch mit

Cette tour d'observation de 30 x 32 x 32 m a été «conçue comme un musée flottant, consacré à la beauté de la terre et de l'univers». L'un des objectifs de l'architecte était de permettre aux visiteurs de contempler la beauté des montagnes avoisinantes, passe-temps populaire au Japon. Il compare sa plate-forme d'observation (haute de 32 m) en forme de boîte cubique ouverte, à un théâtre en plein air,

P 538.539

machine, and light and musical effects. Shaped
like a square, open box, or rather an empty frame,
the Tower allows visitors to walk around its upper
periphery to enjoy the natural view as well as the
show constituted by a "computer-programmed
performance of water with the collaboration of
a 'fog sculptor,' lighting artist and sound artist."

Hilfe von Nebelmaschinen sowie Licht- und Ton-
effekten. Der wie ein leerer Rahmen geformte Turm
erlaubt den Besuchern, um seinen oberen Rand her-
umzugehen und so sowohl den Blick in die Natur
als auch die »computerprogrammierte Darstellung
von Wasser, die unter Mitarbeit eines ›Nebelfor-
mers‹, eines Licht- und eines Klangkünstlers
entstand«, zu genießen.

dont les visiteurs parcourent la périphérie pour
profiter de la vue sur la nature et d'un «spectacle
informatisé sur le thème de l'eau avec la collaboration d'un ‹sculpteur de brouillard› et sa machine,
d'un artiste spécialisé dans la lumière et d'un artiste
sonore».

SHOEI YOH
GLASS STATION
OGUNI, KUMAMOTO, JAPAN, 1991-93

AN UNDULATING GLASS CANOPY GIVES AN
ORDINARY SERVICE STATION AN EXCEPTIONAL
PRESENCE.

EIN VIELFACH GESCHWUNGENES GLASDACH
GIBT EINER HERKÖMMLICHEN TANKSTELLE
EIN AUSSERGEWÖHNLICHES ERSCHEINUNGS-
BILD.

UN AUVENT DE VERRE ONDULÉ CONFÈRE À
CETTE STATION D'ESSENCE UNE PRÉSENCE
EXCEPTIONNELLE.

P 540.541

PLANNING / PLANUNG: 8/91-8/92
CONSTRUCTION / BAU: 9/92-7/93
CLIENT / BAUHERR: HARADA KOHSAN CO, LTD
FLOOR AREA / NUTZFLÄCHE / SURFACE
UTILE: 729 M²
COSTS / KOSTEN / COÛTS: 257 500 000 ¥

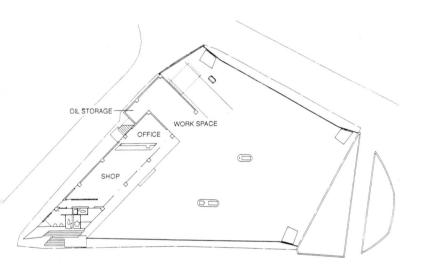

The architect has created an undulating laminated glass canopy to cover a gas station located near a small lumbering town. Shoei Yoh built his Oguni Dome in the same town five years before. The use of an ingenious combination of stainless steel, concrete, polyester films, structural silicone and glass has created an unusually free form that nonetheless meets stringent fire safety standards. At the base, the structure consists of four pour-in-place concrete arches with pre-tensioned steel rods stretched between them. 8 mm thick laminated glass and 3 mm thick perforated stainless steel sheeting were placed in this parabolic web and fastened with structural silicone, according to a technique developed by the architect that is designed to efficiently absorb normal thermal expansion and contraction. Yoh compares this structure to his design for the Naiju Community Center and Nursery School (1994).

Shoei Yoh wählte ein gewelltes Schutzdach aus Verbundglas zur Überdachung einer Tankstelle nahe der japanischen Kleinstadt Oguni, in der er fünf Jahre zuvor seinen Oguni Dome erbaut hat. Durch die Kombination von Edelstahl, Beton, Polyesterfolie sowie Silikon und Glas entstand eine ungewöhnlich freie Form, die dennoch den strengen Brandschutzvorschriften entspricht. Die Basis des Bauwerks besteht aus vier Betonbögen mit vorgespannten Stahlstäben. Verbundglas in 8 mm Dicke und 3 mm dickes perforiertes Edelstahlblech wurden mittels einer vom Architekten entwickelten Technik in dieses parabolische Netz eingesetzt und mit Bausilikon befestigt, um so die natürliche thermische Dehnung und Kontraktion auszugleichen. Yoh vergleicht den Bau mit seinem Entwurf für das Gemeindezentrum mit Kindergarten in Naiju (1994).

L'architecte a créé cet auvent ondulé en verre laminé pour abriter une station-service proche d'une petite ville forestière. Le recours à une ingénieuse combinaison d'acier inoxydable, de béton, de films de polyester de silicone structurel et de verre pour créer cette surprenante forme libre n'en a pas moins exigé de prendre des mesures de protection contre les incendies. À la base, la structure se compose de quatre arches de béton coulées sur place et de tiges d'acier prétensionnées tendues entre elles. Des feuilles de verre laminé de 8 mm d'épaisseur et d'acier inoxydable perforé de 3 mm ont été intégrées à cette toile parabolique et jointées aux silicones, selon une technique mise au point par l'architecte pour absorber les expansions et contractions provoquées par la chaleur. Yoh compare cette structure à son projet pour le Centre communautaire et maternelle de Naiju (1994).

SHOEI YOH
KANADA CHILDREN TRAINING HOUSE
KANADA, FUKUOKA, JAPAN, 1992-94

The triangular wooden structures "are cantilevered from their anchor within the landscape to extend 12 m into the void created by the downward sloping terrain" in this educational facility for children. As the architect points out, the original impression of the viewer may be that these are "forms of primitive housing," but once he approaches he "comes to

Die dreieckigen Holzkonstruktionen dieses Kinderheims »kragen von ihrem Standort im Grünen aufgrund des abfallenden Terrains 12 m ins Leere aus«. Wie der Architekt betont, kann der erste Anblick dem Besucher den Eindruck »primitiver Wohnformen« vermitteln. Kommt er jedoch näher, »wird er über die Technik staunen, mittels derer die

Les structures triangulaires en bois «sont disposées en porte-à-faux par rapport à leur ancrage dans le paysage et s'étirent de 12 m dans le vide généré par la pente du terrain» sur lequel est construit cet établissement d'éducation pour enfants. Comme le fait remarquer l'architecte, l'impression première du spectateur est de regarder des «formes primitives

P 542.543

PLANNING / PLANUNG: 10/92-4/93
CONSTRUCTION / BAU: 4/93-7/94
CLIENT / BAUHERR: KANADA-MACHI
FLOOR AREA / NUTZFLÄCHE / SURFACE
UTILE: 615 M²
COSTS / KOSTEN / COÛTS: 446330000 ¥

wonder about the technology that suspends the structures without the use of posts or columns." The sharp contrast between the green, hilly countryside and the rigid forms of the Kanada Training House is intentional, and has been compared in this respect to his 1977 Ingot Coffee Shop.

Baukörper ohne Pfosten und Stützen aufgehängt werden«. Der scharfe Kontrast zwischen der grünen, hügeligen Landschaft und den streng geometrischen Formen des Kinderheims ist beabsichtigt; der Bau ist in dieser Hinsicht mit Yohs Café Ingot aus dem Jahre 1977 verglichen worden.

d'habitat», mais une fois qu'il s'en est approché, «il s'émerveille devant la technologie qui permet de suspendre ces structures sans l'aide de piliers ou de colonnes». Le puissant contraste entre le paysage vert et vallonné et les formes rigides de ce projet est volontaire. Il a pu être comparé à cet égard au Café Ingot de 1977.

INDEX OF PLACES

ORTSVERZEICHNIS
INDEX DES LIEUX

INDEX OF PLACES

SCOTTSDALE
(ARIZONA, USA)
TEMPLE KOL AMI: 120.121

SENDAI
(MIYAGI, JAPAN)
MIYAGI PREFECTURAL LIBRARY: 048, 198.199.200.201

SEOUL
(SOUTH KOREA)
GANA ART CENTER: 518.519.520.521
RODIN PAVILION: 285.286.287.288.289.290.291

SETO
(NAGOYA, JAPAN)
NAGOYA EXPO 2005 TOWER: 045.046.047, 530.531

SHAH ALAM
(SELANGOR, MALAYSIA)
GUTHRIE PAVILION: 059.060, 524.525.526.527.528.529

SHIZUOKA
(JAPAN)
SHIZUOKA CONVENTION AND ARTS CENTER "GRANSHIP": 027.028, 252.253.254.255.256.257

SIPPY DOWNS
(QUEENSLAND, AUSTRALIA)
SUNSHINE COAST UNIVERSITY CLUB: 051.052, 138.139.140.141

ST. AUSTELL
(CORNWALL, ENGLAND)
THE EDEN PROJECT: 178.179

'T GOOI
(THE NETHERLANDS)
MÖBIUS HOUSE: 021.022, 094.095.096.097.098.099

TOKYO
(JAPAN)
K-MUSEUM: 506.507

TOYAMA CITY
(TOYAMA, JAPAN)
NOH STAGE IN THE FOREST: 306.307.308.309

TSUNA-GUN
(HYOGO, JAPAN)
TOTO SEMINAR HOUSE: 054, 066.067.068.069

UTRECHT
(THE NETHERLANDS)
EDUCATORIUM, UNIVERSITY OF UTRECHT: 048.049,
294.295.296.297.298.299.300.301.302.303

YOUNTVILLE
(CALIFORNIA, USA)
DOMINUS WINERY: 055.056, 216.217.218.219.220.221

ZHUHAI CITY, HENGQIN ISLAND
(CHINA)
HAISHI "MIRAGE CITY": 246.247

PHOTO CREDITS

FOTONACHWEIS
CRÉDITS PHOTOGRAPHIQUES

T. = TOP / OBEN / EN HAUT   B. = BOTTOM / UNTEN / EN BAS   L. = LEFT / LINKS / À GAUCHE   R. = RIGHT / RECHTS / À DROITE

064 ©TADAO ANDO ARCHITECT & ASSOCIATES **066.068.069** SHIGEO OGAWA, © SHINKENCHIKU-SHA **070.071.072.073** © MITSUO MATSUOKA **075** © THIBAUD DE ST. CHAMAS **076.077** © GASTON **078** © GUILLAUME HERBAUT **079** © GASTON **081** © SHIGERU BAN, ARCHITECTS **082.083.084.085.086.087** © HIROYUKI HIRAI **088** © BDM ARCHITECTES **090.091** © PHILIPPE RUAULT **093** © HANS-JÜRGEN COMMERELL **094.095.096.097.098.099.100, 102.103.104.105.106.107** © CHRISTIAN RICHTERS **108** MARCO D'ANNA, © STUDIO MARIO BOTTA **110.111.112.113** PINO MUSI, © STUDIO MARIO BOTTA **115** © MORLEY VON STERNBERG/ARCAID **116.117** © PHIL SAYER **118** © WILL BRUDER **120.121.122.123** BILL TIMMERMAN, © WILL BRUDER **125** © LUCA VIGNELLI **126.127.128.129.130.131** © CHRISTIAN RICHTERS **132** © MORLEY VON STERNBERG/ARCAID **134.135** © RICHARD BRYANT/ARCAID **136** PETER HYATT, © CLARE DESIGN **138.139.140.141** RICHARD STRINGER, © CLARE DESIGN **143** GERALD ZUGMANN, © COOP HIMMELB(L)AU **144.145.146.147.148.149.150.151** © RALPH RICHTER/ARCHI-TEKTURPHOTO **152** © 1998 JOHN EDWARD LINDEN **154.155** © TOM BONNER **156** © JULIUS SHULMAN/DAVID GLOMB **157** © 1998 JOHN EDWARD LINDEN **159** © BRANA WOLF **160.161.162.163** © NORMAN MCGRATH **165** © ANDREW WARD **166.167** © DENNIS GILBERT/VIEW **168** MICHEL PORRO, © FOSTER AND PARTNERS **169** © DENNIS GILBERT/VIEW **170.171.172.173.174.175** WERNER HUTHMACHER, © ARCHIPRESS **176** © NICHOLAS GRIMSHAW **178.179** © IMAGINATION **181.182.183.184.185** ANTHONY BROWELL, © GROSE BRADLEY **186** © MICHAEL RATHEMEYER **188.189** EDWARD WOODMAN, © THE OFFICE OF ZAHA HADID **191** © HIROSHI HARA + ATELIER Φ **192** © MAMORU ISHIGURO **194.195** © SHINKENCHIKU-SHA **196.197** © TOMIO OHASHI **199** T. © HIROSHI HARA + ATELIER Φ **199** B. © TOMIO OHASHI **200.201** B. © TOMIO OHASHI **201** T. © HIROSHI HARA + ATELIER Φ **203** © ARNAUD CARPENTIER **204.205.206, 208.209** © MITSUMASA FUJITSUKA **211** T., B. © DANIEL MAYER **212.213.214.215** © CHRISTIAN RICHTERS **216.217.218.219.220.221** © TIMOTHY HURSLEY **222.223.224.225** HAYES DAVIDSON, © TATE GALLERY OF MODERN ART **226** © JOHNNIE SHAND-KYDD **228.229.230.231** © MORLEY VON STERNBERG/ARCAID **233** © ABIGAIL SCHEUER **234.235.236.237.238.239.240.241.242.243** © FRIEDRICH BUSAM/ARCHITEKTURPHOTO **244** EIICHIRO SAKATA **246** B. YOSHIO TAKASE, © GA PHOTOGRAPHERS **246** T., **247** T. © TAKASHI OTAKA **248.249.250.251.252.253.254, 256.257** © HISAO SUZUKI **259** NACÁSA & PARTNERS **260.261** © PAULINE JALIL **262.263.264.265** © MIKIO KAMAYA **266.267.268.269** © TOMIO OHASHI **271.272.273.274.275** © TOYO ITO & ASSOCIATES, ARCHITECTS **276** © JENNIFER YOOS **278.279** © DON F. WONG **281** RINGO TANG, © WARO KISHI + K. ASSOCIATES **282.283** © HIROYUKI HIRAI **285** © KEVIN KENNON **286.287.288.289.290.291** © TIMOTHY HURSLEY **293** © REM KOOLHAAS **294.295.296.297.298.299.300.301.302.303** © CHRISTIAN RICHTERS **304** © KENGO KUMA & ASSOCIATES **306.307.308** © MITSUMASA FUJITSUKA **311** © LUCA VIGNELLI **312.313.314.315.316.317** © RALPH RICHTER/ARCHITEKTUR-PHOTO **318.319.320.321.322.323.324.325.326.327** © BITTER & BREDT **329** MAKI AND ASSOCIATES **330.331.332, 334.335.336.337.338.339** © TOSHIHARU KITAJIMA/ARCHI-PHOTO **340** © TACO ANEMA **342.343.344.345.346.347.348.349** © CHRISTIAN RICHTERS **351** © LUCA VIGNELLI **352** © JOCK POTTLE/ESTO **353** © RICHARD MEIER & PARTNERS **354** L. © NANA WATANABE **354** R. © CURIOSITY INC. **356.357** © PAUL WARCHOL **360.361.362.363** © REINER BLUNCK **364** © JEANNINE GOVAERS **366.367.368.369.370.371.372.373** © CHRISTIAN RICHTERS **374** © AGENCE MACARY ZUBLENA **376.377** © AUGUSTO DA SILVA/AGENCE GRAPHIX **378** L. © MICHEL ZAVAGNO **378** R., **380** B. © NICOLAS BOREL **383** © JEAN NOUVEL AND LEWIS BALTZ **384.385.386.387.388.389.390.391.392.393** © CHRISTIAN RICHTERS **395** © JOKE BROUWER **396** T.L., **396.397** B. © CHRISTIAN RICHTERS **396** T.R., **397** T., **398.399** B. © NOX **399** T., **400.401** T. © CHRISTIAN RICHTERS **401** B. © NOX **402** © CHRISTIAN RICHTERS **403** © NOX **405** © STEFANO GOLDBERG **406.407.408.409.410.411** © HANS SCHLUPP/ARCHITEKTUR-PHOTO **412.413** © RICHARD BRYANT/ARCAID **415** © DAN STEVENS **416.417.418.419.420.421.422.423** © CHRISTIAN RICHTERS **425** © UDO HESSE **426.427.428.429.430.431.432.433** © WERNER HUTHMACHER **434** © TOM HÖFERMANN **436.437.438.439.440.441** © BERNHARD KROLL **443** ANDREAS STERZING, © SITE ENVIRONMENTAL DESIGN, INC. **444.445** © 1997 SITE ENVIRONMENTAL DESIGN, INC. **447** © TERESA SIZA **448.449.450, 452.453.454.455.456.457.458.459.460.461.462.463.464.465** T. © CHRISTIAN RICHTERS **465** T. ARNAUD CARPENTIER **467** © PETER GROSS **468.469.470.471** © FRIEDRICH BUSAM/ARCHITEKTURPHOTO **472** © GITTY DARUGAR **474.475** © GEORGES FESSY **476** © ARNAUD CARPENTIER **478.479.480.481.482.483** © NACÁSA & PARTNERS **484.485.486.487.488.489.490, 492.493** © TOSHIYUKI KOBAYASHI **495** COURTESY TEN ARQUITECTOS **496.497.498.499** LUIS GORDOA, © TEN ARQUITECTOS **501.502.503.504.505.506.507.508.509** © MAKOTO SEI WATANABE **511** © MICHAEL O'BRIEN **512.513.514.515** © MICHAEL MORAN **517** © ROBERT CÉSAR **518.519** © YOUNG CHEA-PARK **520.521** © WOONGU KANG **523.524.525.526.527.528** © K. L. NG PHOTOGRAPHY **533** SATOSHI ASAKAWA, © SHOEI YOH + ARCHITECTS **534.535** © TOYAMA PREFECTURE **536** YOSHIO TAKASE, © GA PHOTOGRAPHERS **538.539.540, 542.543** © SHOEI YOH + ARCHITECTS

PLANS

NACHWEIS DER PLÄNE
CRÉDITS DES PLANS

IMPRINT

IMPRESSUM

www.taschen.com
© 1999 BENEDIKT TASCHEN VERLAG GMBH
HOHENZOLLERNRING 53, D – 50672 COLOGNE

EDITED BY CAROLINE KELLER
CO-EDITED BY NICOLA SENGER, UTA HOFFMANN,
KARL GEORG CADENBACH, NICOLE BILSTEIN
PRODUCTION THOMAS GRELL
DESIGN AND LAYOUT ANDY DISL
GERMAN TRANSLATION NORA VON MÜHLENDAHL
FRENCH TRANSLATION JACQUES BOSSER

PRINTED IN SPAIN
ISBN 3-8228-6390-4

THIS BOOK IS DEDICATED TO MY WIFE,
ALEXANDRA.